Zentrum Moderner Orient
Geisteswissenschaftliche Zentren Berlin e. V.

Sharing Sovereignty.
The Little Kingdom in South Asia

■ Edited by Georg Berkemer
and Margret Frenz

Studien 20

Klaus Schwarz Verlag Berlin

Die Deutsche Bibliothek - CIP-Einheitsaufnahme

Sharing Sovereignty. The Little Kingdom in South Asia. / Ed. by Georg Berkemer and Margret Frenz. Zentrum Moderner Orient. - Berlin : Schwarz 2003
(Studien / Zentrum Moderner Orient, Geisteswissenschaftliche Zentren Berlin e.V. ; 20)
ISBN 3-87997-626-0

Zentrum Moderner Orient
Geisteswissenschaftliche Zentren Berlin e.V.

Kirchweg 33
14129 Berlin
Tel. 030-80307 228

ISBN 3-87997-626-0
STUDIEN

Bestellungen:
Verlag Hans Schiler
Fidicinstr. 29
D-10965 Berlin
Tel. 030-3228523, Fax 030-3225183
E-Mail info@verlag-hans-schiler.de

Redaktion und Satz: Margret Liepach
Einbandgestaltung: Jörg Rückmann, Berlin
Titelbild: Heldenstein in Nordkerala
Foto: Margret Frenz

Druck: Offset-Druckerei Gerhard Weinert GmbH, Berlin
Printed in Germany 2003

Gedruckt mit Unterstützung der Senatsverwaltung
für Wissenschaft, Forschung und Kultur, Berlin

Table of Contents

Introduction 7

Burkhard Schnepel/Georg Berkemer: History of the Model 11

Georg Berkemer/Margret Frenz: The Role of Hermann Kulke 21

Peter Sutherland: Very Little Kingdoms. The Calendrical Order of West Himalayan Hindu Polity 31

Ulrike Teuscher: Kingship and Genealogy in Mediaeval Western India 63

Margret Frenz: Virtual Relations. Little Kings in Malabar 81

Tilman Frasch: "In an Octopussy's Garden": Of Cakravartins, little kings and a new model of the early state in South and Southeast Asia 93

Akio Tanabe: The Sacrificer State and Sacrificial Community: Kingship in Early Modern Khurda, Orissa, Seen Through a Local Ritual 115

Niels Gutschow: Ranpur – the Centre of a Little Kingdom 137

Burkhard Schnepel: The Stolen Goddess. Ritual Enactments of Power and Authority in Orissa 165

Uwe Skoda: On a tribal frontier – Aghriā-Gauntiā as Village Kings 181

Chandi Prasad Nanda: Validating "Tradition" . Revisiting Keonjhar and Bhuiyan Insurgency in Colonial Orissa 205

Acknowledgements
The editors would like to thank Sunniva Greve for her excellent work in proof-reading the majority of the contributions, and Margret Liepach for her kind and efficient support in all editorial matters. Without them, this book would not have seen the light of day. We thank the Centre for Modern Oriental Studies, Berlin, for allowing us to publish the present volume in their series *Studien*.

Technical Remarks
This volume comprises texts which are based on sources in languages from all over the South Asian subcontinent. We have tried to standardise the spelling of Sanskritic terms only. The spellings of all other, especially living languages, as well as proper names have been kept in the respective author's orthography. For reasons of space we compiled a general bibliography at the end of the volume comprising all bibliographical data provided by the authors. We hope that the readers will not find this arrangement inconvenient.

Georg Berkemer and Margret Frenz
Berlin, November 2003

Introduction

> "The local political system in operation in the eighteenth century was that of the little kingdom." (Cohn 2001c [1987]: 326)

Ever since Bernard Cohn made this statement in 1960, an undercurrent in South Asian historiography has sought to establish a structural base for a "theory"[1] of South Asian kingship and authority. Despite these efforts, there is still "considerable and variable uncertainty about the nature of Indian kings and kingship" (Stein 1998: 133). This quotation from Burton Stein's 1998 essay indicates that historians and anthropologists have been unhappy for quite some time about constructing history with current political administrative or cultural units in mind, as is still the case with mainstream or textbook historiography. The present volume is intended as a contribution to the continuation and extension of various ideas and models relevant to the ongoing discussion. It integrates the most comprehensive of these models, i.e., the little kingdom model, and post-modern historiography. The editors are of the opinion that it is an important and hitherto neglected issue in the current historiographical debate.

Again, it was Bernard Cohn who criticised European conceptions of history as not taking other modes of historical thinking seriously. The binary logic of „objective" histories cannot be applied to orally transmitted historical knowledge or to the textual networks of oral and written tradition, seen at all levels of interaction in South Asia.[2] The manifold and fluid (hi)stories of the people and regions of South Asia cannot be reduced to one single history, neither by political design nor historical or anthropological theory: "The most striking fact about the Sanskritic tradition is that it has never been unified by any event, text, or person." (Quigley 1993: 163). This holds true for all of the textual networks or knowledge systems that contain and transmit (hi)stories in the collective memories of South Asia. Our approach seeks to formulate models in analogy to the textual and anthropological studies that have elaborated the idea of a multifaceted reality as expressed in ritual and performative processes, as well as textual and oral representations. This volume presents essays on the field of equally structured traditional, political and ritual authority in South Asia, and its texts and performances.

What people see as their history in traditional South Asia is focussed on regional and local events. History is told in relation to one's own kin group or community, rather than with the emphasis of mainstream academic historiography, i.e., European academic traditions and the nation state. Despite the abundance of critical literature on India's colonial past, the intellectual efforts they contain have a common tendency to ignore a considerable part of India's own historical tradition, which has been termed endo-history (Berkemer 2001a). Conscious of this state of affairs and intent on showing that the regional and local levels do not represent isolated chaotic situations, the editors invited essays that elaborate aspects of indigenous tradition and its dynamics, which could be perceived as elements of a broad structure of ideas and concepts.[3] Historical thinking in pre-modern India is based on this multi-centred and non-binary structure, spanning several levels of integration from village politics to large empires.

Although some studies focus on small-scale political units, we rarely encounter contributions emphasising the significance of these local institutions for the understanding of local history and its own traditional historiography in South Asia. The local institution perspective provides a solution to the conventional history-writing trap. Some authors have taken Cohn's criticism seriously and become the conceptual fathers of approaches taken since the 1980s.[4] For many readers, they may have been the source of a new awareness about the inadequacy of mainstream historiographical writings. We may even be tempted, looking at our own material, to rethink results and paradigms. The editors consider it essential to show that there are several pasts within the South Asian cultural sphere, where statehood and historical self-perception interact and lead to constructions of various regions of identity. These interactions are based on the above-mentioned structures of ideas and concepts worked out by Bernard Cohn for the Benares region, which led to the first attempt at conceptualising them as little kingdoms. The present book takes into account the most recent development of Bernard Cohn's concept of introducing examples from several Indian regions, using different methodological approaches from a spectrum of disciplines such as anthropology, structural history, political history, architecture and cultural theory.

The book is divided into three parts. A theoretical ouverture introduces the reader to the history of the little kingdom model, especially over the last ten years and in the person of Hermann Kulke. The second part presents essays on several little kingdoms and their attendant situations. Opening the round of case studies, Peter Sutherland exemplifies "Little Kingdoms under Indirect Rule", where aspects of royalty are revealed through the interaction of local cults. Ulrike Teuscher's article is a critical discussion of the Rajput myth and Rajput history that makes use of epigraphical and textual sources. Margret Frenz explores one of the most recent developments in little kingdom theory: the possibility of having a little kingdom situation in a historical setting where the great king has been absent for a long time. Taking the case of Burma, Tilman Frasch proposes a new model for the early Burmese state, constructing his own version of the little kingdom model as opposed to following conventional centralistic ideas. Getting back to India, the next five essays discuss numerous little kingdoms within the cultural region of Orissa, from the textual analysis point of view and the field research perspective. Whereas Akio Tanabe presents the study of a small sub-unit of one of the most important pre-modern little kingdoms in Orissa, the other papers focus on more peripheral situations, such as the replica of the kingdom in architectural styles and rituals (Niels Gutschow), in ritual sovereignty counter-claims in South Orissa (Burkhard Schnepel), the local level of village headmen in West Orissa (Uwe Skoda), and finally, kingship and its relation to tribal groups (Chandi Prasad Nanda). The third part summarises critique of the model, which, as the editors are aware of, is still an ongoing process. Maria Schetelich raises the question of the relationship between historical and anthropological models and indological sources and methodology, while the last two contributions (Georg Berkemer, Heiko Frese) try to fathom both the extent and the limitations of the little kingdom model from different theoretical points of view.

Most of the authors who contributed to this volume have participated in research influenced or even initiated by Hermann Kulke, either as his students or his colleagues. His role as a member and later spiritus rector of the German Research Foundation Orissa projects in 1971-76 and 1999-2005 is particularly significant for our current activities as researchers. The editors and Burkhard Schnepel, who worked jointly on the conference and this volume, wish to take the opportunity of expressing their heartfelt gratitude to Hermann Kulke and dedicate this volume to him on the occasion of his 65th birthday in 2003.

Georg Berkemer and Margret Frenz

Notes

1 In a manner of speaking, the little kingdom model belongs to the realm of "theory". We prefer to talk of a model, i.e., a tool of research, since theory reflects reality in formal language and contains a set of rules that allows for explanations and predictions.

2 It proved helpful in this discussion to refer to concepts of non-European notions of the past, as used in various cultural contexts by Geertz (1966) and Sahlins (1985). Similarly, Andre Wink has applied concepts of Middle Eastern political thinking to 18th century South Asian history (Wink 1986). See also Declan Quigley (1993) for his integration of local and community history in Hindu ritual processes.

3 Several attempts have been made to express the idea of structural unity through historical and anthropological models (Stein 1980; Sharma 1965; Kulke 1976, 1978f, 1979, 1982b) Chattopadyaya 1983; Berkemer 2001b). The most successful little kingdom models so far are those of Cohn and Nicholas Dirks. For a history of these models, see the second chapter in

this volume.

4 See Cohn's writings from the 1970s and 1980s (Cohn 2001d, f, g), Stein (1977, 1980, 1985), Henige (1975), Dirks (1976, 1979, 1982, 1987), Sinha (1987), Kulke (1982b, 1985 [English translation 1995b]).

History of the Model

Burkhard Schnepel/Georg Berkemer

The problem in brief

The papers collected in this volume are the result of a second attempt to organise a conference on the little kingdom. The first one, proposed by Burkhard Schnepel and later by Georg Berkemer and Burkhard Schnepel, was planned for the year 2000 but had to be cancelled due to the bankruptcy of the sponsor. The second, more successful attempt was organised on a much smaller scale by Margret Frenz and Georg Berkemer as part of the 17th Conference on Modern South Asian Studies at Heidelberg in 2002. Unfortunately, Burkhard Schnepel was unable to participate.

The editors of this volume decided to include a somewhat abridged and updated version of the introductory paper originally written by Burkhard Schnepel for the first conference. Since it is a useful historiographical account of the development of the little kingdom model, Berkemer revised it at Schnepel's request. In order not to disturb the argument, the editors decided to add a second historiographical piece, particularly to outline the role of Hermann Kulke in this line of research.

At the centre of the proposed symposium and the subsequent conference stands the politico-ritual unit of the "little kingdom" in South Asia. Since this unit existed in large numbers in almost all historical periods and regions of South Asia, it is its empirical significance alone that urges us to place it more decisively than has hitherto been the case in the focus of scholarly attention.

However, there were "wider" reasons for dedicating a symposium to this unit (to our knowledge for the first time):

a) Organising research with the little kingdom as the main focus and frame of reference brings many new sources to light, which have up to now been ignored all too often by historians, anthropologists and indologists alike.

b) The fact that these sources are not only different in content, but often also in type requires us to rethink the methodological approaches that have conventionally guided the disciplines concerned and, if necessary, to venture into new ones.

c) In this context, the little kingdom proves itself to be an appropriate and heuristically fruitful frame of reference in and through which an intensification of the interdisciplinary cooperation between anthropology, history and indology can be advanced.

d) Some of the most controversial issues in research on South Asia can be shown in a new light, not *despite* focusing on the unit of the little kingdom, but precisely *because* of doing so.

The state of the art

Let us now provide a brief overview of some of the more important studies of little kingdoms in South Asia that have been put forward so far. We will also thereby strive to indicate the questions, problem areas and lacunae discussed by the participants at the conference.

The little kingdoms of South Asia have been ignored for too long by scholars of all academic disciplines concerned. This academic neglect of a form of political organisation that is found in substantial numbers in most historical periods and regions of South Asia indicates an intellectual blind spot, which seems to be rooted in various "orientalist" prejudices rather than in the insignificance of the institution as such. One of these prejudices probably arises out of the conceptual dichotomy between the state and the village, which has dominated Indian research for so long and which, it appears, has left little room for the intellectual recognition of intermediate levels of political organisation. Another reason may be that when it came to interpreting Indian polities the Western centralised state model used to be taken as the main point of reference. As a consequence of this Western bias (which was also taken over by many Indian scholars), the structural unit of the little kingdom has long represented for many scholars not so much an integral component of Indian political systems as a deviation from the norm. Its existence was either completely ignored or taken as a manifestation of the assumed "oriental" inability to put a state, as we know it, into practice.

This state of affairs has changed to some extent, as the study of little kingdoms has been taken up and advanced in various directions in recent years. The term "little kingdom" was first coined and discussed by Cohn (2001b [1987, 1962]) in his analysis of the political system of the eighteenth-century Benares region, where he distinguishes four levels within the Indian political system of that time, from the imperial level of the Moguls down to the fourth, the local level. Here he identifies several types of ruling groups, including what in his view is the most important politico-judicial unit of the pre-colonial "prestige and power system", namely the little kingdom. Commenting on the constant conflicts and skirmishes between the Raja of Benares and the Nawab of Oudh and on the latter's inability to crush the raja militarily, Cohn emphasises that "on the raja's side was the need for legitimacy" and that "power the raja had; but he needed authority as well" (Cohn: 2001b

[1987]: 489). Cohn's analysis must therefore be understood as referring to a hierarchical structure of honour, legitimacy and authority, not to one of relations of command and obedience or of power. Little kings needed authority and honour (manifested in emblems of legitimacy, titles, ritual privileges, etc.), and these were hierarchical and relative, whereas power was not necessarily so.

In his study of the Indian caste system, Dumont (1980: 389f) took up Cohn's concept of the little kingdom, observing that this unit, not the village, was the main politico-economic unit in which actual caste systems were embedded on the ground. However, Dumont only acknowledges the existence and importance of the little kingdom after first subsuming power and the realm of politics on the one hand to status and the socio-religious realm of the hierarchical caste system on the other. For Dumont, the principle of royal authority was encompassed and dominated by the principle of caste. The very existence of kingdoms as little ones is explained as the result of a fragmentary caste force; little kingdoms seem to be nothing other than kingdoms crippled by caste. Therefore, although acknowledging the territorial congruence between local caste systems and little kingdoms, Dumont does not arrive at a positive evaluation of the little kingdom. Consequently, he also fails to see that little kingdoms and their rulers provided crucial links between village, tribal and caste levels of organisation, on the one hand, and regional or imperial levels of organisation on the other.

Stein, too, took up Cohn's lead when he set out to dismantle the conventional historiographical notion of the medieval south Indian state as a centralised and hierarchically organised bureaucratic state, proposing instead that "most, if not all, ancient and medieval states of India are better designated and analysed as 'segmentary states'" (Stein 1977: 5). This form of state, according to Stein, consists of a multitude of political centres. One of them exercises ritual hegemony, although its effective political and military power over the other centres is weakened the further the latter move away from the core in the direction of the periphery. These other centres are simply reflections of the prime centre on a smaller scale. Their rulers exercise actual political sovereignty over their respective segments, while remaining ritually aligned to and dependent on an overlord. That makes a congeries of local political systems into a segmentary state is therefore the acknowledged ritual sovereignty exercised by one of them. Furthermore, in clarifying his model, Stein distinguishes two kinds of sovereignty, one "ritual" or "merely symbolic", the other "actual political". Like Cohn, then, Stein sees legitimacy and authority rather than power and command at the centre of the relationship between great kings and little kings. It was through their acknowledgement of a higher ritual authority that local chiefs were able to gain and uphold their status as kings, albeit little ones.

Tambiah has identified the ancient Indo-Tibetan *maṇḍala* conception as lying behind circular forms of the political organisation in South and Southeast Asia. "What emerges", he says, "is a galactic picture of a central planet surrounded by differentiated satellites, which are more or less 'autonomous' entities held in orbit and within the sphere of the centre" (1985b: 261). In Tambiah's model of the galactic state, the central kingdom – manifested in the person of the king, his residence and the palace – attracts its satellites by being exemplary. It is exemplary in a cosmological sense, as it synecdochically represents the whole world; and in a ritual and performative sense, as it controls and performs the galaxy's most important rituals, regenerating the cosmos and expressing authority in symbolical forms. The numerous components that encircle the centre of the universal ruler or *cakravartin* in their various orbits are simply imitative replicas of the centre. The centripetal and centrifugal forces operating in this galaxy constitute and maintain only a precarious balance of the whole, since the various satellites at the peripheries constantly attempt to split off and join another galaxy, or strive to become central kingdoms themselves. Tambiah's model of the state as "center-oriented space" is a useful alternative to the Western conception of the state as "bounded space". However, one weakness of Tambiah's model lies in the fact that the single components of the galactic polity – in itself open at its peripheries – are themselves regarded as being territorially too bounded.

A historical-developmental perspective to the picture is added by Kulke in his "processural" model of the Indian state. In early medieval India there were, as Kulke (1979) has shown in historiographical detail using Orissan data, several constant nuclear areas from which the larger political units that emerged later on in history were formed. Putting his findings on a more abstract level, Kulke (1995b) has argued that state formation in India took the form of unification of several nuclear areas into larger polycentric realms. These larger sub-regional, regional and transregional kingdoms came into existence through the gradual extension of their spheres of influence in concentric circles, first beyond their core regions into the peripheries of their realms, then over other nuclear areas, defeating their kings and turning them into tributary kings as part of newly-established *sāmantacakra*s or "galactic polities" (Tambiah). Following Kulke, state formation in India therefore represented (in the words of Kosambi) a form of "feudalism from below", and not the degeneration and fragmentation of a formerly larger empire into a great number of smaller segments, as envisaged in conventional images of the Indian feudal state.

All the approaches discussed so far have in common that they recognise the fragmented and composite character of the state in India and try to integrate this recognition into their theories or models in positive ways. They make us realise that the study of South Asian polities will not get very far if it continues to ignore the unit of the little kingdom and place the Western notion of the state as *the* paradigm against which Indian data are to be projected and judged. In addition, these approaches also indicate that it is necessary to reach a substantially different evaluation of actions and attitudes commonly labelled negatively with terms such as rebellion, dissent or insubordination. In this regard, it is especially Wink who points out in his study of Maratha conquest under late Mughal rule that there has been a tendency to explain these and similar competitive and dynamic elements of Indian politics through "a mentalistic jargon" (Wink 1986: 6). "There is at best", he notes, "an acknowledgement of a different system of 'ethics' but never of a different political system" (ibid.). Instead, he urges us to interpret the constant forging, breaking and realigning of political alliances as basic to the art of statecraft in India.

As confirmation and an extension of Wink's insights, Kolff's study on the "military labour market" in Hindustan from 1450 to 1850 can be consulted (Kolff 1990). Kolff illustrates the agonistic character of the state in the north of India at that time. His attention is less on the *zamīndāri* or little kingdom stratum of society as on the well-armed and battle-hardened farmer stratum, that is, on those "almost ungovernable tens of millions of people protected by mud forts, jungles and ravines all over the plains of Hindustan", who were "as free to become rebels as they were to turn auxiliaries" (Kolff 1990: 7). However, the *zamīndārs* or little kings are attributed a decisive role as intermediary "dealers in manpower" (Kolff 1990: 65). Moreover, Kolff argues that the term "Rajput", literally "son of the king", did not initially designate an endogamous caste but was a generic title for a multiplicity of relatively open groups originating in military service. In harmony with more recent theories of ethnicity and the formation of group identities, where the focus of analysis lies more on discursive practices and their social and political logic than on encapsulated social units, Kolff argues that "social identities could be achieved in a manner that was diffuse and dynamic" (Kolff 1990: 66-7) and that "India's multiplicity of identities represented as many integrative concepts, as many communities of memories and expectation" (Kolff 1990: 70). Hence, Kolff aptly stresses the dynamics and flexibility of identities, titles and possessions, even kingly ones, at all levels of the socio-political system, thereby further advancing our understanding of the importance of agency on the part of the actors of all categories.

In the context of the problems of "Rajputishness" and "Rajputisation" that lie at the ideological and empirical base of many little kingdoms, it is also necessary to go further west in India and look at Rajasthan, the region said to have been the cradle of the Rajputs and that was covered with numerous little kingdoms throughout many periods in history. Chattopadhyaya's work is relevant in this context. He focused on the mediaeval period of Rajasthan (8th-12th century) and especially on the processes and mechanisms of early state formation (Chattopadhyaya: 1976, 1995

[1994, 1983]). Hence, in his work we find further insights into the Rajput problem as well as into the processual model developed by Kulke (Kulke: 1995b). Rajasthan is also the focus of a recent study by Teuscher (Teuscher 2000), where the period at the height of Mogul power (15th-16th century) and little-kingly rule in Rajasthan stands at the centre of investigation. In general, focusing on little kingdoms in Rajasthan will provide new insights on how clan-based tribal societies were able to develop into kingdoms in mediaeval India and continue to exist, at first under Mogul and then under British rule.

The difficulty of coming to terms with this and other data does not appear to be merely a question of finding a model for the state in South Asia. The issue of how to interpret the manifold interrelations and mutual dependencies of religion and politics also arises. In modern European ideology, and hence in the conceptual paradigms that guide Western scientific thought, these domains have come to be regarded as two separate entities. This perspective, particular to Western thought, is reflected in and has influenced the interpretation of kingship and the state in India. We saw, for example, that Cohn seeks to come to terms with the interrelationships of kingdoms by distinguishing between power, on the one hand, and legitimate authority on the other. His distinction is reflected in Stein's model of the segmentary state where power is connected with the realm of politics and authority with the realm of ritual. Moreover, Stein ascribes different kinds of effectiveness to these two aspects by presenting ritual as merely symbolic and politics as actually effective. In his research on the relationship between the Gajapati king and the cult of Jagannath, Kulke (for example, 1993) also expresses the view that the ideological and ritual link between the Gajapatis and Jagannath grew more intense the more their actual political power faded. His diachronic view of the relation between politics and religion thus mirrors the synchronic view outlined by Stein. In both models, symbolic ritual hegemony tends to substitute real political power the more the latter proves ineffective, either at the periphery of a kingdom or because power was historically on the wane.

In his study on the south Indian little kingdom of Pudukkottai, Dirks (1987) criticises this point of view, and it is evident that this doyen of present-day studies on the little kingdom (also Dirks 1979, 1982, 1986) arrives at a different picture precisely because and not in spite of his focus on the unit of the little kingdom. With direct reference to Stein, Dirks points out that "the analytic separation of state structure from state ritual ignores the diffusion of ritual forms associated with kingship throughout all modes and levels of political relationships" (Dirks 1979: 172). Elsewhere, Dirks (1987) directs the main thrust of his critique against Dumont in response to the latter's view of Indian society as based principally on a religiously articulated caste system, and criticises likewise his method of interpreting the relationship between politics and religion. Instead, Dirks holds that, prior to the emergence of British colonial rule, "kings were not inferior to Brahmans, the political domain was not encompassed by a religious domain" (Dirks 1987: 4). He further expresses the view that social structure cannot be isolated as autonomous and uninflected by political authority. On the contrary, it is argued that "Indian society, indeed caste itself, was shaped by political struggles and processes" (ibid.: 5) and that "caste was embedded in a political context of kingship" (ibid.: 7). Dirks stresses this point when writing that "the prevalent ideology had not to do, at least primarily, with purity and pollution, but rather with royal authority, and honor, and associated notions of power, dominance and order" (ibid.). He then seeks a better understanding of Indian society by giving greater attention to what ritual does, ritual as a form of action that should not be separated from but regarded as an integral part of the politico-economic domain, related in complex ways. Central importance is given to the role of prestations. These are not seen simply as economic transactions but as rituals of incorporation that play a seminal role in the establishment and maintenance of dominance and political sovereignty.

While this approach offers new insights concerning the interrelation between politics and religion in India, it, in turn, should be discussed. Dirks, as we have seen, criticises Dumont's view of the Indian caste system as a purely religious phenomenon and of religion as encompassing the politico-economic domain. He regards this pre-eminence given to spirituality in the Asian mind as a form of "Orientalism". Consequently, he sets out "to stress the political both to redress the previous emphasis on 'religion' and to underscore the social fact that caste structure, ritual form, and political process were all dependent on relations of power" (Dirks 1987: 5). However, by thus counter-balancing a supposedly Orientalist view of Indian society, Dirks himself appears to be trapped in a Western, "Machiavellian" view. Ritual actions and beliefs are presented primarily as tools in the pursuit of political power. In other words, Dirks does not see them as forces in their own right either, that is, as forces that cannot simply be reduced to evidence of other forms of politics or representations of the dependent variables.

Galey successfully captures the notion of a further change when he writes: "We are here to change our mental habits for we are not dealing with the religion of politics but with the politics of religion" (Galey 1990b: 132). At this point, the significance of Indology in the interdisciplinary study of the little kingdom reveals itself. After all, the studies discussed so far have shown that it is vital to be free of Western conceptions of the state, for example, or of the "proper" relationship between politics and religion. If the situation in South Asia is to be understood in indigenous terms, it will be more necessary than ever to look at emic texts and the conceptualisations held by the actors themselves. There are, of course, quite a number of studies concerned with the political theologies and philosophies embodied in India's classical texts and ancient rituals, for example Drekmeier (1962), Dumont (1962), Heesterman (1985) and Lingat (1973) to mention but a few. This turning to the indigenous "archive" (in Foucault's sense of the term) from the perspective of textual criticism and linguistics could add another key dimension to South Asian research under the following conditions: a) that Indologists combine the level of classical texts and rituals with the analysis of historical kingdoms, as is the case particularly with Inden (1990), Narayana Rao / Shulman / Subrahmanyam (1993, 2001), Shulman (1980, 1985), and Subrahmanyam / Shulman (1990); and b) that the little ones among the historical kingdoms take centre stage and become more sharply focused. This last point should be specified in the context of the proposed symposium.

Indological studies concerned with little kingdoms bring a whole new range of texts into the limelight, texts that are extraordinary but often ignored, such as local ballads; oral traditions; family chronicles of little kingdomly dynasties and local magnates; legal documents, petitions and complaints by competing kings to colonial courts; documents from local archives; manuscripts pertaining to smaller temples and local ceremonies; as well as other expressions of the "little" traditions of subaltern groups. Moreover, Indological studies that focus on material pertinent to little kings are relevant for more theoretical and apparently paradoxical reasons. Let me explain. In studying aspects of royal authority in South Asia, Indologists have primarily dealt with texts written by Brahman ideologues and/or the panegyrists of great kings, i.e., they were mostly concerned with the ideal of kingship. The historical existence, let alone significance of little kings is not reflected in this context at all and if so, negatively (when they become "rebels"). Naturally, when it comes to studying texts produced by little kings or from within little kingdoms, these sources, too, are more often than not idealising and ideological in character. However, studying this material more deeply enriches our view of the ideological and intellectual side of Indian life, since it will make us more sensitive to the fact that ideas and ideologies in South Asia were not monolithic dogmas but dynamic matters of negotiation and contestation. In a nutshell, the Indological side of little kingdom research promises new insights as far as the multifaceted, relativistic, dynamic and contested character of ideology (including religion) in India is concerned, and with regard to the dialectic relationship between these contested ideologies and "factual matters".

Berkemer (1993, 1997, forthcoming a, forthcoming b) and Schnepel (1997, 2000, 2002) have expanded on some of the studies mentioned so far and added their own material from north Andhra and south Orissa, respectively, thereby also stressing the dynamic, relativistic and processual side of the problems discussed so far. Their works show that in order to qualify a king as little, reference should not primarily be made to absolute, measurable units such as the territorial size of a primarily be made to absolute, measurable units such as the territorial size of a kingdom or the number of villages it contains. The description of a king as little, they stress, only acquires heuristic value when it is used to understand the dynamic network of relationships between kings of different ranks. The identification of a king as little should therefore be based on relational, quite abstract politico-ritual criteria, which can undergo rapid historical change and are often subject to contradictory interpretations by the different actors, whether individuals or groups. In brief, a king is little in the shifting tense relationship with another king, who counts as "great" in precisely this relationship. On the other hand, a king is (or becomes) great, not because he is the lord of a clearly marked and rigidly bounded territory but because he is the master of (re–)distribution of land, offices, titles and other gifts that symbolise and constitute royal authority. In this way, he allows others to partake of his "universal" royal authority and binds them into a system of hierarchical solidarity that is simultaneously one of conflictual negotiations.

The works of Galey (1990a, b), Schnepel (1995a) and Peabody (e.g., 1991b, 2003) exemplify that the study of little kingdoms is not confined to archival research. Little kingdoms can indeed be studied by anthropologists with their very own methods and perspectives (such as participant observation) on the ground today. That such research is possible is immediately evident when we point to the fact, stressed and developed especially by Galey, that a distinction should be made between kings, kingdoms and kingship. This latter aspect (one could also speak of the principle of royal authority) has always led a somewhat independent life from the former two. Hence, it is no surprise that it has continued to exist to the present day, although kings and kingdoms have disappeared, albeit with changing aspects. Now, because ideas and values connected with kingship have always expressed themselves strongly in rituals and, as Peabody in particular has shown, the anthropology of little kingdoms re-enters with the fetishisation and circulation of emblems of power. Again, the focus on little kingdoms adds a further dimension to those of traditional anthropological studies, as it looks at legitimising rituals of kings on the ground and at how these rituals are closely associated with subaltern ritual beliefs and the practices of common subjects (rather than with some abstract great traditions and Brahmanical ideals).

Moreover, an ethnohistory of little kingdoms can produce new insights on the administration and organisation of local communities, as shown in particular by Tanabe (e.g., 1999b) and Frenz (2000, 2003) respectively in their studies on little kingdoms in central Orissa and Malabar. For, although the overall administrative and political set-ups in which they are embedded have certainly changed and not left the local community level unaffected, some of the more basic organisational structures and interaction mechanisms that were active in little kingdoms at local level still prevail today. Finally, while most little kingdom scholars have so far worked on the coast, Galey and Schnepel undertook a further interesting step into the mountainous and jungled hinterlands (of Garhwal and South Orissa). As a result, the relationship between king and caste no longer came primarily to the fore. Instead, the relationship between tribal groups and Hindu kings (Schnepel coined the term "jungle kingdoms" for this little kingdom sub-category) emerged as a significant path to be investigated in studies on little kingdoms in the remote hinterlands. How did the legitimising ritual policy of a little king change in the context of tribal ritual practices and beliefs? How were tribal societies administratively linked to the clan-based dominant groups within these little kingdoms? And how were some tribal societies themselves able to develop into little kingdoms?

Hermann Kulke: An Appreciation of His Contribution to the Debate

Georg Berkemer/Margret Frenz

History as we see it is not the discovery of "truth" in objective facts about the past, but the process of selecting and interpreting texts[1] about different peoples and times past and present, which fit into a preconceived notion constructed by historians who are dependent on contemporary ideas in their own cultural context for the formulation of questions and interpretations. Despite being en vogue in present post-modern historiographical critique, this methodological self-criticism is by no means a symptom of the latest fin-de-siècle intellectual crisis. Looking back, we see that shifts of paradigm in historical thinking occurred quite frequently. However, there are a few notions from all but noble antiquity that even the most fervent efforts seem unable to root out, one of which is the idea that there is no indigenous voice in traditional Indian history. It has been rightly criticised that Indian history has been subjected to all kinds of theoretical approaches, conceived outside India's cultural sphere and originally with completely different aims in sight. Thus, many historical interpretations that are used to "explain" things Indian are a by-product of research in other regions, usually Europe.

Even the most ardent critique on the side of post-colonial historical criticism cannot deny its roots in the Anglo-American paradigm, which tends to focus on colonial history in either an apologetic or a critical mode. All critiques may agree that mainstream Anglo-American history writing about India deals with facets of or approaches to modernity. There are other paradigms similarly dependent on non-indigenous notions, i.e., the more continental Indological tradition still predominant in Germany, whereby ancient India is understood more as a sister of Pharaonic Egypt or ancient Greece than as the mother of modern India. In other words, regardless of the leading paradigm, there is a tendency to select and subdivide, and to ignore what does not fit into one's own boundaries of time, ideology and mind. This also holds true for attempts to amend the situation by applying the grand theories (Hegel, Marx, Weber, Dumont) and their epigones (Huntington, World Bank experts etc.).

Since "ideas" as opposed to "facts" structure one's own research approach, a critique of the shortcomings of such an approach cannot be derived from historical sources but can, on the contrary, only succeed with the aid of alternative models and theories. Different non-European historical situations are taken into account in a comparative approach. Thus, the much criticised Nilakanta Sastri (1975, 1984) used the not-so-European Byzantine empire for his comparisons, while his critic Burton Stein took his ideas from the East African state of the Alur (Southall 1956, 1987). Others used methods from neighbouring subjects in the tradition of Bernard Cohn. Despite the criticism showered on these models, they provide useful tools for the small scale of micro-level research. Nonetheless, a fundamental problem remains: all of the alternatives fail to provide a comprehensive theory to bridge the gap between a) ancient India and colonial/post-colonial modernity and b) micro study and world historical theory. This lacuna was painfully felt by many Indian historians, who saw their own "emotional home" completely neglected in history. Although perceived as "one" in the eyes of the "outsider", India falls easily into independent cultural units if looked at from an internal perspective. It can be rightly said that the majority of Indian historians focus precisely on those areas that have been neglected by both Anglo-American and German schools of anthropology and philology. Indian regional histories are usually constructed in hindsight. They establish the current situation of late colonial or early post-colonial statehood from a "glorious" regional past perspective, which, in turn, becomes the starting-point for criticism of the inefficiency of modern politics and education under the ongoing influence of Muslim or European ideas. Here again, the tendency to subdivide history into historic periods and social groups can be observed.

First of all, indigenous ideas and concepts must be unearthed in an attempt to find structures that would overcome traditional "Western" boundaries of periodisation and academic subjects. Indian history essentially calls for a non-Hegelian approach that can surmount traditional typologies and look for long-term developments, hierarchies of cultural processes, and interdisciplinary research. Normally, there is a breach between the approaches of the various disciplines and between large-scale (micro-level) and small-scale models (macro-level). Although efforts have been made to bridge the gap, the meso-level has suffered from a lack of theoretical thoroughness. In short, regional perspectives in history, anthropology, linguistics, for example, are still lagging behind their counterparts, with material based on larger and smaller levels of perception. Here, Kulke's regional approach serves to formulate historical models on a micro- or meso-level, which can be used to criticise or amend the macro-level approaches of comparative and world history. Kulke began his research in the 1970s when he studied the towns of Chidambaram and Puri, using his local knowledge to extend research to the regional level, onto which he applied theories from both the macro and the micro perspective. In the course of his research, he made it clear that regional research constitutes a value of its own. Contrary to constructing a "whole" of which it can never be more than a "deficient" part, a region can reveal itself more comprehensively if seen from its various centres and peripheries.

Behind the difficulties encountered by scholars on the middle level lies the incompatibility of meso-level European models with similar models in other parts of the world. Experience shows that results of regional data are very difficult to fashion into a useful tool for cultural comparison. Macro-level concepts can be used for comparison, as in the case of European feudalism and its Indian counterpart. It is also possible to reach the meso-level by looking at parts of the superior structural level. Furthermore, it is useful to compare micro-level structures such as those of the village, guild or town. There is, however, not much insight to be gained from comparing the history of France, for instance, with the history of Orissa (Berkemer 1998: 185-190).

Kulke himself demonstrated the usefulness of both macro-level comparison (Kulke: 1982c [English translation 1992b]) and micro-level compatibilities in a field where conventional history least expects them, namely historiography (Kulke 1993c, 1998, 2001c, forthcoming b). Here, he shows how Indian societies reconstruct their past in a fairly similar manner to their contemporaries in other parts of the world. Differences occur with regard to how the past is valued and the role it plays for the recipients of these texts. His regional studies extended from political history to historiography, and included various approaches such as art history and anthropological theory, which he successfully applied to historical situations in Orissa ranging from early states and their nuclear areas around 500 AD to the end of British rule in 1947. This regionalist approach has provided a paradigm for students of similar studies both inside and outside India, who widened the scope into other areas using his findings for comparative studies in interregional contexts.

In his numerous writings, Kulke has dealt with the historiography of the princely states of Orissa, their predecessors, the "feudatories" of the Orissan empire, as well as with religious and symbolic legitimation of power on various levels from local to imperial rule. He uses an interdisciplinary approach, adding evidence, such as the representations of rule in art, architecture and town planning, to the written sources by tracing the development of sacred sites from tribal origins to pan-Indian Hinduism or similar symbolic ideas in non-Hindu societies. In short, Kulke was highly influential in making the scholarly community aware of the independent consciousness of Indian cultural regions, as exemplified in the case of Orissa. Here he shows that despite fundamental changes in the course of modernisation, the identity of society has remained intact from its medieval origins up to today.

The critique and close collaboration with some of the above-mentioned scholars led him to formulate his conclusions in a "processural model of integrative state formation". Kulke's model is utilised in this volume as a starting point to illustrate the dynamics behind the history of little kingdoms and thus incorporate aspects of long duree and other processes of change (Kulke 1980, 1995b). A detailed introduction to the model is crucial to understanding the significance of the approach.

Kulke's Contribution to the Debate on State Formation in India

Kulke feels the need to create a model that includes both state formation and the principles underlying the interrelations of the kingdoms in Orissa. Since both the older little kingdom model (Cohn, Dirks) and the segmentary state model (Stein) were unable to describe the complexity of the Orissan situation adequately, he began to amend them, especially by enlarging the time scale. Kulke's emphasis was on process, both as a temporal and a spatial frame. He shows that small straightforward polities that tended, if successful, to grow in complexity and extend in the course of their existence, were established throughout Orissan history. On the other hand, there is a general tendency towards larger and multi-level kingdoms, so that we can talk about an "evolution" of state structure in the region. While early polities after Samudra Gupta (350 AD), which represented the highest level of political development at that time, tend to be confined to single surplus-producing nuclear areas and prove to have been administered by merely a few experts, the later imperial kingdoms span much larger areas and reveal the existence of a methodical bureaucratic apparatus as well as a sophisticated display of grandeur. This progress has not been taken into account in the old little kingdom model, which tends to focus on single case studies of small polities, neglecting thereby the interrelations or possible developments of such small states. The little kingdom of Khurda in Orissa (Kulke 1979) is an ideal case in point for use in comparison with the Putukottai worked on by Nicholas Dirks, since it existed in the 19th century, the time span concentrated on by Dirks, in a similar situation in relation to the British colonial state. Unlike Putukottai, however, it is part of a line of succession in the imperial tradition (Gajapati) and serves as both the centre and the model for all regional little kings of Orissa. Kulke shows that the little kingdom model is not only relevant to British time as an ethno-historic complement to the imperialist concept of the princely state, but also a logical consequence of earlier state structures of pre-British time.

The Three-phase-model

In his model, Kulke adopts an evolutionist point of view in an attempt to generalise processes of Hindu state formation arising from non-state and often non-Hindu societies that came under the influence of earlier states, such as the Gupta empire or medieval regional empires (Colas, Calukyas, Rashtrakutas, Palas etc.). As inscriptional evidence shows, many of the early medieval royal families of Orissa are of local and somewhat "obscure" origin (e.g., Banerji 1928, Behera 1982; Singh Deo 1939). Inscriptions refer to succession from tribal chiefs and divine intervention as prerequisites for the foundation of small Hindu states in previously non-Hindu areas.

1. The Emergence of a State

We assume the existence of local elites who are familiar with the concept of state society, either as an import from outside or as the remainder of a previously existing state structure. When the elites of these societies begin to follow a local variant of Hindu life, the idea of the state is inevitably put into practice. However, their restricted means of communication with the outside and their limited control over their subjects usually keep them dependent on "tribal" support, i.e., they are forced to concede to the symbolic dominance of non-Hindu deities and their rituals at the level of local belief, custom and authority.

A significant example of these processes, which has survived to the present day, is the hybrid structure of religious institutions where tribal priests, for instance, play an important role in Hindu temples (Jagannath), thereby providing a platform for common religious practices among tribals and Hindus in legitimatory rituals (in the politico-ritual scene). This tie to tribal deities provides the king with a vital link to his subjects. Small political units of this type exist in a precarious situation, not only in terms of ideology and legitimation but also in relation to their size. The earliest inscriptions show that only the largest nuclear areas provided sufficient surplus for a continuous growth of the state over a span of several generations. In many cases, however, rulers had to shift back and forth between their existence as a Hindu king on the fringes of the "jungle" and their retreat into this environment that restored their appearance as a "tribal" chief.[2] Kulke has shown that apart from their palaces, these "jungle-kings" maintain one or more forts in the jungle, where both secular rulership and the associated deity are housed in a tribal environment (Kulke 1978a, 1980, 1984b, 2001b, forthcoming b).

2. The Establishment of a Power Pyramid

For the kings fortunate enough to gain a foothold in a larger surplus-producing area, the shift to a new phase of rulership is feasible in the form of a sub-regional kingdom based on the surplus of a large river valley or estuary, where regular surplus and wet rice irrigation provides the materials for a large force of specialists (priests, courtiers, artisans and an army). The second phase is characterised by the establishment of a small power pyramid. Five nuclear areas in Orissa proved capable of supporting a sub-regional state over the centuries (Kulke 1979). Capital cities and fortresses can be traced in these areas, where pan-Indian deities in elaborate Hindu temples take over the role of the Hinduised tribal deities of the first phase. The tribal origin of this state becomes more and more obscured and, in many cases, the state deity (*rāṣṭradevatā*) is taken from the Hindu pantheon, leaving the king's family god (goddess) as the ultimate reminder of the family ties to tribal society. This process repeats itself outside of these areas in the so-called princely states of Orissa during the 18th and 19th centuries, when kings had other means of income apart from agriculture. At the same time, this phase is marked by the beginning of the king's political dominance over smaller kingdoms and the integration of his kingdom into the imperial order of a great king, should one exist.

Part of this process are the new legitimatory styles, such as *praśasti* writings, where the immigration theme supersedes previous tales of local origin that hint too strongly at the possible tribal roots of the dynasty. These developments occur within the context of larger historical processes on a pan-Indian and global scale. In the case of Orissa, the influence of imperial states from outside (Bengal, Andhra etc.) must always be taken into account. In reality, one or more of these changes usually occur simultaneously and it would be appropriate to describe the interaction between the local rulers as a field of social energy (Greenblatt 1988). Kulke's model also provides for strong dynamic short-time changes.

3. The Regional Empire

The third phase subsumes all cases of development whereby one state succeeds in dominating more than one nuclear area. In the case of Orissa, this happened only twice: at first when the Somavamsa dynasty conquered the Mahanadi delta in their nuclear area in Western Orissa, and later, when the Gangas of Kalinganagara established the Ganga empire, again in the Mahanadi delta. Kulke refers to similar developments in Tamil Nadu (Cola empire) and emphasises that these third phase developments never occur without reciprocal influence across cultural regions.

Ideally, a third phase empire is ruled by a king who styles himself *mahārāja-adhirāja*, since he rules over the power pyramid in his own nuclear area, as well as those of others, who are *mahārājas* in their own nuclear area in the second phase of the model.

Further Development of the Model

This model is an ideal addition to the somewhat static little kingdom model developed by Cohn and Dirks and serves as a starting point for our discussions. With his historical examples, Kulke shows how royal families succeed in establishing political dominance and, by emphasising ecology and surplus as well as ritualisation and legitimation, demonstrates the circumstances and conditions under which this development can take place. It is important to note that the processes described in the model continued for centuries and are not based on descriptions of singular events and historical exceptions. It allows us to stress the fact that these historical processes and transformations not only took place in early modern times, when there sources to analyse them abounded, but occurred in a very similar manner from early medieval times onwards, i.e., from when a Hindu state model was available and could be employed for state formation throughout South Asia (Berkemer 1993).

Kulke used this processual model to introduce his students to his method of looking at history as a dynamic process, without forgetting to emphasise again and again that processes as such are determined by specific structural features which, in turn, permit the development of manifold facets and their attendant expression in regional cultures and historical traditions. This approach clarifies that processes of this kind can only be traced if the sources are available. In many regions of India, however, historians are less fortunate than in Orissa, where sources are comparatively abundant and usually accessible.

The sources, which reveal how the processes described in the model actually worked, contain some outstanding texts, some of which were edited by Kulke himself. The most important one is the Kaṭakarājavaṃśāvali,[3] or the chronicle of the *rājās* of Khurda, which provides an insight into the workings of state in all three phases of Kulke's model. Similarly, a group of texts called the Chamu citaus (letters of privilege issued by the late Gajapatis of Puri to subordinate rulers and neighbours) gives a detailed insight into the subtleties of rank allotment by a superior ruler. Apart from interpreting these sources as evidence for the existence of a "theatre state" (Geertz 1980), they shed considerable light on the dynamics of the regional power pyramid that constitutes part of the little kingdom model. The obligation of incorporating sources from the Mackenzie Collection into the review of local Orissan history should be mentioned at this point, since they illuminate the history of South Orissa, providing the Southern jungle kings (Schnepel) with a voice and encouraging researchers to look for similar sources throughout the region. Following in Kulke's footsteps, researchers such as Berkemer, Frese, Nanda, Schnepel, Skoda, and Tanabe have successfully collected and interpreted local "legends" as historical sources in Orissa. Other Orissa scholars such as Biswamoy Pati quote Kulke's works in order to emphasise the importance of long duree developments, even in the social history of the 20th century. During the 1990s, Kulke's colleagues and students worked on a synthesis of his processual model and the older little kingdom theory in order to create a comprehensive, region-based approach. Extensions of the older models are available both in terms of theory and application in new regional contexts. A case study on Kerala (Frenz), for instance, integrates the idea of the virtual king, indicating that the notion of kingship and the role of the king can be seen as separate social categories. Scholars such as Schnepel, Skoda and Tanabe make use of the model's emphasis on social processes to describe little kingdoms from the anthropologist point of view. Frese's historiographical critique contributes, in particular, to revealing the short-sightedness of typological approaches that do not allow for an analysis of the network complexity produced by texts, performances and conflicting traditions in a cultural area. Teuscher provides the hitherto most ambitious amendment to the model by radically re-interpreting the historical traditions of Rajasthan. The dynamics introduced to the little kingdom model by Kulke and his collaborators have made it possible to peruse the extremes in time and space it can trace. It has proved possible to apply it to post-Gupta medieval times (Berkemer 1993) and clarified that it is indigenous to the extent of having its counterpart in the Indian idea of the state (Arthaśāstra 1969; Nilakantha Bhatta 1925).

Finally, we would like to add an anecdote to illustrate the model's usefulness in even the most remote areas of India. An IAS officer came to Heidelberg once to write his PhD thesis – an analysis of the local history of a valley in remote Himachal Pradesh – under the supervision of Professor Kulke. As the scientific paradigm at that time (1980s) suggested, he assumed that his sources could only be read in one way: the valley kingdom was established by Rajputs, who came from outside, took over political rule and established a proper Hindu society. Kulke, however, suggested an alternative interpretation of the sources, using his experience from Orissa. He wanted his student to try and interpret the sources the other way round. Firstly, a local ruler established himself in a small area of the valley, using his own local deity as the focus of legitimation, thereby successfully incorporating Hindu kingship ideas in the little political entity. Only much later did his successors establish themselves as lords of the entire valley, found a hierarchy of smaller kings and religious institutions and, as a final step, establish themselves as outsiders, i.e., Rajputs according to the fashion of the day. This idea corroborates aptly with

Kulke's three-phase-model. When his student returned to Heidelberg after a field trip, he said to Kulke straight out, "You were right, sir!".

Notes

1 "Texts" should be understood here in a very general sense.

2 We are aware that the word "tribal" is ambivalent in the context of anthropological research. Nonetheless, it is used in South Asian studies as a technical term without any pejorative connotation. We take it here in the Indian administrative sense of the term, which is still in use today. For more details, see Pfeffer (2003).

3 Kaṭakarājavaṃśāvali (1987); for commentaries and Orissa predecessors see Kulke (1987), Mādaḷā Pañji 1940.

Very Little Kingdoms. The Calendrical Order of West Himalayan Hindu Polity

Peter Sutherland

> Difficulties in the anthropology of time hinge on the way we conceptualize its connections to space, action, and actor...With these difficulties in mind, I have tentatively sketched a notion of "temporalization" that views time as a symbolic process continually being produced in everyday practices (Munn 1992: 116)

> European reactions to Indian time reveal more about Europe than about India ... [T]here is more at issue than time alone. It is a question ... of time being an integument that joins the individual to the object of a quest, a source of knowledge and meaning, that lies beyond time: the pilgrim's progress toward salvation, or the nation's progress from rudeness to civilization. It is this sense that is baffled and affronted before the immensity of Indian time (Trautmann 1995b: 186).

Analyses of the Hindu state generally go hand in hand with top-down perspectives and centre-out "geometries of power" (Massey 1992). Despite the admitted variety of tropes employed by historians and anthropologists to characterize pre-modern Hindu polity – segmentary, exemplary, theatrical, mandalic, processual, jajmanic, or theophanic,[1] to name a few – all are conceptualized in elitist terms of dominant relations between the king and local groups. As a result, we have little idea of how the Hindu state was imagined and experienced from its margins by peasants. This is no doubt due to the inevitable concern with sovereignty and administration inscribed in surviving forms of historical evidence, which were generally the products of royal patronage – archives, coins, epigraphy, architecture, religious texts, and monarchical ritual. But what alternative geometries of interaction characterized the midfield of power between royal centre and rural periphery and, beyond that, the outfield of power linking peasants or kings with imperial formations? What modes of political communication were involved? How and where should we look for evidence?

To answer these questions in the absence of indigenous texts, I use the practical record of a current west Himalayan institution that villagers call "government by deity" (*devatā kā rāj*) to reconstruct the ritual practices of peasant agency in a pre-modern Hindu regional polity. Combining multi-sited ethnography in the Simla Hills and neighbouring parts of Jaunsar-Bawar and Garhwal with archival research in British colonial texts, and using a geographical approach to historical reconstruction, this essay complicates Bernard Cohn's (2001b [1962]) account of the "little kingdom" and its place in the global political order of 18th century India. I shall argue that evidence of a diminutive, west Himalayan version of the rural little kingdom, registered in contemporary *Pahārī* (i.e. mountain) religion, vividly demonstrates how processional practices integrated Hindu rural polities in a world-ordering scale of peasant, monarchical, imperial and cosmic formations during the period of indirect British rule from 1815 until independence – and, I suggest, under previous forms of foreign rule.

Bernard Cohn's interest in the little kingdom sprang from a similarly broad inquiry into political order. How did 18th century north India's political system actually work given the apparently anarchic conditions of transition from Mughal to British imperial rule? Seeking a more nuanced understanding of pre-modern political order as a whole, its eristical logic, and its cultural integration, he wished to know: "what – if any – were the enduring structures of political relationships, how parts of the social systems involved were connected, and what principles guided not just personal endeavours but the organization and utilization of power and authority" (ibid: 483). Having sketched the four levels that structured the 18th century political system – the remnants of the declining Mughal empire, its successor states, their regional clients, and the minimal local unit, the little kingdom – Cohn's essay focuses on British descriptions of pre-British politico-economic institutions. In particular, he examines the role of "secondary administrators," who acted as "hinges by which the levels of the political system were connected" (ibid: 494). In pursuing the details of administration, however, Cohn loses sight of the broader question, with which his article begins. How were the competing segments of society *culturally* integrated into the political system by the common values of "rituals, traditions, myths and histories through which the political order is legitimized and maintained" (ibid: 484). Revisiting that theme, this essay examines the cultural integration of a scale of west Himalayan little kingdoms by a ritual idiom of communication that elides modern Eurocentric distinctions between "religion" and "politics".

Combining ethnographic research with a critical re-reading of British colonial descriptions of pre-British conditions in the Simla Hills, I use the remarkable record of contemporary west Himalayan festival practice to reconstruct a pre-modern Hindu regional polity in the absence of indigenous textual data. Largely sheltered from the turmoil and change that transformed north India political life in the 18th century, the multi-media arts of Pahari religious performance present historians and anthropologists with a complex archive of peasant political memory, if we can but learn to read it. Understanding the political construction of space and time, I propose, is the key to decoding the historical archive of practice inscribed in the landscape. Focussing on its largest polity, the Bashahr kingdom, I use the regularities of processional movement to demonstrate how the units and relations of pre-modern political organization were defined, and their interactions choreographed, by a region-wide idiom of festival practice.

My evidence complicates Bernard Cohn's account of the little kingdom in two respects. On the one hand, I describe a little documented Himalayan Hindu idiom of shared sovereignty, which local people call "government by deity" (*devatā kā rāj*), and examine its role in integrating a scale of theistic polities of varying size and power. In this characteristic Pahari institution, sovereignty is shared in a ritual practice of collaborative rule, found at all levels of historical political organization, between a territorial tutelary god or goddess (*devatā* or *devī*), who quite literally governs as "king" (*rājā*) or "queen" (*rānī*), and the officers (*kārdārs*) of the "temple committee" that enable the deity to do so. These officers include the indispensable oracle, through whose trance-speech the deity is enabled to communicate with humans, the political leader (be it king, chief, or headman), the temple priest, and the treasurer, storekeeper, accountant, cook, herald, and other minor temple functionaries. Continuing the monarchical trope, the temple is understood to be the deity's "seat" (*kursī*), the kardars are his court of "ministers" (*mantri*) or "cabinet," as one informant put it in modern terms, and the deities of two other local castes act respectively as priest and henchman [I return to these below].

On the other hand, the evidence of government by deity takes discussion of the cultural integration of north Indian political order beyond 18th century conventions of sovereignty and legitimation by examining the historical practices of agency and political mobilization, which set Himalayan Hindu polity in motion under British and earlier forms of foreign rule. The evidence of Pahari government by deity confirms and extends Ronald Inden's (1990) historical reconstructions of political agency in the 9th and 10th century Rashtrakuta "imperial formation." Intent on restoring agency to the analysis of historical Indian society, Inden avoids an essentialist model of caste, rejects the concomitant view of peasants as separate from, and "patients" of, a despotic state, and focuses instead on the active processes of articulation, by means of which rural and urban polities participated in creating a "scale of forms"[2] (Collingwood's phrase) to constitute an imperial formation.

> [T]he acts that did so for the polities of the countryside of a kingdom were those carried out by assemblies of villages or of unions of villages in connection with meetings held in conjunction with the activities of the agricultural year. Similarly, the activities carried out at meetings held in conjunction with the major marketing days were...the acts that had the effect of shaping and reshaping the mercantile and manufacturing polities of the towns (ibid: 217).

Inden argues that the convening of overlapping territorial assemblies were "the acts that made and remade Indian polities." "Far from being opposed ... to an external state," rural castes and urban guilds "actively participated in [the state]. Indeed, by so doing they partly constituted it." Where the "state" was concerned, Inden looks to the army and to "the holding of court and royal progresses [as] the activities which ... reiterated and altered kingdoms as a whole and even entire imperial formations" (ibid). My fieldwork in the western Himalayas confirms the broad applicability of Inden's reconstruction, by revealing the surprising reproduction of similar processes for articulating peasant and former royal formations in contemporary west Himalayan festival practice. What the ethnographic evidence also reveals is the spatio-temporal ordering of a repertoire of processional practices not limited to the progress, which constitute all levels of political organization in the mid-field of power between village and palace. In other word, we see the enactment of pre-modern political practices in the present.

Taking up Inden's (1990, 1998) view of cyclic time as a central ordering principle in medieval Indian polity, I compare and contrast the *spatio-temporal* ordering of two contemporary and overlapping west Himalayan theistic polities by competing calendrical systems, to wit: the kingdom of Bashahr and the regional "empire" of the paramount god, *Mahāsu*.

The imposition of indirect British rule and its policy of "masterly inaction" in the Himalayan fringes of the Imperial Punjab Province, I argue, preserved (more by default than intention) a pre-modern repertoire of Hindu practices of political communication in the Simla Hills States District. The geometries of power that these practices describe are still reproduced in the ritualized movements of tutelary gods at contemporary festivals, albeit with translated meanings in the emergent context of post-colonial India. Paying close attention to the t(r)opology of divine power (*śakti*) traced by the mythic discourse and ritual movements of rural gods, my account adds to current understandings of assemblies in the Hindu state by charting the geographies of travel (i.e. convergence and dispersal), within which assemblies at political centres are embedded.

By paying close attention to processes of mobility, my research revealed two alternative, non-centrist geometries of power in addition to assemblies that still choreograph rural polity under government by deity, namely: circuits and networks. These three geometries of procession form a systematic repertoire of political communication and memory, by means of which *all* levels of organization and interaction, that once ordered historical west Himalayan Hindu polity in the era of kings, are still reproduced at contemporary festivals by processional practice. By seeing how these rural genres of geo-poetics are incorporated in two competing calendrical orders, it is possible to discern the trace of pre-British Himalayan political history – registered in the timescapes of contemporary festival movement.

In particular, what we see is the linkage of a complex *geo*politics of spatial formations (local, royal, imperial, and cosmic) and an equally complex *chrono*politics of temporal cycles (with corresponding periods ranging from one to one hundred years) by the sequencing of festivals in the annual calendar. This articulation of the spacing of time and the timing of space is conceptualized in indigenous terms of a cosmological metaphor, the "conquest of the year," inscribed in accounts of the annual battle of local gods and demons in heaven. Evoked in an oracular prophecy called *bakhān* (report), to which I return at the end of this chapter, this world-ordering military t(r)opology of battle in heaven organizes a transhistorical landscape of political memory, whose incorporation of different eras in the same discursive space defies the chronistic conventions of academic history. Not so much historical record as historical *practice*, the oracular discourse of bakhan instantiates a mode of linguistic agency comparable to 8th century Hindu theistic text production in Kashmir, which Ronald Inden (2000) has described as a "dialogical" and "eristical" mode of "world-articulation" – i.e. of making and remaking the world according to a particular world-vision. Inden suggests that the Kashmir kings who patronized the composition of the *Viṣṇudharmottarapurāṇa* and the *Rājataraṅgiṇī* used these texts not so much as mirrors of the world as it already existed, but rather as blueprints to reshape the world according to the theological prescriptions and reworkings of myth inscribed in the texts. Textual production, in other words, is one of the imaginative processes, by which the future course of history is projected. In the process, myth becomes historical reality. Similarly, bakhan's discourse of Pahari political memory not only inscribes a retrospective record of the past, but also enacts a prospective presentation of the past in order to produce the future – in predictable terms of annual calendrical order.

In so locating Hindu "historical consciousness" (Comaroff/Comaroff 1995, 1987) at the very site of its supposed non-existence, Hindu "cyclical time," as 18th century British Orientalists argued (see Trautmann 1995), it is possible not only to transcend western dichotomies of politics and religion that distort the study of the Hindu state, but also to revise dehistoricized conceptions of Indian, and especially Hindu, time distorted by 18th and 19th century Eurocentric discourse. Stephen Lansing's (1991) study of Balinese rice irrigation offers an exemplary approach to rethinking the historicity of non-linear temporal practices in the calendrical timing of agricultural rituals. Yet, in spite of repudiating Wittfogel's (1957) "hydraulic" theory of "oriental despotism," the author finds it hard to avoid reproducing a dichotomous analysis of villages and the state in the face of the apparently conflicting symbolism of peasant and royal idioms of power (ibid: 132). At the opposite extreme of Greater India, west Himalayan rural religion indicates the existence of a non-dichotomous construction of Hindu political economy in line with Inden's reconstructions, in which peasant and royal idioms of power intersect in the common spatial practices of theistic kingship. Rather than dichotomizing the religious and the political aspects of power, different levels of power are distinguished by the movements of travelling gods according to a calendrical order of processional practices.

Taking my cue from Ronald Inden's agentive reconstruction of Rashtrakuta and Kashmiri imperial formations (1990, 2000), I propose an analysis of the ritual production of time in space, or "temporalization" (Munn 1992), that inserts Hindu cyclical time into historical political practice. Himalayan festival practice bridges the gap between two familiar aspects of Indian time: the metaphysical macro-time of Hindu *cosmic* cycles (*yugas* and *samsāra*)[3] and the musical micro-time of Indic *rhythmical* cycles (*tāla*).[4] Between these two extremes, the *processional* cycles of Pahari festival practice define an intermediate temporality, in which political, agropastoral and cosmic relations are ordered by the ritual calendar.

Within this remembered Hindu polity on post-colonial India's national margins, I examine an alternative Himalayan system of *very* little kingdoms that complicates Cohn's view from Banaras in two important ways: 1) by further reducing the scale of political miniaturization; and 2) by the theistic inflection of kingship at all levels of organization. In particular, I demonstrate how the minimal unit of Himalayan rural political organization, best described as a micro-kingdom, is integrated in a regional scale of theistic polities by the calendrical ordering of festival processions. In this scale of Pahari theistic polities, we have gods as kings all the way down.

Four interlocking fields of government by deity are discussed, which constitute a scale of theistic sovereignties with characteristic processional practices: 1) contemporary peasant polity in Rohru district; 2) historical state-formation in the Bashahr kingdom; 3) the quasi-imperial regime of the regional god, Mahasu; and 4) the integration of all the above in bakhan's oracular landscape of memory.

British Histories of the Simla Hill States

Situated on India's militarized border with China/Tibet, the west Himalayan region I describe is roughly bounded by the Jumna and Sutlej rivers and the former British hill-stations of Mussoorie and Simla. Regional understandings of political location have changed several times over the longue durée according to different reterritorializations in successive foreign imperial formations: British, Gurkha, Mughal, Tibetan (Bhotiya), even possibly Kashmiri-Gandharan. According to many older Paharis, even the modern Indian nation-state is a foreign power. This essay uses British colonial sociology to locate contemporary Pahari religious practice in the historical context of the Himalayan Hindu state of Bashahr under indirect British and distant Mughal rule. Tibetan and possible Kashmir-Gandharan connections are briefly mentioned.

According to British colonial accounts from the first decade of the 19th century, the four great kingdoms of "Cahlore [Kahlur], Hindoor [Hindor], Bussahir [Bashahr] and Sirmoor [Sirmur],"[5] once formed a volatile Himalayan political arena that enjoyed effective autonomy under Mughal rule, acknowledging the Delhi Emperor only as a distant centre of legitimation. Within this arena, rulers vied with each other and the neighboring Kullu kings for regional paramountcy and for receipt of tribute from a congeries of lesser lordships, the so-called Twelve and Eighteen Thakurais (Singh 1982). All this changed dramatically in the first decade of the 19th century, when Gurkha and Sikh imperial expansion converged on the region, threatening to cut off British commercial access to "Tartary" via the Old Tibet Road up the Sutlej valley (Hamilton (1971 [1819]: 303-5); Moorcroft and Trebbeck 1841).

Between 1803 and 1810, indigenous west Himalayan rulers, from Kumaon in the east to the borders of Kangra in the west, were gradually deposed as the advancing Gurkha army swept through the region and established a harsh regime of military rule. In 1815, a joint Anglo-Himalayan force under Ochterlony defeated the Gurkhas at the fort of Rawingarh [Raeengarh] on the southern boundary of Bashahr (Fraser 1820). The political status quo ante was restored – but not without a significant difference. Although nominally reinstated as rulers, Himalayan kings were deprived of their forts and armies and required to pay for "British protection." This effectively disabled the external political agency of indigenous rulers, pacified the region, and established British paramountcy in the mountains, despite the latter's protestations of reluctance at the prospect of assuming additional administrative responsibilities (Hamilton 1820: 612). In 1849, after the East India Company defeated the Sikh king of Lahore and annexed the Punjab (Axel 2001), the kingdom of Bashahr plus the Twelve and Eighteen Thakurais were incorporated in the Imperial Punjab Province under indirect British rule as the Simla Hill States District. At the same time, the former Sirmur districts of Jaunsar and Bawar to the east were annexed by the British as Dehra Dun District.

Combining fieldwork and archival research, I argue that the region's pre-Gurkha territories and practices were administratively "preserved" under the *pax Britannica,* in geographical form if not political power. Currently, in independent India, the practical trace of their memory is reproduced in "fairs and festivals," long since misrecognized by government and tourist agencies as Pahari "folklore" or "heritage."

Now reterritorialized in the Indian nation-state as the eastern districts of Himachal Pradesh and the western districts of adjacent Uttaranchal, the former Hindu polity I describe is broadly coextensive with the cult territory of the paramount regional deity Mahasu,[6] the collective name for a brotherhood of gods from Kashmir, to whose theistic empire I return below. My fieldwork to date has focused on the former territory of the Bashahr kingdom, largest of the Simla Hill States, which is situated in one half of Mahasu's regional domain to the west of the river Tons. This paper focuses on the southernmost of Bashahr's three former districts, Rohru *tahsil*, whose relatively recent annexation by the Bashahr kings after the imposition of indirect British rule insured the preservation of its pre-monarchical political forms and their landscape of rural micro-kingdoms.

The Regional Institution of Government by Deity

I begin by examining the place-making practices that help us define a west Himalayan form of very little kingdom – a rural, dominant-caste, territorial assembly organized as a militia, or *khūnd*, and ruled by a god conceived of as a king. Local people refer to this distinctive Pahari institution of kingship as *devatā kā rāj*, a phrase which one of my English-speaking informants felicitously translated as "government by deity." Central to the practice of government by deity are the movements of gods, which choreograph the internal and external relations of khunds in contemporary Rohru's traditional peasant polity.

In each of these rural caste assemblies, the tutelary god represents, and acts on the behalf of, the territorial community in all relations with other communities and their gods. Addressed by the title, *rājā* (lit. ruler; king), the god of the territory makes decisions on behalf of the community according to a ritualized practice of collective agency that takes the form of oracular consultation. The local leader addresses questions of communal interest to the god, who gives his reply through the trance-speech of his official oracle (*mālī*).

At the westernmost end of his survey of Mahābhārata performances in Garhwal, William Sax (2002:157) makes good *re*use of the hackneyed Orientalist concept of "divine kingship" to emphasize its quite literal instantiation in one example of the institution I call government by deity, by characterizing one rural polity in Rawain as a "divine kingdom" ruled by a "divine king." The Pahari institution in question differs in one significant respect from the kind of divine kingship colonial authors had in mind. Rather than a deified human, the king in question is a humanized god.

The territory of Rawain described by Sax forms the easternmost extent of the west Himalayan regional polity this essay describes, whose totality includes hundreds of similar miniaturized, rural, theistic kingdoms associated with the dominant ethnic group, the Kanaits – a title now considered pejorative. Throughout Himachal

Pradesh, from Chamba in the west, through Kullu, to Bashahr and the Simla Hills States in the east, then over the border to Jaunsar-Bawar and Garhwal, the practice of local governance by deity involves a complex performative repertoire of dance and travel moves, by means of which gods seated in palanquins and embodied by their oracles communicate and interact in human society – to make decisions, settle disputes, appoint ministers, define territory, and engage in rural diplomacy or feuding.

Focussing on territorial and diplomatic practices, this essay examines the movements of rural gods, whose processional itineraries, as I hope to demonstrate, reproduce all important levels of pre-modern political incorporation in the region – from local through royal to imperial – as well as their legitimation in heaven.[7] In the traditional Hindu polities of the Simla Hills, all territorial forms of political organization, from royal to rural, are conceptualized and ordered as divine kingdoms by the mythic and ritual agency of gods acting in conjunction with humans. In each case, political authority takes the institutional form of theistic sovereignty. According to competing mythologies, the establishment of rule by gods in different places inaugurated a variety of new political orders, which superseded an original regime of human sacrifice under "rule by demons" (*rākash kā rāj*) throughout the so-called "northern region" (Uttara Khanda). The territories and relations of competing theistic regimes are reproduced at contemporary rural festivals by the processional itineraries of travelling gods. Some of these domains occupy mutually exclusive spaces; others overlap. My interest in this essay is to tease apart the superimposed landscapes of three competing versions of theistic kingship, which together describe a geographical scale of forms: 1) the very little kingdoms, or micro-kingdoms, of khunds; 2) the little kingdom of the Bashahr state, comparable in size to the little kingdom of Pudukkottai described by Dirks (1987); and what I term the little empire of the regional god, Mahasu, a miniaturized version of the Indic paramount kingship or "imperial formation" that Inden conceptualizes as a "scale of kingships" (Dirks 1987: 214).

The geometries of processional movement are place-making practices that define the incorporation of villages in a theistic micro-kingdom and their further integration in an expanding scale of political networks – with rural peers, former chiefs (not described here), the Bashahr kings, or the regional paramount deity, Mahasu. Together, this scale of polities reproduced by contemporary processional movement memorializes the extent of a former Kanait regional polity, whose relations with distant foreign powers are also remembered in mythic narratives of excursions by mountain gods to the plains (Sutherland forthcoming). The Pahari repertoire of processional practice also demonstrates that geographical theories of mobility, translocality, and flow, which are usually reserved for discussions of post/modernity and globalization, are equally relevant to the historical anthropology of pre modernity.

The Three Geometries of Processional Movement

In a recent essay on globalization, Doreen Massey (1992: 63-64) disagrees with David Harvey's static, bounded representation of place "as the space of a single, essential or integrated identity in the Heideggerian mode" (Coombe and Stoller 1994: 256). Instead, she proposes a dynamic and "*extra-verted*" [my emphasis] sense of place shaped by "interactions," "articulations," and "geometries of power" that converge on, intersect, and extend beyond particular localities, linking them with the "wider world" (Massey 1992: 66). Despite its use in an urban context of globalization, Massey's concept of geometries of power fits well with my own use of geometry to understand a dynamic form of Himalayan landscape – shaped by indigenous categories of procession and the trajectories of power (*śakti*) described by rural travelling gods. Unlike Massey, however, whose use of geometry is merely rhetorical – a figure of speech – my own analysis examines the types of spaces produced by Pahari place-making practices – as politically significant figures of space, or t(r)opologies.

In charting the pathways of numerous processions on British Imperial Survey of India maps of the Simla Hills, I noticed how each indigenous processional category defined a recurring pattern despite the geographical particularities of each different itinerary. "Tours," wherever they went, involved a circular route linking a temple centre with other neighbouring places [see Figs.1 & 2]. "Visiting" described networks of reciprocal exchange between three or four centres [see Figs. 3 & 4]. And "assemblies" described star-formations of convergence and dispersal linking a single centre with a hinterland of peripheral locations [see Fig. 5].

For the sake of clarity, the illustrations I use below are mainly schematic representations of the above three geometries of movement. My aim is to give lasting visual form to the fleeting, and otherwise invisible, spatial logic of processions, which integrate rural micro-kingdoms in a scale of competing, overlapping, and intersecting networks. Owing to practical restrictions, only one map of actual processional routes is used, to show how geometry translates into geography. After examining the deployment of these three geometries in rural, royal, imperial, and cosmic contexts of communication, I demonstrate their temporal integration in two competing festival calendars.

The Rural Context

The Geometry of Circumambulation / *Daurā*

Every year in the month of Baisakh, after the snow has melted, the images of local dominant-caste gods are taken out of their temples, seated in palanquins, danced, consulted, then taken on tour to visit the villages incorporated in their local jurisdictions. Two names are given to this local territorial progress: in Rohru, it is known in Pahari [P] as *daurā*; in Tukpā to the north, it is known in Kinnauri [K] as *boning*. The indigenous classification of these festivals as *zātra* (H. *jātra*, S. *yātra*, lit. journey) refers to their processional form, which describes a geometry of circumambulation [see Fig.1].

Fig. 1: The Geometry of Circumambulation / Daurā

In Rohru and Tukpa (the ancestral seat of the Bashahr kings in Kinnaur), the rural territories of local gods defined by circumambulation are called *ghoris*, a Pahari term for which I have found no indigenous etymology. Ghori is also used in two other spatial contexts for the pastoral territories that organize communal flocks and for the minimal, sub-pargana, revenue divisions of the former Bashahr state. The dominant-caste assemblies resident in ghori territories are called khunds, a Pahari term meaning "warrior," "territory," and "militia" in different contexts.

The khund is a territorial community, whose agentive mode of incorporation unsettles essentialist theories of social identity in rural India, framed in genealogical terms of "encapsulated social units." (cf. Schnepel/Berkemer in this volume). One of Cohn's three types of little kingdom, the *taluka*, conforms to this essentialist model. "The taluka is the territory controlled by a lineage of agnatically related kin of the same *biradari* (exogamous local caste group)" and should not, according to Cohn, be confused with the pargana, an administrative or revenue subdivision "not based on longstanding sociological grounds." (Cohn 2001b [1962]: 489). All land in the taluka was shared and controlled by the lineage on the basis of "genealogical" descent from a "common ancestor" (ibid: 491). Talukas were acephalous groups unlike Cohn's other two types of little kingdom, the rajadom and the jagir, each of which was governed by an acknowledged ruler or *rājā* who was either hereditary or appointed.

According to Pahari villagers, however, the territorial unity of a khund is based on neither kinship nor clan as in Cohn's taluka. What they describe is more commensurate with Ronald Inden's political reconception of the unit of rural caste society in medieval times as a *jānapada* – "one of the seven 'limbs' or 'constituents' (*anga*) of a 'rulership' or polity (*rājya*)" described in ancient Indian texts such as the *Arthaśāstra* and the *Laws of Manu* (Inden 1990: 218). The khund, as found in Rohru and immediately neighbouring areas, is a complex political community, whose inclusion of many different lineages of the dominant *Khash-Rājpūt*[8] agro-pastoralist caste *and* their dependent castes closely resembles Inden's characterization of the janapada as a "subject-citizenry." Not based "exclusively" on kinship or caste, the unity of a khund is "inclusive" (Inden 1990:219), politically constituted by overlapping forms of interlineage *and* intercaste collaboration, competition, dominance, and conflict. All interaction among castes within the khund is governed by ritual relations between caste tutelary gods, among which the dominant caste, "territorial god" (*ghori devatā*) has ultimate authority over the khund as its king. Although British gazetteers often classify the latter as a "family-" or "lineage god" (*kul devatā*) as well as a "territorial deity," and describe khunds as Kanait "tribal sections" or "*khels*," all the members of khunds I consulted in Rohru fervently denied they were descendants of a common apical ancestor. Instead of blood, four modes of association currently hold this complex community together: 1) the shepherding of a communal flock of sheep and goats formed by combining household flocks under the protection of the territorial god; 2) the formation of a local militia to protect the community and its pastures; 3) participation in a territorial assembly to determine matters of collective importance; and 4) the ritual reproduction of caste relations in a caste system of gods. All four modes of association are ordered by the institution of government by deity, in which the territorial god rules as king and incorporates other caste gods as attendants in his rural micro-kingdom.

Confusion between family and territory in British gazetteers may have to do with the dual meaning of the Hindi term, *kul*. In addition to such social glosses as "race, family, community, tribe, or caste," that are usually found in British colonial texts, *kul* or *kula* also has residential or spatial connotations such as "seat of a community" or "inhabited country" (Monier-Williams 1984: 294).

These latter spatial usages of kul fit more closely with the sense found in many Pahari origin myths, which tell of a deity's search for a place to "settle" (*bāsna*) and found a "seat" (*kursī*) of his own, from which to establish his rule. In all such myths, government by deity brings political order to pre-existing communities, in the wake of oppression by demons, in the absence of a god, or sometimes after the ouster of an incumbent deity. The political constitution of the khund is clearly established by the deity's first official act, which is to appoint many *different* local lineages to fill hereditary offices in his temple committee. The president (P. *mahattas*) of the temple committee is often drawn from the dominant landowning lineage, but the oracle, through whose voice the deity issues his orders, usually belongs to a different lineage, sometimes from a different village, as do other offices, thus balancing the president's power by representing the families of original settlers.

The multi-caste composition of a khund underlines the relevance of a spatial/political rather than a social/genealogical formulation of its construction. In addition to the dominant, Khash-Rajput caste, the micro-kingdom of a khund also includes two other localized caste communities: the "hamlets of *Kolīs*" (*kolwāra*), members of the landless subaltern caste, and at least one "village of *Bhāts*" (*bhātolī*), members of the Brahman caste (formerly called Bhat), both of which serve the dominant caste: the former as artisans and servants, the latter as hereditary priests of particular households or the temple of the territorial god. Together with the dominant caste assembly, Brahman and Koli communities are also represented by their own tutelary gods in the regional pantheon of government by deity, each performing a different function in the local ritual polity in a scaled-down version of Hocart's (1950; 1970) sacrificial model of caste and kingship. In the ritual idiom of government by deity, the dominant-caste, territorial god is king and "sacrificial patron" (*jajmān*); the Brahman god is his sacrificial priest or "*purohit*," as local Brahmans say; and the subaltern Koli god is both his "chamberlain" (*wazīr*) and exorcist, contributing to the sacrifice only from afar by policing demons (*bhūt-pret*, or *rākash*) at the margins of the settlement. Clearly, the khund is politically constituted as a theistic kingdom not a family.

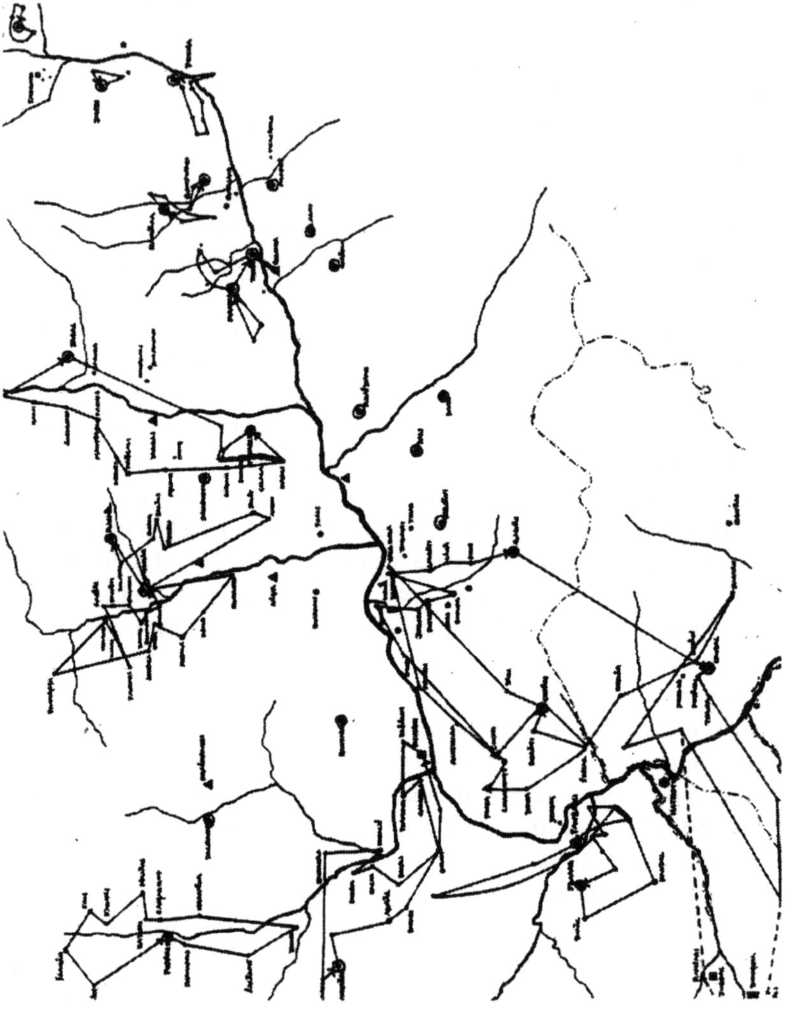

Fig. 2: Circumambulatory Tours of 19 Micro-Kingdoms in Rohru District

To give some idea of the complex landscape of khunds and micro-kingdoms associated with rural forms of government by deity, Fig. 2 charts the geographical variety of spaces defined by the circumambulatory tours of ghoris in Rohru district. In particular, the map illustrates the processional routes taken by nineteen Khash-Rajput deities that link the villages of each ghori in a conventionalized itinerary during the spring festival season (and sometimes in the monsoon season). The use of the gloss "territory" for ghori, it should be noted, does not properly describe the spaces so defined. Rather than the discrete, homogeneous, and externally bounded space of modern contract law, the political space of each micro-kingdom is "center-oriented" (Tambiah 1976:112) in two ways. It is defined both by the radiation of power outward from a static centre (the capital) and by the projection of power in a mobile centre – the deity's palanquin on its processional progress. Nancy Munn characterizes such a space as the "'mobile spatial field' of the actor in contrast to a determinate region or locale … It is space defined by reference to an actor, its organizing center" (Munn 1996:451). It is choreographed space.

The Geometry of Dyadic Exchange / *Deoālī*

The second processional mode (P. *deoālī*; K. *bāyoling*) refers to the dyadic exchange of visiting and hospitality among khunds and their gods associated with a second category of festival, also called zatra [see Fig.3].

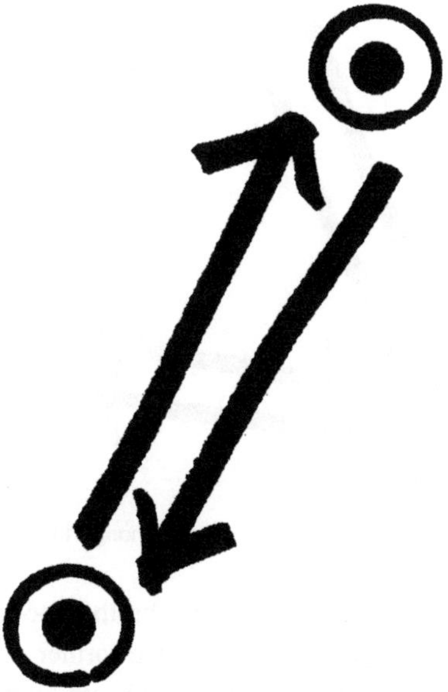

Fig. 3: The Basic Geometry of Dyadic Exchange / Deoālī

In the monsoon months of *Sāvan* and *Bhādom* (mid-July to mid-September), as soon as the collective work of planting out the rice-seedlings is done, the gods of khunds exchange visits of reciprocal hospitality with each other in cycles of varying length. Khunds are thereby geographically linked in a ranked scale of alliances by a mythic discourse of kinship. Three typical relationships among gods are common, listed in decreasing order of closeness and endurance: "brotherhood" (*brādarī*), that of "adopted brother" (*dharmbhai*), or "friendship" (*dostī*). Dyadic exchange of visiting among gods so related is associated with calendrical festivals timed by a scale of cycles ranging from three to six years, depending on the closeness of the relationship. In the case of a brotherhood of gods, reciprocal visiting defines a multi-local network of regularly sequenced, dyadic exchanges, whose choreography defines a complex timescape of movement [Fig.4].

Fig. 4: Network of Dyadic Exchange Among Three Brother Gods

The kinship networks of three such divine brotherhoods span the high-altitude passes of the Dhauladhar range, linking all three former districts of Bashahr: Rāmpur, Chīni, and in particular Rohru and Tukpa. Origin myths describe these gods as the sons of chthonic mother-goddesses from Kinnaur, who once migrated from their maternal homes to establish seats and kingdoms of their own. Since that mythic time of their "pre-social histories," gods now rely on their human subjects to carry them in palanquins to visit their mothers or brothers at festival times.

The rural diplomacy performed at such festival "reunions," or *milin,* is choreographed by a characteristic palanquin move, in which brother gods touch their heads together, while their oracles embrace. After their initial meeting, brother gods are usually seated side by side on stone platforms (variously called *śūprī, thaur,* or *thāt*) associated with the power of a "goddess of place" (*jagah devī*) or "goddess of the ground" (*bhūmi devī*). The multiple reunion of gods at such monsoon festivals gives dramatic expression to current relations and tensions between traditionally allied khunds in the jostling and often violent contortions of their palanquins as they meet and greet each other. This is the occasion for gods to act up and show their displeasure, which they demonstrate by causing their palanquins to keel over and capsize, as it were, on the ground. In 1994, at the Laila rural fair, I witnessed one god stubbornly refuse to join the assembly of his four brothers grouped side by side on the platform, pointedly sitting apart from them until, as he subsequently explained through his oracle, an on-going dispute was resolved once and for all. Gods, in other words, express the political will of the groups they rule and represent, and their meetings are the occasion for rural forms of diplomatic negotiation through the agency of their oracles and ministers.

Again preferring agentive to essentialist modes of explanation, villagers consistently *denied* that the mythico-ritual discourse of divine brotherhood linking khunds in networks of cyclical exchange is in any direct way socially determined by prescribed, preferred, or pre-existing relations of kinship or affinity. In fact, my repeated questioning revealed the opposite principle that, in the absence of prescribed forms of marriage (including village exogamy), interlocal unions were formed between families, which already knew each other as a result of pre-existing visiting relations between the gods of their respective khunds. Villagers also consistently denied any genealogical basis for the linkage of khunds by divine brotherhood such as lineage fission and migration, always pointing for evidence to the different lineages in the places so joined. If brotherhoods of gods once were coterminous with Kanait tribal sections, or khels, as British gazetteer authors maintained, such formations have apparently been systematically forgotten in Rohru. Alternatively, British authors were mistaken.

Nowadays, brotherhood between khunds refers to an historically constituted, diplomatic process conceptualized in discursive terms of divine kinship and performed in rites of domestic hospitality and male-bonding by the serious political business of drinking. If any shared substance is involved, it is alcohol not blood. The performative construction of divine brotherhood is confirmed by the immediate interruption of visiting relations among gods and khunds caused by the outbreak of hostilities and "feuding" (*boīrāla*). This usually results from disputes among shepherds in the alpine pastures.

Such an agentive conception of rural political community in India contradicts a long line of modernist and orientalist discourse about "ancient" or "primitive" society – from Ferguson through Hegel, Marx and Maine, to Cohn and Dumont – that not only *opposes* "nature to history," "repetition to development" (Trautmann 1995: 172-173), kinship to contract, and community to territory, but also *reduces* politics to genealogy and agency to custom. By contrast with such essentialist representations, political brotherhood between khunds is categorically *and* calendrically distinguished in government by deity from domestic relations of kinship and affinity among households by distinguishing two festival types: those with, and those without, the participation of gods in palanquins. Thus, to understand what government by deity means to local people, we must rethink western *secularist* oppositions of "politics" and "religion" in Himalayan *theistic* terms of kingship and kinship. I return to this important distinction below, and its seasonal/musical marking in the annual calendar.

The Geometry of Assembly / *Sangera*

The third processional geometry of "assembly" (*sangera*) is associated with sacrifices to the goddess Durgā or Kālī, which mark the third and final festival season of the year between mid-October and mid-January (*Kārttik* to *Pauś*) [see fig.5].

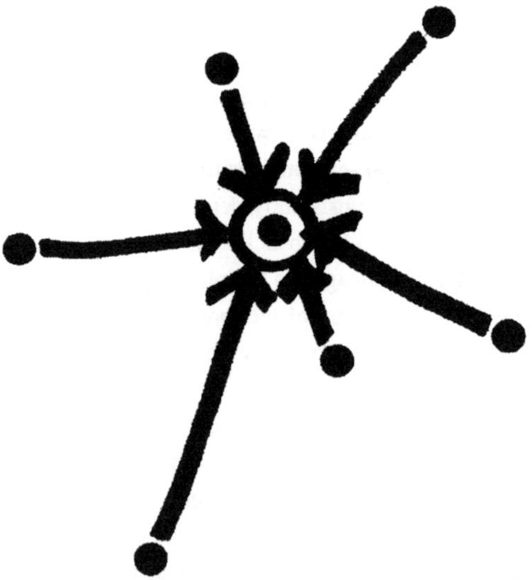

Fig. 5: Geometry of Assembly at a Central Place / Sangera

In Rohru's peasant polity, the geometry of assembly is associated with the staging of the great "peace sacrifice" (*śānt yajna*) [henceforth śant] once every twenty-four years by each khund in Rohru, or with extraordinary rites of (re)consecration (*pratishthā*). Invitations to śant are issued by three categories of host to three categories of guest, defining three fields of communication: 1) by the host deity, acting in his role as king, to other Khash-Rajput gods (his royal peers) and to the gods of Brahman communities (his divine priests); 2) by the host khund to other, allied khunds (its peers); and 3) by each household in the khund to its own social circle of kinsfolk, affines, and friends. Thus, hospitality is enjoyed among gods, khunds, and households.

Continuing the conceit of theistic agency, each divine king and divine purohit journeys in procession to the sacrifice accompanied by retainers. On arrival, the seating of Rajput and Brahman deities in assembly around a *mandala* of the goddess dramatizes the Puranic myth of Durgā's creation by the aggregation of individual male powers.[9] The unifying female power, or *śakti*, of the goddess so defined demonstrates the historical political significance of gender in the construction of the sacrifice as a shifting site of shared sovereignty in Pahari rural polity. I return to this below.

The sacrificial ritual is performed collaboratively by the gods and temple officials of guest communities directed by the host god. Khash-Raputs bring sacrificial victims, which they present to the host khund to "cut." Brahmans perform the work of *tantra-mantra,* as it is often facetiously called – the construction of world-ordering diagrams and the recitation of verbal formulae of closure, exorcism, and empowerment. In Rohru, the three-day ritual of śant rearticulates world-order by pacifying demons, closing the quarters, invoking the power of the goddess, and re-empowering good relations among allied khunds and client castes within a particular local circle by sharing in the performance and consumption of the sacrifice. The ritual involves an unusual, two-part performance of multiple sacrifices called *śikhā-phīr* (lit. top and turn). In the first, victims are offered simultaneously in the five directions on the temple roof (*śikhā*) at the centre of social space, in the second, sequentially during a circumambulation (*phīr*) of the settlement boundary.

The sacrifice itself is embedded in a timescape of interlocal processional movement defined by the travel routes of deities and their khunds coming to and returning from the event. This nicely illustrates Massey's *extra-verted* conception of place. By collecting lists of gods who are invited to attend the sacrifice by a number of different host khunds, I was able to chart the historical political geography of rural interlocal relations linking some 15 micro-kingdoms in Rohru with their local circles of allies – and enemies. Significantly, the invitation lists I collected always included the names of gods and khunds, which are no longer invited due to some former incident of feuding, but whose relationships are nonetheless remembered, albeit by their absence. The historical trace of such rural political networks remains invisible in the top-down, centre-out view of the Hindu state inscribed in royal archives.

The distinguishing feature of śant, on which I wish to focus here, is neither its gendered construction of the sacrifice, nor its mandalic assembly of caste-ranked gods, nor the history of rural politics this records, but rather the temporal geography of shared patronage and prestige produced by its shifting locus of performance. Given that each of some 35 khunds in Rohru is obliged to host the sacrifice once every twenty-four years, a performance of the festival inevitably takes place every three to four years in one part of the district or another, albeit unpredictably. Scheduled by this random procedure, śant is a truly movable feast, whose circulation from one local peasant centre to another is intended to insure the equal distribution of prestige bestowed by hosting the event. Put in another way, the spatio-temporal mobility of śant insures equality among dominant caste peers by preventing the monopoly of patronage by any single khund, on the basis of which asymmetrical relations of permanently centralized sovereignty might develop. Such an analysis recalls Deleuze and Guattari's (1987: 357) use of Pierre Clastres' view of war in "primitive" societies as a positive "mechanism directed against the formation of the State" and its centralized hierarchical "conservation" of power.

This constitutes a previously undescribed, egalitarian practice of shared and shifting sovereignty among Hindu peasants, which is significant for three reasons. As a nomadic or levelling practice, it presents a much-needed corrective to exclusively hierarchical representations of Hindu society. As such, it also provides an institutional baseline, from which to trace the historical emergence of hierarchy, as I argue below. But following Deleuze and Guattari's anti-evolutionist argument that states do not develop from egalitarian societies, it is important to note that despite the imposition of a monarchical state hierarchy on the peasant polities of Rohru, the anti-hierarchical practices of peasant polity have neither ceased to exist nor developed into part of a hierarchy. They remain distinct within a superimposed scale of overlapping territorial formations – the Bashahr little kingdom and various greater imperial or national formations – by virtue of the fact that they constitute on-going modes of ritualized resistance. Thus, if the participation of Pahari peasants in overlapping practices of political communication (in part) constituted the Hindu state of Bashahr, their participation sometimes involved resistance against the state.

The Royal Context
The Spatial History of State-Formation in Bashahr

The periodic assemblies of ... rural and urban citizenries with imperial and royal courts were the acts that made and remade Indian polities (Inden 1990: 227)

A spatial history of state-formation in Bashahr may be traced in the emergence of expanding networks of asymmetrical patronage focussed on single political centres, according to two distinct ritual registers of political memory: 1) the spatial ordering of śant in a hierarchy of other assemblies; and 2) the political ordering of assembly in relation to circumambulation and exchange by calendrical sequence. In each case, local gods travelling to attend a sacrificial assembly to the goddess at the invitation of a former chief or king trace centralized geometries of power, procession, and patronage in the landscape. Elsewhere (1998), drawing on British colonial descriptions of now defunct festivals, I interpret the expanding scale of assemblies so defined as a spatial record of the superimposition of hierarchical/centralized on egalitarian/nomadic modes of patronage and sovereignty. This record represents not so much the evolution of the Bashahr state out of peasant polities but rather the integration of the latter in a calendrical regime of chiefly and state practices that choreograph an expanding scale of spatio-temporal fields of power. Thus, as with those egalitarian social forms that Deleuze and Guattari call "bands," the political networks of peasants both participate in and are "irreducible to the State." They exist "in terms not of independence, but of coexistence and competition [with the state] *in a perpetual field of interaction* ... The same field circumscribes its interiority in States, but describes its exteriority in what escapes States or stands against States" (Deleuze/Guattari 1987: 361).

The most inclusive spatial network of centralized patronage in this scale of assemblies was/is the annual holding of court by the Bashahr kings at the Dasara assembly. Formerly, in the era of kings, I was told, some 185 local gods from all parts of the kingdom assembled at the *Bhīmākālī* palace-temple complex in Sarahān for a great sacrifice performed at the king's expense. According to my own observations at two performances of the festival in 1988 and 1994, nowadays the number of visiting gods may be reduced to about ten, but the timescape of political mobilization they defined provides practical evidence for reconstructing the historical performance of kingship in Bashahr and, in doing so, for fleshing out Ronald Inden's view of procession and assembly as the crucial modes of collective agency in the medieval Hindu state. The geometry of assembly that once was traced by these 185 gods, as they travelled to and returned from Dasara at the king's expense, vividly demonstrates the role of processions in articulating relations between king and khunds according to a hierarchical and centralized construction of patronage and sovereignty.

On arrival, the dual and gendered construction of theistic sovereignty is demonstrated in parallel acts of submission and allegiance: by local gods to the state and royal dynastic goddess, Bhimakali, and by local leaders and khunds to the king.

Rather than dwell on this performative reinvention of the Durgā myth as a gendered rite of political incorporation, the aspect of Dasara I wish to emphasize answers Cohn's question about the *cultural* integration of political order: in this case, by eliding a west Himalayan Kanait idiom of travelling gods and assembly with an all-India Brahmanical idiom of kingship focussed on sacrifice to Durgā. This convergence of top-down/brahmanical and bottom-up/Pahari idioms of power in the festival's syncretic performance lends weight to the claim by at least one member of the Bashahr royal family that, unlike most kings in the Simla Hills, who trace their origins to Rajput dynasties in the plains, the Bashahr royal dynasty derives from indigenous Kanait stock.

The Imperial Context

Mahasu's Quasi-Imperial Progress

At the Dasara festival, the royal goddess of the Bashahr state never moves from the centre, while the gods and khunds of local micro-kingdoms travel in from the peripheries to attend her assembly at the king's expense. The sovereignty of the great king's deity is thereby constructed as central, female, and grounded, while that of lesser kings (in this case, the gods of khunds) is distinguished as peripheral, male, and mobile. Power, in other words, is inversely related to mobility in Bashahr's centralized hierarchy of theistic kingship. In Mahasu's regional cult, however, we see the territorial progress as an alternative idiom for incorporating local groups in a paramount kingship by a more complex, dual construction of power and mobility. In Mahasu's characteristic processional practice, centralizing and localizing modes of sovereignty are linked in a perpetual territorial progress, in which power is simultaneously grounded at the centre and projected into the peripheries by Mahasu's characteristic practice of perpetual progress. My description refers to the period before Indian kings were deprived of their "Privy Purses" by the Government of India in the 1950s, and hence of their ability to fund Mahasu's expensive demands.

Mahasu is the collective name for a brotherhood of four immigrant gods from Kashmir, whose regime displays a distinctive, historical idiom of procession. While the eldest of the four brothers Mahasu, *Bothā* or *Bauthā* (his name means "seated"), never moves from the cult centre, Hanol, the youngest brother, *Caldā* (his name means "mover"), projects his power by being permanently on tour. Travelling out into the peripheries of his domain to visit his own territories and those of lesser gods, supposedly spending one year with each host, Calda and his enormous retinue were traditionally entertained at the expense of the local rural communities they encountered in the course of their progress. In addition, the two middle Mahasu brothers, *Bāśik* and *Pabāsī*, also perpetually circumambulate their lesser domains spending one year in each of the communities they control in respective circuits of four and eight years. Thus, time is the measure of Mahasu's power as he tours territory in multi-year cycles.

According to current accounts, Calda's regular visits brought fertility to each agro-pastoral community that hosted him by infusing the land with his divine power (*śakti*). Misfortune (*dosh*) and recurrent agricultural problems signal the need to invite Calda to visit, but nowadays the impoverishment of kings makes it hard for small peasant communities to fund the deity's reception unassisted. And so, nowadays, the regular schedule of Calda's once perpetual progress is interrupted by periods of immobility.

In addition to dispersing divine power, however, Calda's procession also once provided the occasion for a characteristic process of competition for prestige, in which rural communities along his itinerary vied to host the god for the longest stay. In this way, Calda's touring provided a convenient means for depleting the resources of local aspirants to power as his retinue ate its way through the realm. At the same time, justice was dispensed, healings performed, and taxes collected, which eventually found their way back to the treasury in Hanol.

Encompassing the twin tracts, *Pāmshī Bīl* and *Shāthī (or śatī) Bīl*, on opposite sides of the Tons river, Calda Mahasu's twenty-four year progress formerly integrated a scale of local, tribal, chiefly, and royal formations during the 19th and early 20th centuries under indirect British rule. His origin myth describes his migration from Kashmir as a military manoeuvre that constituted Mahasu's regional paramountcy in classic Vedo-Puranic terms of defeating an incumbent demon-king (Kirmat Dānū) then conquering the quarters by a great territorial progress. Such tropes are still central to government by deity and its ordering linkage of exorcism and empowerment at every spatial scale from household to kingdom. In addition to defining the extent of his domain and given its potentially endless duration, Mahasu's progress also performs a conquest of time, thus equating both geo-politics and chrono-politics as complementary practices of Hindu paramount kingship.

The mythic geography of Mahasu's domain suggests the origins of his regional cult as a Kanait *jānapada* or *sangha* – an "early" North Indian form of "tribal republic" that one historian of Himachal (Ahluwalia 1993: 42) describes as dating from the "period of the Mahabharata" and as having ended with the rise of Gupta paramountcy in the 4th century C.E. (ibid: 46). Significantly, and by contrast with other forms of government by deity in the region, I have not been able to link Mahasu's theistic regime with local memories of any historical Hindu kingdoms. This may well indicate its pre-monarchical origins in a period of tribal political institutions, which placed less emphasis on centralized and hierarchical forms of sovereignty.

The geographical division of Mahasu's domain into twin tracts uses the Mahabharata's eristical discourse of kinship and feuding to organize Kanait communities in regional factions. Pamśi Bil, or "region of the five," to the west of the river Tons, is named for the virtuous five *Pāndava* brothers and Shathi (or śati) Bil, to the east, for their villainous *Kaurava* cousins who are variously said to number 60 or 100 in different parts of the region. But in Chaupal and Rawain, the factional organization of space is further complicated by the social ordering of communities in moieties by the same factional discourse (Vidal 1982; Sax 2002). Such divisions no longer structure local community affairs in Rohru, but I did come across one remembered trace of the institution inscribed in the peroration of bakhan spoken by the subaltern oracle of Maslī, who formally addressed the community by naming its *Pāmśiya* and *Shāthiya* factions. At regional level, the presence of separate halls of assembly, one for Pamśiya, the other for Shathiya, next to Mahasu's main temple in Hanol presents an architectural trace of the same epic discourse of factional organization. The spatial separation of local leaders in these two halls at Mahasu's great annual assembly called *Jāgara* (vigil), reproduces at a regional scale the divided seating of "*pāmsāī*" and "*shātī*"[10] factions I observed in Dyora, capital of Karan's micro-kingdom in Rawain, on opposite sides of the assembly hall. I take this as a historical trace of Mahasu's regional sovereignty, which once unified factional divisions in the annual institution of a great Kanait tribal assembly.

The Cosmic Context
Bakhan and the Conquest of the Year

And so we come to the final, global level of incorporation by an imagined performance of procession and assembly in heaven. Every year, at the start of winter, in a final *extraterrestrial* event, government by deity is hypostatized in the oracular report and prophecy, bakhan. According to the video-recording I made of one such report by the oracle of the subaltern god, *Kilbālū,* of Masli in 1985, "all the gods and demons of the world" leave the human world for two to four weeks and travel to heaven "in their spirit-form" (*śakti kī rūp mem*) to attend a great assembly at the court of the ultimate sovereigns, *śiva* and *Kālī*. Significantly, during their absence from the human world, religious practices of collective agency are suspended. The images of gods are locked in their temples, palanquins are dismantled, temple-drums remain silent, and another category of festival called *sāza*, associated with domestic agency, is performed – significantly *without* the participation of gods.

After recharging their power at the cosmic source in heaven, local gods and local demons join battle to fight for control of the coming year. After the battle, they return to their territories in the human world and immediately possess their respective oracles, who prophecy conditions in the coming year for each local territory in the region, according to the fortunes of their respective gods in the battle with the demons. Although the gods always win in the end, the difficulties some of them encounter in battle, or on the course of their journeys home, are conventionally interpreted as omens to predict: the coming year's weather, the relative success of the wheat and rice harvests, immanent social problems, or the need for some cleansing ritual or pilgrimage in their respective territories. Notice is also given to particular khunds of the approaching time to perform the śant sacrifice, so that preparations for this costly 24-year festival can be set in motion several years in advance. Bakhan, in other words, is partly a farmer's almanac.

In addition to agricultural prediction, bakhan evokes regional memories of different historical political formations embodied in the mountain locations of their "ontological centers" (Inden 1990: 257). I learned of three alternative locations for bakhan's assembly in heaven: 1) the peak of mount Raldang Kailaś in the kingdom of Bashahr, 2) lake Mansarovar in Tibet, and 3) the unspecified mythic location, Ashtakulī (lit. "eight mansions"). I interpret the latter as a mandalic epithet for the plan of the city of the gods atop Mount Meru, the Hindu-Buddhist *axis mundi*, where the palaces of the eight guardians of the directions are peripherally located around Vishnu's central palace as described in the *Viṣṇu Purāṇa*, Book II, 2, 29-30 (1980: 254). References to lake Mansarovar in the text of the bakhan I recorded point to a location in Tibet at the foot of the archetypal Mount Kailaś. I interpret this as a distant memory of the period of Tibetan (Bhotiya) regional paramountcy in the 8th and 9th century prior to the formation of the Bashahr kingdom.

More detailed memories of historical political geography are also inscribed in bakhan's oracular discourse. On the one hand, the account of the battle between gods and demons invokes a transhistorical (if not to say anachronous) view of a static global landscape of memory, where political actors of different rank and from different historical eras occupy the same oracular temporality. In the foreground, the gods of Rohru khunds, local chiefs, the Bashahr king, and Hanol Mahasu are listed by name as victorious in battle with the demons; in the middle distance, down in the plains, kings are at war, and the capital of the Mughal emperor is specified in Delhi; and far beyond, in the metropolitan background, according to one bakhan of the Bashahr state goddess, Bhimakali, from 1918, the British army is mentioned as victorious in the trenches of World War One in Europe.[11] Simultaneously linking different historical eras and distant locations in its synchronic purview, bakhan's oracular version of "time-space compression" (Harvey 1989) describes a much-expanded sense of post-colonial memory, based on an alternative Himalayan experience of foreign rule, not limited to European colonialism.

On the other hand, bakhan's prophetic discourse describes a dynamic circuitry of cosmic power that shapes the political structure of the year in terms of kingship. Retaining bakhan's god's eye-view as we follow the gods back to earth, we can track the subsequent trajectory of their power through the year, as it circulates through the political centres and divisions of the state according to the calendrical order of processions. In this way, Hindu cyclical time may be understood politically as a framework for practically ordering a ranked scale of interactions that constitute the state, in each of which the rural micro-kingdoms of khunds are incorporated in different networks of association. This confirms Inden's observation that "people within the same kingdom could be and were [...] organized into relatively plural rulerships" for a variety of purposes and strategies "pursued on the part of the ruler and ruled" (Inden 1990: 221). As we have seen, some were egalitarian alliances formed among peers (i.e. brotherhoods of gods and khunds); others were embedded in hierarchical relations with traditional chiefs (*thākurs*), district administrators (*wazīrs*), the Bashahr king, or a paramount divine king (Mahasu).

By charting the course of this calendrical circuit, the entirety of west Himalayan regional polity may be grasped in its remembered global context – interstitially located between a variety of Indic cosmic centres above (in heaven as represented by sacred mountains) and various foreign imperial centres below (the Mughal emperor in Delhi or the British army in the trenches of World War I). I was told that, in some bakhans, current government policies in Delhi are mentioned. In this sense, then, bakhan gives a marginal, Pahari sense of global historical awareness, in which the rural forms of government by deity are remotely incorporated in Tibetan, Hindu, Mughal, British, and current Indian national forms of foreign rule.

To complete our understanding of the cosmo-political order structured by Bashahr's calendrical cycle, one final feature of bakhan must be mentioned that brings us back to earth and families. Its description of the great assembly in heaven splits the year into two unequal periods of ritual practice. For most of the year, we have terrestrial festivals involving the processions of gods in their palanquins, which constitute different kinds of *political* formation. But during the winter, when the gods go to heaven, their palanquins are immobilized and the gods are put to sleep. During this hiatus in processional practice, when snow lies on the ground, the political festivities of zatras are replaced by a social category of festival called *sāza*,[12] in the course of which *domestic* relations of friendship and marriage are celebrated in the absence of gods.

Travelling is still a central idiom of saza festivals, but only neighbours and kinsfolk go visiting. This either involves the exchange of hospitality among male heads of households within a single village, or the travelling of brothers to visit their out-married sisters and brothers-in-law in other villages. The distinction between politics and kinship so defined in the calendrical order of Pahari festival practice presents a Himalayan Hindu alternative to the modernist opposition between politics and religion characteristic of post-Enlightenment discourse. Festivals with gods perform collective relations between political agents (khunds and rulers), while festivals without gods celebrate personal relations between households. The two modes of communication intersect when feuding occurs between khunds, as a result of which all relations both personal and collective are discontinued. This prohibition is total and includes official visiting between gods, intermarriage between families, even the exchange of food between individuals of the feuding khunds.

Bakhan's imagined procession and assembly presents a Kshatriya discourse of legitimation that I characterize as a Himalayan mandate of heaven. It is neither subordinated to brahmanical priestly authority (as Dumont insisted following the *Dharmaśāstras*) nor reduced to genealogical terms (as essentialist representations proposed). The great gods of heaven, Śiva and Kali, are represented as universal monarchs holding court. The tutelary powers that meet in their assembly are not representations of family or caste but divine kings of rural territorial assemblies protecting their domains. And the oracles, through whose trance-speech this assembly is evoked, are the Khash-Rajput or Koli officials of similarly casted gods. No mention is made of Brahman gods at this gathering in heaven. Unlike the world-ordering sacrificial knowledge of Brahmans deployed at śant and Dasara, the theistic epistemology of bakhan apparently belongs to a pan-Himalayan oracular idiom more akin to Tibetan Bon-Po or Nepali shamanic traditions. The Pahari theistic polity hypostatized in bakhan's oracular discourse substitutes for Brahmanical sacrifice the Kshatriya legitimating practice of war. What it legitimates is not caste status or hierarchy in the abstract but the plural and specific powers of local political agents.

Calendrical Time and Hindu History

The burden of my argument rests on demonstrating the historical political meaning of government by deity and its calendrical ordering of processional movement. Unlike other Hindu conceptions of time (Underhill 1921; Freed and Freed 1964; Babb 1975; Pugh 1981, 1983; Wadley 1983), the Pahari calendar is more than an eco-ritual schedule for integrating agricultural and festival work with the seasonal cycle. It is also a dynamic articulation of the power of agency, by means of which time and place are politically ordered [see fig.6].

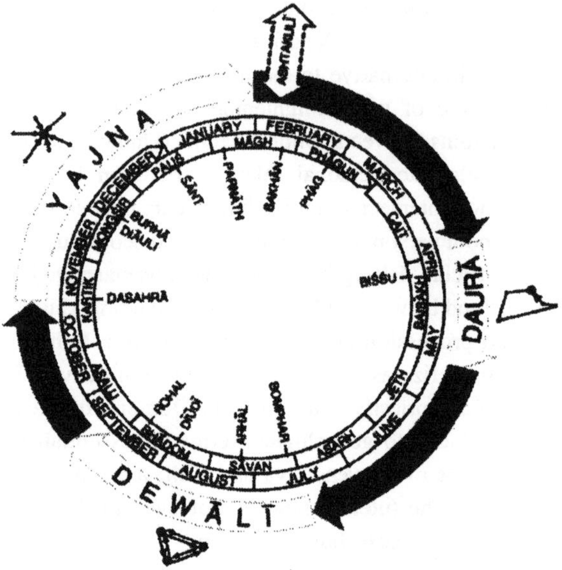

Fig 6: Diagram of the Bashahr Calendrical Cycle

Examination of the calendrical sequencing of ritual movement in the Bashahr calendar shows the temporal logic of political organization in the state marked by the flow of tutelary power (*śakti*). The circulation of power through the year hierarchically sequences an expanding scale of formations by festival timing, in the course of which the minimal political units of the state (i.e. the micro-kingdoms of khunds) perform ritual acts intended to: 1) define their territories, 2) engage in interlocal alliances, and 3) variously assemble at rural, royal, and heavenly centres. Significantly, however, the timings of Mahasu's main festival, Jagara, and his annual territorial relocation do not belong to the hierarchical order that shapes the Bashahr state and its calendar. As we have already seen, Mahasu's perpetual progress imposes an alternative spatio-temporal regime.

How then does the calendrical ordering of festival practice help us better understand the cultural integration of pre-modern north Indian polity? In the absence of a western-style political constitution, it would seem, the legitimation and ordering of power in the oral culture of west Himalayan theistic polity was not textualized but "temporalized." That is to say, adapting Nancy Munn's (1992) concept of temporalization quoted in my epigraph, a regional order is *performed* by processions and assemblies in the landscape, not *inscribed* in legal texts. The abstract geometry of circles and lines so often employed in orientalist discourse to distinguish European from Indian time is clearly inadequate to theorize the contemporary timescapes of Pahari Hindu memory so defined, let alone to interpret their historical political meaning.

By charting the flow of tutelary power traced in the landscape by the movements of gods, a spatial analysis sensitive to time has revealed two competing historical practices for projecting and legitimizing power. Most of the processional itineraries discussed in this chapter are ordered by what Andrŗ Wink (1990: 227) has called the "*vertical* organization" of the Hindu state linking peasant, royal, and heavenly domains within the space of the former Bashahr kingdom. But one exceptional, superordinate itinerary contradicted this paradigm by crossing the boundaries of Bashahr and neighbouring states to reproduce what Wink views as the "*horizontal* organization" characteristic of erstwhile Indic imperial formations.[13]

Mimicking the imperial "conquest of the quarters" that made the 8th century Kashmir-Gandharan king, Muktāpīda Lalitāditya, ruler of all North India, Mahasu's perpetual regional progress also follows the complementary Indic practice of the "conquest of time," by means of which paramount Indian sovereigns prior to and including Lalitaditya inaugurated whole new politico-moral eras. Establishing his mythic status as divine successor to the Krishna of the Mahabharata epic and as demon-slaying saviour for the *Kali Yug* (the present, degenerate "world-era"), Mahasu's perpetual touring enacts a calendrical strategy that imposes a 24-year temporal order on space. By contrast, the Bashahr calendrical cycle follows the opposite strategy of imposing spatial order on the year. The distinction between "nomadic' and "rooted" conceptions of sovereignty so defined, I have argued, may indicate a constitutive and practical difference between two historical forms of sovereignty in the development of north Indian political systems: the tribal/regional and the theistic kingdom.

Central to the west Himalayan spatial history I describe, the mythic construction of Kashmir as the origin place of theistic kingship poses an intriguing question of historical origins for further research. What does the mythic Kashmir have to do with the historical Kashmir in the formation of west Himalayan political consciousness? What, if anything, does Mahasu's mythic migration and conquest have to do with the Kashmir-Gandharan origins of theistic kingship (Inden 2000) and Muktapida Lalitaditya's great north Indian conquest of the quarters? What, if anything, does the earlier Kashmir of Huna immigration from Central Asia have to do with the name of Huna Bhat – the mythic protagonist who summons Mahasu from Kashmir to liberate the Northern Region from the depredations of demons? But that is another project.

Conclusion

Using evidence of the spatio-temporal practices of processional movement and assembly in contemporary west Himalayan religion, I have argued for a politicized and historicized reconception of Hindu "cyclical time" as a calendrical idiom for ordering theistic forms of governance. If the evidence from Himachal is anything to go by, the historical political anthropology of time merits more attention in other parts of South Asia and Greater India (I am thinking in particular of Bali), where festival calendars still choreograph processional practice and mountains still organize the field of power.

In conclusion, it remains for me to add to the list of tropes for the Hindu state, with which I began. In the west Himalayan idiom of government by deity, the ritual incorporation of rural micro-kingdoms in a scale of networks articulates two competing forms of *calendrical* state: the Bashahr little kingdom and Mahasu's little empire. Geographically sheltered from the anarchy of 18th century north Indian politics and from subsequent British and Indian modernization, the calendrical choreography of rural gods reproduced in these overlapping systems may give some insight into the otherwise invisible cultural practices of mobilization that ordered Indic theistic polities prior to and during Islamic rule.

Notes

1 These metaphors refer respectively to alternative characterizations of the Hindu state by Stein (1977), Geertz (1980), Tambiah (1985), Kulke (1995), Dirks (1987) and Inden (1990).

2 Inden (1990: 22-25) uses Collingwood's concept of a "scale of forms" to avoid simplistic, unitary or mechanistic representations of agency with respect to persons, societies, or empires. "Persons as agents are ... composed of entities that *overlap*." "The name Collingwood gives to the sort of system which such overlapping entities compose is a 'scale of forms'." This is a special kind of "system," in which "the relationships among these entities are not simply those of physical force, as in a mechanical system. They are what Collingwood calls 'dialectical' ... and 'eristical'". "Through this double process of interaction, agents, or even parts of agents, attempt to retain or alter their positions in a system or systems."

3 A *yuga*, or world era, is the minimal temporal unit in the cyclical cosmology of creation, decline, destruction and recreation characteristic of Puranic thought. The term *samsāra* refers

to the Indic conception of existence as an enduring cycle of birth, suffering, death, and reincarnation from which Buddhist and Hindu soteriology propose alternative visions of liberation as *nirvāṇa* and *mokṣa*.

4 The term *tāla* refers both to the cyclical structure of particular metres in Indian classical music theory and to the practice of marking them during performance by clapping.

5 See *Punjab Government Records* (1911: 256).

6 See also Berreman (1963), Galey (1980, 1986) and Majumdar (1960).

7 Relations with distant Mughal and British imperial powers are also evoked in the mythic and oracular forms of political memory.

8 Khash-Rajput is currently the preferred title of rural members of the dominant agricultural caste in Rohru. The title Kanait, by which they were formerly known under British indirect rule, is now considered pejorative due to its association with British colonial stereotypes of hillfolk as degenerate, promiscuous, drunken and unreformed.

9 According to the *Devīmahātmya* myth, the goddess Durgā is created by the aggregation of the individual powers of the 33 male deities of the Vedic heaven (Indralok) in a singular female persona.

10 I am quoting William Sax's Garhwali spelling of titles he recorded in Dyora (2002: 180).

11 See *The Administrative Report of the Bashahr State for the Sambat Year* 1974 (Mar. 13 1917-Mar. 12 1918).

12 A Pahari category of festival held at the beginning of each lunar month.

13 I am following André Wink's distinction between the "*'horizontally'* integrated infrastructures of extensive empires, such as those of the Mauryans and Kushans, incorporating ethnically diverse military and mercantile elites" (Wink 1990: 227) and the "*'vertical'* linkages" provided by "Brahmanical cults and rituals performed in ... new temple establishments" that characterized Hindu kingdoms after the dissolution of the Buddhist empires (ibid: 228) [my italics].

Kingship and Genealogy in Mediaeval Western India

Ulrike Teuscher

For some years now the numerous regional, subregional and local kingdoms and lordships that existed between "the empire" and "the village", the so-called "middle ground of social and political organization" (Schnepel 1997: 3), and their internal dynamics have received at least moderate attention from historians. This put an end to the negative attitude towards them and opened up the possibility of studying them in their own right. Many problems still remain, however, one of which is the emergence of regional differences. In this respect, I would like to focus on mediaeval Western India, on a cluster of states and lordships that later came to be known as the Rajput states. I will deal mainly with two related traits. The first is the peculiarity of the political systems and the structure that developed between the 10th and 15th centuries A.D. The second is how this peculiarity in essence informs pan-Indian strategies of royal or lordly legitimation and helps develop a characteristic regional culture.

Western India is a particularly interesting case in this context, to which very little attention has been paid in the past. The structure and ideology of political units that emerged there, especially from the 10th century onwards, were to become paradigmatic for the greater part of Northern India until the vast destruction incurred by the Delhi Sultan ʿAlaʾ al-Dīn Khaljī and his armies around 1300. Even after that, a distinct cluster of greater and smaller kingdoms emerged to reconstruct their regional peculiarities, which proved to be exceedingly stable, existing well into the 20th century. However, research on pre-Mughal history is highly uncommon, mainly for two reasons. Firstly, the concepts that gained ground particularly in the Mughal and colonial eras are so strong that they overshadow earlier developments completely. The pathetically meagre sources compared to those of contemporary South India, for instance, constitute the second obstacle. The sources consist mainly of inscriptions (copper plates are rare) now seldom found *in situ*. Drawing a coherent picture of the political systems and structures that prevailed before ca. 1500 A.D is therefore difficult. The development of certain elements, however, can be traced, giving us at least an idea of the relations and forms of power of the greater and lesser political units at different levels.

In Western India, as in other regions of South Asia, a great many attempts were made by those that exercised power to stabilise the patterns of dominance and submission. The symbolic means of stabilisation altered in accordance with political change. Its development indicates that many units used specific patterns that were taken up again and again whenever necessary, reinterpreted and combined with new elements and adjusted to changing circumstances. Due to the spread of Brahmanical knowledge, the means and their significant differences can be found in many of the regions of South Asia. A case in point is the widely used genealogies drawn up for rising kings, which often contain long rows of mythical ancestors as a means of bestowing an exalted position on the respective monarch. These are often seen as paradigmatic, even indispensable for constructing the institution of kingship in the rising dynasties of the post-Gupta age (Thapar 1984: 53; Spencer 1984; Ali 2000). Ali writes that the kings were placed within the world history of the *paurāṇic* paradigm, which was highly competitive since overlordship of the world existed as an ideal but was not given; it had to be secured over and over again.

> "The genealogical lists, then, were conscious means of organizing politics and their histories along the lines of the larger universal histories of the Purāṇas, and not "natural" holdovers from a tribal society or an earlier mode of production in the process of being transformed into states" (Ali 2000: 179-180 with reference to Thapar 1979).

> "The inscriptions ... were related also to the political representations of other kings. ... They represent the world as consisting of a highly ordered hierarchy of kings, at the centre of which sits a single ruler, the paramount overlord or king among kings (*cakravartin, rājarāja, rājādhirāja* and so on)" (Ali 2000: 185).

In Western India, although genealogies became a source of legitimation of utmost importance, the construction of a mythical ancestry hardly played any role at all. My hypothesis asserts that there is evidence here of an independent historiographical tradition, which was strongly oriented towards the local or subregional political structure and concentrated on information gained from the careful examination and assessment of older inscriptional sources. It differs greatly from the later historical writing,[1] so-called bardic chronicles, which has been much maligned for its "fictitiousness".[2] Furthermore, the employment of this independent historiographical tradition is interconnected with the peculiarity of the social and political development of the area, an influence "from below", as it were, at the level of the little (or even the small) kingdom.

I

In a process Chattopadhyaya calls "early mediaeval state formation" (Chattopadhyaya 1983: 2), a group of political units emerged in Western India from the 7th century onwards. One in particular, the great kingdom of the Gurjara-Pratihāras, overshadowed all others from the 8th to the middle of the 10th centuries. It eventually declined only to re-emerge and build up a large cluster of political units at different levels, including powerful great kingdoms like Malwa and Gujarat, where countless other kingdoms and lordships developed both within and on the periphery, some dependent, some independent, their relationships in a constant state of change.

This paper will focus attention on two that were located in peripheral areas to the great powers of the region. The first, Mewar, lies in the southeast of the Aravalli mountains, the second, Marwar,[3] in the southwest of the Aravallis in an area that has now become Southern Rajasthan. They were neighbours, belonging to the same cluster of political units. Their royal families entered into marriage alliances and wars. They were not only related in this sense but also by a common orientation towards the greater power of the South, the kingdom of Gujarat, occasionally becoming dependent little kings. Mewar was one of the first areas to be subjected to early mediaeval state formation in the 7th century. It made a bid for greater power in the 10th century, similar to other, greater kingdoms that were eventually crowned with more success in this competitive venture. Marwar, a core area of the Gurjara-Pratihāras, was again subjected to monarchical forms of power from the end of the 10th century after their decline, having been occupied by families from Śakambharī in the north of the Aravallis.

Whereas these entities are normally referred to in lineage terms such as the Guhilas (of Mewar), the Cāhamāṇas (of Marwar) and the Caulukyas of Gujarat, I have used geographical terms up to now. Lineage denominations are particularly significant in the present context, however, since lineage ideology became a primary organisational principle in the area[4], leading to the development of *lineage domains* (entitled Mewar etc.).[5] This term was coined by Chattopadhyaya, who identifies them at the beginning of all mediaeval state formations in South Asia (Chattopadhyaya 1983: 11), although they seem to have directed the course of events more strongly in Western India than in other regions. The sources show that lineages derived from a larger, older clan existed in Western India even in the 7th century,[6] although no hierarchy could be discerned. Two processes of expansion in certain lineages seem to have taken place subsequent to the source gap caused by the Gurjara-Pratihāras overlordship. The first is of the "leapfrog variety", opening up new regions for settlement and rulership of lineage members. In Mewar lineage expansion seems to have taken place in the following manner. Around 943 a king of the

Nagda / Ahar Guhilas expanded his domain considerably into the South East. Although this expansion was not permanent, several new power centres sprang up in this wider area in the years that followed (between 950 and 960). They were ruled by the king's sons, their successors or other close kinsmen.[7] There is no evidence that a hierarchical relationship existed between these centres from the start. In subsequent decades, however, heavy competition for overlordship of these small neighbouring areas began to surface. A similar development took place in 12th century Marwar. Five different centres of rulership successively emerged between 1090 and 1182. They were created by younger sons or brothers of the kings. Some of them sought to extend their control over the neighbouring centres as well.[8] These kinsmen either went out alone to look for new land or they were stationed in the newly-conquered areas. However, this was not the only means of proliferation, nor was it the most common one. If such fissions had taken place in every generation, expansion would have accelerated. The more frequent case seems to have been to provide younger sons of a king with land within the original power centre itself. Several sources speak of kings' sons as dependent landholders. The eldest in particular was furnished with large holdings and responsibilities, while the younger ones were given land in the role of a *bhoktṛ* ("enjoyer"), coupled with administrative responsibilities.[9] Contrary to the eldest, who (ideally) became king and passed on his possessions, the younger ones sank into oblivion after a generation. None of them could pass on their status to others and in some cases, it is obvious that their land was later given to someone else.[10] Having probably lost their privileged position when they were no longer the younger sons of kings, they began to form a class of landholders on a lower level, known as the *rājaputra*s or the *rāṇaka*s of a certain area.[11] This phenomenon may account for the building up of a tight infrastructure of kinsmen both close to and further away from the ruling king in the respective centres. Simultaneously, a hierarchisation of lineage segments arose, possibly according to the seniority principle – seniority being defined by the proximity of kin to the ruling king.

Chattopadhyaya is of the opinion that "... monarchical forms of polities often developed through integrating pre-existing lineage areas, and that power distribution through lineages can very well function alongside other, bureaucratic forms of rulership" (Chattopadhyaya 1983: 15). The oldest inscriptions of the area in question show the unchanged import of pan-Indian "classical" terms of kingship and administration, such as *mahārāja, māṇḍalika* etc. But in the course of time, the terminology, structure and content adjusted itself more and more to the political reality, in which kin orientation and the distribution of land at different levels constituted an extremely vital factor in the stabilisation of hierarchies. The older, imported terms became less frequent and were augmented by new ones such as *ṭha-*

kura, *rāṇā*. It seems as if an integration of the two systems took place between the 11th and 12th centuries. Several hierarchies existed alongside each other, intersected one another and could even be assembled into a single hierarchy[12]. They were, however, built up according to different value systems and organisational principles that also functioned independently.

Hence, several categories of rulers or landholders produced by different political systems emerged in Marwar and Mewar from the 11th century onwards. Whereas the widely-used term *ṭhakura* was not linked to royal lineages,[13] the inscriptions abound with titles that denote members of royal lineages only, such as *rāutta*, *rāṇaka*, *mahārāvala*, *mahārājakula* and *rājaputra*. The term *rājaputra* was often reserved for sons of ruling kings, at least in the area under review, although in some cases it seems to denote a class of "nobles" set apart from the others or as an equivalent for the other titles mentioned.[14] *Rāutta*, *rāṇaka* or *mahārājakula*, for example, denote lineage membership and were not primarily landholding terms.[15] A *rāutta* could also be a *ṭhakura*.[16] Different periods where one of the previous terms was used more often than others can be distinguished. The terms seem to have been employed to differentiate between various groups within a lineage. The database is unfortunately too small to indicate evidence of a hierarchy.[17] However, these titles became so meaningful that some were gradually used as royal titles from the 12th century onwards.

The other category of rulership hierarchy can be found in pan-Indian terms referring to the "classical" *sāmantamaṇḍala* concept, such as *mahāsamantādhipati* or *māṇḍalika*, *mahāmaṇḍaleśvara* . These terms also form a category distinct from *rāutta* etc., which is evident in the fact that they occur in the same title.[18] Their use reveals a strong political influence within the lineage domains. Here they were obviously used in certain contexts only, in particular to denote dependent little kings or governors outside the respective lineage domains. They are never used within the latter. Few kingdoms refer to these categories, as, in our context, the kingdom of the Caulukyas of Gujarat, which expanded substantially, especially in the 12th century, and sought to stabilise its power over areas inhabited by lineages belonging to other clans. Moreover, the influence of lineage domains shows how these offices and titles were allocated by the overlord. Normally one would expect little kings to be reinstalled in the wake of defeat or replaced by a governor (*māṇḍalika* etc). It seems, however, that younger brothers of deposed kings were frequently chosen for this position, which means that either the overlord installed someone legitimised by lineage but in a personally unstable position or that this step was part of a contract already settled between the overlord and an aspiring younger member of the lineage. The Guhila king, who was *māṇḍalika* in the second half of the 11th century, stated that he belonged to a younger lineage (*EI* XXXI, pp. 245-246). In the middle of the 12th century, the various power centres of Marwar also came under the overlordship of the Caulukyas. Having installed a foreign *daṇḍanāyaka* (a military officer) for some years, they transferred the whole area to a younger brother of one of the deposed kings. The overlords seem to have taken the power structure of the lineage domains into careful consideration. Installing a foreign *daṇḍanāyaka* with no local authority was as precarious as leaving a defeated king in power, who had too much of it.

It seems quite clear that little kings who were prepared to serve as *māṇḍalika*s enjoyed the active protection of the overlord and could strengthen their position against their own kinsmen. It is conspicuous, on the other hand, how strongly little kings avoided terms of submission. The less stable their position on being installed in completely strange surroundings,[19] for instance, the more likely they were to refer explicitly to their position towards the overlord. The more 'indigenous' they were, the more they tended to circumscribe their position in evasive terms.

Thus, it seems that the "right" ancestry became crucial to a king interested in maintaining power. Non-lineage members were completely excluded from independent rulership. A differentiation of legitimacy within the lineages occurred by separating segments through "seniority", i.e., nearness of kin to the ruling king.

II

Under these conditions, genealogies became one of the most powerful strategies of legitimation. They are, as Malinowski stated long ago, primarily legal charters and not historical records (Fortes 1953: 28). But they are also histories and have histories, as they are constantly reconstructed, their "codes of meaning ... manipulated from text to text" (Ali 2000: 175). Here, in my opinion, they represent an independent historiographical tradition, since the Brahman authors charged with the meticulous treatment of a lineage past demanded by rulers whose justification was under constant scrutiny by their kinsmen, who , in turn, had genealogies (or genealogists), developed the method of ignoring their *paurāṇic* accounts and using older genealogies as sources to place their patrons. The use of these inscriptions in some respects resembled modern historiography – they were used as historical sources. Those who were nearest in time to a certain king who was to be included in the list were always considered the most reliable. The authors were not satisfied with later works that had already been reconstructed, regardless of how elaborate they were. Instead, they took all known inscriptions into consideration and probably even hunted for others. They then tried to reconcile the information, integrating only kings for whom they had a sufficient number of preferably contemporary sources, unless there was a vital reason for the patron to have (mostly very recent) predecessors eliminated.

Before the destruction of the respective kingdoms by the Delhi Sultan around 1300, the genealogies of the Guhilas and Cāhamāṇas had been rewritten several times. A unilinear genealogy is primarily a means of documenting the right to mobilise force. The longer it is, the more successive the layers that can be incorporated and the more force mobilised.[20] However, in a ranked society with monarchical institutions, the differentiated access to power along the logic of seniority may well have been the second main object. Whenever a new political situation arose, as a rule with an unusual extension of power by one king, rewriting became necessary. The first genealogies in the Cāhamāṇa area emerged in 1161 when a younger kinsman succeeded in extending his power, probably under the protection of the Caulukyas, deposing his brother in the process, who was the designated *yuvarāja* and the latter's son, and later again in 1272 when the power centres of Marwar were united under the independent rulership of a *mahārājādhirāja* Udayasiṃha. In Mewar, the first elaborate genealogy emerged in 977 after considerable expansion, followed by that of 1083 in connection with the rise of a new king as *māṇḍalika* (probably subordinate to the Caulukyas). The most refined and lengthy ones occurred between 1274 and 1285, after the Guhilas had successfully expanded into the fertile Banas plain to the east of the Aravallis, an area that had formerly belonged to the Caulukyas.

The first Cāhamāṇa genealogy in Marwar from 1161 (*EI* IX, pp. 64-65) spans twelve generations and was compiled for a king named Alhaṇa. It shows that its main object was to legitimise the king as a rightful member of the Naḍol lineage, having branched off from the elder Cāhamāṇas of Śakambharī, to which all the kinsmen of the lineage domain belonged. His succession was questionable, as his brother Kaṭudeva had rightfully been king before him (he was *yuvarāja*). This brother had already designated his son as successor (*EI* XI, pp. 33-34). In all probability, Alhaṇa became king under the protection of the Caulukyas after they had defeated Kaṭudeva. There were two ways of handling irregular successions. In the earlier part of the genealogy, the relation between predecessor and successor is always specified. Apart from the sons of kings, brothers are mentioned four times and a paternal uncle once. These successions could probably be justified as rightful on the assumption that the predecessor had died without heirs. The brother of the inscription's patron and former ruling king, on the other hand, was omitted. Successions of this kind in the past were specified to give the ruling king legitimacy (since it could be presumed that the latter had rightfully stepped in), but a recent deposition might be glossed over, perhaps by declaring the deposed king as unworthy.[21]

This method of drawing up genealogies gains momentum when the latter are used as sources for later reconstructions of a king's ancestry. Thus, the genealogical part of the inscription of 1272 (*EI* IX, pp. 74-79) was obviously modelled on the original from 1161. The specific relationships between predecessors and successors of the past are reiterated. Moreover, one of the kings on the list (having probably ruled in the 10th century), Āṇahilla, who was described in 1161 as the son and successor of Mahendra, acquired a new ancestry. It stated that Mahendra had a son Aśvapāla, who had a son Ahila. He was succeeded by a paternal uncle, Āṇahilla, (i.e., a brother of Aśvapāla). This means that a son and his successor disappeared from the list in exactly the same manner as the elder brother of Alhaṇa, the patron of the genealogy of 1161 had done. It is highly probable that this irregularity was concealed by omission in earlier times and found its way into the genealogies of the 12th century in this manner. By consulting inscriptions from an even earlier date than 1161, the authors of the genealogy of 1272 hence unearthed an irregularity that had long been glossed over.[22]

The same phenomenon crops up in the Mewar genealogies. The first two from 977 (*IA* 1910, p. 101) and 1083 (*EI* XXXI, p. 245) are identical up to a certain point, when the kings of the second genealogy "branch off" into a younger lineage. The *praśasti* was commissioned by a king claiming to be from a younger lineage that had taken power (or had been installed) after the elders were defeated by the Caulukyas. Genealogists writing in the 13th century, as in Marwar, rediscovered the names of these kings and inserted them in the list of succession (Peterson 1890: 76, 85).

It is clear in both cases that the authors must have used older sources, either inscriptions (which is likely, since even the formulations are similar) or matching sources. They went back in time instead of relying on contemporary narratives, believing that old sources would tell them more about lineage history. Proving legitimacy in the face of lineage members was obviously of crucial interest to the kings, whose view rarely extended beyond the lineage domain. They never got beyond the dependent legitimation that made all kings who had branched off from senior ones members of younger lineages. The absence of mythical heroes, *paurāṇic* allusions or *paurāṇic* settings in the *praśastis* is common to all of them. There was no room to create an ancestral myth in their position; it would always have gone via the older lineage. Furthermore, it would not have been of much use. Through it, all the other power claimants would have gained the same legitimation . Neither would it have served to differentiate the legitimacy of e.g., brothers. Even the foundation legends were decidedly localised. Whereas the Cāhamāṇas of Marwar never developed a legend, the Guhilas acquired one when they began to opt for greater power in the second half of the 13th century. Contrary to the Cāhamāṇas of Śakambharī,[23] the senior branch of the Guhilas, from which they claim to have branched off, was probably unknown at the time. They began to derive themselves from a Brahman Bappa, who had obtained the right to rule from an ascetic Harita (Peterson 1890: 75). This, too, can be concluded from older inscriptions, as, for instance, that of 977 indicating a Brahmanic origin (*IA* 1910, p. 101) and the inscription of 971, in which a king named Bappa genuinely appears, albeit not as the founder of the lineage.[24]

There was, of course, communication with lords of other kingdoms. The 10th century, especially, was a formative period of consequence for all mediaeval Western Indian dynasties. The kings of the entire region began to recognise that their respective status was equal. An essential feature of the first genealogies seems to have been the fact that it enabled royal lineages to indicate notable marriages to other clans and the suitability they had attained to engage in these alliances. The wives and their clan names figure prominently in the genealogies of the 10th and 11th centuries. It is likely that these wives were daughters of neighbouring kings or important landholders of other clans and, at least in part, very probably of subordinate ones. A system of hypergamy had certainly not yet developed by the 11th century. Although the Guhila king was at that time a dependent little king, a *māṇḍalika*, he was still able to proclaim several marriages to princesses of the powerful Paramāras. Even a daughter of the mighty king Udayasiṃha was among them.[25] It seems as if marriages were a powerful marker for alliances, but could not serve as a mechanism to legitimate overlordship and subordination. Albeit of politically different status, the Rajput clans were presented as equal in these inscriptions.

It is conspicuous that even the great mediaeval Western Indian powers followed the restrictions dictated by the lineage domains, so that no great pan-Indian mythic genealogies emerged in these lofty regions either. On the contrary, they remained regionally oriented throughout, their foundation legends exceedingly moderate. The Caulukyas derived themselves from God Indra's water pot (*culuka*); the Paramāras declared that their founding father had sprung from the fire pit of the sage Vasiṣṭha on Mount Abu.[26] Beyond that, no mythical heroes can be detected in the genealogies of these mighty mediaeval dynasties, which themselves are rarely elaborated upon in the inscriptions.

What counted for all of them, great or little king alike, was "being the eldest" in an uninterrupted line of succession. This probably became an exclusive type of status category that bound independent kings in mutual recognition. Up to 1300, however, the main competitors for power over the respective kings were members of their own lineage. The peculiar form of the genealogies can be attributed to the Brahmanical authors' method of relying exclusively on older inscriptions as their sources, one they employed thoroughly. Almost no king's name from the past gleaned from old inscriptions escaped them and none were added to simply prolong the lists.

III

The 14th and 15th centuries have not been addressed in any great depth by historians of Western India, either. Admittedly, the sources for this period are still few and far between. The more powerful kingdoms had ceased to exist after the invasion and conquest of ʿAlaʾ al-Dīn Khaljī and became provinces of the Sultanate. The smaller ones also disappeared, were obliged to bear a Sultanate governor or recognise the suzerainty of the Sultan (Habib 1981; Ahluwalia 1978: 102f, 120, 136f, 151f). In the course of the 14th century, however, the authority of the Sultanate over the conquered areas began to wane again. Malwa and Gujarat, the former states of the Paramāras and the Caulukyas, developed into independent sultanates. In the remoter areas that comprise today's Rajasthan, new families who were partly descendants from older landholding families of different levels began to wage a power struggle, especially in Western and Southern Rajasthan. They included another Guhila lineage of unknown origin that built up a stable power basis in South East Rajasthan during the 14th century. Three great powers existed in the region around 1400, namely the Sultanates of Malwa and Gujarat and Mewar. The Sultanate of Delhi was, at that time, only one of many powers.

In the light of later sources, in particular the abundant so-called bardic literature of Rajasthan, the 14th century constitutes the beginning of a new chapter in Rajput culture and subsequent centuries are seen as a kind of continuum with later times. However, a closer look reveals that there was a distinct phase of development in the pre-Mughal age, the 14th and 15th centuries, which was later overshadowed completely by concepts of the Mughal and ensuing eras. Bardic literature, for instance, originates in the second half of the 16th century and is remarkably ill-informed about earlier developments (Tessitori 1918: 21f).

Prior to 1300, the Guhilas had never been lords of a *rājamaṇḍala*[27] or *sāmantamaṇḍala*. Now, for the first time this type of state structure began to emerge. The Guhila kings gained considerable power from mid-14th to mid-15th century, acquiring a veritable circle of lesser kingdoms that happened to be at the border of the Guhila core region.[28] It can be deduced from inscriptions in the first half of the 15th century that all the kingdoms on the periphery had suffered military defeat. Sources from the Sultanate of Gujarat show that these little kingdoms, which simultaneously faced numerous attacks from the Sultan,[29] were a bone of contention between the two emerging powers. Strong contest obviously arose as to who could force the smaller neighbours into a permanently subordinate position. The little kings, on the other hand, tried to play them off against each other and frequently reversed their alliances, albeit involuntarily.

Unfortunately, contemporary sources have proved scant. It is difficult to assess whether the tradition to give land at the peripheries or the centre to younger brothers was revived at this point or whether an alternative solution was found to settle their demands. There appears to have been an attempt to centralise. It is, nevertheless, remarkable that no lineage domains ever transpired again. There is no mention whatsoever of a younger lineage in any of the inscriptions of the time. Even the Guhilas, who reigned at that time in Vagor in the South of Mewar, were an independent lineage that had branched off long before 1400. It seems as if the dense network of kinsmen holding land had ceased to exist.

Thus, the political situation in Mewar distinguished itself in many respects from that of any of the previous great Western Indian states. It became the only powerful state to be ruled by descendants of the old lineages in the first half of the 15th century. There were no other powers to compete with or imitate. A ring of tributaries had emerged around the core region and behind them, the Sultans, who were the main competitors for overlordship of Western India, consolidated their power according to their own value system.

Under these circumstances, considerable effort was made to create new legitimatory strategies. These were complex and directed towards different levels of addressees. Suffice it to mention some that might have had a bearing on their relationship to little kings. A comparison with later traditions, so amply found in so-called bardic literature, reveals tremendous differences. The legitimation of the 15th century was completely free of the relations and objectives that became so dominant in this literature, of which the oldest examples probably stem from the second half of the 16th century and which, according to many historians, were strongly influenced by the relationship of the Rajasthan kings to the Mughals (Henige 1974: 206).

The kings of Mewar chose a means of legitimation oriented to the past. They drew on older strategies in a manner described by Meister as 'post modern', piecing together elements of quite diverse origins (Meister 1994: 166). In recompiling the genealogy, they probably drew on traditions current in the smaller successor states of the Caulukya empire. The mediaeval art of writing with its strong orientation towards a lineage audience was once again employed. Between 1439 and 1460, a genealogy was compiled for the third time in the history of Mewar, again with the help of old inscriptions, and could be called the culmination of the mediaeval historiographical tradition I mentioned earlier. The authors had to start from scratch. Most of the inscriptions they needed had to be hunted down in the debris of destroyed buildings or other similarly difficult locations. Even today, it is easy to assess the inscriptions used by the authors. The list of kings was reconstructed almost to perfection back to the 7th century. Again, contemporary sources seemed more reliable to the authors than the lengthier later ones. Old changes of lineage such as the one that occurred in the 11th century were unearthed yet again, although no longer evident in the *praśastis* of the 13th century. A foundation legend that was the result of an interesting combination of facts elicited from old inscriptions from the 10th and 13th centuries was propagated. It tells us that the founder of the Guhila dynasty was a Brahman from Ānandapura (a tradition from the 10th century) called Bappa, who obtained the right to rule Mewar by favour of the deity Ekaliṅga through the preceptor Harita (a 13th century tradition). The authors obviously created this legend according to the same method used in reconstructing the list of kings. It is interesting to note that the legitimacy of the Brahman origin of the royal family that had been discerned from 10th century sources was not questioned, although the family had been made Kṣatriya in the 13th century. On the contrary, this element was willingly taken up and even elaborated on in a *māhātmya* that was written to promote the cult of the old "state" deity Ekliṅgji.

Although many new elements were included in the legitimation at that time, the way the genealogy was written drew on conservative values. It is very possible that an adjustment to the actual political circumstances had not been thoroughly worked out in this phase of fast change. It seems striking that these *praśastis* were not a great success. They were heavily remodelled subsequently and a completely new tradition emerged a mere 40 years later. The most problematic competitors for power were little kings who now claimed to be from other clans (and Sultans) and not their own kinsmen. There were other rising kings, however, who could not imitate this legitimatory strategy because many of them were complete upstarts with no prospect of gaining a foothold.

The relationship of Mewar and its neighbour Marwar in this context should be examined in more detail. The predecessors of the new kings of Mewar were very probably members of a peripheral Guhila lineage that had succeeded in gaining power in the 14th century. They had the advantage of being able to establish a genealogical connection to the Guhilas from the 10th to 13th century. The new kings in Marwar were, however, Rāṭhoḍs, not Cāhamāṇas, and probably stem from a Rāṣṭrakūṭa lineage of an earlier period, which had led a subordinate existence somewhere on the periphery of Marwar. They appear now and then as marriage partners or dependent landholders of the Cāhamāṇas. In the first half of the 15th century, they are found among the dependent little kings of Mewar. In a 1460 inscription, Maṇḍovarapura, the erstwhile capital, is spoken of by the Guhilas in the same terms as other subjugated kingdoms. The reigning Guhila king Kumbha is described as the destroyer of Maṇḍovarapura (*EI* XXI, p. 287). Nevertheless, this subjugation seems to be somewhat obscure. The kingdom had a large hinterland and, according to Ferishta, was never attacked by the Sultanate of Gujarat. All other smaller kingdoms, in comparison, were constantly under pressure by contesting powers. Another inscription from 1460 formulates the relationship of the Guhila king more evasively. It describes how Kumbha placed his foot on the foreheads of (unspecified) kings and having brought a [statue of] Hanumat from Maṇḍavyapura (Maṇḍovarapura), erected it in [his fortress] Kumbhalameru (Nath 1999: 152). This contrasts with the description of other areas conquered, which he had "seized" or on which he "furnished tributary status".[30]

It must have been during Kumbha's time (c. 1436-1468) that the Rāṭhoḍs gradually began to consolidate their power. Jodhpur, the new capital, was founded in 1458, most probably after the destruction of Maṇḍovarapura. Around that time they also opted for a new status. It might be expected that the strategies developed by their powerful neighbour Mewar would have served as a model. There is, however, absolutely no evidence of any stone *praśasti*s of the Rāṭhoḍ kings. They either decided to contest the Mewar model right from the start or they tried to imitate it and came to the conclusion that they would fail. Unfortunately for them, almost all pre-1300 inscriptions from the area belong to Cāhamāṇa. According to lineage logic, the Rāṭhoḍs were not at home in their own country.[31]

Hardly any inscriptions pertain to the Rāṭhoḍs. There is one Cuṇḍa known from a grant for the *kuladevī* "Cāmuṇḍā" in the year 1394, which seems to be the oldest source and clearly belongs to an ancestor of the ruling Rāṭhoḍs of the 15th century (Reu 1938: 60f). Two earlier inscriptions, however, do exist, one belonging to a certain Sīha Rāṭhaḍ from 1273 and one to a Dhuhar from 1309. These appear as ancestors of the ruling family in later sources but there is no reason to connect them to this lineage or attribute them with royal status (Henige 1974: 204f). Tessitori is of the opinion that these two were added to the genealogy as late as the 16th century (Tessitori 1918: 263), and since there are no known sources that are older, their discovery could well be attributed to an attempt at finding older inscriptions in order to compile a genealogy along the lines of the Mewar model. This might be a hint that the Rāṭhoḍs tried to emulate the Guhila model but were soon frustrated.

In any case, they had to find another solution. The most interesting inscription in this respect is from 1460 and informs us that a predecessor of the ruling Rāṭhoḍ king Jodha had brought the *mūrti* of the *kuladevī* Mātājī Aḍpaṁṣṇijī from Kanauj (Karan no date: 267). It is the first reference to the Rāṭhoḍ tradition of origin as successors to the mediaeval Gahāḍavāla dynasty of Kanauj (situated in the Ganges Plain). In the rich bardic literature of the 16th and later centuries, this legend is elaborated and serves as proof of origin from a paradigmatic Rajput clan of the pre-1300s and also for the fact that the Rāṭhoḍs were Sūryavaṁśa Kṣatriyas.

It is impossible to say whether this was the main objective around 1460. However, contemporary development in Mewar itself is quite remarkable. After Kumbha's death in 1468, Mewar underwent a long period of crisis that terminated once and for all its claim to being the greatest power in Western India. Marwar was thereafter at least as powerful and a short time later saw the emergence of other powers such as the Kacchvāhas of Amber. It seems that this situation was also responsible for a radical change of legitimation in Mewar, which was to become the paradigmatic Rajput legitimation of later times. A common system of values that would legitimate all these powers and not just the Guhilas had to be introduced. The next great *praśasti* in Mewar comes from the year 1488, showing evidence of the first changes. A Kṣatriya origin, for instance, had never been mentioned up to this time. Now, Bappa (Bāṣpa), the founder, is introduced as a Brahman, but the king Kṣetrasiṃha, who ruled around 1400, is described as a Kṣatriya (Peterson 1890: 119). In 1500, the heir apparent of Mewar described himself as being a descendant of the *sūryavaṁśīya-mahārājādhirāja-śilāditya-vaṁśa* (Peterson 1890: 140-142), proving that *paurāṇic* Sūryavaṁśa (or for other clans Candravaṁśa) origin is not an invention of the Mughal era, as authors like Tessitori and Henige presume, but the product of a distinct formation period of Rajput ideology belonging to the second half of the 15th century (Tessitori 1918: 20; Henige 1974: 202). Moreover, the core of a legend of foreign origin is also incorporated here, possibly a reaction to the incipient "legends of foreign origin" of other clans, i.e., the Rāṭhoḍs. But its creation still betrays the methods of the Brahman genealogists, not the later bards. It is based on the unmitigated search for old inscriptions. King Śīlāditya genuinely exists in the Guhila genealogy. According to an inscription of his reign, he ruled around 646,[32] and has now become identified with the Maitraka king of Saurāṣṭra called Śīlāditya.[33] This identity of names was evidently used to construct a connection to an older dynasty that would provide the Guhilas with a Solar origin.[34]

Hence, the way was paved for a comparable origin in both royal dynasties, Guhilas and Rāṭhoḍs, around that time. As adequately documented in bardic literature, both were Sūryavaṁśin and developed huge mythical genealogies linking them with Rāma, his sons and the Ikṣvākus from the 16th century on. Originally, both of them came from other lands. That they obviously stopped (or in the case of Marwar never started) relying on a Brahmanic genealogical tradition but began to promote bards as panegyrists, a tradition that very much deviates from the older royal one, was a common feature they shared. The bards came from another caste and wrote (or sang) in another language. Tessitori exclaims in wonder: "... there is probably no bardic literature in any part of the world, in which truth is so masked by fiction, or so disfigured by hyperbole, as in the bardic literature of Rajputana" (Cit. Henige 1974: 201). In other words completely new objectives concerning legitimation grew imminent. The drawing up of succession lists according to older inscriptions was bound to lineage orientation and lost its importance.[35] The new carriers of historical tradition found no access to the older ones. They were thus forced to reconstruct the earlier past by other means and with other aims.

A key feature of bardic literature is its immense capacity for variations on similar themes. The position of the bards as at least partly self-employed enabled them to develop several different traditions in accordance with the demands of their employers but beyond the latter's direct control. It is not clear when these bards first emerged, but they were very probably there in the 15th century. It is possible that the Brahmanic genealogies of Mewar were already understood as a conscious attempt to establish a countertradition that could not, however, provide neighbouring and competing states with a common value system due to the nature of its sources.

Mewar was forced to bow to the newly-emerging system in the end and from 1500 onwards established a completely new set of genealogical traditions. The kings never ceased to have *praśasti*s written in stone, although the genealogy used in the later inscriptions emanate from bardic genealogies and show only few traces of the older Brahmanic works. The genealogy of 1675, for instance, bears scant resemblance to the works of up to 1460. It opens with 150 mythical kings via Rāmacandra, Kuśa, the Ikṣvākus to the "Ādityas", whereby Śīlāditya was the one that bridged the gap to the "more human" part. This, too, had been strongly altered compared to the lists of 1460 and those before. Very few names are identical, their positions often mixed up, and many new names introduced, partly due to popular hero legends surrounding feats of older generations.[36] Bardic legitimation proved vital in legitimating the kingdoms of Rajputana and bound them into a network of values, alliances and conflicts. The origin probably goes back to a contest between an overlord and a little king who began to gain power and opt for a newly-acknowledged status among his neighbours, rather than to the influence of the Mughals. In summary it can be argued that from the 16th century on, when the strong lineage network had declined and the emergence of a new cluster of political units saw the introduction of the Rajput states and their culture, the early mediaeval lineage method of writing history was superseded by one that was oriented towards the existence of several clans.

Notes

1 Chattopadhyaya already notes this peculiarity in passing, writing that the early Western Indian dynasties were very eager to place themselves in the pan Indian strategy of Kṣatriyadom's pan-Indian strategy of mythical ancestry (most likely referring to the Gurjara-Pratihāras) but that later gaining access to the new highest status group, subsequently called Raj-

puts rather than Kṣatriyas, seems to have been of greater significance (Chattopadhyaya 1994: 181).

2 I am well aware of the ambivalence of the term "fact" as opposed to "fiction" in historical writing. However, I would like to use them here as relational terms in the sense of two different points in a continuum. They are not in any way meant to separate "true" from "false" history but refer solely to methods and objects of historians.

3 Both regional names have been in use since the 10th century and are not meant to denote a territory with fixed boundaries. Names can refer to both small centres as well as large areas, according to the expansion of the respective ruling lineages.

4 I am aware of the connotation the term "lineage system" carries and would not suggest its use here, particularly since other organisational principles were in operation, such as monarchical forms.

5 Although the strong lineage orientation of the Rajput polities has often been acknowledged, distinct early medieval developments, separated by an enormous time span from early modern ones, have not always been adequately recognised in this context. The static existence of lineages and their ideology and organisation seem to have been taken for granted.

6 Four Guhila lineages were known in Mewar in the 7th century (Somani 1993, 78-88).

7 In 943, king Bhartṛpaṭa expanded to Partabgarh. Two sons of his wife Mahālakṣmī are found to have been kings in Jagat and Ahar in 950 and 953. A third independent kinsman was later found in Jiran on the eastern periphery and another in Unwas in 960. *Varada* VII, pp. 7-15; *Indian Antiquary* XXXIX, pp. 186-191; *IA* LVIII, p. 161-162; *Epigraphia Indica* XIV, pp. 176-188; Peterson 1890: 67-69; Somani 1976: 57.

8 The first source speaks of a king Jojalla in Naḍol in 1090, who established a dynasty there that lasted until c. 1145. In 1110, his younger brother Aśvarājan is in neighbouring Balī. In 1152 a younger brother of this lineage moved on to Kirādū and later conquered Naḍol, most probably under the protection of the Caulukyas. His son Alhaṇa unified all three centres under one rulership around 1160, and shortly afterwards (1182) two new centres sprang up, Jalor and Bhīnmāl, both ruled by a brother and a son of Alhaṇa's successor Kelhaṇa, the latter initially styled as a *bhoktṛ*, i.e., installed landholder, but soon becoming independent due to the sacking of Naḍol by the Delhi Sultan. *EI* XI, pp. 26-28; ibid. pp. 28-30; ibid. pp. 43-46; ibid. pp. 46-54.

9 In 1115 a younger brother of the king was a *bhoktṛ*. In 1160 a king's younger brother was the donee of 12 villages in the vicinity of the capital. In 1176 two younger brothers are called *bhoktṛ* by their elder Kelhaṇa. In 1132 a younger son is mentioned as a (joint) holder of land, and in 1152 a younger son is depicted as holding administrative offices. *EI* IX, pp. 66-67; *EI* XI, pp. 49-50; ibid. pp. 50-51; ibid. pp. 29-30; ibid. p. 35; ibid. p. 45.

10 The village Sonāna , for instance, was given to a king's younger son Kīrtipāla in 1161, but in 1171 belonged to a Guhila *ṭhakura*, who obviously did not receive it from the said Kīrtipāla. *EI* IX, p. 69; *EI* XI, p. 48. See also for the following Mita 1999: 92-102.

11 A class of "nobles" is implied in the expressions ... *rājaśrīrāyapālādīnāṃ rāṇākānāṃ valepi graṃthir nāsti n ca dū[ṣa]aṃ kimapyastīti* ...; ... *deśaṃto rājaputrān janapadagaṇāṇ* ...; *rāṇakānaṃ pārśvāt pālanīyaṃ* ‖ *EI* IX, p. 65; *EI* XI, p. 40; *EI* XXXIX, p. 181. A collective is denoted in each case and seems to have a special standing in a given area. Precisely what status they had and what their source of income was unfortunately cannot be discerned.

12 A hierarchy of this kind is described in an inscription of 1171 that integrates "old" and "new" terms. Overlord was the *mahārājādhirāja* Kumārapāla Caulukya, *mahārāja* was the local Cāhamāṇa king Kelhaṇa, next in the hierarchy was a landholding subordinate *rāṇaka* and at the end of the ladder was a *ṭhakura*, a landholder of one village. *EI* XI, pp. 47-48.

13 *Ṭhakura* was a title for small landholders who could be members of royal lineages but also *kayasthas*, *sonis* and even *mahājanas*. *EI* VIII, p. 208-212; *EI* XI, p. 37; ibid. p. 55; ibid. p. 60; *IA* 1877, p. 194f; ibid. p. 204; Peterson 1890: 219.

14 Especially in Mewar, *rājaputra* also occurs as a term for members of non-Guhila lineages

such as the Solaṃkis. *EI* XXXI, p. 248; *EI* XXX, p. 12.

15 Mita (1999: 97) is of the opinion that these titles always denote landholders belonging to other clans. It seems, however, that they were also Cāhamāṇas in Marwar (*EI* XI, p. 37) and Guhilas in Mewar (*Journal of the Asiatic Society of Bengal* LV,1, p. 19). In many cases, the clan's name is not mentioned.

16 Such a term seems to exclude others such as *rāṇaka* etc. for the same bearer, whereas they can occur together with *ṭhakura*. *IA* XI, p. 42.

17 In Marwar the terms *rāṇā* and *rāuta* occur frequently in the 12th century. The term *mahārāja-kula* comes into use in the 13th century, now as a royal title. In 13th century Mewar, the royal title becomes *mahārāvala(kula)*. *EI* XI, pp. 34-36; pp. 41-42; pp. 42-43; pp. 47-48; *JASB* LV,1, p. 19. In the Caulukya domain, in comparison, the title *rāṇā* occurs much more often than in Marwar and Mewar. The use of the term *rāutta* has its peak in the 11th century and later declines. *IA* VI, pp. 180-214.

18 We can at least deduct this from the Caulukya area, where titles such as *mahāmaṇḍaleśvara rāṇaka* occur. *EI* VIII, p. 204.

19 Similar to the Cāhamāṇa *māṇḍalika*, who was installed on the banks of the Narmada by Jaya-siṃha Caulukya around 1175. *IA* 1889, p. 80.

20 I.e., father's brothers and their kin, then grandfathers' brothers and their kin etc.

21 The specification was not always so thorough. For instance, Alhaṇa's son Kīrtipāla (not the *yuvarāja* but denoted as "younger" after receiving land as a *bhoktṛ*) wrote another genealogy (*EI* IX, pp. 68-70) in the same year and had some kings, denoted as "brothers", omitted from the list, thereby adjusting the text to the demands of unilinearity.

22 I must admit that Kaṭudeva, the predecessor of the patron of the inscription of 1161 was not reinserted in the genealogy of 1272. The object of the authors was to legitimate their patrons as opposed to creating an independent "historical truth" in the modern sense. Maybe the rightful succession of Alhaṇa was still too crucial for the then ruling king. This is corroborated by the great pains taken by the authors to represent Alhaṇa's son Kīrtipāla as the rightful successor, although his brother and his brother's son had been kings. Kīrtipāla was nothing but the founder of a younger lineage segment who stepped in after the sacking of Naḍol by the Ghurids around 1197. The legitimacy of the ruling king of 1272 heavily depended on that connection.

23 Having been defeated by Mahmud Ghur in 1192, they lingered on in Northern Rajasthan on a diminished scale throughout the greater part of the 13th century.

24 *Journal of the Bombay Branch of the Royal Asiatic Society* XXII, pp. 151-167.

25 *EI* II, p. 13-16, v. 17-22. This must have greatly privileged the Guhila *māṇḍalika* . In 1155 the Kalacuri king mentions that he even married a daughter from this union. *EI* II, pp. 251-267.

26 *IA* XII, p. 199; *EI* II, p. 180-194. These moderate legends were hardly ever used. Most genealogies of the Caulukyas, for instance, use a rather nondescript Mūlarājan as the founding father.

27 In1428, the reigning king was first described explicitly as "having gained a spotless *Maṇḍala*" (*āruhyāmalamaṇḍala*, Peterson 1890: 99).

28 The acquisition can easily be followed from the inscriptions. It started with the conquest of a tribal area in the Aravalli mountains, continuing on to Hadauti, Idar, Sapadalakṣa, Nagaur, Jalor and Mandor (which is Marwar) and Śakambharī.

29 Ferishta reports several wars with Mandalgarh (Hadauti), Idar, Nagaur, Mewat, Dungarpur (Vagor) and Sirohi (Briggs 1981: 40-43).

30 *Gṛhītvā, karadaṃ vidhāya* ... (Nath 1999: 152, v. 4).

31 Here it may be noted that it was obviously impossible for the Rāṭhoḍs to claim Cāhamāṇa ancestry. It was not as easy to fabricate a status as many historians might believe.

32 *Proceedings of the Royal Asiatic Society Western Circle* 1908-9, p. 48.

33 This king is dated back to the 8th century (Ray 1936: 1154).

34 Unfortunately, the Maitrakas never defined themselves as belonging to the Sūryavaṁśa. Sir-

car is of the opinion that the connection was the result of a special relationship to the Sun God Mitra (Sircar 1969: 5).

35 It is interesting that *paurāṇic* dynasties occurred here only after the genealogies had been transferred from the hands of the Brahmans to the bards.

36 There was a king named Samarasiṃha, for example, known from his own inscriptions from about 1283 to 1300. He is now described as a contemporary hero and brother-in-law of the great king Pṛthvīrājan Cāhamāṇa, who was killed in the Ghurid attack of 1192. *Journal of the Asiatic Society of Bengal* 55, pp. 6-65; Peterson (1890: 145-154).

Virtual Relations. Little Kings in Malabar

Margret Frenz

As the previous essays have shown, the discussion on the model of the little king plays a vital role in the wider debate on state formation in South Asia. In Germany, Hermann Kulke's role in this debate should not be underestimated, firstly because he himself was passionately engaged for decades in historic research about small and princely states based on indigenous sources and, secondly, because he motivated his students to devote their time to similar questions. He encouraged them to concentrate on indigenous sources and advised them not to focus on one region of India (Orissa) only, but to broaden their approach and apply it to similarly structured regions all over the subcontinent. In an effort to contribute another facet to the the little kingdom model, this article will analyse the situation on the Southwest coast of India, namely Malabar. Some of the features found here provide points of reference for comparison with the situation in Orissa, Kulke's main region of research. The model developed by Kulke and his "school" allows for a comparative perspective, thus extending the outlook presented by studies based on indigenous sources.

The main hypothesis of the present essay asserts that in late 18th and early 19th century Malabar, the peculiarity of the regional power structure was the result of influence by a virtual – i.e., at that time non-existent or imagined – great king (Frenz 2003: 148). Against the background of the virtual great king and focusing on the interrelationship of little kings in Malabar, the arguments in favour of this proposition will be discussed. Historiographic evidence concerning little and great king(s) is difficult to come by, spread as it is over different sources such as, for example, the *Paḷaśśi Rēkhakaḷ*, a compilation of letters between several little kings of Malabar and representatives of the British East India Company from the late 18th century, when it conquered Malabar (Paḷaśśi Rēkhakaḷ 1994). Colin Mackenzie's collection of manuscripts from the early 19th century constitutes a significant contribution to the otherwise scant array of source texts. Mackenzie had local people in South India collect and record historical documents (Dirks 1993). Malayāḷam manuscripts are not represented in great profusion here, however, since the majority were destroyed during the Maisūrian invasions (Mahalingam 1972: 298).[1] The quantity of manuscripts dealing with the southwestern part of India, therefore, is comparatively smaller than those dealing with the southeastern part, i.e., today's

Tamil Nadu and Andhra Pradesh. Besides these sources, there are reports by several European travellers to Kerala, of which the more famous are Visscher's letters containing his impressions of his stay in Kerala, and Mr. Rottler's notes on his journey to Ceylon and the Southwest coast of India (Rottler 1790; Padmanabha Menon 1989). Both mention the relationships between great and little king(s) incidentally in various contexts.

The Virtuality of a Great King

An account of a local historical tradition preserved in various versions in the Mackenzie Collection hints at the mutual relationship between the great and little king. It describes how the ruler of Malabar, Cēramān Perumāḷ, left his kingdom in the 9th century. Of particular interest is a scene describing how he divided his land among several little kings within his sphere of influence. His departure was announced as a journey either to Mecca or the Ganges – or possibly both. [The sources are not clear about the religion he seems to have turned to: Buddhism and Islam are mentioned in equal part.] The "enigma" surrounding Cēramān Perumāḷ's departure lies in the fact that he never returned to Malabar to rule again. How the "missing" point of reference in the concept of rule, in this case of the great king, was symbolically marked in the decades after his departure is noted in the Mackenzie Collection as follows:

> "Thus the Congu Dasum being governed by the Chera Rajahs, when the Chēra King was taken up into Kăilāsam he directed his Minister to take the reins of Government during his absence; & therefore it is that from that time to the present, the descendants of Ram Rajah of Măleyālăm sit not in their palanqueens in the usual way, but are carried with their legs hanging down, for they look for the return of their king and by this attitude they denote attention to the affairs of his state." (MSS EUR/Mack Gen 1)

Cēramān Perumāḷ is described in numerous sources as having distributed the land belonging to his kingdom amongst little kings. It is also said that he established places that functioned as repositories of knowledge about him and gave away royal insignia, such as his crown, sword and shield (Mahalingam 1972: 283). One could argue that the sources intend to describe these events as his desire to keep the balance between little kings by distributing his property and rights in as equal measure as possible. For little kings of later periods, these politico-ritual acts by Cēramān Perumāḷ were among the most important sources of legitimation for their rule.

Taking the example of Konnilakkonadiri, the ruler of Koḻikkōṭu at the time of Cēramān Perumāḷ's departure from Malabar, I will show how he and his successors used a link with Cēramān Perumāḷ to legitimate their rule in Koḻikkōṭu. In the particular case of Koḻikkōṭu it is of interest to note that in addition to the land mentioned in the quotation below, one element of the royal insignia was the title *tāmūtiri*[2] (also known as *samuri* or *zamorin*), i.e., king by the sea.

> "One of the early kings of Koḻikkōḍu, Konnilakkonadiri by name had done great personal service to Cēramān Perumāḷ for which he, at the time of his departure to Mecca (?), granted him a piece of land around Koḻikkōḍu over which he was asked to rule and extend his rule over the adjacent territory." (Mahalingam 1972: 283)

The question that arises here, assuming that the little kings in the study believed in the historicity of the Cēramān Perumāḷ story, is what consequences the departure of the great king of Malabar had for the concept of rule in Malabar. Did little kings lose their legitimatory base. What problems arose for little kings in legitimating their rule without a great king? How was the structure of rule adapted to the new circumstances? To explore these questions, let me first recapitulate one of the general characteristics of a little king according to the model and then move on to the Malabar situation in particular.

According to the model, the relationship between a little and a great king is comprised of the following elements: parallel to his internal autonomy, the little king acknowledges an external ruler of higher standing, who is able to support this status in political and ritual terms by military superiority. The system of ritual redistribution allows a little king to partake of a great king's power, on the one hand, but makes him dependent on the latter to ritually legitimise his rule in his own territory, on the other.

The supreme ruler in Malabar during the 9th century was known as Cēramān Perumāḷ. Since the great king of the Cēramān Perumāḷ dynasty was the most successful *rājā* among the rulers in Malabar with respect to his military undertakings, he acquired the status of *mahārāja*, which was underlined with royal insignia, as is vividly described in the following account:

> "The Brahman of the sixty four Gramams gave Chayrooman Payroomal [Cēramān Perumāḷ] a commission to rule with sovereign array the kingdom of Kayralam consisting of one hundred and sixty caadams and bestowed upon him the privilege Egathatraadeepadee [Ekacchattra-adhipati] or a right to use the insignia of Royalty. They put flowers and poured water in to his hands as a pledge of performance." (OIOC MSS Eur Mackenzie 5)

Military success and the associated expansion of conquered land were prerequisites for this achievement. The question of a successor emerged at the end of a great king's reign. Since the Cēramān Perumāḷ dynasty belonged to the Nāyars in Malabar, they followed a matrilineal line of succession, the *marumakkattāyaṃ*. The low level of importance attached to genealogies in the usual inscriptional form is one of the characteristics of matrilineal society. It is, therefore, far more significant in this context to be able to trace a *taṟavāṭu* (Nāyar house-and-land-unit) back to an ancestress.[3] In the case of one little Malabar king, for instance, the sole vestige discovered after research in numerous archives and conversations with his descendants in Kerala was the name of his mother and his mother's mother – the comment attached signifiying that nothing else was of importance.[4] His family apparently did not have a *vaṁśāvali*.[5] A possible explanation for this might be that *vaṁśāvali*s are a typical North Indian phenomenon based on and geared towards patrilinear hierarchies in line with purāṇic tradition. This in turn is linked to the authority of the father of the family, which is decisive in patrilineal society, as was (and still is) found in the majority of cases in North India. In Malabar, however, the matrilineal concept implied that the mother's brother had greater decision-making powers than the children's father. Consequently, the *vaṁśāvali* is not given great prominence as a source of status legitimation, since it does not correspond to the social norms of the Nāyars, who were appointed as little kings in Malabar. Malabar shows no signs of the purāṇic tradition familiar in North India. Oral traditions had far greater weight than recorded written texts and inscriptions (Claus 1978: 1). It was the son of the last Cēramān Perumāḷ's sister, and not his own son, who inherited the kingdom. Under this system, the son of the great king was merely bestowed with a subordinate position of power – a fact that could lead to conflict with his theoretically superior cousin. Thus, the *marumakkattāyaṃ*, the matrilineal line of succession (see figure), harboured a structural opposition between the great king's son and his sister's son.

The matrilineal line of succession made it more difficult to form long-reigning dynasties. The *marumakkattāyaṃ* passed on the status of *mahārāja* in a a manner that did not correspond to the *dharmaśāstra*.[6] In practice, a conflict was likely to arise between the great king's son and his matrilateral cousin (the son of the great king's sister) as a result of the structural opposition inherent in the system. In the extreme, this contradiction could lead to a breaking up of the *mahārāja*'s kingdom. The following hypothesis is derived from these considerations: the political structure of a pre-modern Indian society based on matrilineal descent among ruling elites (little kings), such as Malabar, was more stable on a long-term basis under a 'virtual' great king. The rules of inheritance made it impossible for a regional kingdom to achieve stability over several generations under a sequence of *mahārāja*s. The situation resembles the taluka, the little kingdom type dominated by a landowning kin group as described by Cohn (2001b [1962]: 489), insofar as such a group shares political power in the Malabar situation as well – with the exception of one aspect: the kin group in Malabar was matrilineal. In dealing with royal succession, the result was a host of problems.

The following examples illustrate the kind of "problems" associated with matrilineal succession. Distribution of power is expressed in similar terms to those used in the case of the above-mentioned report by Kaṭattanāṭu *rājās* on Konnilakkonadiri, the ruler of Koḻikkōṭu (Mahalingam 1972: 288). A different version of Cēramān Perumāḷ's transfer of power is given in another report: Cēramān Perumāḷ is said to have promised his wife's maidservants, two Vellala girls, that any sons born to them would enjoy the status of independent rulers. The descendants of the younger maid are said to have ultimately produced four branches, of which the eldest member became the ruler of Kōlattanāṭu (Mahalingam 1972: 287) – thus the descendant of Cēramān Perumāḷ belonged to the circle of Malabar rulers but was not master of the circle of little kings as his father had been. Even the Nambyars of Iruvaḻināṭu, who ruled over 1000 Nāyars, traced their reign back to Cēramān Perumāḷ: '[...] the kingdom granted to them by Cēramān Perumāḷ extended north to south [...]' (Mahalingam 1972: 288). The even smaller principality of Payyermola, whose rulers could only call upon 500 Nāyars, was alledgedly created by Cēramān Perumāḷ before his departure. It is said that by the time Cēramān left for Mecca, the rulers of Kurumpranāṭu received confirmation from him that they were legally entitled to rule over their area (Mahalingam 1972: 289).

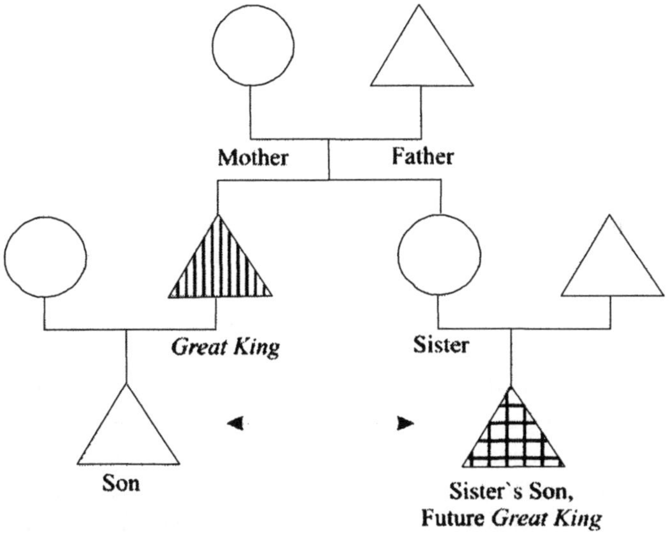

Structural opposition between the great king's own son and his sister's son

Despite some elements of uncertainty, the end of the last Cēramān Perumāḷ's reign is commonly associated with the beginning of the Koḷḷaṃ era in 825 A.D, when the town of Koḷḷaṃ was most probably founded.[7] This is one of the local eras used in

Kerala, apart from counting the number of years that made up a king's reign. This calendar is also linked to the end of the great king's supremacy, when the little kings who resided in Malabar took over joint responsibility for the land in the absence of the great king – always keeping the memory of the *mahārāja* alive in their legitimating accounts and awaiting his return (Logan 1989 [1887]: 243, 245).

A distinctive feature of power relations in Malabar in the 18th century was that, despite the absence of a *mahārāja* since the 9th century, legitimation of local *rājās* hinged on a supreme ruler, as revealed by titles, inscriptions and oral records. The status of the parties involved depends on the particular stature of a king in relation to his position as great or little among other kings; i.e., a ruler can be a great king in the eyes of someone weaker than himself, and at the same time, be a little king in the eyes of someone more powerful. On the one hand, he is perceived by others as the occupant of a particular position, whilst on the other, he behaves, in accordance with his own ideas of levels of superiority. The relationship between the two levels, i.e., the macro- and the meso-level, is the process that defines the kind of connection or alliance fostered by both parties. Therefore, an analysis of the relationship should focus on this process, which defines the status attributed to the respective partners. There are two possible patterns of conduct for a little king in the face of a great king, who is either unable to attack him or who does not actually exist. The little king can either act as if he were a great king or he can remain a little king should his legitimation necessitate the existence of a great king. Examples of this often crop up in Indian history source texts, where rulers award themselves titles, such as *talavāra* (bailiff), *rāṣṭrakūṭa* (Regent of the Empire) or *pratihāra* (gatekeeper), none of which are imperial titles and thus implicitly refer to the dynasty of a great king who no longer exists or never did (Berkemer 1993: 157). There are, however, almost no self-awarded titles to be found in the case of Kerala. The supreme ruler bore the title *perumāḷ* – in rare cases other titles such as *śrī rājādhirājā paramēśvara bhaṭṭāraka*,[8] whilst less powerful rulers used the title of *rājā* at the very most (Narayanan 1996: 79).

Despite limitations in the Mackenzie Collection, the documents tell us how during the 18th century a great king in Malabar, who no longer existed or may not have existed at all, was imagined and continued to live in people's memory. In addition, he was important for the practical legitimation of rule. The respective documents mention Cēramān Perumāḷ as Malabar's most powerful ruler. In a manuscript about the *rājās* of Kōḻikkōṭu, the *rājās* of Kocci, who had received their crown and sword as insignia from Cēramān Perumāḷ, are also mentioned (Mahalingam 1972: 282). Furthermore, there are records of a report about Cēramān Perumāḷ which reads that he was the 18th king in the line of Perumāḷs and had ruled for 36 years before becoming interested in Islam and undertaking the journey to Mecca.[9] The transfer of power to his subordinate rulers is described thus: 'At the time of his departure to Mecca, Cēramān Perumāḷ distributed his kingdom among his subordinates.' (Mahalingam 1972: 285). The Malabar *rājā*s in many cases attributed the establishment of rule, or their participation in rule, to Cēramān Perumāḷ's initiative. He was obviously keen to put his land in good hands before leaving for Mecca – the recipients appear to have been ,his' little kings.

With regard to the situation in 18th century Malabar, I therefore put forward the thesis that, while no great king actually existed, a 'virtual' great king was prevalent in the minds of little kings, and that this concept had far-reaching consequences within the principalities of Malabar. Since most documents were destroyed at the time of the Maisūrian invasions, we can only assume that the surviving documents date from after this period. Thus, if Malabar rulers in the 18th century still reverted to the personage of Cēramān Perumāḷ as a great king, i.e., a legitimator of rule, the logical conclusion is that he served as a 'virtual' great king to the little kings of Malabar. A parallel to this phenomenon is the concept of rule endorsed by the Nāyakas in 17th century Tamiḻ land, who legitimated their rule by relating it to the *rājā*s of Vijayanagara. Their political vocabulary was evidently borrowed from the Kakātiyas (Narayana Rao / Shulman / Subrahmanyam 1992: 7, 12, 38; Subrahmanyam / Shulman 1990). In the context of temples, even today priests legitimise their priesthood in the Mīnākṣi temple in Maturai through descendants of a royal appointee; neither the British nor the succeeding government of Tamil Nadu is accepted as the legitimate successor of the Nāyaka dynasty that appointed the temple priests during the 16th and 17th centuries (Fuller 1991: 109, 111).

The Virtual Relationship in a Historical Case Study

The following examples refer to Kēraḷa Varmma Paḻaśśi Rājā, a little king who ruled in Kōṭṭayaṃ in North Kerala. His case exemplifies the role played by the great king in the processes of legitimating the rule of a little king and the relationship between these two figureheads, which was of utmost significance to both. The little king referred to the great king mainly to legitimise his rule over his own little kingdom, manifested in politico-ritual acts during the annual festival cycle. The great king, on the other hand, needed the submission and appreciation of a circle of little kings to display his own greatness. Much more so in the special case of Malabar, where the matrilineal line of succession left the great king without the support of a hereditary power base cum *vaṁśāvali*.

Paḻaśśi Rājā, along with other little kings – such as the Rājā of Ciṟakkal and Vira Varmma of Kurumpranāṭu – and one little queen, the Bibi of Kannūr, formed a circle of neighbouring rulers with similar strengths and monitored one another within the Malabar *kūṭṭaṃ*. Paḻaśśi Rājā, as a member of the aforementioned circle of little Malabar rulers had a twofold relationship with the other rulers. On the one hand, he was linked to them by family ties, while he maintained, on the other hand, changing political alliances. This meant that he sometimes sought amicable and at other times hostile relations with neighbouring rulers, who might at the same time be his relatives – depending on the political and economic situation. These fluctuating relations can be attributed to the constantly shifting socio-economic, political and cultural set-up. Vira Varmma of Kurumpranāṭu, for instance, was related to Paḻaśśi Rājā and yet relations between them were decidedly strained on account of Paḻaśśi Rājā's desire to resist large-scale British interventions in matters of domestic policy. Paḻaśśi Rājā's resistance to intervention, however, surfaced only after the British had broken the agreements they had made with him. Vira Varmma, on the other hand, opted to co-operate with the British. If we take this as an example of forming alliances within the circle of little kings as well as with a new potential great king, it becomes obvious that scenarios with constellations of political power grouped unfavourably would have caused Paḻaśśi Rājā to look around for new allies. This search for new allies was a traditional element in Indian government – it was also considered a feasible solution to the ongoing establishment of British colonial power at the end of the 18th century. In this instance, Kēraḷa Varmma Paḻaśśi Rājā found himself facing political opponents who disputed his authority within his little kingdom and intended to exploit his people economically. He seized every possible opportunity to prevent this from happening.

Let us now turn to the relationship of the little kings of Malabar to a great king, of which there are traces in several sources. According to them, Paḻaśśi Rājā and the other rulers in Malabar still referred to Cēramān Perumāḷ as the rightful occupant of the title of great king, i.e., as their superior ruler. Here I would like to reiterate the quotation at the beginning of the paper that vividly describes how "the descendants of Ram Rajah of Măleyālăm sit not in their palanqueens in the usual way, but are carried with their legs hanging down, for they look for the return of their king and by this attitude they denote attention to the affairs of his state." This is how they still show their respect for the great king, who is expected to return one day. They not only refresh their memories of him but also conduct politico-ritual acts in accordance with this idea or with imagination. They derive their legitimation from their participation in his rule. A great king could 'live on' as a 'virtual' great king, provided little kings relied on him as the basis of their legitimacy in their own territory. In Europe, Charlemagne was ascribed a function similar to that of the virtual great king of Malabar. Even after his death he was seen as the *pater Europae* and became an integrative force for the counts and dukes of Europe (Fleckstein 1991: 955-959; Becher 1999: 118).

The position of the last Cēramān Perumāḷ seems to have been very strong even in the memories of the little kings at the end of the 18th century. When the Tāmūtiri of Koḻikkōṭu tried to assume the position of great king after the discontinuation of the Cēramān Perumāḷ dynasty, he was not accepted by the little kings as such (Padmanabha Menon 1989 [1924] (Vol. 1): 263). Moreover, his struggles against the Rājā of Kocci for status as great king of Northern Kerala were not crowned with success. These instances illustrate that not only was it difficult for a little king to leave the circle of little kings by creating differences or waging war against others, but that the question of legitimising an envisaged overlordship also played a vital role. My hypothesis suggests that the new impending great kings were not able to install a lengthy tradition that would rival the long-lasting memory and legitimising powers of the last ruler of the Cēramān Perumāḷ dynasty, as embodied in the politico-ritual acts he carried out. Like Paḻaśśi Rājā, the other little kings and queens still linked their rulership to the great king Cēramān Perumāḷ. Taking into account the elements constituting the Malabar concept of rule hitherto presented, Paḻaśśi Rājā was positioned at the meso-level – between the 'virtual' great king, at the highest level and the *nāṭuvāḻis* or *dēśavāḻis* levels directly below him, as I have shown elsewhere (Frenz 2003: 150).

Why then did the little kings not accept one of the foreign powers, such as Maisūr or the East India Company, as a new great king? The invasions by Ṭippu Sulttān in the course of the 18th century, which were accompanied by forced conversions to Islam and high taxes, along with the British attempt at conquest – with its European conception of bureaucracy and high taxes – contradicted the local conception of the state and the traditional methods that regulated how power was shared amongst the little kings. Furthermore, neither Ṭippu Sulttān nor the British were able to produce any form of sacral legitimation for their claim to power, since they were not integrated into the ritual system in Malabar. The little kings in Malabar considered the merchants and employees of the EIC to be ritually inferior, something which they themselves would scarcely have realised (Deyell / Frykenberg 1982: 21). This explains why Paḻaśśi Rājā was unable to accept either of the powers as a superior authority in spite of the initially temporary and later conclusive military supremacy of the British. Since Paḻaśśi Rājā considered his role to be that of little king in relation to the 'virtual' great king of Malabar, as did other little kings,[10] he recognised neither Ṭippu Sulttān nor the British as supreme rulers or as the new great king.

Had Paḻaśśi Rājā acknowledged the British as the great king, he would have been forced to leave his traditional circle of rulers, who were positioned below the virtual great king. As an integral part of the British system, Paḻaśśi Rājā would have had no choice of being anything but a British subject, since the British system did not provide for power-sharing, and neither would the British have been interested in including participatory rule in their concept. His basis of legitimation would thus have been removed by outside forces. Consequently, in order to maintain legitimation of his rulership, he preferred in this matter to refer to a virtual great king.

Summing up, we can observe the renaissance of an older tradition of rulership – despite the arrival of the British and their policy of conquest. This revival of a concept of rule associated with a great king in the paradigm of the little kingdom is admirably illustrated in the picture described in the text above: little kings with their legs hanging out of the palanquins, thereby blazoning their reference to a great king and their expectation of his return.

Conclusion

With these remarks on the concept of rule, I have underlined my hypothesis that the little kings of Malabar solved the problem of social structure and Hindu kingship by referring to Cēramān Perumāḷ, the last great king, whom they either invented or used as a convenient tool to legitimate their rule as equals. Even during the 18th century, they symbolically legitimised their rule by referring to their relationship with Cēramān Perumāḷ as the *mahārāja* or great king of Malabar. These virtual relations, although rarely detailed explicitly in the sources, seem to have had stronger bonds for many of the little kings of Malabar than powers that genuinely existed, such as the Maisūr army or the East India Company. With the renaissance of the older tradition of rulership set in the paradigm of the little kingdom, little kings also established a form of opposition to the administrative attempts of the British to control the country with bureaucratic measures.

Notes

1 Mackenzie Local Tracts Malabar in Tamil [MLTMT] Ms. 77, No. 9 (Mahalingam 1972: 298): "On returning home in the year 966 (M.E.[Koḷḷaṃ or Malayāḷaṃ Era, beginning in the year 825 A.D.]) after the invasion by Tippu Sultan, they found that all their records were destroyed."

2 Sanskrit: *samūdrī*, Malayalam: *tāmūtiri*.

3 "As descent and succession within the kin-group was organized on matrilineal principles, it was important for these taravads to trace their lineage from an ancestress." (Arunima 1998: 117).

4 Research trip to London, Tamil Nadu and Kerala 1998.

5 Summary of events from 1796-1798 in Kōṭṭāyaṃ (miscellaneous), in OIOC H/607.

6 Claus (1978: 18) argues against Hocart that the socio-religious complex of Southern India is not derived from Aryan sacrificial rituals, but is the result of an unmistakably Southern Indian development. Anthropologists may be more reminded of Polynesian complex chiefdoms and kingdoms such as Tahiti and Hawai'i.

7 In the light of historiographical critique, it should possibly be interpreted the other way round – the legend was probably tied to the date and not the date to the legend. Śaka saṃvat, which was customary elsewhere in India, was not employed in Kerala. Contrary to the type of calendar generally linked to the establishment of a temple, the Koḻḻaṃ era begins with the founding of the town of Koḻḻaṃ. (Cf. Sircar, 1965: 269f; Narayanan 1996: 34f) Koḻḻaṃ was founded after it was liberated from the rule of the Pāṇḍyas.

8 Roughly translated as „the glorious king of kings, highest devotee of Śiva, venerable lord".

9 It should be remarked that 18 and 36 are ideal numbers, strongly indicating that the text in which they are used refers to historical legend and not to historical fact (cf. Kulke 1987, 1998).

10 The Cēramān Perumāḷ dynasty is still recalled by the Malayalees even today, which serves to indicate that little kings had attached themselves firmly to the dynasty's intellectual world and patterns of conduct almost 900 years after it had ceased to exist.

"In an Octopussy's Garden": Of Cakravartins, little kings and a new model of the early state in South and Southeast Asia

Tilman Frasch

Our image of ancient Indian kingship, whether Hindu or Buddhist, has long been one of the absolutist ruler governing a more or less strongly centralised, highly hierarchical polity or state. It was shaped by two factors. On the one hand, historians were influenced by their own political environment, the strictly centralised political set-up of the British Raj with the Viceroy, Council and central government agencies at the top, provincial authorities at the middle level and, finally, the district magistrates and collectors that formed the basis of public administration. This set-up was taken over almost unaltered into the constitution of India, with either a political party or, during the Emergency proclaimed by Indira Gandhi, a single ruler exerting political power formerly held by the British Crown and its representatives. On the other hand, the sources from which our information on the early Indian state is derived clearly represent a corresponding top-to-bottom perspective. Even a superficial survey of the sources reveals a highly formulaic pattern of medieval (i.e., post-Gupta)[1] Indian inscriptions.[2] The king is usually exalted through the lineage of rulers into which he was born, as well as through a host of officials of various grades and responsibilities that surround him and obey his command. This courtly approach is juxtaposed to the self-sufficient peasant village which, though partly autonomous, is at most times completely subject to the state. It has to pay taxes, deliver corvee labour and can be transferred to other overlords including religious institutions (temples, vihāras, agrahāras etc.). Normative texts such as the Artha-śāstra lend additional support to this approach, which does not come as a surprise given the environment in which they were produced – the authors were mostly Brahmins or members of a scribal group known as the *kāyastha*s and *lipirekha*s, who had strong ties with the court.

For Buddhist rulers, the situation was not very different, as Buddhism contributed little to a kingship theory of its own. The most original Buddhist kingship theory is found in the Agañña-Sutta, which describes the gradual spread of crimes such as murder and robbery among the people. However, before total anarchy broke out in a society where people were originally born free and self-determined, it was agreed upon to elect someone from their midst (the Mahāsammata or "Great Elect") to restore and maintain law and order. In return, he was to receive a share of the produce. [3] The power of a Buddhist king is thus derived from men rather than from god, although it is still thought to be universal.[4] This finds expression in the concept of the *cakravartin* or "wheel-turning" monarch, a concept that may have become prominent in Buddhism due to the fact that it complements the career of a Buddha.[5] Apart from being a *cakravartin*, Buddhists also expect their king to be a *dhammarāja*, a person who is not only supposed to generally maintain law and order, but more specifically to support and protect Buddhist monks and institutions. The model to be followed in this respect, at least in the eyes of Theravada Buddhists, was the Mauryan king Ashoka (c. 268-231 B.C.). Although a historical figure, this king was idealised in early Sinhalese historical writings as the blueprint for Buddhist kingship.[6]

With kingship deified and exalted to the point of absolutism or even despotism, subjects had little scope to act against royal power. Evasion, occsionally accompanied by emigration, seems to have been the most effective method.[7] Buddhism developed an additional right that permitted regicide in the case of despotism, provided someone took over the throne and prevented the kingdom from falling into anarchy. According to a popular tale in Buddhist countries, this could even be the assassin himself if no one else was around.[8]

Re-assessing Feudalism

What then did the relations between the court and the village look like? The model that has gained widest publicity among historians is that of (Indian) feudalism. Given its complexity and significance for further discussion of the medieval state, it will be presented here in great detail. Introduced by Kosambi in the late 1950s[9], it was fully developed during the 1960s, especially in the work of Sharma, now regarded as a classic.[10] Both authors (to begin with the ideological elements of the model) and their epigones had strong Leftist inclinations. For them, feudalism was not simply a model of the medieval Indian state but a necessary historical stage on the road to communism, as outlined by Marx.[11] To justify this claim, they drew heavily on European medieval states where feudalism apparently existed.[12] This comparative analysis, however, was quickly abandoned, since the most fundamental element of European feudalism, manumission (or commendation), whereby a peasant entrusted himself to the overlord, who promised protection and support in return for a share of the product, was absent in early India. Instead, historians from the feudalist school developed the Indian feudalist model, which emphasised the handing out of villages to Brahmins as proof of the existence of feudal relations. It was shown how rulers allotted land as fiefs to Brahmins, sometimes called in from distant regions and expected to settle on the land. This system was intended as one of mutual benefit. The Brahmins received material support while serving as agents of the state, as outposts of royal power, frequently even bringing peripheral or uncolonised areas into the realm of the ruler. [13]

Other participants in this type of feudal state were the court officials, who held various posts in the administration. Their services were usually rewarded with high-flown titles, which in some areas of India occupied a considerable part of the donative inscriptions. Again, the bestowal of titles and offices had a double implication. They reassured holders of their status, while the full set of office-bearers exalted the king and legitimised his claim to stand at the centre of a symbolic microcosm, surrounded by a host of subordinates. Recorded on a copper plate, this set-up could be propagated to the remotest areas of the dominion, at least when the messenger of the plate (*dūtaka*) read its contents aloud in front of the local population affected by this act. In comparison to grand fiefs, bestowing titles and offices on the kingdom's worthies was a relatively cheap way for the king to reward his followers. Fiefs, however, continued to remain important, as the officials could not live on immaterial wealth alone.

The internal feudal structure of the court could extend to the world outside the kingdom, too. In this case, subjugated neighbouring rulers (*sāmanta*s) were re-invested with their former possessions after taking an oath of loyalty.[14] Normally, this would imply their annual appearance at court as part of a grand ceremonial audience day. In a process that Kulke has aptly termed "samantaization", the overlords sought to increase control over the *sāmanta*s by retaining them permanently at court, while their territories were given as fiefs to members of the royal family or loyal courtiers.[15] This, however, bore the risk that fief holders would themselves become a threat to the overlord, should they begin to struggle for independence. Indian history reveals a number of cases where chiefs at the periphery established their own independent polities once central rule had weakened, sometimes even replacing it.

In theory, all fiefs were revocable when the reason for their origin ceased to be. They could be withdrawn if the holder grew disloyal or on the occasion of his death. Similarly, a new king could revoke all fiefs established by his father to make certain that the holders took their oath in his name. Moreover, the need to bring his own followers into office and power required the withdrawal of a number of fiefs, as they could not be increased ad infinitum. To sum up, the feudal system described here tended to create a stable state with relatively well-defined albeit mechanical relations between the ruler, his administrative apparatus and the country. The system looked different in practice, however, as all office holders made a more or less blatant attempt to gain permanent hold of their otherwise temporary, revocable possessions. This tendency was not only evident in peripheral regions, where sheer distance prevented overlords from maintaining permanent control, but also in core areas of the state where court officials endeavoured to make their fiefs hereditary (while ideally still enjoying their benefits, such as tax exemption) and thus carve out semi-independent principalities – little kingdoms. The situation in Bengal under king Ramapala is an excellent example of the precarious balance of power between the king and the various local power holders. To fight the Kaivarta uprising, the king had to reassure the loyalty of the *sāmantas* – who in fact acted like little kings in this situation – by delivering large presents to them (Bhattacharya 1989: 54-66). A king too weak to keep internal unrest in check or, worse still, to defend himself against occasional attacks from neighbouring rulers, was forced to fall back on his family possessions as the ultimate remaining economic resource.[17]

Feudalism as a processual model, therefore, constantly poses the danger of completely overturning the centralised structure of the state by transferring power along the lines of "feudal relations" to regional and local power holders and landed magnates. In fact, Sharma's seminal study on Indian feudalism ends in precisely this manner, pointing out the perils of the system. Although he does not elaborate on it further, it seems obvious that feudalism as a process (or feudalisation) ultimately tends to boost the dissolution of central rule rather than strengthen it.

The most radical criticism of the feudalism model came from Stein. He introduced it for the first time at a conference in 1973[18] and worked it into a book soon afterwards.[19] In contrast to the feudal state, which anticipates a strong, centralised power at its centre, the segmentary state (which is more or less confined to South India)[20] begins at the lowest level, the village and village-based, socio-economic units (*nāṭus*), the "nuclear areas of corporate institutions" and primary units of peasant organisation.[21] These *nāṭus* can combine horizontally should the need arise (e.g., for irrigation purposes)[22] or accept incorporation into vertical organisation.[23] While the state was constituted on a local or at best regional level, royal power was confined to its religious, ritual suzerainty. According to Stein, the imperial kingship of the Chola kings from the 9th to the 12th centuries was a product of their successful implementation of a belief system acceptable to the members of all *nāṭus*. Their royal power emanated from the central temple in the capital (e.g., the Rajarajesvara temple at Tanjavur) where the kings served as the foremost supporters and protectors. Contemporary inscriptions from South India reveal that the imperial temples built by the Cholas acquired religious and economic functions (Spencer 1969; Talbot 1991, 2001).[24] At the same time, certain leading men from the *nāṭus* continued to receive grants from the Chola kings, who tried to reinforce the vertical integration of their state with these local power holders. Though starting from the opposite end to the feudal model, Stein's ultimately arrives at a similar point, namely where supra-local or regional land owners and office holders become crucial to the constitution of the state.

It comes as no surprise that in developing a model for the early state of South Asia, under review here, the third significant group of historians concentrated on this group of supra-local or regional power holders. Though certainly less coherent than the "feudalists" (Stein can be omitted here, since his model has hardly been applied outside his own writings, although it did provide immense stimulation for scholarly discussions),[25] proponents of the "little kings" model share a common set of assumptions and methodological approaches. Methodologically, they tried to interpret their data with the help of anthropological theories, explaining social relations. Assuming the changes that took place over centuries to be negligible, they have begun to study current Indian society to learn about its past. Written texts such as inscriptions or non-epigraphical historical works (as far as they are available),[26] or any cultural artefact can thus become a potential source for the study of history. The seminal work for this "school" was certainly produced by Dirks, who investigated how the little kings of Putukottai state were transformed into a landowning, managerial elite in 18th century British India (Dirks 1987). It is shown that the status of little kings does not depend on economic conditions alone, but derives from a social and religious environment where power, authority and subordination are permanently re-negotiated and reaffirmed in daily ritual and social practice. Though Dirks' study focuses on a later period, he made it clear in a successive contribution that he regarded his model as relevant for the discussion on the pre-modern state in India.[28]

In a way, Tambiah's study of kingship in a Southeast Asian Buddhist context can also be considered as belonging to the work of the little kings' school. His "galactic polity" presupposes a set of equally strong and potential "little kings" (he does not use the term) struggling for superiority. The successful one becomes the centre of a new "galaxy"[29] and his kingship becomes exemplary for other contenders. The polity is held together as long as the centripetal forces of the central ruler, which derive in particular from his ability to comply with Buddhist notions of just rule and the preservation of law and order, are slightly stronger than the centrifugal forces of the rulers surrounding him. As soon as this balance of power shifts, the whole system collapses into its former state of equally potential principalities. Although Tambiah is silent on how the emergence of the stronger actually takes place (apart from some vague allusions), his model clearly regards little kings as the agents of state formation.

While the proponents of the various "schools" were eager to emphasise the difference between their respective models,[30] I would like to stress the similarities of the three models, which seem to go beyond the tacit acknowledgement of the importance of mid-level power holders (or little kings) as far as their common structure is concerned. All of them are oriented towards a centre (although this may be depicted as more ritual or symbolic than real) and relations between power holders on various levels tend to be linear, static and mechanical, irrespective of whether they describe exchanges of protection and tax between feudal lord and peasant or the powers in force between a planet and a satellite. As already mentioned above, this centripetal orientation is not solely a problem of modern-day historian perception, but a reflection of the medieval perception of the state as a representation of cosmic order, seen as well-organised and unchangeable; inscriptions were produced by the political and social elite of the state and more often than not took the top-to-bottom perspective that makes it difficult for the modern historian to adequately portray that part of the state and society that existed beyond the narrow confines of the court and the capital. The major weakness of the models, however, lies less in their centripetal structure than in their inability to capture the internal dynamics, the changes that took place within the structure itself. The processual models we have are more concerned with long-term developments that transformed the structure of the state.[31] Even Dirks' anthropological approach, which provides the best analytic tool for understanding short-term political developments, shows a strong tendency to produce yet another static structure centred round little kings, whose power remains more or less unchanged. On the basis of the inscriptions from the kingdom of Pagan (12th-13th century Burma), with which I am familiar most, I will develop a new model for the early state that accounts for both internal *dynamics* and the political space of the little kings.

As few scholars of Indian history are well-versed in the history of the Pagan kingdom, some basic features need to be described at the outset of this chapter.[32] Founded (i.e., enclosed by a wall) around the middle of the 9th century, Pagan is now a small town in the dry zone of Central Burma. Although its oldest epigraphic and architectural traces originate in the 10th century, the proper history of Pagan only began during the reign of King Anawrahta (c. 1044-1078 CE). Anawrahta left signed votive tablets at each of the important religious sites he visited, so that reports according to which he led campaigns to the far North and South of Burma, culminating in the conquest of several city states in Lower Burma, could be true. Although occupied with extensive travel, he began with the construction of large stupas in his capital, Pagan. As Anawrahta's son, Saw Lu, was not in a position to maintain his father's achievements, a usurper, known by his former military title of

Kyanzittha (c. 1081-1112/4 CE), took over the throne. Like his son and successor, Alaungsithu (c. 1112/4-1168 CE), he campaigned widely to pacify the country, continuing at the same time with the construction of religious monuments in the capital. Under Alaungsithu, the western coastal strip of Arakan came under the sway of Pagan for a short period, though in contrast to the principalities of Lower Burma, it seems to have maintained a high degree of independence throughout the Pagan period. This particular king has not only been credited with a vast itinerary (during which his "followers and army suffered much ado", as later chronicles put it), he is also said to have standardised weights and measures. Moreover, there are indications that he encouraged the colonisation of the area north of the river Irawadi, as suggested by a number of temples he built there. After a short period of anarchy, yet another usurper seems to have gained possession of the throne. A striking change took place under Narapatisithu, who reigned from 1174 to 1211 CE and evidently preferred to stay in the capital rather than travel the country like his predecessors.[33] Indeed, "village inspectors" (*rvā rhu*), who carried out royal functions such as deciding the outcome of law suits, are mentioned for the first time under his son and successor Jeyyasingha (aka Nadaungmya, 1211- c. 1230/2 CE). Narapatisithu concentrated on further transforming the capital into a sacred centre. He appears to have constructed more temples than any other Pagan king, including the Dhammayazika stupa, which stands out as the oldest dated pentagonal monument in the world (completed in 1198 CE). It was built in honour of the five Buddhas of the present world (*kalpa*) but may also have served to commemorate a purification of the Buddhist *sangha*, which the king had performed in the area where the stupa was built. In the course of this reform, Burmese monks underwent re-ordination at the hands of five monks who had been ordained anew in Sri Lanka.

In the years after 1200 CE, Pagan emerged as a major (if not the most important) centre of Theravada Buddhism. The contemporary capital of Sri Lanka, Polonnaruwa, had to be abandoned after a series of attacks, forcing the Sinhalese kings to shift their capitals and states from the dry zone in the North to the wet zone in the Southwest of the island. In India, Muslim troops advanced through the Ganges valley down to Bengal, destroying and plundering numerous monuments of the "infidels" including the Mahabodhi temple at Bodhgaya. The Burmese had developed a special relationship to Bodhgaya going back to the time of King Kyanzittha, who had sent an embassy there. Thereafter, pilgrimages from Pagan seem to have been quite frequent. When the Muslims conquered the site, king Jeyyasingha decided to "transport the holy land" (Griswold) by constructing an almost full scale replica of the Mahabodhi temple in Pagan around 1218 CE. Supposedly, this was not solely an attempt to safeguard the temple symbolically in an area inaccessible to potential religious adversaries, but a powerful demonstration by the king that his capital, Pagan, had become the centre of Theravada Buddhism.[34]

The reign of King Kyazwa (1235-1249 CE) saw imperial kingship at its peak. Temples were constructed in great numbers, with more and more members of the royal family, courtiers and even common people appearing as builders. The king himself is credited with only one smaller pyatthad (*prāsāda*). Instead, he seemingly engaged in writing religious treatises that later earned him the title of the "philosopher king". His familiarity with Buddhist scriptures is also manifested in the edicts on thieves, which he issued towards the end of his reign. The punishments that awaited thieves in hell according to these edicts were compiled from various Buddhist suttas.

The reign of King Narasihapati (1256-1284/7 CE) was in some aspects similar to that of Kyazwa. The chronicles describe a lavish life of luxury, while dedicatory inscriptions show that the construction of religious monuments remained initially at its high level. Lower Burma, where the rule of the Pagan kings had always been precarious, was incorporated fully, with princes serving as governors of significant towns (Pegu, Tala). Like his predecessors, Narasihapati went on pleasure trips to his palaces in the South. However, the Mongolian conquest of China and their advance towards the border of Upper Burma began to disrupt the prevailing tranquillity. The visibly weakened authority of the king in Pagan encouraged chiefs at the periphery to strive for independence. This was most apparent in Arakan, which had in fact not been genuinely dominated by Pagan, and in Lower Burma, where Wareru, the ruler of Martaban, seems to have been ultimately successful in establishing an independent principality.[35] Narasihapati, however, made his biggest mistake after thc Mongols had taken a stockade in the far North. Instead of marching against the enemy, he abandoned his capital city of Pagan and fled to a place further south, from where he sent an envoy to Kublai Khan's camp to negotiate a truce. This cowardice was such a severe violation of kingly duties that it not only sealed the fate of the king personally, who was assassinated by one of his sons and later acquired the nickname "Tayokpye Min" or "king who ran away from the Mongols,[36] but also the fate of Pagan's sacred kingship altogether. Although his successors continued to occupy the throne of Pagan until the middle of the14th century, Pagan kingship was no more than a shadow of its former splendour. Even in Central Burma, the heartland of the former kingdom, they had to share authority with numerous other chiefs and rulers, who struggled for supremacy over the core area of the former empire. Among them were three Shan brothers who continued to direct the affairs of the former capital even after they had moved into their new residential towns away from Pagan. Despite this political decline, however, Pagan continued to be a religious centre well into the 16th century, receiving great attention as a religious and historical centre once again in the 18th and 19th centuries under the last kings of Burma.[37]

Ideologically, kingship in Pagan closely followed the norms of a supreme being and holder of absolute power.[38] The king was considered as the highest of men and as residing in a sacred centre, he was held responsible for the securing and maintaining of cosmological principles of order. To this effect, he was given far-reaching powers as the ultimate judge (including the right to impose capital punishment) and access to the products of the kingdom. The latter was expressed in the epitome "lord of all land and water", which either meant a monopoly (as in the case of teak, gems or oil) or a share of the revenue. Though often described as absolutist or even despotic (especially by Western observers in the 18th and 19th centuries) and notwithstanding the grand vocabulary used for his exaltation, royal power was by no means unrestricted. As mentioned at the outset of this paper, the king as a person was not sacred and could be removed as long as anarchy was not the outcome. A king could be slain accidentally (as in the case of the cucumber king) or intentionally. In the latter case, members of the royal family were usually involved, e.g., the assassination of king Narasihapati by one of his sons or the plot against king Jeyyasingha that followed his accession in 1211.[39] The most ruthless person in this respect seems to have been Sihasu, the youngest of the Shan brothers, who came to the throne after deposing the last ruler in Pagan and perhaps even poisoning his elder brother.[40] Apart from members of the royal family or courtiers, we sometimes find commoners involved in rebellions against the king. Thus in 1275, "royal anger" descended on a certain *Rājapuiw* who had "sinned against the king", as it was phrased at the time. Capital punishment of the king was remitted when his aunt begged pardon on his behalf, but his possessions were confiscated.[41] Another uprising occurred in 1245 in the district capital of Prome (*Praññ*). In order to punish the rebel (who clearly bore a commoner's name), the headman of Prome was obliged to acquire an elephant at the expense of a considerable amount of land.[42] This example serves to illustrate how the king solved the dilemma described by Lingat. If the need arose, he was in favour of pardoning rather than killing the culprit. In doing so, he maintained his position as a *dhammarāja* and even increased his religious merit.

It has been said that kings were styled as "lords of all land and water" and theoretically had unlimited access to the material resources of the state, especially land and products, such as rice, wood, precious metals and gems. In practice, however, existing ownership rights restricted the amount of land the king could effectively claim in addition to fields that were already his own property (e.g., crown domains) or that had not been claimed by anyone else.[43] The land handed out as a fief was called *mahādān* in the Pagan kingdom.[44] A personal grant, a *mahādān* was given as a reward for services rendered to the king; it was revocable when the occasion ceded and could not be transferred to a third party by the grantee without the consent of the king. That the kings of Pagan were occasionally powerful enough to enforce this became patently obvious after the ascension of king Kyazwa in 1235 CE. The king, an inscription reads, "revoked every single fief (*mahādān*) in Upper and Lower Burma".[45] Unfortunately, we have no further records that might shed more light on the background of this act. It appears, however, that between the reigns of Kyazwa's father, Jeyyasingha, who died in an accident around 1230/31 CE, and Kyazwa, another king – presumably his elder brother[46] or a usurper or both – ruled for a short period. Whatever the case may have been, Kyazwa apparently found it necessary to discontinue completely with his predecessors and disempower their cronies in favour of his own supporters. Two years later, in 1237, he held an audience day in the course of which several courtiers received large amounts of *mahādān* lands.[47]

Though the large-scale revocation of fiefs was a single event, it is obvious from numerous inscriptions that the kings of Pagan in general retained their rights over *mahādān* fiefs. Fief holders, in turn, had to ask the king before they could transfer the land to a religious institution, though kings seem to have consented in general. Thus, when a donor stated in an inscription that his dedication included a *mahādān*, the king's consent was implied.[48] Members of the royal family such as queen *Mrakan-saññ*, who handed over to her grandchildren 50 *pay* of fields she had received as a *mahādān*, were no exception.[49] It appears that *mahādān* lands could even be sold, as the minister *Mahāsaman* endowed his monastery with the *mahādān* lands he had bought from various owners.[50]

A special type of fief was given to royal wives. This group included the queens (regularly but not necessarily numbering four), the lesser wives and the royal concubines, as well as their daughters, the princesses. All of them were eligible to become "holder of a town", usually indicated by a title consisting of the name of the town and the suffix *-saññ* (meaning "holder"). The most significant case is king Jeyyasingha's mother, *Mrakan-saññ*, (she had originally been a concubine but was later elevated to the rank of queen).[51] Other towns given out as fiefs were Mashet, Sigon and Singaing (all in the granary of the kingdom, the Kyaukse district), Halin and Kyabo near Myingyan.[52] The number of holders increased markedly during the second half of the Pagan period, rising from one under king Narapatisithu to at least five under king Narasihapati.

As far as can be discerned, all fief holders seem to have spent most of their time in the capital, administering their fiefs as "absentee landlords". Yet the feudal lord (or lady) did have personal ties to the fief, demonstrated, for example in the construction of a temple, usually in its central town. King Narapatisithu is said to have built a temple in each of the towns he had given to his queen Veluvati,[53] and Khin

Un, daughter of King Kyanzittha, built a temple at Natogyi. The latter received another donation from prince Pyamkhi in the course of his visit there almost a century later.[54] These temples had the dual function of representing the power of the fief holder from Pagan (who in turn had received it from the king, thus ultimately translating these temples into the superiority and omnipresence of the ruling king), and at the same time of bringing a small fraction of Pagan's splendour, sanctity and glory to the countryside. Moreover, and as the second example above indicates, courtiers and members of the royal family would sporadically visit their fiefs outside Pagan and perhaps attend the consecration of the temples. The personal ties between court and administrative centres, between the rulers and the ruled, were thus occasionally reinforced.

Through these links, provincial towns served as regional administrative centres for the surrounding villages, grouped into units such as *tuiṅ* and *khvaṅ*. They were the points at which taxes in both cash[55] and kind, ranging from rice and coconuts to cloth and baskets, were collected and partly stored,[56] and partly transmitted to the capital, Pagan. They also frequently served as venues for the legal administration of the kingdom, presumably when the king or other courtiers came to visit the place. In general, however, legal administration was a village affair and rarely went beyond this local level.

Finally, the provincial towns had a military function, housing a small detachment of soldiers and sometimes had fortifications (*mruiv*). An inscription from the mid-14th century indicates what a garrison might have looked like during the Pagan period: "1 young elephant, 30 strong shields, 15 bows, 5 guns (*mi-pok*), 1000 [unit not specified] of rice, 50 cows, 100 goats". In addition, 31 people, including one mason, were assigned to live there.[57] Ngahsaungkyan near Bhamo in the far North was arguably the most important stockade during the Pagan period. Its conquest in the early 1280s gave the Mongols free access to Northern Burma. In the East, a string of stockades defended Central Burma, particularly the Kyaukse district, against possible invaders from the Shan Plateau. According to the chronicles, these stockades were established by king Anawrahta.[58] The only one mentioned in the inscriptions is at Hseittaung.[59] Other stockades guarded strategic positions such as the town of Myinmu, situated at the confluence of the Mu and Irawadi rivers.[60] Since it also guarded the spot where the great overland route from China to Upper Burma crossed the Mu river, the town was home to a customs officer (*kaṅ-sū-krī*).

References to headmen in these towns and villages are too scant to allow conclusive statements. It appears, however, that their office was hereditary to a large extent and that they were usually recruited from the local population. The customs officer from Myinmu, for example, bore a commoner's name, indicating that he had been recruited locally and not sent to Myinmu from Pagan. A similar case may have been the headman of Prome.[61] It seems that only in the latter half of the 13th century were members of the royal family from Pagan installed as governors of towns (*mruiw-sū-krī*) outside Pagan, where they then resided. At least this is the picture we get from the chronicles.[62] The custom may have served to distinguish provincial towns from villages, where headmanship remained hereditary throughout the Pagan period (and perhaps throughout Burmese history before the advent of the British). Thus, the father of the *Sapok* village headman had also been the village headman before him,[63] and in other instances the sons of headmen ranked among the leading men of the village.[64] In general, villages were administered by a headman and his council, although it seems that relevant decisions such as land transactions had to be agreed upon by all free men from the village. Many of these names were listed in the inscription.[65] The sale of village land was concluded regularly with a feast, in which all villagers participated, consuming considerable amounts of meat and alcohol.[66] The common meal seems to have been a key element in the transaction, as villagers in one case remonstrated against the sale, complaining that they had not partaken of the meal.[67] The distribution of the money was organised by the headman and other leading village figures.[68] If village land was indeed administered jointly, it does not seem too far-fetched to assume that taxation was also a village affair rather than the concern of individual peasants.

The village headman was clearly the most distinguished person in the village. He presided over village council meetings, acted as a judge in disputes and represented the village on higher state levels, especially when dealing with the court. His judicial functions are alluded to in an inscription from the year 1197 CE, which records three attempts to solve a dispute within the village. Only when the headman and the council had failed to find a solution acceptable to all parties, were courtiers from Pagan called in to decide the case and supervise the erection of boundary pillars.[69] The representative function of the headmen is illustrated by an inscription from the year 1246, when no less than eleven headmen from towns in the Kyaukse district (including Pinlay, Tamut and Myingondaing) were present at Pagan to join a dedication of the future king Uccana (1249-1256 CE) in favour of Mahakassapa, one of the leading monks of the day.[70] It is not clear whether they had gone to the capital "on duty" or on a pilgrimage, although – as Stein reminds us – both purposes could converge.

As in many instances in the later history of Burma, royal power depended to a large extent on the king's ability to secure the loyalty if not support of the village headmen.[71] Yet, although politically significant, these town and village headmen were not the only group of intermediate power holders whose advocacy was crucial to the survival of kingship. Another group figuring prominently in the Pagan inscriptions is the *sū-krway* or "men of wealth", who could include landed magnates and rich merchants. They were possibly both at the same time, receiving their income from land revenue and trade alike, and we can also assume that some of them combined their economic strength with political power, acting as village headmen or even taking up an office at the court. Information regarding land owners is astonishingly scarce, given the role land ownership played in an agrarian society. One of the prominent families was very likely the "lords of Nyaungyan". There is a "grandee of Nyaungyan" (*ÑÑoṅ-raṁ-krī*) and his younger brother (*ÑÑoṅ-raṁ-ṅay*). They came from Nyaungyan, a small town in Central Burma, south of the Kyaukse district, which is famous for its old tank that presumably predated the Pagan period. It is quite possible that their wealth derived from well-irrigated fields in the vicinity of the tank. The family entered history in 1248 CE when the daughter of the grandee made over her possessions to three Pagan monasteries, a dedication in memory of her deceased husband, prince Gaṅgasu, the son of king Narapatisithu.[72] Similar to the lord of Nyaungyan, there was a "grandee of Sagu" (*Caku-krī*), one of the administrative centres south of Pagan that governed the rice fields of Minbu district. He made a donation to a monastery in 1167 CE, and his descendants were still living in the area a century later.[73]

Marriage alliances with local headman or magnates, such as the one between prince Gaṅgasu and the lord of Nyaungyan's daughter or the elevation of the sister of a "man of wealth" to the rank of a lesser queen by king Uccana[74], was a typical royal strategy to unite the economic forces of the kingdom for their mutual benefit. The king gained an economically strong ally beyond the narrow confines of the capital and his son (and perhaps his daughter, although there is no decisive evidence for this) was able to participate in the wealth. Gaṅgasu, one of the younger sons of Narapatisithu, who had little chance of ascending the throne, was thus apportioned an appropriate livelihood. The magnates, in turn, enjoyed royal protection, if only for the length of one particular reign. They occasionally received a boost to their status by being admitted to live at the Pagan court, and were further acknowledged by times when the king bestowed them with titles. Beyond the sphere of social prestige, the stay at Pagan gave them an opportunity to acquire religious merit in this merit-making field (*puññakhetta*) through donations and constructions.

The *sū-krways* are perhaps the most neglected group of people in the historiography of Pagan, despite their frequent emergence as witnesses and donors. The term *sū-krway* simply means "rich person", though the usage of the day carried a good deal of contemporary admiration. Their high status is attested in numerous inscriptions where they appear foremost as lay witnesses, next in line to village headmen but ahead of other functionaries from the village.[75] This indicates that *sū-krways* were originally rich landowners who then engaged in other businesses such as trade and perhaps money-lending. It is certainly no accident that the second highest number (next to Pagan) of *sū-krways* is found in or around the town of Pakhangyi, the trading centre at the crossroads of the overland route that connected Southwestern China, Upper Burma, East India and Lower Burma.[76] Either traders or rich landowners, the *sū-krways* constituted a strategic group for the kings, who endowed them with protection and social prestige. The highest recognition they could expect was to be raised to the status of a *seṭṭhi* or even *jayaseṭṭhi*.[77] Both these honorary Pali titles were conferred on them by the king. The brother of king Uccana's lesser wife, referred to above, is one such example; other *seṭṭhis* who became members of the (extended) royal family had married either a daughter or a granddaughter of king Narapatisithu[78] or a daughter of king Narasihapati.[79] That *seṭṭhi* was a honorific title can be seen from an inscription that reports how King Kyawzaw made the *sū-krway Ṅā Phun Saṅ* a *jayaseṭṭhi*.[80] Although it is always dangerous to draw a conclusion from a single instance, it seems likely that the bestowing of Pali titles on the rich was a royal reward not unlike the examples of courtiers and officials who were given titles such as Asaṅkhaya, Anantasūra or Mahāsamanta. The official awarding of titles was definitely cheaper than handing out a *mahādān*, although this was also granted to *sū-krways*.[81]

In an Octopussy's Garden

If we now try to link the empirical data from the Pagan inscriptions to the existing models of the early Indian state, the results are quite ambiguous. The ideology of kingship created a strong centre that could theoretically monopolise and in effect mobilise a large share of the economic resources of the state. The king was the pivot of society and therefore responsible that cosmic order be reduplicated in the human sphere. The city of Pagan, with all its elements of a sacred centre, further emphasised the centralised, hierarchical structure of state and society. With regard to the handing out of land grants and titles to the bureaucratic staff, Pagan was a typical feudal kingdom, almost representing the ideal type considering the successful revocation of all *mahādān* fiefs in Upper and Lower Burma by king Kyazwa. This latter example shows that a feudalist structure had the potential to preserve and strengthen a central ruler rather than lead to his weakening and the dissolution of the state.

At the same time, a considerable amount of political power remained in the hands of local and regional headmen. Village headmen normally held a hereditary office and despite their responsibility to the royal court enjoyed a high degree of autonomy. The district and town headmen, whose power was spatially more extensive, were placed at the next highest level. Judging by their names, many of them had been recruited from the local ranks and not been sent in from the court. Along with the landed magnates and rich traders, these headmen were "little kings" within the state, who could effectively challenge and eventually replace a central ruler. Depending on the perspective, the state could therefore be considered either as galactic or as a patchwork of little kingdoms. Only the segmentary model appears to be inappropriate (even though certain socio-economic units such as the *kharuiṅs* from the Kyaukse district or the *tuiṅs* along the Irawadi can be discerned), as the uniformity of religion hardly allows for power struggles along religious lines and the power of the kings in Pagan was clearly political and less religious.

Neither model, therefore, seems capable of supplying a framework for the situation in Pagan, nor did, as we have seen, attempts to conflate or integrate them enhance our understanding. In fact, all of the models share a similar deficit of depicting internal power relations as well-defined, centre-oriented (though flowing in both directions) and linear, making the structure of the state appear static, if not unalterable. They are thus unable to represent relations of power in a permanent state of change within a certain structure, which were re-arranged by military power or re-negotiated in rituals and ceremonies. Any attempt to replace the feudal, segmentary or galactic state models would of necessity have to be rewarded by one that captures these internal dynamics and accounts for the political and social spaces occupied by agents other than the ruling elite.

As a first step towards a new model, a distinction will have to be made between the intensity of power and its extension. Limits to the extent of power may be either natural (sea coast, unsurmountable mountains) or political (neighbouring state); in either case, it defines the maximum outline of the state that could be or has been reached by a central ruler. This idea was also current in 12th and 13th century Burma, where kings mentioned the sea coast in the South and West, the Salween in the East and the mountain ranges of Tibet and Yunnan in the North as the boundaries of their kingdom.[82] The areas within this outline were regarded as being under the dominion of the Pagan rulers. With reference to intensity, the degree of power a Pagan king could exert did not follow a linear pattern, nor did it decrease with distance from the capital or the court. Royal power might have been extremely intensive in peripheral districts if the latter fell into the category of crown domains or were administered by a loyal supporter of the king. In contrast to this, areas in the heartland of the kingdom might have experienced low-intensity rule, e.g., if their economic significance was negligible or they belonged to a little king who managed to keep royal influence in check. However, the intensity of power was always a temporary matter. It could decline or even vanish completely as the result of a rebellion, but could also increase in the course of a visit by the king, a member of his family or one of the courtiers, an event that would have strengthened the ties between the locality and the court. The imperial circuit soon after accession is a well-known example of how new kings tried to widen their power bases and gain general acknowledgment. The instalment of new headmen loyal to the ruler was frequently the result of such an occasion. Rule became extremely intense in times of war, affecting in the first instance the corridor through which the army passed and which had to sustain the soldiers. Beyond that, society was affected as a whole, since villages and districts were forced to contribute batches of soldiers, at the risk of severe punishment in the case of refusal to do so. In short, the distinction between intensity and extension of power is fundamental to understanding that the power structure of an early state was never static, but that royal claims and traditional rights, superiority and autonomy had to be rearranged and renegotiated in a permanent process.

As a second step, we should define the requirements a new state model has to fulfil. It must acknowledge a certain degree of centrality, the existence of a king, a court and perhaps a kind of capital,[83] while allowing at the same time for autonomous spaces of little kings of all shades. It must define the limits of the state without claiming boundaries in the modern sense. Finally, it must reflect the flexibility of power relations beyond the categories of strong/weak rulers. A model that seems to meet all these requirements is that of the Octopus. Its somewhat oversized head represents the court, headed by the king, the royal family and all the ministers and courtiers around him. Regardless of whether the long lists of administrative staff found in inscriptions paint a true picture of the court structure or were purely composed to herald the magnificence of the ruler, they constantly give the impression of an oversized court/capital in relation to the rest of the state. The head also has eyes, enabling the ruler to perceive what is going on in his state. The early kings of Pagan, as mentioned in the introduction, were itinerant and could gather information personally. The turning point came around 1200, under king Narapatisithu and king Jeyyasingha, who preferred to stay in the capital and rely on village inspectors and other informants. At a more symbolic level, the omniscience attributed to Buddha could be linked to the kings as well, since they were perceived as future Buddhas, (*bodhisattva*). Unlike Angkor, where Jayavarman VII had it prominently displayed on the multi-faced towers that dominate the Bayon of Angkor, the kings of Pagan would at best pray for "omniscience which is to see all and to know everything", as contemporary translation puts it.Finally, the head has a mouth, symbolising the king's claim to the economic resources of the state and his capacity to consume (or redistribute) them in toto.

The claim for dominion over the eight directions of the compass is manifested by the eight tentacles. Their tips mark the outer boundary of the kingdom, the sphere of royal influence. The suckers of the tentacles mark the areas of intense rule: the crown domains, district and garrison towns or villages of loyal headmen, all of which provide a firm support for the body of the Octopus. The tentacles can provide chains of command and represent the channels along which revenues and taxes flow. By moving the tentacles, it can change its grip to power and take different places under intense rule. Allowing the Octopus to move into a new position altogether takes into account states that have no clear capital or core area (such as the Pala kingdom in Bengal), a voluntary or forced shift of the capital (e.g., the transfer of the capital from Anuradhapura to Polonnaruwa in 11th-12th century Sri Lanka) or simply a king's tour through his dominions and finally, of course, a military campaign. If the Octopus moves into a new position, it can also extend the outer limits of intervention, which means that it can widen its economic base through plunder, at least over a certain period.[84]

Yet, regardless of the position of the Octopus or the arrangement of its tentacles, there are always areas – which can at times be quite vast– not covered by intense rule. As mentioned earlier, these could begin immediately beyond the walls of the capital (a constellation that could reappear in every district capital under intense rule, while the surrounding villages remain largely autonomous), but also comprise the estates of landed magnates and petty rulers and are, in short, the realms of the little kings. Situated within the reach of the tentacles, they could remain unaffected by royal power over long periods. Ultimately, they represent the new power centres when central power perishes. This can again be seen clearly in Burma, where a number of local rulers emerged after the decline of Pagan at the end of the 13th century bearing the title of *maṅ* (previously reserved for members of the royal family) and continued to struggle for supremacy even after Ava had been founded in 1364 CE. It was only in the late 15th century that the headmen of Taungoo succeeded in creating a new Octopus's garden by conquering neighbouring rulers including those of Lower Burma.

Summary

It was not the intention of this paper to give a complete overview of the discussions addressing the nature of the state in early India. Instead, a variety of models fundamental to shaping our picture of it have been presented. They share a common set of shortcomings, primarily their perception of the state as a statical machine-like construct, the structure of which can be transformed but does not account for its internal dynamics. To overcome these shortcomings, an attempt has been made here to perceive the state as a living body in the form of an Octopus. Its oversized head symbolises the court with its pompous ceremonies, its inflated body of courtiers and the potential to gather intelligence or consume the product of the state. Its tentacles mark the extension of the state, its outer limits of concrete political control. The centrality of the state, usually marked by the capital, is lifted to a certain extent, as the Octopus is able to move (accounting for royal tours within the state and warfare), thereby largely blurring the limits of the state, unless they are fixed by natural boundaries. The possible extension of political power is kept separate from its actual intensity. The power of kingship is felt only in places under the immediate control of the suckers, while the intensity remains low in all areas between the tentacles. Thus, the "Octopus's garden" contains space for other state "bodies" to exist autonomously provided, of course, they acknowledge the dominance of the Octopus whose tentacles surround them.

Notes

1 The question of whether the term "medieval" can be used in the context of Indian history is still a matter for considerable discussion among scholars. According to traditional periodisation, Indian history can be divided into three phases : "antiquity" (up to the end of the Gupta dynasty), "middle age" (again divided into "early middle age" up to c. 1200 AD and "late middle age" up to the end of the Mughal empire), and finally the "modern period" that begins with the advent of the British. Disregarding all socio-religious connotations of the three periods (Hindu antiquity, Muslim middle age, Western modernity), recent approaches to highlight an "indigenous modernity" (see Sanjay Subrahmanyam, Penumbral Visions, Oxford 2001), and finally claims that only a rediscovery ("renaissance") of an underlying antique culture can create a "middle age", I use the term here without inherent value to describe the centuries following the Gupta period.

2 Striking examples of this can be seen in the inscriptions of the Pala kings of Bengal (Mukherji/Maity 1967) or the Maitraka kings of Gujarat (Njammasch 1997: 111-124). For a discussion on this, see Kulke (1997) and Njammasch (1997).

3 Dīgha Nikāya III. 27 (1911: 80-98).

4 Ibid.

5 According to the Sihanada-Sutta (Dīgha Nikāya (1890) I.3), the future Buddha Gautama decided to become a Buddha rather than a worldly ruler while preparing for his final existence as a human being in Tavatimsa heaven. During the night of his Enlightenment, he defended this decision against Mara, who made an attempt to draw him back to a worldly way of life.

6 Lingat (1989); Lingat also draws attention to the ambivalent situation of the king, whose actions could be both beneficial and detrimental, since they included the possibility of taking life.

7 André Wink (1984, 1986) discusses this phenomenon under the term of *fitna.*

8 The story of the "cucumber king" involves a peasant who accidentally slew the ruler when he broke into his garden to steal cucumbers. The courtiers forced the peasant, whose deed had been discovered, to stand as king. It seems to be a specifically Southeast Asian theory in defence of regicide, since most versions come from Burma, Cambodia and Indonesia.

9 Kosambi 1956.

10 Sharma 1980.

11 At the risk of saying the obvious, it should be noted here that Marx himself denied India the

potential to enter this phase of historical materialism without help from outside. Instead, he developed a concept he described as the Asiatic Mode of Production, according to which India had remained stagnant throughout its history.

12 Sharma made use of several works dealing with Europe, e.g., François Ganshof's *Feudalism* (Ganshof 1961), a translation of his "*Qu'est-que-ce la féodalité?*".

13 It has been noted that the use of religious experts to expand or maintain royal power bore some resemblance to the "Reichskirchensystem" of the Ottonian and Salian emperors of 10th and 11th century Europe (Bhattacharya 1989).

14 A well-known example of this method is recorded in the Allahabad pillar inscription of Samudra Gupta (Fleet 1888; Chhabra/Gai 1981). Having conquered twelve rulers of South and Southwest India, the king claimed he had re-installed them in their former positions. Similarly, the inscription of Rudradaman at Sudarsana lake in Gujarat praises the king as the "restorer of deposed kings" (*bhrsṭa-rāja-pratisṭhāpaka*; Diskalkar 1977: 1-16).

15 For the term, see Kulke/Rothermund (1982: 144). For the role of the *sāmanta* in general, see Gopal (1963).

16 Cp. Swapna Bhattacharya, Landschenkungen, p. 54-66.

17 The role played by family possessions and crown domains in the formation of the state has rarely been researched up to now. Most historians (not only those from the "feudalism camp") stuck to the traditional claim that the king as "lord of all land and water" had the economic resources of the state completely at his disposal. This assumption ignores existing property rights, which limited the king's access to the tracts not claimed or tilled by any one else (as the "rule of the fallen land", *bhūmicchidranyāya*, holds).

18 Stein 1977, p. 3-51.

19 Stein 1980.

20 In a way, this reflects the different nature of the sources Stein used for his research. South Indian inscriptions contain much more information regarding the situation in the village than epigraphs from any other area in India. For Pallava inscriptions that contain frequent references to village committees (*erivāriya perumakkal, sabhaiyar*) responsible for the maintenance of irrigation works, see Mahalingam (1988), inscr. no. 102, p. 342, or inscr. no. 223, p. 573.

21 Stein 1980, p. 167.

22 It is astonishing in this connection that despite emphasising peasant domination and its far-reaching powers to associate, Stein hardly mentions irrigation, the primary cause for cooperation.

23 Stein 1980, p. 207.

24 This has been highlighted by many scholars, see e.g. Spencer 1969, p. 42-56; Talbot 1991, p. 308-340; idem 2001.

25 Among the few works are Hall (1980) and Biller (1986). Outside India, it was applied to the Thai state by Chutintaranond (1990).

26 This somewhat clumsy expression tries to summarise diverse "historical texts", from historical *mahākāvyas* (e.g., the Rājataraṅgiṇī) and family records (*vaṁśāvalis*) to hero stones and songs, all of which are ways of memorising the past in South Asia. It would be wrong to interpret the distinction between inscriptions and these texts as "Tradition" or "Überrest", a concept that was basically developed to examine medieval European history sources but does not fit the South Asian context satisfactorily.

27 Nicholas Dirks, The Hollow Crown. Ethnohistory of an Indian Kingdom, Cambridge 1987.

28 See e.g Dirks 1976, p. 125-157.

29 The term is obviously a synonym for "cosmic mandala", since in strict astrophysic terms "galactic polity" would be a misnomer and should in fact be called a "solar system". Galaxies, it may be recalled, have a black hole at the centre.

30 Stein's book in particular received a rather cold reception in journals on Indian history. For more moderate criticisms, see e.g., Sharma (1993) and, specifically dealing with South India,

Veluthat (1993). An enlightening overview of the debate is supplied by Kulke in the introduction to his *The State in India, 1000-1700* (Kulke 1995a).

31 Most notably Kulke (1995b) and Chattopadhyaya (1995 [1994, 1983], 1997).

32 Most of what is said here can be found in greater detail in the corresponding chapters of my thesis (Frasch 1996).

33 This can be inferred from an inscription from the year 1194 CE that relates of a campaign in Lower Burma without participation of the king: She-haung Myanma Kyauksa-mya [Old Burmese Inscriptions, hereafter OBI], vol. 1, Rangoon 1972, p. 360 = no. 146 of Duroiselle (1921).

34 Frasch 2000, p. 27-37.

35 According to later Mon historiography, Wareru was just one of several Mon rulers struggling for supremacy over Lower Burma (Schmidt 1906). In contrast, late Pagan inscriptions claim that Lower Burma had been reconquered by the rulers from Upper Burma: Inscriptions of Burma, vol. I (Luce/Maung Tin 1933), plate 276a [hereafter Pl.] = OBI 3, p. 158, l. 1-3, or Pl. III 292 = OBI 3, p. 196, l. 18.

36 The nickname is almost contemporary, appearing for the first time in an inscription from 1312 CE: Pl. IV 416b = OBI 3, p. 298, l. 10. I might add here that Michael Aung-Thwin's recent attempt to re-write late Pagan history contradicts epigraphical evidence and lacks credibility (Aung-Thwin 1998).

37 For a short history of Pagan after the imperial period, see Frasch (2002a).

38 Cf. Aung-Thwin 1983, p. 45-85.

39 The details of this affair are far from clear, as the information comes mainly from a report by minister Asaṅkhaya, who was given a reward for bravery (or loyalty) a year after Jeyyasingha's accession. The land had been taken from Singhapicaññ, a half-brother of the king, as punishment for his disobedience. It seems that Pyam-khi, another half-brother of the king, was involved as well. For a more detailed account, see Frasch (1998).

40 Kyawzwa was dethroned in 1298 CE and subsequently became known as "the king thrown from the throne" (*nan-kla-maṅ*): Pl. III 286 = OBI 3, p. 185. The assassination of his brother is recorded in the chronicles (U Kala 1960: 316).

41 Pl. III 249 = OBI 3, p. 103, l. 28-9.

42 Pl. II 143a = OBI 2, p. 32, l. 13-5. The price of the elephant was 50 *pay* (land unit), which is half the amount awarded for an elephant in other instances. It is thus very likely that the headman of Prome confiscated rather than bought the animal.

43 Several law suits concerning the land ownership in the Pagan period suggest that the "rule of the unused land" (*bhūmicchidranyāya*), a term that frequently occurred in contemporary Indian inscriptions, prevailed in Pagan as well, cf. Frasch (1996: 231-243).

44 It should be noted that the term *mahādān* in Pagan never had the same connotation of describing a religious donation that it had in contemporary India.

45 Pl. I 90 = OBI 1, p. 267, l. 15-6.

46 The elder brother appears in Pl. I 67 = OBI 1, p. 22, l. 1.

47 Pl. I 102 = OBI 2, p. 159. It may be significant in this context that in the course of 1236 and 1237 a very high number (perhaps the highest of any two-year period during the Pagan kingdom) of religious institutions were established. One gets the impression that former members of the court preferred to invest in religious buildings (and therefore in merit making) than risk being stripped of their possessions by the new king.

48 In Pl. I 90, an elderly minister donated his *mahādān* in two lots to the Jeyyaswat temple; in Pl. III 231b, the victorious general of the battle at Tagaung was allowed to transfer the fief he had received as a reward to his monastery.

49 Pl. II 153 = OBI 2, p. 66, l. 11.

50 Pl. I 102 = OBI 2, p. 159.

51 Pl. II 153a = OBI 2, p. 66, l. 10.

52 Pl. II 150-151 = OBI 2, p. 61, l. 8 (Mashet); Pl. I 74 = OBI 1, p. 156, l. 9 (Sigon); Pl. III 228b

= OBI 3, p. 65 l. 16 (Singaing); Pl. II 162 = OBI 2, p. 93, l. 13 (Halin); Pl. III 272 OBI 3, p. 147, l. 25 (Kyabo). The problem with the interpretation of the suffix *-saññ* as "holder of ..." is its use as an indication of a place of origin. and, to make matters even more complicated, it was also used to denote an office at the court.

53 Glass Palace Chronicle 1923, p. 149.

54 Pl. IV 373c+d = OBI 1, p. 214 and p. 148.

55 Pl. IV 392 = OBI 4, p. 185 (SIP no. 51, p. 145), l. 6, has "pond tax" (*aṅ-khvaṅ*) of 10 vizz copper, and Pl. III 244 = OBI 3, p. 92, l. 23-5, refers to "land from which 2 harvests are possible and which [therefore] can be taxed at 10 [kyat silver ?]".

56 Pl. I 63 = OBI 1, p. 128, l. 12, records a royal granary at Minbu, Pl. II 162 = OBI 2, p. 93, refers to a granary somewhere in the Kyaukse district.

57 Pl. V 589 = OBI 5, p. 214, l. 26-29 (1345 CE). In Modern Burmese, *mi-pok* denotes a "gun" or "cannon", though it seems impossible that the Burmese werre in possession of fire weaponry at such an early stage.

58 Glass Palace Chronicle, p. 95.

59 Pl. II 140b = OBI 2, p31, l. 19.

60 OBI 1, p. 365 and OBI 3, p. 230, l. 27.

61 Pl. II 143a = OBI 2, p. 32, l. 13-5.

62 According to the Glass Palace Chronicle, two sons of king Narasihapati served as governors of Prome and Tala respectively (Glass Palace Chronicle 1923: 178-179).

63 Pl. II 193 = OBI 2, p. 196, l. 22.

64 Pl. I 55a = OBI 1, p. 183, l. 3; Pl. II 115 = OBI 1, p. 46, l. 14.

65 Pl. III 319a = OBI 2, p. 230, l. 10-12 (22 names altogether).

66 Pl. IV 395 = OBI 3, p. 206, l. 16-8.

67 Pl. V 583 = OBI 3, p. 279, l. 21-25.

68 Pl. I 55a = OBI 1, p. 183. The inscription is difficult to understand but it seems that two villagers had insisted on their former rights and received 60 kyat silver in compensation.

69 Pl. II 117a = OBI 1, p. 64. Several passages of the OBI reading need to be improved to make the inscription intelligible, e.g., in l. 9 the verb *thwak* ("to say") should read *phlat* ("to decide").

70 Pl. II 162 = OBI 2, p. 93, l. 24-29. Interestingly, they are referred to as *rvā-sū-krī* or "village headmen", although their home towns were obviously not villages.

71 According to the chronicles, one of king Kyanzittha's concubines was the daughter of the Htilaing headman (Glass Palace Chronicle 1923: 105).

72 Pl. II 143 - 147 = OBI 2, p. 33 sqq.

73 Pl. IV 381 = OBI 3, p. 14.

74 Pl. III 229 = OBI 3, p. 66, l. 2 and 10. Cp. a similar case in the chronicles related for king Narasihapati (Glass Palace Chronicle 1923: 152).

75 Pl. I 52 = OBI 1, p. 152, l. 19, and Pl. III 282 = OBI 3, p. 109, l. 10, both have a *sū-krway* at the head of the witnesses; in Pl. II 123 = OBI 1, p. 179, l. 27, he is preceded by a headman and one *saṅ-krī*; Pl. II 199 = OBI 2, p. 146, has five monks in front of the *sū-krway* who, in turn, come before the village headman.

76 Pl. IV 471 = OBI 4, p. 50, l. 7, and OBI 1, p. 330, both mention the "*sū-krway Saman-cata* who came from Majjhimadesa [India]", and Pl. II 158 = OBI 2, p. 78, l. 11, has an Indian (*kula-*) *sū-krway* residing at Pagan.

It may be worth mentioning in this context that a member of the Nānādesi merchant guild made a donation to the Vishnu temple inside the walled city of Pagan (the Nat-hlyaung-kyaung). The temple seems to have served as a focal point for the group, both for trade and religious services.

77 The only instance known for the latter title dates from the reign of king Kyawazwa (1287-98 CE): Pl. III 282 = OBI 3, p. 174, l. 2-3. This king apparently deviated from the tradition of his predecessors more than once. He also provided the only known instance of a *mahādān* being

given to a *sū-krway*: Pl. III 293 = OBI 3, p. 196, l. 10 (1299 CE).

78 Pl. I 15 = OBI 1, p. 60, l. 4; l. I 93 = OBI 1, p. 287, l. 3. The latter reference applies to a daughter of prince Rājasū.

79 Pl. II 200 = OBI 3, p. 62, l. 3.

80 Pl. III 282 = OBI 3, p. 174, l. 2-3.

81 Pl. III 293 = OBI 3, p. 196, l. 10 (1299 CE).

82 Pl. I 19 = OBI 1, p. 65, l. 7-10; Pl. III 276a = OBI 3, p. 158 l. 1-3. Due to the expansion of Angkor under Jayavarman VII, the Salween was a also political boundary. Listing the coastal strip of Arakan among the provinces of the kingdom, however, shows a considerable amount of wishful thinking, as the advance into Arakan over the Arakan Yoma passes remained troublesome until the 19th century. For the routes, see Leider (1994), for the status of Arakan under the Pagan kings, see Frasch (2002b).

83 This expression takes into account that not all states in early India had a clearly defined urban centre as a permanent capital. For example, a number of Pala inscriptions was issued from the "victorious camp" (*jayaskandhavara*), a term that can be understood here as capital .

84 In a way therefore, Spencer's famous system of tax, tribute and plunder can also be incorporated in the Octopus state (Spencer 1976).

The Sacrificer State and Sacrificial Community: Kingship in Early Modern Khurda, Orissa, Seen Through a Local Ritual

Akio Tanabe

Kingship, Community and Ritual

The aim of this paper is to elucidate the nature of kingship in Khurda, Orissa, in relation to the characteristics of the local community and the people's subjectivity in the historical context of the early modern period. The end of the Orissan empire in 1568 marked the beginning of a major transformation not only at the level of state politics but also with regard to the social system and individual identity. That it led to a rising importance of "little kingdoms"[1], especially in the hilly tracts of Orissa known as the Garhjat area, which had a significant influence in many spheres, will be of particular interest for this volume. Although it can be argued that the Khurda kingdom (circa 1572-1804) dealt with in this paper was one of the little kingdoms in complex interrelationships with each other and with the paramount power (Mughal and later Maratha), it was not strictly just one of them.[2] The Khurda king was unique if not politically predominant, since despite his comparatively small territory, he was regarded as the Gajapati (*gajapati*: the lord of the Elephants)[3] or the paramount ruler of Orissa, at least in name and authority. Thus, he is characterised by a combination of symbolic greatness as "Gajapati Maharaja" and politico-military susceptibility as a "little king". In this sense, the Khurda kingdom can be said to have been a "great little kingdom".

In previous studies on state and society in India, historians were inclined to deal with the level of the large state, such as the Mughals and Marathas, and anthropologists with that of the village. Recent focus on the "little kingdom" level between the village and the large state, however, provides a new perspective on the politico-ritual process of interactions and exchanges that existed between the different polity levels.[4] Studies on little kingdoms also paid attention to the ritual-religious significance of the workings of kingship, which has led to an appreciation of how vital indigenous conceptions of sovereignty and dominance are for the understanding of state and society in India.[5]

The analysis of the local situation in pre-colonial Khurda presented in this paper draws on these studies of little kingdoms and attempts to expand on them by concentrating on the interactions of kingship with the micro-regional socio-political units of the local community.[6] The local community in Khurda consisted of several villages centring around a fort. They were called *gaṛa* (garh, fort) or *bisi* (county) and I refer here to this micro-regional or local unit as the "fort area" or "local community". The fort area seems to have formed the basic constitutive unit of the kingdom in the hilly areas of Orissa, and the primary unit of social reproduction.[7]

Rather than limit the scope to the interaction between kings and feudatory rajas, as previous little kingdom studies have tended to do, I will concentrate in this paper on state interaction with the fort area. To understand the overall nature of state and society in pre-colonial India, it is vital that attention be paid to the aspects of both kingship and local community in the context of their interaction. Previous studies on the pre-colonial state have also focused on the relationship between the state and the localities in their attempt to understand the nature of state sovereignty and power.[8] The study of the fort area seems promising from this perspective, since the workings of kingship and the social system met and interacted in this field.

In this paper, I will shed some light on what seems to me to be the new character of kingship in relation to the local community and its people in early modern Orissa of the seventeenth and eighteenth centuries. After examining the historical context, I will proceed with an analysis of a community ritual called "Ramachandi festival" in Garh Manitri, which displays a marked symbolic royal presence. I carried out intensive fieldwork and historical research in Garh Manitri, which was one of the forts under the Khurda kingdom. The content of the ritual strongly suggests that its present structure, which I observed, was mainly constructed after Garh Manitri had become part of the Khurda kingdom in the late sixteenth century. As far as I could ascertain, only minor changes were made to the content of the ritual during and after the colonial period. I have dealt with the changes in the overall semantics of the ritual during colonial and post-colonial period elsewhere (Tanabe 1999b). Here, I would like to concentrate on what the ritual can tell us about the late pre-colonial or early modern situation. The ritual representation of Ramachandi festival does not, of course, give us a complete picture of what the state and community were actually about. However, if the ritual details are read against the background of historical knowledge of early modern Orissa, they provide us with excellent material for understanding people's notions and emotions – their mentality – regarding the king, chief, goddess and Jagannath. Through this, we get an idea of people's sense of identity and subjectivity in relation to the new development of politics and religion in early modernity. Particular attention will be paid here to the politico-religious significance of the symbolic permeation of the divine king in the local community and how this functioned in connecting people in the locality to the wider world.

The seminal works of Bayly, Perlin and others, have made the vibrant economic activities in early modern India well known (e.g., Bayly 1992; Perlin 1993). In order to grasp early modernity in India as a whole, however, it is important that we understand the economic changes in relation to other aspects such as transformations in state politics, social structure and religion.[9] Therefore, I will look at how the nature of kingship and local community changed in the early modern period and how this change is related to a transformation in values, religious practice and the meaning of people's everyday activities in the locality. If a significant quality of modernity lies in its conjunctural character, which brought relatively isolated societies into contact and connected the local to the wider sphere, the penetration of the king's power into the locality certainly linked people's identity and ethics to the wider sphere while they themselves remained in the locality, and can be said to be a form of modernity.[10] I will attempt to explain its politico-cultural logic in the following and hope that the paper will contribute to a further understanding of a form of early modernity in India.

Historical Context and the Paradox of Early Modernity in Orissa

The relationship between the state and the local community in seventeenth and eighteenth century Khurda is formulated here as "the sacrificer state and sacrificial community". This intricate relationship came about as a result of a new intensified interaction between local communities and the little kingdom from the late sixteenth century onwards. It was a historical process that transformed the nature of the state and local communities irreversibly.

In order to understand the early modern transformation of relationships between the state and society, let us compare the early modern with the medieval situation. Numerous semi-independent chiefdoms existed in Khurda until the late sixteenth century. They belonged to the Orissan empire, but since they were located in the hilly tracts at the periphery, they probably had purely prestation relationships with the emperor-king. Each chiefdom had a chief and his *iṣṭadebatā* (often a goddess) as the tutelary deity. The system of entitlements or sacrificial organisation was complete within the chiefdom, as the chief played the role of the sacrificer and the entitlement holders in the chiefdom carried out their respective duties. Land and other shares as well as duties in the chiefdom were considered as granted to the entitlement holders by the local chief and not by the king. Sacrifice to the goddess was the key idiom of the socio-political system at the local chiefdom level. The members of the chiefdom offered their work as a sacrifice to the tutelary goddess, with animal sacrifice as the paradigmatic representation of the sacrificial principle. This kind of situation can be inferred from traces of a few chieftaincies in Khurda that remained semi-autonomous until the British arrived, such as *sauri khaṇḍāyat, śuddha khaṇḍāyat* and Haladia *rāja.*[11]

The tutelary god of the state (*rāṣṭradebatā*), of course, was Jagannath, the real ruler of Orissa, with the emperor-king as his deputy on earth.[12] Orissan emperor-kings performed worship rituals (*pūjā*) to Lord Jagannath in Puri and orchestrated administrative-military affairs from Cuttack. It is important to note that the idiomatic relationship between the king and the god was not about sacrifice but *pūjā.*[13] The king was the worshipper-devotee of Jagannath through *pūjā* at the imperial level, where animal sacrifice was merely of peripheral importance. Under this politico-ritual structure, there was a clear structural and functional difference between the level of the state-empire and that of the local chiefdoms. The king worshipped Lord Jagannath with *māhāpraśād*, while the chief performed animal sacrifice to his tutelary goddess. The king managed state affairs and the chief managed local everyday affairs with the system of entitlements. The king remained at the level of state-empire outside the local community, so to speak, as the relationship between the state and the local community was mainly restricted to tributary exchanges between the king and the chief. The king did not have direct authority or surveillance over the entitlements of each and every member in the local social system.[14]

This situation changed in the late sixteenth century when the regional-imperial state ceased to exist and the Khurda kingdom was established as a sub-regional polity with all-Orissa level authority. As the power of the early modern state gradually permeated the local community, the relationship between state and community became more intermingled and complex. Many of the semi-autonomous chiefdoms were knit into a more closely related structure of early modern kingship.

In seventeenth and eighteenth-century Khurda, a development took place in the administrative technology of surveillance, recording and accounting applied to the locality. A study of administrative records on palm-leaf scripts shows that the flow of resources and their distribution in the local community were minutely surveyed, and entitlements of different members defined in monetary numbers and recorded systematically (Tanabe 1999a, forthcoming a). Importantly, while the local community maintained its autonomous character with regard to the division of labour for everyday reproduction, the community rights and duties of each entitlement holder came to be considered as granted directly and legitimised by the king. The association of individual entitlements with royal authority and their evaluation in terms of cowry numeration can be said to have contributed to giving entitlement value a more universal character, rather than a specifically local one. This universalisation of entitlement value led to an increased alienation of some office entitlements in the plains.[15] The offices of village head and village accountant were bought and sold (Sterling 1904: 57-61),[16] illustrating how a local entitlement gained a more universal value and eventually acquired a market price. Thus, administrative development was concomitant with commercialisation of the social system. As I have argued elsewhere, the "introduction of more advanced and universal administrative technology in the local communities in the process of state formation, such as accounting, measuring and use of money, meant not only that these communities in the jungles of the hilly tracts of Khurda were more closely incorporated into the royal redistributive system, but also that they came to be connected to the wider network of the flow of money and goods, specifically the trade and commerce articulated with the growth of the world economy" (Tanabe 1999a: 196).

So far, so clear. However, there are other – namely religious and ritual – aspects of early modern Orissa that should also be considered if we are to aim for an overall understanding of state and society in that period. In this regard, we can point out that the king's relationship with the Jagannath cult intensified. This resulted in the ritualisation and divinisation of the king, who by this time was represented as the *thākur rājā* (divine king) and *ādya sevāyat* (first servant) of Jagannath (Kulke 1978e). At the same time, the *bhakti* cult began to develop, especially among the non-Brahmin population during this period, represented by the Chaitanya movement and popularisation of the Oriya Bhagavatam.

Thus, two phenomena were evidently at odds with each other on a superficial level during the early modern development of Orissa. On the one hand, there was a growth in what might be called "rationalisation" in terms of the development of administrative state technology and a flourishing of the market economy, while there was an increase, on the other hand, in "spiritualisation" in terms of the king's divinisation and ritualisation, coupled with the emergence of *bhakti* and its popularisation. It is this simultaneous development of the "rational" and the "spiritual" that characterises early modernity in Orissa. I have already suggested elsewhere that these socio-religious and politico-economic phenomena should be considered as suggesting concomitant developments of early modernity in India, rather than mere historical coincidence (Tanabe 2000). But let me explain here what I mean by this.

That the advent of modernity, with its characteristic rationality, leads to the gradual confinement of spiritual and religious aspects of state politics and society to the private sphere is a common assumption in modernisation theory. However, evidence from the present late-modern situation where so-called "religious nationalism" (Juergensmeyer 1993, van der Veer 1994) and "fundamentalist movements" (Marty/Appleby 1991, 1993a, 1993b, 1994, 1995) have emerged clearly demonstrates the fallacy of such an assumption. The question I would like to ask here is, "Are these merely phenomena of late modernity?" While today's "religious nationalism" and "fundamentalist movements" certainly have characteristics peculiar to the conditions of late modernity, the history of Orissa tells us that there was in fact a concomitant rise of the rational and spiritual/religious from the early modern period and that this is not an invention of late modern times. There was clearly a development of the spiritual/religious in early modern Orissa that cannot be reduced to mere residue of the medieval. The concomitant development of the rational and the spiritual could be called – in an attempt to articulate the problematic – the "paradox of early modernity" in India. Thus the question we should now ask is, "How can we explain the internal logic of the relationship between these two aspects of early modernity?" That is to say, if they were not a mere historical coincidence, there must have been an internal politico-cultural logic that led to their concomitant development. The logic must be found if the question is not to remain an incomprehensible paradox.

With the analysis of a local ritual, I will attempt here to provide a preliminary answer to this very difficult question. The key seems to lie in how the king became the sacrificer for localities. The transformation of the nature of kingship in early modernity was pivotal in influencing the local social structure as well as the subjectivity and identity of the people. The local ritual provides excellent material for understanding what the establishment of "sacrificial king and sacrificial community" meant for the local people, and how it influenced their perception of king, community, deities and self. By attempting to grasp the implications of ritual materials in the historical context of politico-economic change, we hope to find some clues towards solving the paradox of early modernity in India. Let us now take a look at the ritual of Ramachandi festival itself.

Ritual Sequence and Its Interpretation

The festival of Ramachandi takes place over seventeen days, between the ninth day of the dark fortnight of *Āśvina* (September-October) and the tenth day of the bright fortnight. The first sixteen days correspond to *Durgā Pūjā* and the seventeenth to *Daṣaharā*, although they are treated in Garh Manitri as one continuous festival. The period between the first and the thirteenth day is the preparatory phase for welcoming the goddess. Here, a description and interpretation will be given for the fourteenth day (*mahāsaptamī*, the seventh day of the bright fortnight) onwards (see map). Since I have presented details of the festival elsewhere (Tanabe 1999a), I will merely illustrate the essence of the ritual process and present the interpretation insofar as it is relevant to the present argument.

Worship and possession of Goddess:
The ritual of *mahāsaptamī (The Great Seventh)* begins with a Khond priest (*jāni*) worshipping the goddess in rock form on the hill. Two water pots (*kaḷaṣa*) are also prepared. Characteristic for this worship by the Khond priest is the making of an offering known as *puñji*, which is a mixture of rice, milk and egg made into small mounds with a little local liquor poured on top. The goddess possesses a Saora medium, who represents the goddess in the *mahāsaptamī* ritual. The sacrifice of a cock is offered, after which the medium, the Khond priest, Khond attendant carrying the water-pots, sacrifice-executor and drummers proceed down the hill and enter the village with the barber holding a torch at the head of the group (this group will be referred to below as the medium group).

This phase of the ritual is full of "tribal" elements. Only the indigenous people can mediate the "primordial power" (*ādi śakti*) of the goddess, which is extremely strong and dangerous. The location of the hill in the forest also suggests the undomesticated and untamed nature of the power of the goddess. The offering of *puñji* adds tribal colour to the ritual. Needless to say, egg and liquor are not usually offered in *pūjā*. As regards the historical conception of the people, this phase corresponds to the "ancient" time when tribal culture dominated, prior to the advent of "Hindu" civilisation and kingship.

Submission of the chief:
After the cock sacrifice at the "village mouth" (*gāṃ muha*), the procession of the medium group proceeds through the village accepting offerings from each household. Only uncooked "dry offerings" (*śukhilā bhoga*) are allowed to be given. In front of Ramachandi's temple, the chief lays the "royal sword" (*rājāṅka khaṇḍā*) on the ground and challenges the goddess. The sword symbolises the sovereignty of the king, who had endowed the chief with authority as the legitimate ruler in the fort. Legend has it that the chief had his suspicions about the divinity of the Saora medium and, testing him, challenged him to lift up the twelve-foot sword. According to the legend, the medium not only lifts up the sword but starts swinging it fiercely. In this dramatic moment, the sound of drums grows louder and the excited villagers shout *Hari bola* (Hail the God) several times. From this point on, the king's sword is in the hand of the Saora medium, now recognised as an incarnation of the goddess.

Here, the chief's authority is symbolically removed by the indigenous tribal medium. and his challenge to the latter met by humiliation. The symbolic response shows that the chief alone is not capable of controlling the local goddess's primordial power and, by implication, the tribal population. The people – including the chief – must submit to the power of the goddess mediated through the tribal medium and tribal priest.

Invitation of goddess to the palace, offering of cooked meals and red sari:
Thereupon, cooked offerings (*saṅkuḍi bhoga*) are made for the first time to the medium in the king's name in the royal court (*kacheri*).[17] Offerings of animal sacrifices are then placed in front of a small shrine dedicated to goddess Mangala, next to the temple of Ramachandi. Here, sheep and goats are sacrificed for the first time. The medium group proceeds to the Upper Fort, accepting cooked offerings and animal sacrifices on the way. In front of the scribe's (*koṭha karaṇa*) house, the scribe spreads a piece of cloth made from two red saris, on which the medium performs the sword play (*khaṇḍā kheḷa*) .

It could be argued that elements of the "great tradition" increase with the addition of cooked offerings and sacrifices of goats and sheep.[18] It is worth noting that the increase of these elements is initiated by the king when he invites the medium into the palace. We can see how the king is portrayed here as playing a pivotal role in introducing the elements belonging to the great tradition. The sword play contains sexual connotations, since the villagers claim that the goddess "lies on the sari in joy" and that the red sari has a strong symbolic connection with marriage. The goddess is pleased and gradually appeased by these royal offerings, a hint that the power of the goddess is heading towards union with royal authority.

Royal Sacrifice:
After the medium has accepted cooked offerings and animal sacrifices from individuals, he goes to the "sword hut" (*khaṇḍā ghara*). A Brahman priest throws rice and flowers on the medium, chanting a *mantra*. The medium then places the sword in the hut. The Brahman sanctifies the sacrificial goat by chanting a *mantra* into its ear, whereupon the sacrifice of the goat, known as the "royal sacrifice" (*sarakārī baḷi*), takes place.[19] As soon as the goat is sacrificed, the medium drinks the blood flowing from the goat's body and falls down. The goat is later divided up and distributed among the villagers according to custom. The chief is given the penis and testicles in which the *śakti* is said to be concentrated, while the head of the goat goes to the "state" (meaning the king's court cum sub-tahasildar office in the village of old, but today presented to the villager who used to be an officer there and happens to be the Brahman officiating at the royal sacrifice). The rest of the body is divided into eighty-five equal portions. Four portions are spare parts. The eighty-one portions go to the "state" (three portions), chief, sub-chiefs (six families), ex-*sarabarākāras* (ten families), Garh Manitri *pāikas* (peasant-militia: it is believed there were twenty-four families, but extended to thirty families), Chhiama *pāika*, Barabati *pāika*, Baliberani *pāikas* (two families), *koṭha karaṇa* (scribe), *baithi karaṇa* (scribe), Potters (ten families), carpenter, gardener, sweetmaker, blacksmith, washerman, astrologer, barber, Bāuris (three families), medium, *kabāri* (fuel-wood provider: Saora, two families), Baliberani *kabāria* and Chhiama *kabāri*.

The royal sacrifice differs from previous sacrifices offered in that the subject of the offering is not the individual or household but the whole community represented by the king as the sacrificer[20] and that the sacrificial animal is sanctified by the Brahman. The Brahman's *mantra*, which represents the ordering principle,[21] succeeds in separating the royal sword from the body of the living medium, as the latter puts down the sword in the sword hut and collapses after accepting the royal sacrifice. The villagers say that the power of the goddess now leaves the body of the medium and resides in the sword. The sword as the divine medium is more convenient, unlike the uncontrollable and unpredictable tribal medium. When the power of the goddess resides in the royal sword, it is under control and in union with royal authority. Here, we see that it is a combination of the Brahman's ritual authority and the king as royal sacrificer that brings about complete control of the power of the goddess.

Sacrifice functions here as a basic mechanism for the transformation of the divine power of the goddess and the community. Sacrifice, in a word, is a process of self-transformation through symbolic death and regeneration. By destroying the sacrificial animal identified with the sacrificer, the sacrificer and the community represented by him undergo a process of death and regeneration. Through symbolic death, the community without borders acquires immanence with the sacred that lies beyond it, and the community thus re-structured is recharged with sacred power.[22] Sacrificial ritual is a powerful mechanism for identity formation, which works by redefining social order. In the community festival dealt with here, the community as a sacrificial organisation, with its hierarchy and centrality of the king as the sacrificer, emerges through the sacrificial process of submission and self-destruction to achieve its re-establishment.

In the royal sacrifice, which is the climax of the *mahāsaptamī pūjā*, the king comes to be finally accepted by the goddess as a worthy sacrificer. The incomplete and helpless community finally achieves re-establishment of the complete self with the royal sacrificer. Acceptance of the king as a fit sacrificer by the goddess results in union of the power of the goddess with royal authority. This union is symbolised by the sword, which represents royal authority, and is also filled with the power of the goddess. Thus, the sword is both the "king's sword" and "Ramachandi's sword". As a result of this union, the goddess's power of generation bears fruit. The meat of the royal sacrificial goat that is consumed during the festival symbolises the fruit of the union. The meat is said to be full of divine power and brings about benevolent manifestations of the goddess's generative power in the form of procreation of the people, abundant crops and military success. The "system of entitlements" is paradigmatically represented by the distribution of the meat from the sacrificial animal in the royal sacrifice. Each entitlement holder has a share in this "body politic" of sacrifice. The sacrificial process was made possible by the cooperation of people and the division of labour based on the "sacrificial organisation" of the community. Each family that contributed service to the ritual gets a share.[23] The meat is taken to be the product of the sacrifice, with the king as the "sacrificer" and the community as "sacrificial organisation".

Worship of the goddess in the form of the sword and mahāṣṭamī sacrifice:
In the morning and evening of the *mahāṣṭamī* (The Great Eighth) day to the last day of the festival, the sword and the water-pots representing the goddess are worshipped[24] in the sword hut, with the Brahman acting as the priest and the chief as the worshipper (*karttā*).[25] Iron pens and palm-leaf scripts collected from the traditional administrative authorities of the region, namely chief, sub-chiefs, scribes (*koṭha karaṇa* and *baithi karaṇa*), and accountant (*kauṛi bhagiā*), and from the ex-*sarbarākāras* (tax-collectors from the colonial time) and others patrons of the festival, are placed next to the sword and worshipped. The *mahāṣṭamī* sacrifice is performed at midnight. The cooked offering and meat from the sacrificed animal are distributed to villagers later on according to the custom. The head of the sacrificial sheep goes to the "state" (actually to the Brahman, who used to work at the king's court), while the rest of the body is divided into twenty-seven portions that go to the "state" (three portion), chief, sub-chiefs (six families), accountant (*kāuṛi bhagiā*), *koṭha karaṇa*, *baithi karaṇa*, ex-*sarabarākāras* (ten families), *barakandāj* (assistant officer at king's court), *pūjāri* Brahman, sword house *pāika* (*khaṇḍā ghara pāika*), barber and Govind Pattanayak.[26] Cooked offerings (*āṣṭamī sarā bhoga*) go to the "state" (three portions), chief, sub-chiefs (six families), *koṭha karaṇa*, *baithi karaṇa*, ex-*sarabarākāras* (ten families), *barakandāj*, sword house *pāika* (*khaṇḍā ghara pāika*) *pūjāri* Brahman, Vedic Brahmans (twelve portions), blacksmith, potter, carpenter, astrologer, gardener, washerman, Bāuri and Govind Pattanayak. Two portions are kept for the performance of *pūjā* during the immersion of the water-pots (*bisarjana*) but later go to the Khond priest.

Here, the chief regains the sword he once lost to the tribal medium as an object of worship. It is by royal and Brahmanical intervention that the chief is able to retrieve the sword. Through the workings of the king and the Brahman, the indigenous power of the goddess, hitherto carried into the village by the Saora medium and the Khond priest, is transferred to a sword that can be worshipped in a temple (sword hut) in a peaceful manner. This ritual drama tells us that the chief alone is not capable of ruling the locality and that he needs the support of royal authority and the Brahman in order to receive the local goddess's blessings. The worship of the divine-royal sword by the chief in the company of the Brahman is illustrative of this relationship. The iron pen and palm-leaf scripts, which are placed alongside the sword and the water-pots, were writing instruments in the olden days and were indispensable for administration. The palm-leaf scripts from the eighteenth century contain details of the system of entitlements. They symbolise not only the honour and prestige of the traditional administrators in the region but also the penetration of the royal government's surveillance and authority into the region and the royal acknowledgement of the system of entitlements in the local community. It is shown that the king controls both the power of the goddess as well as the distribution of its fruits in the form of products of the land, goods and money. It is conspicuous that shares of the *praśād* meat from the *mahāṣṭamī* sacrifice are only distributed to high office-holders related to the state administration. This distribution of sacrificial meat functions to distinguish the privileged from the rest of the people. Concerning the distribution of cooked offerings, we note that Vedic Brahmans accept the *praśād* for the first time in the ritual, whereas the tribal Saoras are denied shares. This clearly shows the shift towards establishing a social system whereby those related to royalty and the Brahman are privileged.

Daṣaharā procession:
On *daṣaharā*[27] day, the tools of profession are laid out and worshipped in each household.[28] It is also the first day of prescribed duties in the system of entitlements. The Brahmans and other service castes visit patron households (*daṣaharā bheṭi*) and begin their work (*anukuḷa*). In the evening, the chief lifts up the sword in his hand and leads a para-military procession accompanied by the Khaṇḍāyats, Khond priest, Brahman, scribe and barber with the torch and drummers. When they reach the *daṣaharā* field, the chief, followed by others, write "We seek protection at the feet of auspicious Ramachandi" (*śrī śrī śrī Rāmachaṇḍī charaṇe śaraṇa*) three times on a piece of palm leaf with an iron pen[29], tear it and throw it away. The act of writing words seeking the goddess's protection reconfirms the position of community members as devotees of the goddess. The use of the iron pen and the palm leaf in writing words of devotion, however, strikes us as very different from how the tribal medium expresses his devotion, namely by submitting his own body for possession, and the priest by offering rice, egg and liquor. In the context of the relationship between this ritual act and the conditions of early modernity, the specific act of writing words of devotion can be said to be a form of "literate devotion" that distinguished the elite from the rest in the "literacy aware society" of early modern India (Bayly 1996).

The Khond priest discards (*visarjana*) the water-pots into the pond at the *daṣaharā* field. The chief and the remainder of the procession go to the Jagannath temple where they receive "water and leaves of holy basil" (*tuḷsī pāni*) from the temple priest. The procession then continues on to the temple of the tutelary deity of the chiefly lineage, Govinda Jiu, which is also in the form of Jagannath. Here too they receive *tuḷsī pāni*. On reaching the chief's house, he is greeted with a ritual of respect and welcome (*baṇḍāpanā*) performed by the barber. The Brahman then performs *pūjā* on the sword, returns it to its case and hangs it up in the sword room in the chief's house. This last act marks the end of the festival.

Daṣaharā is the day when the process of re-establishment of socio-political order enacted by the ritual comes full circle. The duty of each family defined in the sacrificial system of entitlements is reconfirmed by the worship of professional tools and the beginning of service exchanges.[30] In the para-military procession, the chief holds in his hand the sword he has been worshipping as the symbol of unity between royal authority and the divine power of the local goddess. The chief acts here as the local representative of the king, and only in this capacity would the local goddess grant the chief and his community protection and success. It is worth noting here that the royal sword is known to be held by the *daḷabeherā* (military chief) in almost all forts in Khurda on *daṣaharā* day. In this way, although the king's corporal body is absent in the locality, people are very much aware of the king's symbolic presence.

Power and Subjectivity: The Transformation of the King and the Subjects

Let us now examine the framework of the sacrificer state and sacrificial community as represented in the ritual against the historical background. I have drawn two figures here for comparison. Figure 1 shows a model of medieval socio-political structure in Khurda before the sixteenth century, in which there was a multi-layered structure of polities as described above. In this political system, the regional-imperial king was the political representative of the real ruler Jagannath on earth. Semi-independent chiefs in Khurda had a tributary relationship with the king. Each chief had his local tutelary goddess to whom he and the community sacrificial organisation offered sacrifice. The system of entitlements in the locality was managed by the chief as sacrificer.

Figure 2 represents early modern transformation. The sub-regional king's authority and surveillance penetrated into the locality, and every single entitlement holder became directly connected with the king in the sacrificial organisation. Not only did the king hold information about individual entitlements with the aid of early modern administrative technology but local connection to the king became indispensable at the level of politico-cultural legitimacy and ritual efficacy.

As can be seen from the festival of Ramachandi, the king's presence in the locality was ritually represented by royal symbols. The royal sword and royal sacrifice are the most prominent symbols of royalty present in the local ritual. The king is represented as the central sacrificer around whom the sacrificial community is organised. In the early modern period, the king was no longer merely a worshipper of Jagannath at the imperial level. He also became sacrificer for the local goddesses as his symbolic presence – often represented by the king's sword in individual forts – and thus more ubiquitous, so to speak, at the local level. In this way, the local goddess representing indigenous power was united with the king, who increasingly became deified as the representative of the supreme state god Lord Jagannath during this period. In the course of the ritual process, the chief is shown to be incompetent as the sacrificer in controlling the power of the goddess. This can be seen in the ritual representation of the incident of his challenge to and defeat by the local goddess when his sword is taken away. It is only after royal intervention that the goddess is satisfied and transformed into the benevolent protector of the region. The role of the sacrificer is taken over by the king, while the sacrificial organisation of the locality remains the same. The combination of the sacrificer king and sacrificial community emerges at this point. Thus in Figure 2, the chief is replaced by the symbolic presence of the king at the centre as sacrificer.

Under the early modern transformation, the centrality of the king in the community's sacrificial organisation was extended from the ritual arena to everyday practice, where the duty of each member was carried out as sacrificial service. The ritual commencement of duty on *daṣaharā* day clearly illustrates this. The system of entitlements in the locality, represented and reconfirmed in the ritual activities and sharing of sacrificial meat and *praśād*, also functioned as the basis of everyday activities. The symbolic presence of the king as sacrificer and legitimising centre of the sacrificial organisation in the locality made it possible for the people to connect themselves to the king as royal subjects, while remaining in the locality and paying service to the local goddess and the community. Since each duty and entitlement were seen as defined and granted by the king, the people were able to convert their everyday activities into service for the kingdom. Moreover, since the king was seen as the representative of the Lord Jagannath on earth, work performed for the community and the kingdom could also be taken as service to the Supreme God. Thus, the same duty in the locality, defined in the local system of entitlements, simultaneously became an act of service to the kingdom as well as an act of devotion to Lord Jagannath.

This development in people's positioning and subjectivity is related, I would suggest, to the popularisation of the *bhakti* cult, in which the aspect of "*bhakti* yoga" (path of faith) and "*karma* yoga" (path of action) were combined to provide religio-spiritual meaning to the performance of everyday activities as sacrificial duty to the Supreme, represented by Jagannath-Krishna in early modern Orissa. It was a means of connecting a "secular" duty in the "here and now" to the "divine" without the ritual involvment of a Brahman priest. People's everyday work in the locality was thus given a more universal spiritual meaning. To understand the implication of this, it would not be out of place to mention Max Weber's argument in *Ethics of Protestantism and Spirit of Capitalism.* Weber looks at how secular duty in the world was infused with religious meaning in the ethics of Protestantism. It was a way of sacralising secular duty and of secularising religious values. It can be said that early modernity in Orissa also suggested a means by which local everyday activities could become grounded on the more universal ethics of *bhakti* relevant to Jagannath. *Bhakti* ethics appear to have provided a means of transforming everyday activities into universal divine service. In contrast to the asceticism of Protestantism, its character could be described as devotionalist where actions are offered to the divine and their fruits are accepted as divine blessings. People were no longer embedded in the local social structure but acquired a self-reflective subjectivity through which they could translate and connect the specific and local to a more universal value.

How was it possible for the people to acquire this kind of self-reflective subjectivity that connected local existence and activities to the wider and more universal value? I have already suggested that this was made possible through the king's connection with each entitled member. But then, how was it possible for the king to permeate the individual level? Here, I would like to pay attention to the transformation of kingship and its relationship to early modern subjectivity. Insofar as the formation of subjectivity is said to be linked to the workings of power (Foucault 1979, 1983), the subjectivity of individuals in early modern Orissa can be seen as related to the effects of power and authority in kingship. Before coming to this argument, however, let us first see how the transformation of the nature of royal power influenced people's relationship with the king, the goddess and Jagannath.

It is interesting to note that as royal power penetrated the locality, the symbolism of the king's presence increased. The authority of the king as head of the administrative surveillance, the source of legitimacy of each entitlement and the fit sacrificer of the local goddess are connected and represented by symbolic presence in the locality. This symbolisation of royalty can be considered one of the characteristics of early modern royalty along with its deification and ritualisation. Indeed, for the king to become the ubiquitous sacrificer for the many local goddesses, his presence had to be symbolised. The king was no longer a physical presence "out there" in the imperial capital. His essence grew more conceptualised as the divine representative of Jagannath and the symbolic sacrificer of the local goddesses.

Needless to say, this ubiquitous symbolisation of royal power was also related to the workings of power that permeated the early modern state. Since the king was considered to have given the entitlements and prescribed duties to the community members, people in the localities accepted their position and their duty in the local community as royal subjects, performing their work as service to the king and Jagannath. Thus, the subjectivity and identity of community members were no longer simply embedded in a local social structure. Although duty was still defined by the local sacrificial organisation and performed thereof, people's identity was defined reflectively in relation to the larger sphere of the kingdom and the universe. This quality of self-reflection that links people to a larger sphere beyond the locality constitutes early modern subjectivity, and was nurtured by people's relationship to the symbolic presence of the king in the locality.

As the people's relationship with the king became the basis of their subjectivity and identity, it can be argued that subjectivity was shaped by the subtle workings of early modern royal power penetrating the individual level. In this way, following Foucault's analysis of the relationship between subjectivity and power, we can argue that early modern subjects in Orissa, who took everyday duty as service to the king and Jagannath, became subject to the workings of royal power. However, we must also be careful to note the difference between the disciplinary power that Foucault has argued to be internalised by the modern European subject, and the kind of power that was internalised by early modern subjects in Orissa. In Foucault's rendition of disciplinary power, the transcendental gaze was internalised by individuals and accepted as their own. Individuals thus willingly disciplined themselves in accordance with social norms and ethics. This relates to the typical Kantian scheme in which a dichotomous distinction is drawn between mind and body, and reason, seated in the mind, was supposed to control and discipline the desiring body as the basis of civil man. In the case of early modern Orissa, however, bodily existence and desire were never totally denied. Till today, the corporal aspect constitutes an important aspect of personhood and identity as the body is constructed in relation to marriage, food and land, the determining factors for position in society (Tanabe 1998). In addition, desire was to be neither suppressed nor denied but channelled towards God. Even sexual desire was good as long as it was directed towards the deity (usually Krishna), as propagated in the Bhagavatam.[31] Thus, channelling body and desire towards the divine was more in demand than controlling them by reason. And this is precisely what early modern royalty did – connect and channel specific bodies and desires in the locality towards the universal deity of Jagannath. The early modern king mediated and enabled the channelling of the self in the service of God. Thus, we could say that the channelling power of royalty was internalised, embodied and practiced by early modern Orissan subjects. In the case of early modern Orissa, sacrificial practices were embodied by individuals who offered up their entire selves including their bodies, desires and actions. In this sense, early modern Orissan subjectivity contained both aspects. On the one hand, people were self-reflecting subjects with a free will to devote themselves to a higher cause and, on the other hand, they were subject to the channelling power of royalty.[32]

Concluding remarks

This paper has attempted to identify the structure of "sacrificer state and sacrificial community" as ritually represented in the Ramachandi festival and to consider its influences on people's perception of self as regards the king, the community and the deities. In this sense I examined the mentality of the people of Khurda and its history in the early modern context in an endeavour to find a holistic and overall explanation for the development of administrative technology and market economy as well as divine kingship and the popularisation of *bhakti*. More specifically, I tried to unearth clues for the understanding of the internal politico-cultural logic behind the apparent paradox of the concomitant development of the rational and the spiritual in early modern Orissa. The key, as presented in this paper, was the local permeation of royal power, which affected the configuration of the state, the community and people's subjectivity in an irreversible manner. Let me summarise my argument below.

During the early modern development of the Khurda kingdom in the seventeenth and eighteenth centuries, the administrative surveillance of kingship penetrated the local level with increased state power. During this period, the state introduced a process of measuring, numerating, monetising, accounting and recording each individual entitlement. In the early modern context, this contributed to the process of connecting remote localities to the wider market network, with its flow of money and goods.

Along with the "rational" developments in the field of state politics and economics, there were also notable developments – that could be termed "spiritual" – in the nature of kingship, social configuration and people's subjectivity. The hinge connecting these two aspects of early modernity was the king. In his sovereignty, he was in a position to totalise the administrative, coercive aspects of power as well as those of the symbolic and the religious.

Significantly for the social configuration and the subjectivity of the people, the king was established as the one who bestowed entitlements on members of the local community. This meant that from their point of view positions and duties in the locality were connected to the king, who came to occupy a central place as a reference point for the subjectivity and identities of individuals. This, however, did not mean that a single sacrificial organisation was established in the kingdom that centred around the king (*pace* Dirks 1987). The sacrificial organisation of the system of entitlements remained based in numerous communities in the kingdom. What the king actually did was to reconfirm and sanction the roles of individuals in the local system of entitlements. The king stayed outside the communities, granting authority for the assignment and power of each entitlement holder through various prestations,[33] and acted as the central organiser of sacrificial activities. It is essential to note here that the king's presence in the locality was symbolic. The king did not have a substantive relationship of bureaucratic hierarchy with the locality as in the case of European absolute monarchy. It was his symbolic representations – royal sword, royal temple, royal sacrifice etc. – that worked to maintain the legitimacy and value of the local system of entitlements. Each entitlement holder in the sacrificial community performed his duty in the locality as a sacrifice for the reproduction of the whole, centring around the symbolic presence of the king. This royal intervention, however, meant that the ritual-symbolic autonomy of the local community was irreversibly lost. The local community and its individual members became dependent on the king's presence for its reproduction, which is clearly illustrated in the example of the Ramachandi festival.

As the function of the kingdom-state grew in significance even at the daily local level, local communities in Khurda were were ideologically made incomplete in themselves. That is to say, local communities no longer constituted "the whole" to which the sacrificial activities could be dedicated. The chief of the local community ceased to be a self-sufficient sacrificer. The symbolic presence of the king was required for the reproduction of the community. The king became the sacrificer, indispensable as the symbolic centre of the sacrificial organisation in the locality. The local presence of royal symbols functioned as a representative of the more universal value of Orissa kingship and Jagannath, to which the people in the locality could connect themselves as a means of establishing their identity beyond a particular locality.

The establishment of the symbolic centrality of the king as the sacrificer around whom the sacrificial organisation of the local community was constituted can be observed in the elaborate rituals of the Ramachandi festival. Although the king himself is physically absent, the strong symbolic royal presence plays a crucial role in the ritual. In its performance, the king's presence is represented as being imperative to controlling and transforming the power of the local goddess to benevolence. Sacrifice as the process of death and regeneration is shown to be achieved through the system of entitlements in the community, with the king as the sacrificer. The fruits – wealth, abundant crops, military success – gained through the work of the community members are accepted as the fruits of sacrificial service, with the king as sacrificer, and shared in accordance with the system of entitlements.

Thus, the reproduction of the local community in early modern Khurda became dependent on the subtle workings of the power of kingship that permeated the locality. The king's body remained outside the local community, yet the relationship with his symbolic presence was internalised by the individual members as the basis of their identity. Each member's duty and entitlement was defined by the state and accepted as a duty not only to the community and its goddess but also to the king and Lord Jagannath. The link to Jagannath is represented in the ritual by the act of visitng the temples of Jagannath to receive blessings at the end of the festival. Here, sacrificial service in the locality is eventually connected to devotion to Jagannath, the state deity. Thus, while remaining in the locality and serving the local community and its goddess, individuals are also connected through the king to Lord Jagannath.

The establishment of the locally ubiquitous symbolic authority of the king went side by side with the permeation of state power in the form of surveillance and control over individual entitlements and the local distribution of resources. The power of state knowledge also had its symbolic side as the central sacrificer around whom the local community was organised. The power of the early modern state in Orissa must be understood as having had administrative and symbolic aspects that corresponded to the rational and spiritual aspects of the early modern period. The people became subject to the workings of this power in the early modern state, but at the same time developed a self-reflective subjectivity allowing them to evaluate and give meaning to their work in a wider perspective. This was achieved by each community member positioning their duty and entitlements in relation to the sacrificer-king. The king represented both the rational aspect that channelled the local to the wider state and market as well as the spiritual aspect that channelled each member to Jagannath.[34] Thus royal channelling power connected the local to the universal and the rational to the spiritual.

Thus, the penetration of the workings of kingship into the local community in the seventeenth and eighteenth centuries meant that the community remained the site of sacrificial organisation, while the king took the position of the sacrificer. The sacrificial organisation of the local community was rendered ideologically incomplete without the king as the sacrificer. The permeation of royal power throughout the locality connected each individual to the state, the market and the Universal deity, Jagannath. The "sacrificer state and sacrificial community" in early modern Khurda point to this new development in the relationship between state and community, and implies a new transformation in people's subjectivity.

Notes

1 The term "little kingdom" was first applied to the study of the Indian state by Cohn (1959, 2001b [1962]) and further developed by Stein (1980), Dirks (1979, 1987), Peabody (1991a, 1991b), Berkemer (1993) and Schnepel (1995a, 2002). Berkemer appropriately defines "little kingdom" and "little king" as follows: "A political system whose ruler can consider himself in domestic politics to be independent and who also pursues a ritual policy within his own territory, but who at the same time recognizes an overlord who is both politically and ritually above him and militarily superior, whose authority he shares and who needs him for the acknowledgement of the authority of his own rule within his own kingdom and in his dealings with other *little kings*, should be considered a *little kingdom*" (Berkemer 1993: 320).

2 On Khurda kingdom, see Kulke (1974, 1978d, 1978e, 1993b).

3 Narasiṃha I (1238-1264 A.D.) was the first Orissan king to use the title of "Gajapati", indicating its sovereign status in East India (Kulke 1978c: 201). On the traditional account of rulership in India, see also Sterling (1904: 62).

4 The focus on little kingdoms does not, of course, deny the significance of studying great kingdoms and villages. With my formulation "sacrificial state and sacrificial community" in this paper, I have primarily focused on the "little kingdom" and "fort area" levels, a domain that has been insufficiently researched up to now, and have thus not been able to take the function of large states or villages fully into account. Hence, it must remain a subject for future research.

5 In this connection, I would also mention the names of Fox (1971) for North India, and Mahapatra (1977) and Kulke (1978c, 1993b) for Orissa, whose works were instrumental in inspiring research in this direction, although they did not employ the term "little kingdom".

6 This is an attempt to provide an answer to the problem put forward succinctly by Chattopadhyaya as follows: "In trying to understand the presence of autonomous spaces of authority within the structure of a State it is therefore necessary to understand how sources of authority were perceived and how they were sought to be related to the authority of the State" (Chattopadhyaya 1997: 8).

7 This seems to correspond to the importance of the unit of *nāḍu* in South India (Subbarayalu 1973; Stein 1977; Beck 1972; Srinivas 1989: 56-69). Bhatt summarises, "In pre-British India, regions of nadu type were significant in establishing ritual, social, and political identities" (Bhatt 1980: 55).

8 Geertz (1980); Tambiah (1985); Peabody (1991a, 1991b); Stein (1980); Chattopadhyaya (1997). See Kulke (1995) for review of theories on the medieval state in India.

9 Bayly (1998), Perlin (1993, 1994) and Narayana Rao/Shulman/Subrahmanyam (1992) are examples of work in this direction.

10 On the conjunctural character of modernity, see Subrahmanyam (1998).

11 *Sauri khaṇḍāyat* and *śuddha khaṇḍāyat* were semi-autonomous semi-tribal chiefs and Haladia *rāja* was a mini-king who ruled over five villages under the Khurda king.

12 On the idea of Gajapati as the deputy of Jagannath, see Kulke (1978e).

13 It is certainly true that *pūjā* has a sacrificial structure (Tanaka 1991) and in this sense is also permeated by the sacrificial principle. However, I am concentrating here on the different form of ritual in relation to *pūjā* and sacrifice (most typically animal sacrifice).

14 This kind of medieval situation where the lesser autonomous unit was encompassed within the greater unit is captured by Kulke's integrative model. When the imperial regional kingdom was established by integrating the surrounding chiefs and kings, "local autonomous corporate institutions ... continued to exist within and autonomous tributary kingdoms outside these enlarged imperial core areas". Significantly, many of these institutions – temples, pilgrimage centres, monasteries, local cults and lesser polities – retained their own identity and occasionally even enhanced their importance after integration (Kulke forthcoming a). Medieval state formation can thus be characterised as an integrative process of incorporation and

subjugation of lesser autonomous units by a greater polity. Integration was achieved by establishing tributary and indirect administrative relationships with existing institutions without interfering directly in internal matters. There was therefore a multi-layered state structure of regional-imperial, sub-regional and local level polities.

15 However, there seems to have been no alienation of offices in the hilly tracts.

16 It is well known that several offices were alienable in other parts of pre-colonial India, too (Fukazawa 1982: 251; Bayly 1992; Kotani 2002; Mizushima 1990).

17 The royal court was used as a sub-tahasildar's (a tax-collecting officer) office from Ekharajat Mahal, the land whose right of tax collection was granted to the Puri king as the superintendent of Jagannath temple by the British government. In the 1960s, the king of Puri occasionally visited the place to hunt and picnic. Today, offerings are made by a villager who used to be an officer there. Significant is the fact that offerings are still made in the king's name even today.

18 A reminder of the legend of Lord Jagannath in which the deity is said to have eaten only fruit, nuts and roots with the tribal population. He was offered cooked meals on arrival later in Puri.

19 As its name indicates, the sacrificial animal is supposed to be given by the king. There is evidence in the palm-leaf document of 1776-77 that the king used to donate expenses for offerings at the palace in Garh Manitri including two sheep and a buffalo for Ramachandi festival, presumably for the respective *mahāsaptamī* royal sacrifice and *mahāṣṭamī* sacrifice (Tanabe 1999a). Even after colonisation, when there was a sub-tahasildar's office of Ekharajat Mahal in Garh Manitri, they used to give a donation for the animal in the king's name. When Ekharajat Mahal was abolished in the 1960s, the Jagannath temple office in Puri agreed to contribute one hundred rupees towards the royal sacrifice, a custom that has survived to the present day.

20 It should be noted that the idea of "sacrificer state and sacrificial community" is illustrated here.

21 The delivery of a *mantra* is considered extremely important precisely because the sound, that is, the vibration as the basis of creation, brings diversification and order into the world.

22 For theories on sacrifice, see Hubert and Mauss (1964 (1898) especially pp. 9-18); Bataille (1976); Hocart (1970); Inden (1998); Schnepel (1988); Tanaka (1991).

23 The special position of the king and the chief is represented by the portion they take. The king takes the animal's head and the chief its sexual organs.

24 The form the ritual takes is the same as that of a normal Hindu ritual, using the *mantra* to worship"forest Durgā" (*bana durgā*).

25 In order to protect the sword, guard *pāika*s (*khaṇḍā ghara pāika*) are supposed to protect the sword hut at night. It is said that the original sword, which was twelve feet long, was stolen by the king of Ranpur. From then on, guard *pāika*s were asked to watch over the sword hut. Members of the accountant family (*kauṛi bhagiā*) belonging to the chiefly lineage then went to the palace of Ranpur and took away the king's front door in revenge. This door is still used as the front door of the accountant's house today.

26 Govind Pattanayak belongs to the Scribe caste and became very influential in the village from the 1970s to the 1980s. He received ritual privileges as a result of his personal authority.

27 Daṣaharā is the day of goddess Durgā's victory as well as the day Rama prayed to Durgā to grant him victory. Hence, it is thought to be an auspicious day to begin battle and other deeds.

28 Swords and agricultural tools are worshipped in the houses of the Khaṇḍāyat caste, for instance, while scissors and combs are worshipped in houses of the barber caste.

29 Some, especially children, just write on a piece of paper.

30 It is worth noting that the service exchange relationships enacted on *daṣaharā* day have been preserved in the village as part of everyday exchange relationships.

31 The Oriya translation or rather retelling of the Bhagavatam was done by Jagannath Das in the sixteenth century. This Oriya Bhagavatam became the bible of the *bhakti* cult in early modern Orissa. Houses for Bhagavatam (*Bhagabata ghara*) were constructed in hamlets for the vil-

lagers to recite and listen to the Bhagavatam.

32 The points I have made in this paper regarding subjectivity in early modern Orissa are admittedly somewhat more conjectural than the data presented here can confirm. However, I hope these points will serve useful for future research on the topic.

33 See Tanabe (1999a) for details of prestations between the king and privileged entitlement holders in the locality.

34 This refers to the king's nature as "a twinned being", possessing both human and divine aspects (Kantorowicz 1957), which made it possible for him to function as a hinge between the two aspects of early modern development. Schnepel has focused on the twinned nature of Orissan kingship in an interesting manner (Schnepel 1995b). Unfortunately, however, the analysis was conducted with a predominantly ahistorical approach. It is furthermore necessary to investigate how the twinned nature of kingship in Orissa was transformed in history.

Ranpur – the Centre of a Little Kingdom

Niels Gutschow

Historical background

Fifteen hundred years ago, eighteen 'jungle states' were recorded in the hinterland of coastal Orissa. At the same time, Maṇināgeśvarī appeared as a Hinduised tribal deity, worshipped on a small hill plateau near Bhubaneswar some 50 km southeast of the capital of the former dynasties. Hermann Kulke describes the subsequent formation process of feudatory states (or 'Little Kingdoms') west, southwest and northwest of Bhubaneswar:

> "The Gajapatis encircled their fertile coastal granary and their political and religious centers, Cuttack and Puri, by a large number of feudatory states which bore the name *gaḍajāta*, meaning 'born from the fort' (*gaḍa*). Several decades after the downfall of the Gajapatis in the year 1568, the Moghuls assigned the small Garhjat (=*Gaḍajāta*) states of central Orissa to the *rājā*s of Khurda who had meanwhile become local successors to the imperial Gajapatis. Under the Khurda rājās, the Garhjat states achieved a semi-autonomous status which they retained even when the Marathas conquered Orissa in 1751. When the British conquered Orissa in 1803, the autonomy of the Garhjat states even received imperial sanction when the East India Company acknowledged them for a quit-rent as their allied feudatories" (Kulke 1980: 30-31).

Symbols of Hindu royalty and the settlement of Brahmins were needed as legitimation of power in the early phase. In the case of Ranpur, the development of a settlement in addition to a power place of tribal origin certainly had an immense strategic advantage in terms of a variety of associations tied to one of the Eight Mother-Goddesses (Aṣṭamātṛkā), who apart from Jagannātha as the state deity (*rāṣṭra-devatā*) exerted power on a sub-regional level. A local chronicle (*Rāṇapura Rājavaṁśa Itihāsa*, basically a 19th century compilation) tells us that in 1727 BC 'God' ordered a local chief to establish Maṇināga, the Jewel Serpent, as an act with cosmogonic associations. In a second step, the chronicle constructs a suitable past for the legitimation of the Ranpur *rāja*: In the 15th century he secured the necessary Hindu kingship paraphernalia in Puri, returned with a Mādhava image as a representation of Jagannātha and subsequently constructed a temple. The fort soon moved from the top to the foot of the hill, signifying the first step towards a larger settlement. Events in the late 17th century may already belong to what Hermann

Kulke has coined "remembered past" (Kulke: forthcoming b), which says that one *rājā* established seven main roads and 42 small streets. A conflict with Puri created a peculiar discontinuity in Ranpur's development. In the early 18th century, the rājā was obliged to include what Hermann Kulke called a "subsidiary *ishtadevata*" in the royal pantheon (Kulke 1980: 32). He needed the support of a Jungle Goddess (Khiḷāmuṇḍa) to re-establish his local power. By the middle of the 18th century – the Marathas had conquered Orissa – Ranpur's religious infrastructure must have already been fully established and the present temple of Jagannātha constructed, since the *rājā* established his new quarter in a wide compound adjoining the temple. From then on, the Little Kings of Ranpur placed memorial stones depicting themselves riding on elephants at the temple of Taḷamaṇināga.

The chronicle reveals that the "twelve festivals/rituals" tied to Jagannātha were introduced by an early 16th century *rājā* and, significantly, established a strong ritual tie between the peripheral 'Little Kingdom' and the centre. As this notion is clearly part of a constructed past, we must assume that these rituals were introduced or re-introduced by the middle of the 18th century. The Jungle Goddess Khiḷamuṇḍa was then brought with great pomp to the centre of the "Little Kingdom" in the shape of a long bamboo pole on the occasion of *daśahara*, the autumnal ritual of renewal par excellence. As a convenient counterpart, the *doḷameḷaṇa* festival must have been established a little later to celebrate another ritual of renewal at full moon in March, signifying the equinox of spring. This sequence communicates a sense of hierarchy. On the regional level, the Jungle King demonstrates loyalty towards Jagannātha, the state deity, and on the sub-regional level, the king renews his ties with the Jungle Goddess, who was somehow instrumental in renewing his kingship. On a third level, the tutelary goddess of the *rājā* and protective power of his territory, the Jewel Serpent (Maṇināga), calls for a demonstration of loyalty from 'all' (in reality 108) village gods, even those from Ranpur, including Jagannātha.

The urban fabric (Fig. 3)

An immaterial axis dominates the urban site along the east-west direction. Maṇināga is located high above 'everything' and since the powerful tribal goddess originally became manifest in non-iconic form in the shape of a stone, she ultimately represents 'place' in an otherwise unordered and potentially chaotic landscape. As such, she cannot be moved, transferred or otherwise manipulated. she marks a specific place of power, immovable. The Ranpur chronicle "remembers" that a temple was constructed for her in the middle of the 16th century. Lightning destroyed it on 3rd April 1943, however, giving rise to the construction of the present temple on a more humble scale. The Jewel Serpent looks down upon the temple of Jagannātha and its neighbouring 17th century palace, to which three imposing structures were added around 1910 in what one could call Orissan Baroque with a vernacular touch.

The temple faces strictly east, towards the main street of a settlement that was established in the late 17th century – Samukha Sahi (fig. 4). This road develops into an S-shaped curve before it passes one of Jagannātha's five 'ministers', Svapneśvara, who presides over the eastern direction. The bends are smooth enough not to obscure the dominant axis. Approaching the abode of Jagannātha, Maṇināga appears at a certain point almost as a crown high above the temple. Perpendicular to the main axis, which also divides the town into two halves of six neighbourhoods (*sāhi*) each, runs the ritual axis of the settlement, appropriately called *baḍadaṇḍa*, literally the "main stick". It originates at the main gate of Jagannātha's compound and ends at the gate of Guṇḍīcā, Jagannātha's summer residence at a distance of some 700 metres. Opposite the gate of the summer residence, the ritual axis opens up to form a large square or field (*padiā*) in answer to the needs of two major urban rituals. The three chariots of Jagannātha, Subhadra and Balabhadra are placed here in early June for five days in a waiting position until the Triad returns 'home', while 108 gods convene here on the occasion of *pañcadoḷayātrā* to demonstrate loyalty to the great tribal goddess, Maṇināgeśvarī. Thus, this ritual space was created as a stage for the performance of the two principal events in the calendar of the Little Kingdom: the car festival – *rathayātrā* – in honour of the Lord of the World "legitimises the Hindu kingship" (Kulke 1980: 36) of the Little King and *doḷameḷaṇa* (Fig. 9) secures territorial integrity.

Shifting the royal residence documents a change from fortress to settlement, traces of which can still be seen. The first kings must have settled on top of the hill, near the non-iconic image of Maṇināga. According to the chronicle, the king moved in the early 16th century to a plateau below the hill and above the later settlement. Almost two hundred years later the king is said to have worshipped Maṇināga in his house, implying the existence of a movable image of the goddess in iconic form since that time. Shortly before the middle of the 18th century, Rāmachandra Narendra, who regained kingship with the help of the jungle goddess Khiḷamuṇḍa, once again moved his 'palace' (in reality no more than a one-storey structure around a large square courtyard) close to the Lord of the World, whose temple must have been rebuilt by him at around the same time. The establishment of a new proximity of palace and temple, the most powerful symbol of kingship, at the centre of the developing settlement completes the spatial configuration. Further temples dedicated to Kṛṣṇa were built in the 19th century and a new iconic image of Maṇināga was enshrined in a new temple (fig. 11). The construction of yet another palace in the early 20th century adjacent to the temple's compound wall merely accentuates the existing pattern. A gate now provides direct access from the palace courtyard to the temple.

In imitation of patterns known from Puri, the Lord of the World is encircled by five 'ministers' (fig. 5) – Harihareśvara within the deity's compound (the centre), Svapneśvara in the east, Daṇḍabaluṅkeśvara in the south, Candeśvara in the north and Baluṅkeśvara way beyond the limits of the settlement in a western direction. Eight monasterial institutions (*maṭha*) are scattered throughout the 12 neighbourhoods, with one more located in the village of Purnavasanta, close to the temple of Baluṅkeśvara. A recent addition is the temple dedicated to Baḍibaluṅkeśvara at the ritual square and in 1998 the construction of a temple dedicated to Gaṇeśa close by. Apart from the temple dedicated to Nārāyaṇī, the most important goddess, there are eleven Maṅgalā shrines (often portrayed in a non-iconic form by a pair of reeds) as well as temples dedicated to Brāhmaṇīdevī (in Nuagaon), Bhuvaneśvarī, and Habudasinghī.

A second shrine to Nārāyaṇī was constructed in a more simple form in 1996, with a small shrine dedicated to the popular goddess of northeast Orissa, Tariṇī, added next to it in 2002. The latter was built with donations from neighbouring Kansari Sahi. The latest development features the construction of a Hanumān temple on the slope between Taḷamaṇināga and the temple of the tribal goddess at the top of the hill. A crude concrete structure was made possible by the initiative of a group of young men from Ranpur. Slogans such as "Jay Hanumān, Śrī Rām; Hare Kṛṣṇa, Hare, Hare" are painted on the rocks flanking the structure, with an additional slogan excluding non-vegetarians from visiting the shrine. These latest additions enable the former Little Kingdom to integrate successfully into what is known on a higher level as 'globalisation'. All Indian and all Orissan trends have come together, if only on a modest scale.

Seven Bhagavatamaṇḍapas, small buildings where the Bhagavata is read out in the evening, add to the religious infrastructure, as well as Bibhahamaṇḍapas and two Kamanaghars, towards which the competing groups of Daṇḍayātrā are oriented. Translated into a diagram (fig. 4), the urban fabric and religious infrastructure show a circular arrangement. The centre is occupied by the double representation of divine and profane kingship, with a settlement in the eastern half of the circle. The division of the settlement by an east-west axis stresses the cosmic orientation towards the four directions, although the cross appears amputated. The duality of the two settlement halves resurfaces with the existence of two Kamanaghars and two Bibhamaṇḍapas. This well-known pattern allows for the potential competition or even aggression that can arise in the course of urban rituals in times of crisis.

Likewise, the social topography adds to the spatial duality. Clearly 'beyond' the northern end of the ritual axis, the Untouchable quarter unites lumbermen, bamboo weavers, sweepers, cobblers, fishermen and watchmen, while a less distinct quarter at the southern end unites fishermen, washermen, the tribal priest (Jani) and the (landless) Muslim community as butchers, who acted as caretakers of elephants and horses in the days of the Little Kingdom. The original settlers here belonged to the tribal community of Behera, whose members produce items made of reeds, such as the ritual stick needed for the Daṇḍayātrā.

In contrast to what is known about Śāsana villages in Orissa, which were originally planned to settle Brahmins, Ranpur's social topography appears mixed. A number of *sewakas* (Brahmins who serve Jagannātha) have settled along the east-west axis, for example, but side by side with blacksmiths, carpenters and the *diwān*, the Little King's minister, and the *karana*, the accountant of the temple. The ritual axis, *baḍadaṇḍa*, was originally lined with only a small row of houses on the eastern side, as the opposite side belonged to the royal family. This pattern changed in the 1920s when a Marwari trader occupied a plot on the western side and constructed a pretentious building, an imitation of the king's palace. Since then, *baḍadaṇḍa* has turned into a market street where old houses with thatched roofs have been replaced by multi-storeyed reinforced concrete structures.

The north-south orientation of the settlement is even reflected in the location of the cremation ground. About two kilometres north of Ranpur, the cremation ground for commoners and members of scheduled castes is situated on the banks of a river. The royal cremation ground remained near the site of the former fort, Upargaḍa. The Muslim cemetery (Mosani Padiā) lies at the southern end of the axis, which is not straight but inclines with the slope of the hill. Not surprisingly, the inhabitants of Nuagaon, the 'model village' planned after the great fire of 1943, have a separate cremation ground beyond the Muslim cemetery. Ritually speaking, Nuagaon is treated as a separate entity that cannot be absorbed by the original settlement.

The urbanistic pattern (Fig. 4) of Ranpur clearly reveals a plan, the basic element of which is a neighbourhood (*sāhi*) with quarters that differ considerably in size. Two rows of houses face a broad area, similar to what in England is known as a common or in Germany, an 'Anger'. It is strictly a rural element that was multiplied to form the centre of a Little Kingdom. The surrounding villages demonstrate this spatial organisation more clearly, where a large open space in front of the house belongs to the plot. The actual 'public' space is thus much narrower than visually discernible. The house itself extends over two or three courtyards in depth and marks the centre between the forecourt and a long back yard that is accessible from the back by a narrow 'service lane'. The lane provides access on both sides. Half of Ranpur's quarters are organised in an east-west direction, the other half in a north-south direction. This change in direction produces a T-shaped pattern that makes small connecting lanes obligatory. The original fabric is much obscured by the changes made in the wake of the fire in 1943 that devastated most of the town. Long rows of houses were reduced to smaller ones, creating additional access lanes that altered the basic linear system to a grid pattern.

Each settlement in the coastal belt of Orissa requires ponds to bridge the dry season. Some are architecturally framed, with steps leading down from an artificial dam. Sixteen of them surround the settlement. The chronicle even mentions the "digging of a tank" named Baḍa Sāmukā and two ponds, joined at the end of the 19th century, were pretentiously named "Sagara" (ocean).

Doḷameḷaṇa – the festival of renewal in spring (Fig. 5-9)

Almost every ritual in the calendar of festive events that occur in Ranpur is enacted according to models developed in Puri itself or in the context of the agricultural cycle as observed in the fertile valleys of the major rivers of Orissa. They include *doḷameḷaṇa*, literally "the meeting of swings", which is widely practiced around full moon in Phālguṇa (February/March), known in Orisssa as Doḷapūrṇimā. In Ranpur, the entire festival is called *pañcadoḷayātrā* in memory of the final event on the fifth day after full moon, when all the swings (*doḷa*) of the 'Little King' of Ranpur's former territory are carried in a procession (*yātrā*) towards a central ritual ground. As Heinrich von Stietencron observes, "the swing festival (*doḷotsava*) for Kṛṣṇa or Rādhā and Kṛṣṇa (...) is common to many parts of India" (Stietencron 2001: 364), but only in Orissa does it herald the most significant of the many festivals related to spring as the beginning of the agricultural season.

Ranpur does not have a tradition of constructing separate swings. It is the small portable shrine (*vimāna*) that houses the movable image of a god (*calantī pratimā*) for a certain time, one that represents the god enshrined in the temple. During a procession, the god visits the houses of devotees in response to an invitation. The god is praised on this occasion and receives offerings in exchange for granting *darśana*, "the eye contact or vision that confers divine blessing" (Stietencron 2001: 365).

The small shrine is shaped like a real temple with an open ground floor, complete with four or twelve elaborately carved columns if it is to be based on a square or eight for an octagon. The superstructure is mostly two-tiered, complete with a pinnacle in the shape of a *kalaśa* and *triśūla* or snake-hood. If the shrine shelters a form of Viṣṇu, the pinnacle has a disc form. In rare cases (like No. 56, Baluṅkeśvara from Mangarajpur), the supported structure is open, with a lobed arch adorned with *makara* creatures at the base. The roofs and individual columns are covered with red velvet. Frills in white or yellow emerge from the eaves, flower garlands form a second layer over the architectural shape, with a flag on top completing the impression of a temple.

Two bamboo poles are fixed below the shrine or at the sides, converting it into a palanquin, which is then carried by four *sewakas* from its original temple. A *sewaka* from the Mali community heads the procession, banging a metal plate (*ghaṇṭa*). In many cases, another Mali follows with a ceremonial umbrella.

Having arrived at the square, which measures roughly 100 by 70 metres, the palanquin is placed on one of the 108 platforms (*doḷamaṇḍapa*) that are lined up in groups of twelve along the edge. Throughout the year, many of these platforms are covered with food stalls. The stalls are removed for the *yātrā* and the platforms repaired and coloured in a light blue.

Similar to most places in Orissa, the Ranpur swing festival extends over eleven days and can be divided into three phases. It begins with *phālguṇa śukla daśamī*, five days prior to full moon and extends five days beyond full moon. The first phase ends before full moon, the second is performed on the day of full moon and the third begins after full moon.

First phase: tenth to fourteenth day preceding full moon

The festival starts with Rasayātrā, i.e., a form of Kṛṣṇa kept in the Rasabihari Maṭh is paraded along the ritual axis of the town with the four Śaiva 'ministers' of Jagannātha, namely Harihareśvara, whose temple is located within the compound of Jagannātha, Candreśvara, Svapneśvara, and the two Mahādevas who guard the southern and northern directions, Baluṅkeśvara in Purnavasanta and Daṇḍabaluṅkeśvara near the large Sagara Pokhari. They all meet Doḷagovinda or Madhanmohana, the representation of Jagannātha that leaves the temple every night.

The night before full moon, a momentous procession is undertaken in anticipation of the concluding event. Around nine o'clock in the evening, only two palanquins arrive at the gate of the Jagannātha temple, since the other three are not removed from the respective temples. Thus, Harihareśvara and Daṇḍabaluṅkeśvara join Svapneśvara in his palanquin and Baluṅkeśvara joins Candreśvara. An hour later, Doḷagovinda appears in a palanquin with Lakṣmī and Bālakṛṣṇa, a representation of Kṛṣṇa as a child. All of them are iconographically identifiable bronze images, ritually transformed for this purpose into a living body of god. In the context of the Doḷameḷaṇa, the divine pair of Govinda (in the shape of a four-armed Viṣṇu with his four attributes) and Lakṣmī can be identified as Rādhā-Kṛṣṇa. This palanquin rushes immediately towards the north-south axis, heading north in the direction of the ritual ground. Svapneśvara's palanquin follows suit with the third one close behind (Fig. 1). Five servants of the Jagannātha temple head the procession: a Sankhua with his conch shell (*śaṅkha*) and a Bariko (from the community of barbers) with a torch in front, followed by three Mali with a metal plate (*ghaṇṭa*). A formal halt is observed in front of the Caitanya Maṭh and a few more stops in answer to requests by devotees along the road. In this case, the four carriers from the community of farmers (Cyasah) put down sticks of equal length to support the carrying poles.

The three palanquins are place in a row facing east at Pañcadoḷa Padiā, the ritual ground. A Ratha Brahmin performs a ritual at the centre of the ground to the sound of the metal plates before a straw fire dedicated to Maṇināgeśvarī is lit. The fire marks or indeed purifies the spot where the powerful goddess that protects the Little King's territory will be placed on the final day of the swing festival.

The procession returns along the ritual axis without further stops, turns to the temple of Svapneśvara in the west, adds a detour through the southern quarters of the town and arrives back at the temple of Jagannātha two hours after midnight.

Second phase: full moon – doḷapūrṇimā

In the morning of full moon, the palanquin carrying Doḷagovinda, Lakṣmī and Bālakṛṣṇa appears at around nine to be placed on the Doḷavedi in front of the palace. Since the arch of the structure was lost decades ago, the palanquin is placed on the ground of the large platform. Two ceremonial umbrellas are placed on either side, while a large canopy covers almost the entire platform (Fig. 2). The sons of the last acting king, who still resides in the palace behind the platform, worship the gods in the palanquin and offerings are brought by many of the people. The most meaningful act, however, is the offering of green mangos and jackfruit to the gods, which heralds the beginning of the spring season.

All 109 gods of the territory of Ranpur that join the Pañcadoḷayātrā are brought to their respective platforms. On 9th March 2001, however, when I was present at the ceremony, I did not notice a single palanquin swinging. They are simply placed on a platform for a couple of hours and returned to their temples in the afternoon. In Ranpur itself, five Mahādevas and the gods of nine Maṭhas and the Nṛsiṅgha temple arrive at their respective platforms. The five Mahādevas leave their temples again in the evening to join Doḷagovinda in his nocturnal excursion, doing so for the last time the following day, which is observed as Holipūrṇimā.

This day stands for another aspect of changing seasons. Young men make their rounds throwing colour. Whoever is caught will fall victim to their desire. As the borders of social behaviour and hierarchy are obliterated, obscene shouting is a regular and accepted feature of this event. Shops remain closed and houses firmly locked for a couple of hours to confine the youngsters to their chosen battlefield, the Baḍadaṇḍa. Holi is very much a liminal event. It is placed neither here nor there. As an in-between, it defies accepted rules of social behaviour and serves as an outlet to channel aggression that cannot be expressed otherwise.

Third phase: Pañcadoḷayātrā

The administrative servant (Karana) of the Jagannātha temple, Gopināth Mohanty, sends an invitation to all movable gods in Ranpur territory well in advance: 15 altogether in Ranpur itself and 92 in villages that mark the cultivated and to a large extent irrigated tracts of land. Only Rādhakaṇṭha (No. 36) comes from Siko, from that legendary place where Śiva in the form of Bankaniddhi was instrumental in the reconfirmation of Ranpur as a place of kingship.

These gods leave their temples on the fifth day (*pañcamī*) after full moon and arrive in Ranpur after midnight. The majority of 41 palanquins come from the southern villages, seven alone from Gopalpur. Four come from the southwest, where cultivated land stretches like a finger into the forest, and Khilamuṇḍa resides. Five come from the west and five from the east (including Siko, located beyond the territory of Ranpur Tahasil and identical with the former princely state). The remaining 36 arrive from the north, three alone from Sunakhala, an important market place at the border to the former neighbouring state of Khandpara.

The palanquins are paraded with tremendous pomp towards the designated ritual ground, Pañcadoḷa Padiā. Colourful animals in bizarre forms are brought on cycle rikshas. The night passes with dancing for the gods and with songs of praise (*kīrtana*). Collective excitement fills the access roads in Ranpur. They say, however, that in the old days performances accompanying the event were much more lavish and varied. People were armed as guardians of the gods in the shape of serpents (*nāga*s) or demons (*asura*s), preferably on wooden horses (*gohora nacha*).

The people from Gopalpur were so disappointed that they organised a similar congregation known as *satdoḷa*, which referred to the seven gods of Gopalpur who participate in the Ranpur congregation. Moreover, a further 11 shrines (*vimāna*) from Gopalpur and three from neighbouring villages (Champapedi, Dimiria and Mahatpala) also take part. On the seventh day (*saptamī*) after full moon, 21 doḷas roam around Gopalpur to present *prasāda*, the gift of grace.

The congregation at the Pañcadoḷa Padiā is strictly organised. Each doḷa has its 'innate' place to which it turns annually. There are 108 platforms to support the palanquins. The sequence around the square does not reflect the topographical reality of the kingdom, primarily because the square itself is divided by an imaginary line. The host or master of the place (*thānapati*, Skt. *sthānapati*), in this case Jagannātha represented by Doḷagovinda, is placed at the centre. The western part of the almost circular congregation is reserved for images of Viṣṇu, i.e., Jagannātha and Kṛṣṇa or Rādhā-Kṛṣṇa, and the eastern part for those of Śiva. This configuration suggests a strong element of what Stietencron (2002: 379) coined as the meeting of Viṣṇu and Śiva (*hari-hara-bheṭa*). In contrast to the case studies presented by Stietencron, the Śaiva element dominates in Ranpur. In March 2000, 63 images of Śiva were placed to the left of Doḷagovinda and 44 of Viṣṇu to his right. A further image of Kṛṣṇa, Brajavihari from Brajavihari Maṭh in Purnavasanta, is placed between Doḷagovinda and the five Mahādeva ministers of Jagannātha, starting with Svapneśvara. People say that Doḷagovinda cannot be placed next to Śiva and Brajavihari is needed as a mediator between them to soften a somewhat critical constellation. The division of the circle, which follows an iconic imperative and avoids reflecting a spatial order of the Little King's territory, the alternative option, results in a sequence that does not suggest an order of any kind. Convincing, however, is the fact that Doḷagovinda is framed by his retinue from Ranpur itself, six on his left (including Brajavihari from Purnavasanta) and eight on his right. Jagannātha appears twice as Dadhivāmana, eight times as Patitapāvana, the "Purifier of the Fallen Ones", and twice as Trutīyādeva, literally the "Third God" – another name provided by the rural population for their favourite god of the triad of Puri, represented by Jagannātha, flanked by Balabhadra and Subhadra (Stietencron 1978: 471). In all three cases the wooden image of Jagannātha is referred to. Dadhivāmana (*vāmana* refers to Kṛṣṇa as a child, not to Viṣṇu as the dwarf incarnation) first appeared in the 12th century, while the concept of Patitapāvana – referring to a painting of Jagannātha, which in Ranpur is found inside the eastern compound gate as well as at the southern entrance to the Jagamohana of the temple – originated in the 18th century. Likewise, Trutīyādeva is singled out from the Triad of Puri as the only one belonging to low-class people. As Stietencron puts it (1978: ibid.): "Only Jagannātha really belongs to the region and loves his people even if their social status is low". The majority of Viṣṇu's representations, however, appear as Gopinātha, Caitanya, Brajavihari (five times) or Rādhāmohana (six times), to name but a few. Among the representations of Mahādeva, most of the nineteen are present in the form of Baluṅkeśvara, followed by Nīlakaṇṭheśvara, the "Blue-throated", which represents Śiva swallowing, at Brahmā's request, the poison entitled *halāhala* that emerged during the Churning of the Ocean. Śiva is also present six times as the 'Lord of the place' (Lokeśvara), as the 'Lord of magical power' (Siddheśvara) or as the 'Immortal One' (Amṛteśvara). Each village can produce an explanation or a legend that accounts for the emergence of the specific deity enshrined in the village temple, duplicated at a later stage in order to be movable and participate in a number of ritual events.

In March 2001, a total of 107 gods convened in Ranpur to occupy 106 of the 108 platforms, which were duly renovated and ready to receive guests. Ramalalaju from Kankia (No. 27) and Mukteśvara from Mayurjhalia (No. 20) were absent. A new representation of Kṛṣṇa, Banabihari from Nathapur (No. 44), has occupied the last platform in the row of images of Viṣṇu/Kṛṣṇa (No. 44) since 1991. The platforms of the absent gods cannot be taken by newcomers. Therefore, the second god from Jamadeipur, Brajabihari (No. 22), had to share a platform with Patitapāvana, who traditionally represents Jamadeipur. This process demonstrates that the sequence of the gods is not necessarily fixed. If a god remains absent for a number of years, a new one will take the seat.

The congregation culminates in the arrival of the representation of Maṇināgeśvarī, which has been kept on the ground floor of the Little King's palace for the last couple of years. The goddess arrives in a small shrine with a second layer on top of it, in a light temporary bamboo and paper structure composed of two columns flanked by lions, the goddess's mount, that support a five-lobed arch with *makara* creatures at its lower points and a disc (*cakra*) as Jagannātha's emblem on top. Seven plaques of wood with paintings of kingship symbols are fixed to the broad structure that rests on three carrying poles. The palanquin is placed at the centre of the ritual ground, facing east.

On the following day, the sixth day after full moon, the 'Lord of the Place', Jagannātha, feeds the 108 guests who convened at the centre of his sacred realm (*kṣetra*) in response to his invitation. The guests had left their immediate *kṣetra*, defined by the cultivated area of their respective villages, and represented them, as it were, at the centre. It is here that Jagannātha, who never leaves his micro-realm, is faced with the visual representation of his meso-realm. On such an occasion, however, the congregation aims at reaching beyond: Doḷagovinda presides over the circle, flanked by his four powerful ministers, the guardians of the cosmos, but at the same time he joins his retinue to submit to the powerful mountain goddess. Maṇināgeśvarī symbolises the origin of the place that was colonised by Jagannātha and his followers. On the meaningful day that marks the passage of the seasons and as such provokes renewal, the 'new' gods that colonised her territory demonstrate their loyalty and revive their ties with the chthonic power of the place.

Levels of understanding

Space and Time

The spring equinox is a perfect occasion for rituals of renewal throughout the northern hemisphere of the world. Calendrical diversity, however, permits fixing this day differently. The Gregorian solar calendar designates the 21st March as the day. Incorrect calculations caused its gradual shifting towards the 14th April, the first day of the month of Vaiśākha, which in many subcultures of the Subcontinent is still celebrated as New Year. In Orissa, the March full moon, Doḷāpurṇimā, represents the alternative according to the lunar calendar.

New Year calls by definition for a ritual of renewal to ensure continuity of time and space, continuity of individual and collective life, human beings and even gods in a given territorial situation, be it a single structure, a village, an imperial city, a royal or a divine territory. In Ranpur, the ritual adresses the territory of the 'Little King', which is identified on the occasion as a divine territory presided over by Maṇināgeśvarī. Her presence in the centre of a circle of a substantial number of gods ensures and confirms the territorial set-up. Taking similar ritual events into account, one could even talk of a rebirth, in which context the fire lit on the congregation site the night before full moon probably indicates death or at least a comprehensive cleansing of the place of evil influences.

One does not have to turn to Babylon, where the gods representing urban quarters were paraded through the streets to celebrate their presence for another year, to find similarities. Much closer, in the urban culture of the Newars in the Kathmandu Valley of Nepal, all movable images of the gods and goddesses who accept blood sacrifices as the primary offering (Bhairava, Durgā and Gaṇeśa) leave their 'house' (*dyaḥchē*) in town on Caitra *māsānta*, the last day of the 12th month. They are brought to the place of their non-iconic representation in the form of a stone (*pīṭha*), often located beyond the limits of the settlements. These secondary representations of divine power return in a sense to their place of origin to be created or born again for the period of another year. They return to their 'house' along a processional route that addresses the respective quarter of the god or goddess – a suitable occasion to be welcomed by the people.

The idea of renewal and birth are additionally expressed on yet another scale – the entire territory of the Newars. Legend has it that the valley was drained by the act of cutting the mountain ridges. The *bodhisattva* Mañjuśrī, who stands for wisdom, learning and creation, achieved this with his powerful sword, removing ignorance and any other obstruction. In this case, land was made habitable and a *koṭwal*, a guardian in the shape of Bhairava, was placed where the draining river Bāgmatī leaves the valley. A ritual for the New Year, Vaiśākha Saṃkranti, is enacted on precisely this spot – probably not solely to remember a mythical event but to celebrate its renewal and thus confirm its cosmogonic relevance.

To return to Ranpur: the mobile representation of Maṇināgeśvarī, the *iṣṭadevatā* of the 'Little King' and thus the tutelary deity of his territory, leaves the palace shrine to what could be described as a demonstration of loyalty by all the village gods and above all by Jagannātha and his 'ministers'. At this point, the notion of the 'Little Kingdom' turns into a 'Divine Kingdom'. Maṇināgeśvarī rules the divine kingdom, while the 'Little King' becomes her tool in profane matters. Hermann Kulke referred to Jagannātha's annual coronation ceremony, during which he is visited by sub-regional deities, including Maṇināgeśvarī. This event has been translated into the image of a tent, with Eight Mother Godesses forming the tent pegs and Jagannātha representing the supporting central pole (Kulke 1980: 31). This idea is certainly applicable to Ranpur, when we consider the 108 gods that represent the tent pegs, with Maṇināgeśvarī depicting the centre, and even more so than anywhere else, since the congregation of gods at the Pañcadoḷa form a circle around the tutelary goddess.

Symbolic associations

The figure 108 is well-known feature in a number of ritual and spatial contexts. We know of 108 names of Annapūrṇā in Vārāṇasī, of 108 sources of Gaṅgā in the Himālaya and of 108 *rudrākṣas*, berries used to make Śaiva rosaries – to mention but a few. A popular association in Orissa is the occasional illustration of Jagannātha, the Lord of the World, is illustrated accompanied 108 pots of water.

The notion of 108 as an auspicious number is not confined to the sphere of religion, if we recall the return of a Chinese spaceship on 1st April 2002. The Chinese administration announced that the spaceship had landed safely in Inner Mongolia having completed 108 orbits around the earth and that it took 162 hours (i.e., two times 81, which is nine times nine etc.) to complete the celestial journey.

To begin with, 108 represents nine times twelve, while the sum of the digits is nine. A more simple analysis reveals that nine represents space by referring to the four cardinal and intermediate directions as well as the centre, while twelve represents the twelve annual cycles of the moon, which in the solar context became months. Indeed, a perfect number to represent or demarcate space. The *doḷameḷana* in Ranpur achieves both. The congregation of 108 gods represents the territory of the former feudatory state, while at the same time the deities create a circle-like (*maṇḍala*) space around the presiding goddess at the centre.

Built in the 7th century, Borobudur forms a three-dimensional *maṇḍala* that is based on a multiple of 108. On a more simple level, the Khalkha Mongols reintroduced Buddhism to Central Mongolia in 1586 by founding a monastery with a wall enclosure that is said to have once supported 108 *stūpas*. And Geser Khan, Mongolia's legendary hero, is reported to have built a town with 108 bastions after his victorious battle against the enemy (Heissig 1992: 104).

Finally, the sacred journey along the perimeter of Kāśī/Vārāṇasī, *pañcakrośīyātrā*, should be remarked on. A circumambulatory path, punctuated by temples, shrines and sacred places can be traced to the 16th century. One century later, 108 of these places were numbered to make the pilgrimage significant on another level.

In the case of both the monastery in Mongolia and the processional path at Kāśī, a spatial entity is defined by a number that opens up the obviously required cosmic associations. Likewise, the *rājā* and his Ranpur Brahmins aimed at shaping the 'Little Kingdom' according to norms that appeared to be 'universally' recognised.

Conclusion

In his case studies on Harirājpur (Puri District) and Arilo (Cuttack District), Heinrich von Stietencron identified an overwhelming dominance of Vaiṣṇava kīrtanas and dances and has no doubt that the festival basically addresses Rādhākṛṣṇa. He did, however, question "the justification, the meaning and the purpose of the festival", as he saw "little sense" (Stietencron 2001: 381) in such a congregation from a theological perspective. He continually searched for "the 'true' motif that led to the introduction of this festival in bygone days". To my understanding, he found the right answer when he claimed that "a network of loyalty" is renewed and thereby confirmed. He further acknowledged that "once a year the deity of the landowners [unites] with the deities of their labourers and clientele in a common festival" (Stietencron 2001: 383). While this is certainly true for the case studies Stietencron refers to, the landowner turns out to be the 'Little King' in Ranpur, where the deities of the clientele are those of the village, the *grāmadevatās*, who demonstrate loyalty to the tutelary goddess, represented by Maṇināgeśvarī, a Hinduised tribal deity. Hermann Kulke stressed this point by declaring that "in order to keep tribal loyalty and support, patronage of the great goddess and her cult was still most essential for internal and vertical legitimation" (Kulke 1980: 36).

The congregation of 108 gods on the occasion of *doḷameḷana* in Ranpur supports this notion and provides a good answer with regard to the driving force, the 'true' motif behind the "unusual and concerted mobility of so many gods" (Stietencron 2001: 378). After the *rājā* had moved his palace towards the newly-established urbanised settlement in the second half of the 18th century, the festival was probably introduced to ensure, if not enforce, a demonstration of loyalty from the surrounding villages, loyalty to the tutelary goddess of the entire territory, which was simultaneously the *iṣṭadevatā*, the tribal deity 'chosen' by the 'Little King' in support of his divine affiliation.

Among the many rituals of the festive calendar, *doḷameḷana* was and still is one of numerous events where ties between the king and his subjects, the tutelary goddess and her retinue, are renewed.

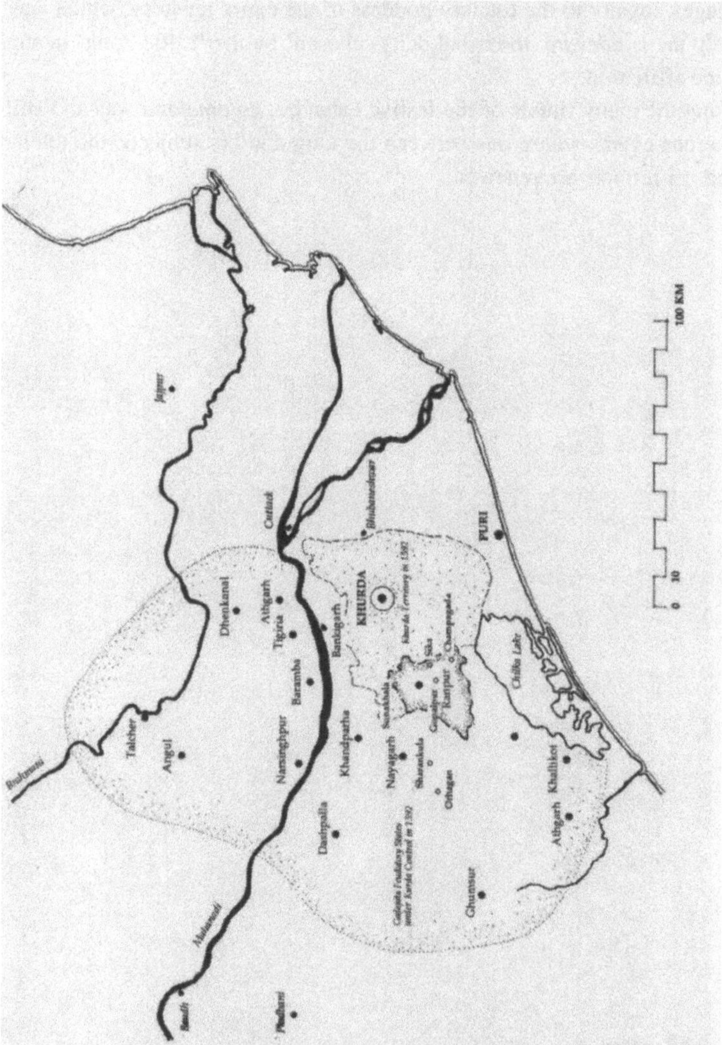

Fig. 1: Identification of the capitals of the 15 feudatory states (or 'Little Kingdoms') that, with the exception of Ranpur, were under the control of the king of Khurda from the end of the 16th century. Sika belonged to Ranpur while Sharankula in the west was at times contested.

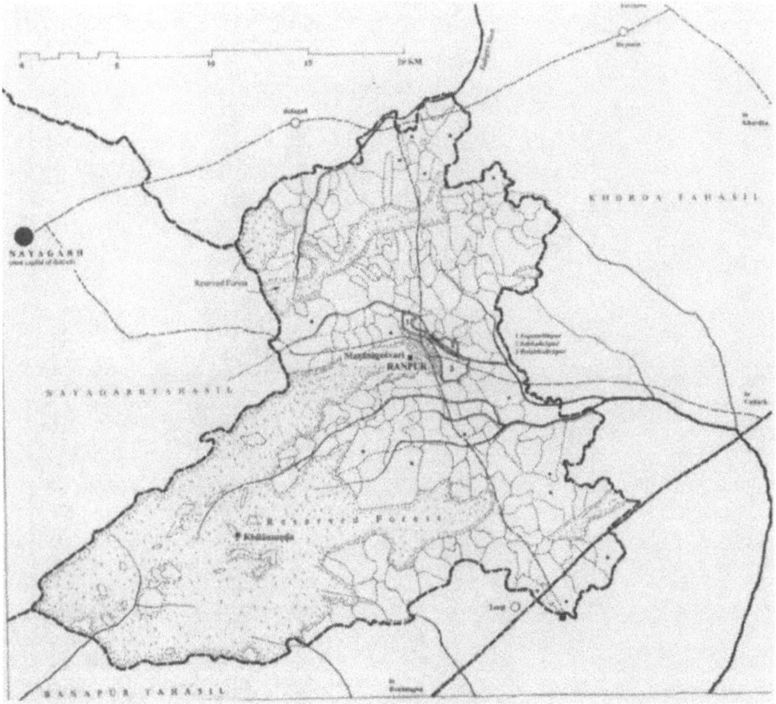

Fig. 2: The boundaries of Ranpur Tahasil, which correspond to those of the former Ranpur State. The map prepared for the 1981 census shows that more than a third of the entire area remained "reserved forest".

It is said that the king of Ranpur originally had three places or "forts" (*gada*) to resort to, Ukutukumei in the Southwest with its Khila Munda shrine, Champagada in the Southeast, and Sanagada located north of the hill that penetrates into the eastern, largely cultivated area. East of the hill lies "Ranapur Gada" with its Jagannātha temple just below the temple of Maṇināgeśvarī. Ranapur Gada is surrounded by a belt of three revenue areas without a settlement, namely Jagannāthpur, Subhadrapur and Balabhadrapur.

On the occasion of Durgāpūjā and in the shape of a bamboo pole, the goddess Khila Munda is brought to Ranpur by procession from her shrine near Ukutukumei.

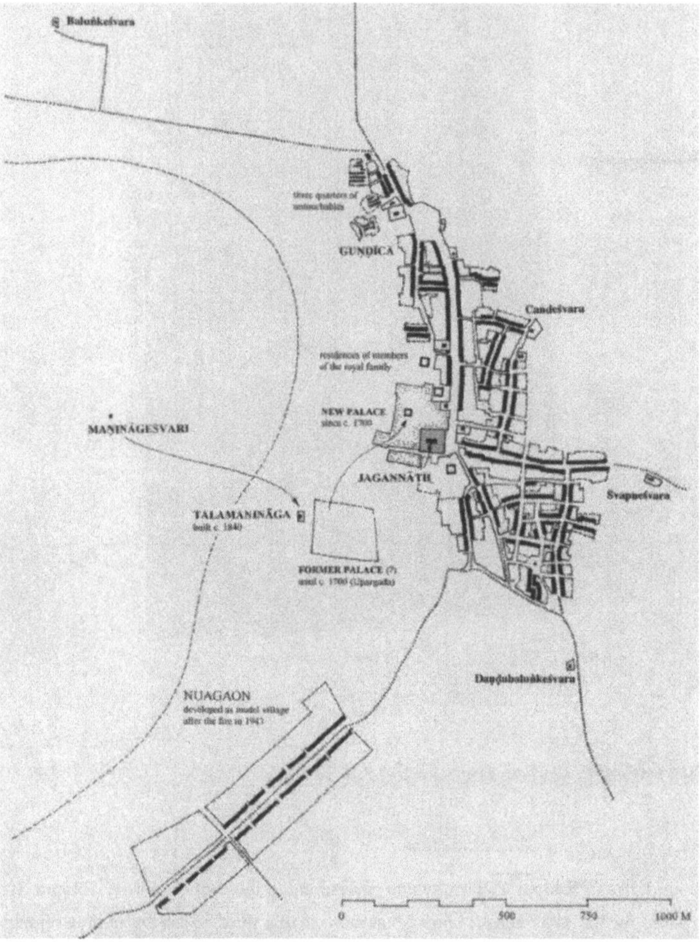

Fig. 3: Spatial and institutional development of Ranpur from the 17th century to the creation of a model village after a fire had devastated the original village in 1943.

The cronicles mention the relocation of the palace from Upargaḍa to north of Jagannātha by Rama Chandra Narendra, who ruled from 1692 to 1727, and the construction of a temple for Maṇināga by Braj Sunder Bajradhar Narendra, who ruled from 1821 to 1842. The surrounding Śiva temples towards the east were built earlier, while the temples of Harihareśvara, Daṇḍabaluṅkesvara und Baluṅkesvara were built by Banamali Narendra, who ruled from 1628 to 1663. The latter "developed the town, its main road and the streets" – an activity that involved major extension.

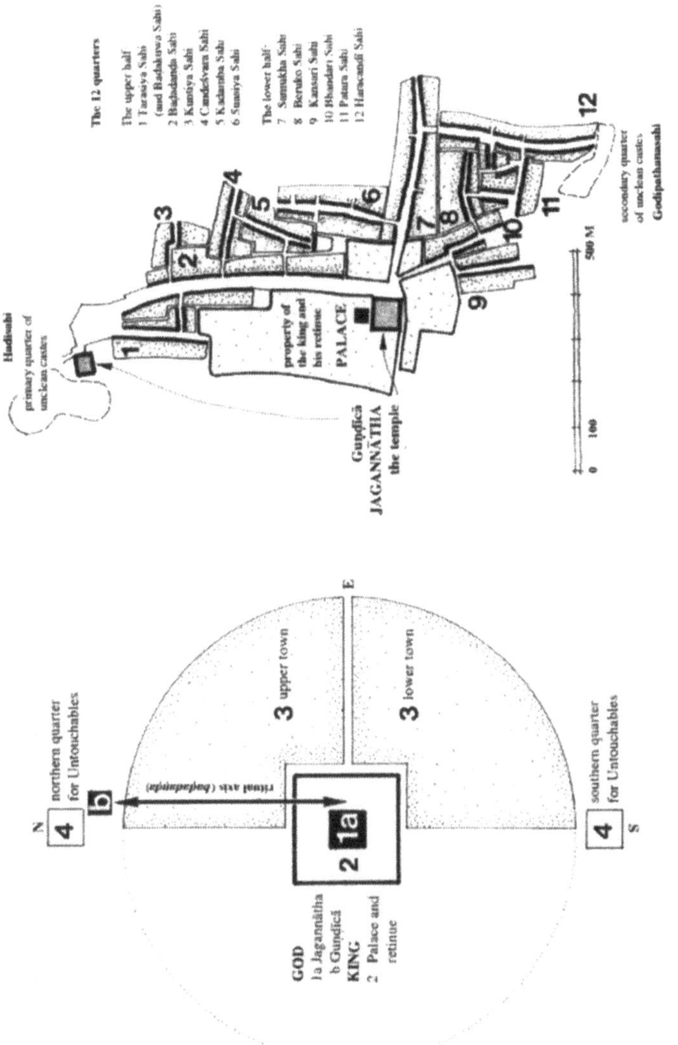

Fig. 4: Diagrammatic representation of the urban territory – sacred and profane.
Jagannātha (1) with his temple (1a) and his summer residence at Guṇḍīcā (1b) form the ideal centre, almost identical with the adjacent palace (2) and courtier quarters.
The ritual/processional axis (*baḍadaṇḍa*) between the temple (1a) and the summer residence in Guṇḍīcā (1b) forms the "backbone" of the urban development.
The urban area (3) is divided by an east-west axis (Samukha Sahi) with six quarters in the "upper" town and six in the "lower" town. This spatial division into two halves is mirrored by two quarters designated for scheduled castes (Hadisahi in the north and Godipathanasahi in the south) and Muslims (4).

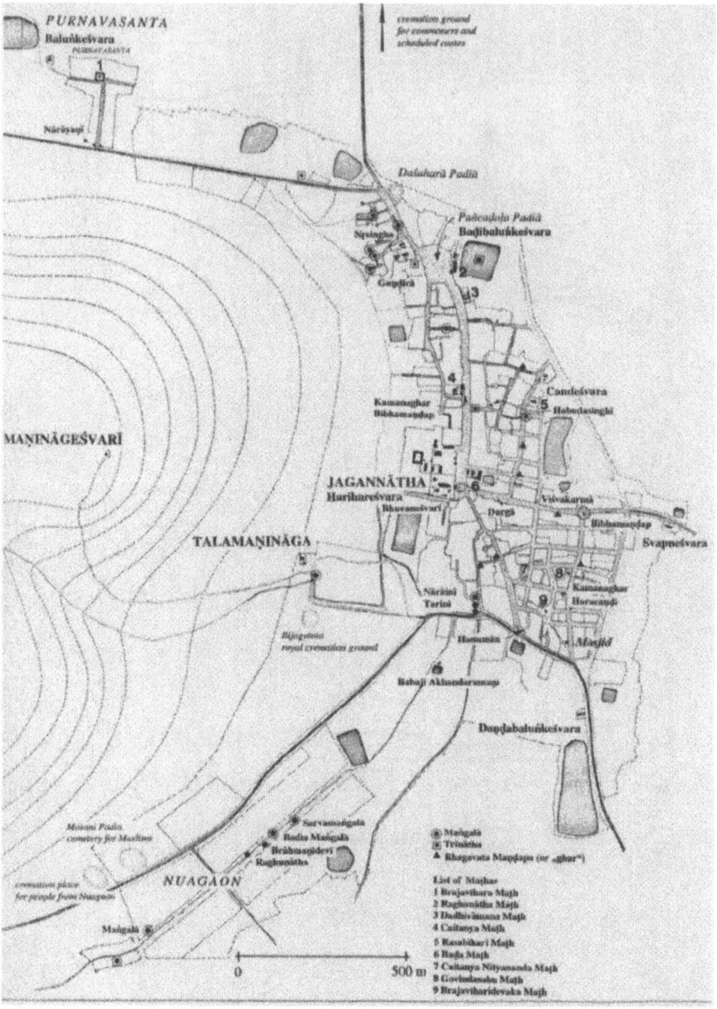

Fig. 5: Religious infrastructure

Besides the temples dedicated to Jagannātha, Maṇināga and Durgā (like Bhuvaneśvarī, Haracaṇḍī, Brāhmaṇīdevī), the five Mahādevas and the nine maṭhas, ten shrines are dedicated to Maṅgalā and four to Trinātha. There were also seven houses in honour of Bhagavatī.

Four cremation places are reserved for people of royal descent (near Talamaṇināga), for commoners (a few hundred yards to the north), for Muslims (north of Nuagaon) and for residents of Nuagaon (southwest of Nuagaon).

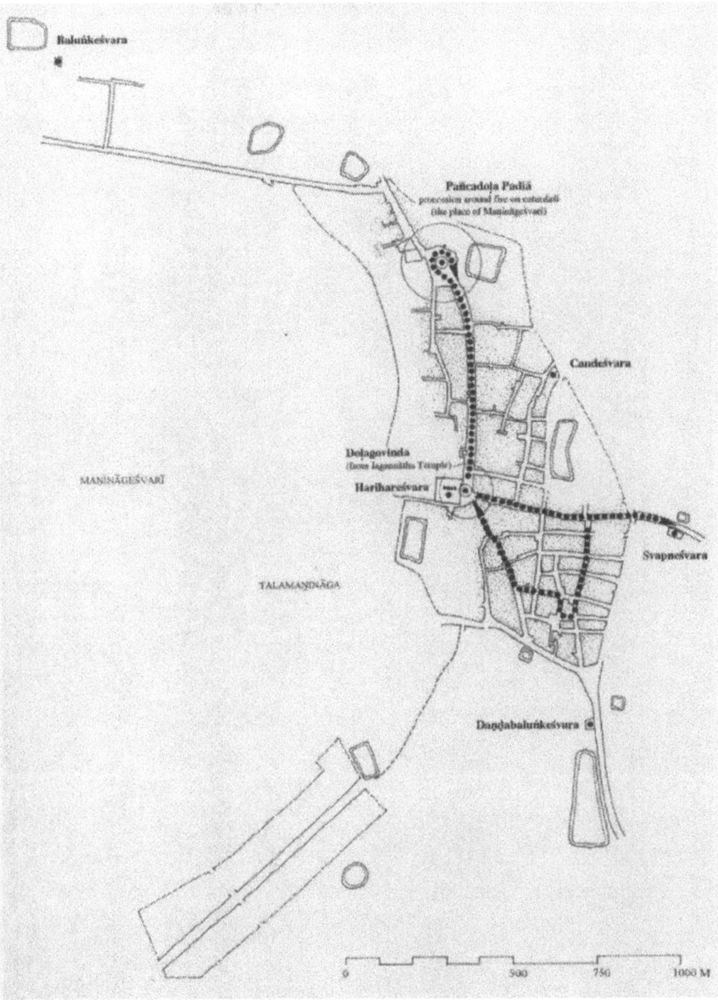

Fig. 6: Doḷameḷaṇa – the five Mahādevas, ministers of Jagannātha marked by a dot, convene at the centrally located temple for a period of seven days to accompany Doḷagovinda (also called Madanmohana) and Lakṣmī on a nocturnal procession. The night before Doḷapūrṇimā, this troupe parades to the festival ground, Pañcadoḷa Padiā, where a fire marks the spot Maṇināgeśvarī will be placed on five days later. From there, the procession leads to the temple of Svapneśvara in the east and returns to Jagannātha after a detour to the maṭhas of the southern quarters.

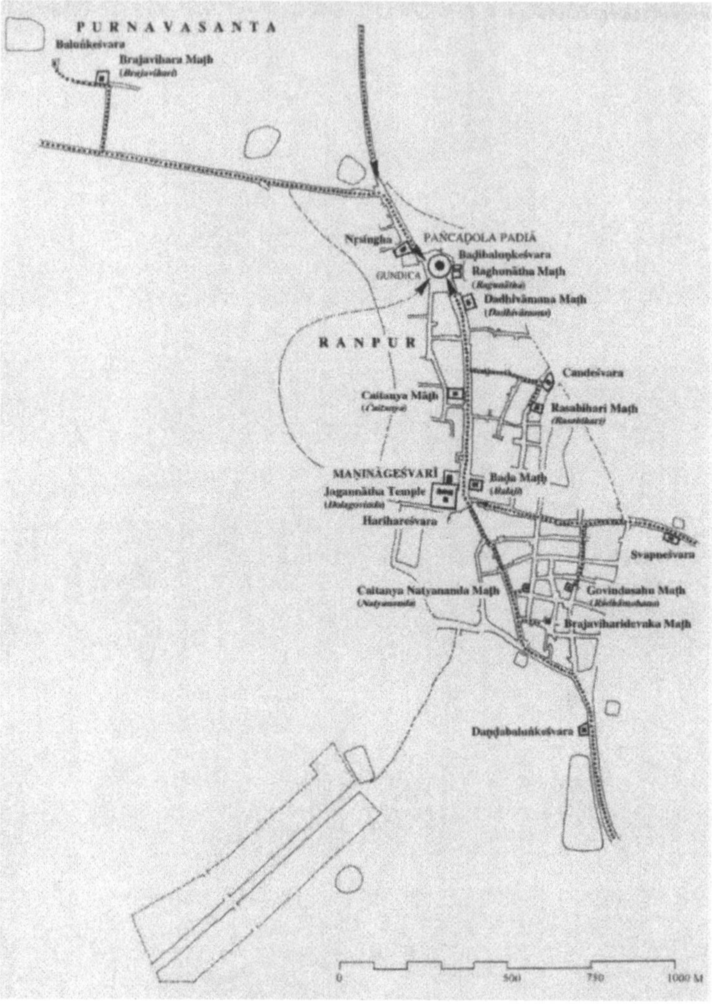

Fig. 7: Pañcadoḷayātrā, – on the fifth day after full moon in March (14th March 2000), 109 gods and goddesses from the territory of the former Ranpur State (including one from Siko) convene at Pañcadoḷa Padiā, the large square at the northern end of Baḍadaṇḍa road. They form a full circle around Maṇināgeśvarī, who is brought there from the palace. From Ranpur itself, the gods from nine maṭhas and the Nṛsingha temple as well as the five Mahādevas are carried to the square in their litters (*vimāna*).

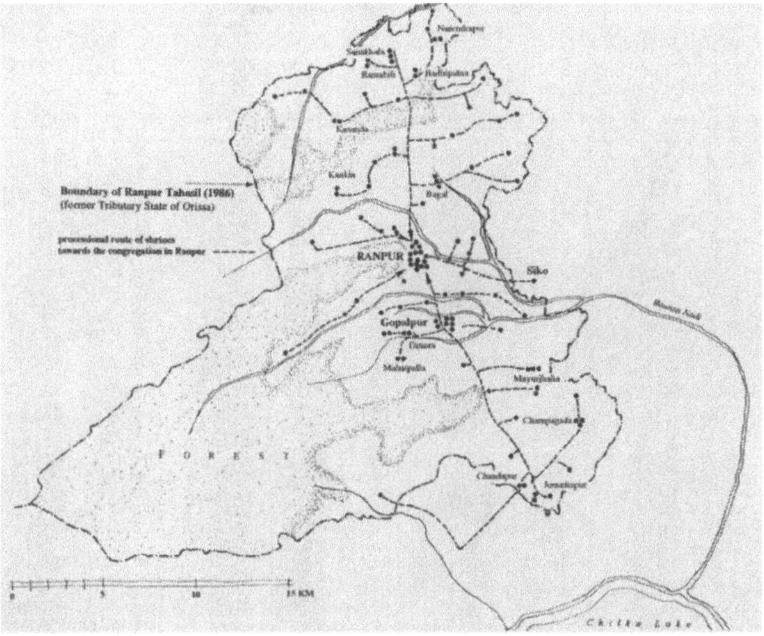

Fig. 8: Pañcadoḷayātrā – on the fifth day after full moon in March (14th March 2000), 109 gods and goddesses from the territory of former Ranpur State (including one from Siko) convene at the ceremonial ground, Pañcaḍoḷa Padiā. Most arrive in processions that originate at Sunakhala in the north (39 *vimānas*) or from Champagada and Chandapur in the south (34 *vimānas*).

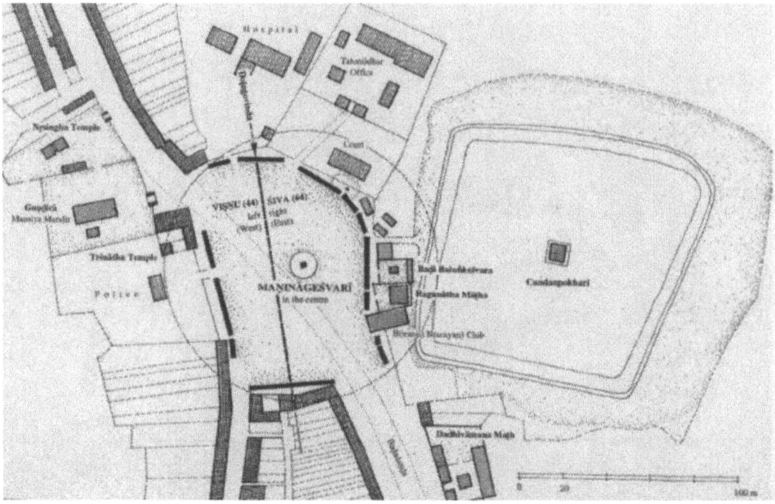

Fig. 9: Pañcadoḷayātrā - on the fifth day after full moon in spring (in the month of Phālguṇa, 14th March 2000), 109 gods from Ranpur and the territory of the former Ranpur State (including one from neighbouring Siko) convene in movable representation (*calantī pratimā*) at the ceremonial ground, Pañcadoḷa Padiā. Maṇināgeśvarī, the tutelary goddess of the king, takes up the central position to which all portable shrines (*vimāna*) are oriented. The gods and goddesses of her territory are placed on platforms (*maṇḍapas*) in such a way that they almost form a circle – a maṇḍala – around the centre.

The circle is divided by an axis that follows the direction of the main urban ritual axis, the Baḍadaṇḍa: 64 representations of Śiva are located on the eastern side, 44 representations of Viṣṇu/Kṛṣṇa are located on the western side. The (unnumbered) central position in the north is held by Doḷagovinda as a representation of Jagannātha.

Fig. 10: Doḷapūrṇimā
The portable shrine sent from the temple of Jaganātha with movable representations of Madanmohana (representing Jagannātha), Lakṣmī and Balakṛṣṇa on the Doḷavedī, the royal platform placed along the ritual axis in front of the early 20th century palace.

Photograph: Niels Gutschow, March 9, 2001

Fig. 11: Pañcadoḷayātrā on the fifth day after Doḷa- or Holipūrṇimā: 109 portable shrines (*vimāna*) from the villages of the former Ranpur State convened in 2000 at the ceremonial ground, Pañcadoḷa Padiā, to be worshipped the following day. Detail of the northeastern corner of the ritual ground with portable shrines (see list nos. 16-43) placed on platforms (from left to right).

Photograph: Rashmi Ranjam Patnaik, March, 26, 2000

Fig. 12: Talla Maṇināga, the lower Jewel Serpent in the shape of Durgā, complete with shield and sword, whereby the sword and subsidiary elements of identification are veiled by a layer of vermilion.

Photograph: Niels Gutschow, 16 January 2002

Fig. 13: Memorial stones of unidentified kings of Ranpur (17th / 18th centuries) placed along the rear wall of the temple of Talla Maṇināga.

Photograph: Niels Gutschow, 16 January 2002

The Stolen Goddess
Ritual Enactments of Power and Authority in Orissa

Burkhard Schnepel

Preface

Kulke has been well-known and rightly praised for his studies of the cult of Jagannath and its multi-faceted interrelationships with the Gajapati kingship. However, he is, unjustifiably, less well known for his equally significant studies of the ritual policy of the little kingdoms or "Feudatory States" in the hinterland of central Orissa.[1] As early as 1976, at a time when little-kingdom studies were far from being *en vogue*, did he realize the heuristic value of looking into these seemingly marginal kingdoms. And he saw that, given the polycentric and multi-levelled nature of the traditional Indian state, even the smallest and remotest kingdoms could be important players in the larger politico-ritual systems to which they belonged. Thus, Kulke's little-kingdom studies are not just supplementary, but in many aspects vital and basic to his Jagannath-Gajapati research and to his later, more theoretically minded, works on the nature of the pre-modern state in India (Kulke 1982, 1985, 1995 (ed.), 1995a and 1995 b). Therefore, it comes as no surprise that Kulke, apart from tirelessly encouraging the little kingdom-researches of younger scholars (resulting already in several theses, with further to come), has himself again taken up this topic more forcefully in recent years, so that further significant publications by him are to be expected. The present article which deals with aspects of the ritual policy of the jungle kingdoms of south Orissa is therefore a tribute to this line of Kulke's intellectual enterprises. To be sure, my indebtedness to Kulke does not just concern his publications, but I have been privileged during the last decade to have had many stimulating conversations with him, as well as to devise and conduct some research projects together with him. And gradually he became more than just a mentor and senior colleague to me but a cherished friend.[2]

Introduction

In the former Hindu kingdoms of South and Southeast Asia the two domains of politics and religion were closely interconnected. Their interrelatedness comes to light not only when we look at the ideological aspects of royal authority as manifested in classical treatises propounding an indigenous theory of kingship or in historical inscriptions remembering the deeds of great kings. It also shows if one looks at the expressive or performative side of power and authority, that is, if one considers ritual or ceremonial ways of staging and enacting royalty. In theoretical terms, this mise-en-scène character of Hindu kingdoms was most significantly accounted for in Clifford Geertz's model of the "theatre state", which he developed on the basis of material relating to Bali. Geertz's model rests on the premise that Balinese kingship, paradigmatically manifested in the Negara royal court, represents an exemplary centre. According to Geertz, this centre is more than just the motor or the heart of the state, it *is* the state: "The ritual life of the court and in fact the life of the court generally, is ... paradigmatic, not merely reflective, of social order" (Geertz 1980: 13). The pompous state rituals and courtly etiquette were "the ends in themselves, they were what the state was for" (ibid.) and "mass ritual was not a device to shore up the state, but rather the state was a device for the enactment of mass ritual" (ibid.). Therefore, symbolic actions and royal paraphernelia were not used to establish and legitimate political power; the ritual and ceremonial dramas of the theatre state had no subordinate or instrumental function regarding the exercise, enhancement or maintenance of power. On the contrary, "they were the thing itself (Geertz 1980: 120). And: "Power served pomp, not pomp power" (ibid.: 13).

In this article, I would like to show that Geertz's view of ritual and ceremony as theatre and play fails to grasp important aspects of political ritual and the ritual enactment of power and authority in Hindu kingdoms. The ethnographic and historical data supporting my argument refer to pre-modern Orissa. Within Orissa, my own investigations focussed primarily on the former jungle kingdom of Jeypore in the remote and mountainous hinterland of southwest Orissa, which is roughly congruent in territorial extension with what later became Koraput District. The kingdom of Jeypore was ruled by a dynasty of Hindu kings, who had assumed power by the end of the fifteenth century and held on to it until 1952, when all princely states in Orissa, like their counterparts elsewhere in India, were abolished.[3] Jeypore's Hindu kings only managed to exert and hold on to their power throughout this period by practising a kind of ritual policy which took account of the fact that their subjects were predominantly tribal in character. By doing so, they gradually helped to Hinduize tribal forms of ritual, though it can also be noted that various Hindu concepts and forms of worship of the kings and their followers were tribalized in turn.[4] Apart from feeling the need to legitimize their rule internally, i.e. vis-à-vis their tribal or low-caste rural subjects, these kings also had to legitimize themselves externally, i.e. vis-à-vis other kings of the region and especially the all-Orissa overlords.[5] These were traditionally represented, as is well known, by the so-called "Gajapatis" or "Lord of the Elephants", whose seats of power were in or near the fertile delta of the river Mahanadi in central Orissa.

Traditionally, then, Orissa was home to a considerable number of kingdoms, one of which was the acknowledged centre and apex of the political system of the region. The various little kings often stood in rather tension-ridden relations to one another and to the great king or Gajapati. In this latter relation, they were "little" not because their kingdoms were small in size, but because they stood in politico-ritual relations of inferiority towards a superordinate king who was himself "great" (not "large") in these relations, though sometimes "little" in respect to kings of other regions or to supra-regional and even pan-Indian powers such as the Mughals, the Marathas and the British.[6]

The political system of pre-modern Orissa (and India generally) therefore consisted of a polycentric and multilayered network of royal positions. The ensuing polities, whether we call them kingdoms or even states, achieved their coherence and vitality through various forms of ostentatious display of solidarity among kings and chiefs at various levels of the political system, but frequently also through the display of a conflictual and rebellious attitude on the side of subordinate or subaltern persons and groups. Hence, in traditional or pre-modern Indian political systems, power and authority were not reified or petrified into distinguishable monolithic blocks with fixed boundaries and a stable monopoly of force at the centre. Rather, their functioning was dynamic and relative in character. The hierarchical solidarity, competition and rivalry of the various holders of power and authority found expression in innumerable wars, feuds, punitive expeditions and, more theatrically, in the threatening display and brandishing of one's weapons.[7] And, as I wish to show in this paper, they were propounded by using a ritual idiom, that is, by staking one's own claims or by contesting a rival's claims to power and authority in the domain of religious belief and practice.

In the rest of this paper, I shall first introduce, in Section 3, eight ethnohistorical cases of the ritual enactment and construction or attempted destruction of power and authority in Orissa. These various "acts" are each elaborated using interludic remarks. Due to limitations of space, I can only highlight, or point out, some of the more important facts and characteristic traits pertinent to the particular cases in question. However, in their totality they will provide a kaleidoscopic impression of the politico-ritual life of Orissa, on the basis of which it will then be possible to discuss the role of ritual enactments of power, authority and territorial sovereignty in Hindu kingdoms in more general terms (in Section 4). Finally, in Section 5, I shall develop my argument in a theoretical direction, concentrating especially on the question of how concepts like "theatre", "performance" and "theatrality" might be usefully applied in socio-cultural and historical studies.

Acts and Interludic Remarks

First Act. Time: End of the 15th century. Place: The temple town of Puri in central Orissa. This is the sacred abode of Jagannath, the undisputed "state deity" (*rāṣṭradevatā*) of Orissa.

During the annual car festival (*ratha yātrā*) in July in honour of Jagannath, Gajapati Purushottama Deo (1467-1497), one of the most powerful Hindu kings on the subcontinent at that time, climbed on to the wooden car of Jagannath, sprinkled the platform in front of the deity with water and then swept the floor, using a broom with a golden handle. This ritual act resulted in war. According to a popular Orissan legend,[8] Purushottama had intended to marry the beautiful Princess Padmabati, the daughter of the king of Kanchipuram in south India. However, the prosepctive father-in-law withdrew his consent when it was reported to him that Purushottama had done the work of a "sweeper". Purushottama considered this withdrawal an affront to himself and Jagannath, and he set out to seize the princess by force. He marched south with his warriors, defeated Kanchipuram, captured Padmabati and, after some hesitation, took her as his wife.

Interludic Remarks. The war between Puri and Kanchipuram was induced by the so-called *cherā pāhamrā* ritual, which up to the present day is conducted by the Gajapati in Puri in front of tens of thousands of exultant pilgrims. Through this act of ritual humiliation the "Lord of the Elephants" publicly expresses his great devotion to the god, but also emphasizes his privileged position in the cult of Jagannath.[9] In our case, this splendid ritual performance by a Vaishnavite king was scorned by a rival Shivaite king and led to a ritual of a quite different kind, namely to Purushottama's war-expedition against Kanchipuram. The ritual of devotion resulted in a ritual of violence and exhibition of power. However, it did not end tragically (from the Orissan point of view), but, like many romances, in marriage.

Second Act. Time: The same. Place: A jungle path bordering the little kingdom of Jeypore.

When Purushottama returned from his successful campaign against Kanchipuram he was attacked by Vijaya Chandra (1467-1510), the second king of the dynasty of Jeypore, while traversing a jungly path on his estate. Following a brief fight, the jungle king and his indigenous warriors managed to take hold of one of the Gajapati's elephants and flee with it into the bush. This animal was carrying part of the war booty taken by Purushottama from Kanchipuram, most prominently a golden statue (*mūrti*) of the Hindu goddess Durgā. The family chronicle of the Jeypore royal dynasty, where this incident is remembered, also reports that this *mūrti* was installed in the capital with great ceremony. Durgā was proclaimed the tutelary deity (*iṣṭadevī*) of the kingdom, and the annual celebration of the Durgā *pūjā* in Jeypore is said to have been performed so splendidly that it brought "good name and fame all over India" to the kingdom (Sarma 1938: Verses 147-155). The family chronicle of the Gajapatis of Orissa, on the other hand, does not even mention this, to them, very humiliating theft.[10]

Interludic Remarks. The trope of the theft of the *mūrti* of a goddess can be found in many parts of Orissa and, beyond, in India generally (Dirks 1987: 87-88; Peabody 1991a, b; Sax 1991: 167-169; Schnepel 1995, 1997: 231-242, 2002: 257-268). It would be too simplistic to concentrate merely on the historicity of the Jeypore legend, on "*wie es eigentlich gewesen*" ("how it really was") in Ranke's sense, for, even if it can be proved that this theft was only "invented" by the Jeypore kings and their Brahman agents in order to boost their standing, what is important here is the very fact that this act was remembered or invented or, as in Puri, passed over in silence. And it is worth stressing that this event represents the appropriation of a ritual emblem and source of power. The theft of *mūrti*s or at least the trope of some such theft is therefore the object of a politics of remembrance or, as the case may be, of a politics of forgetting or of surpressing memory.

Third Act. Time: October 1991. Place: Bissamcuttack, the former seat of a powerful "feudal" retainer of the King of Jeypore in the northeastern part of this kingdom.

When I first noticed Mohapatra consciously, he was just about to sacrifice a goat with the single stroke of an axe through her neck. It was around midnight, and we were in the temple of the village goddess Markama, who was to receive a number of sacrifices that night, the eighth night of Durgā *pūjā*. About one hundred worshippers were assembled at the temple during this hour, the air was dusty, the atmosphere tense and ghostly. The music of the "untouchables" reached from the outer yard of the temple to its sacrum. Mohapatra was to kill four more goats.

Interludic Remarks. The photograph lying in front of me depicts Mohapatra immediately after his sacrificial acts. His eyes are wide open and he has a glassy stare, which reveal terror and relief at the same time. The next day I learnt that Mohapatra is of Brahman descent. He was therefore quite out of place at this temple of a tribal goddess longing for blood sacrifices, and even more so as an active sacrificer. Mohapatra runs a small business. His old bus had repeatedly broken down in the months preceding the Durga *pūjā* of that year, and it cost more than 60,000 rupees to repair. Pondering the reasons for these ruinous events, Mohapatra at last remembered that immediately before his bus had broken down for the first time, a woman clad in red had got off. He reasoned that this was the goddess Markama leaving in anger, probably because a menstruating women was sitting next to her. By acting as sacrificer Mohapatra sought to appease the goddess, hoping that in future his bus would run smoothly.

Fourth Act. Same place and time as the third act.

Immediately after being chopped off, the heads of the goats were taken from the sacrificial posts to the image of the goddess situated in the temple's sanctum by a young priest speedily making his way through the excited crowd of spectators. Next to the goddess sat a priest, who was possessed by her and who revealed her messages to the worshippers by speaking in tongues. A second priest, standing next to the possessed person, translated this glossolaly into Oriya for those thronging close by. The image of Markama consists of a stone, coloured red and covered with numerous silver eyes and a long red tongue. During *pūjā*, this head of the goddess is adorned with garlands of white and red flowers. On the floor in front of the *mūrti*, there are burning candles, pieces of coconut, green leaves and numerous red, blue and yellow flowers. This "stage" is framed by a structure of stone, in front of which the priests sit and perform their services. If one steps back a little and looks at the mis-en-scène as a whole, one gets the impression of looking into a lion's mouth.

Interludic remarks. In the religious life of Orissa, an important part is played by mother and earth goddesses, who are worshipped in the form of stones, trees, wooden posts, earthen mounds and other non-iconical symbols. Characteristically, these goddesses possess a strong territorial rootedness. Often their fields of influence fade out at the borders of their own village or clan locality. However, within their sacred domains (*kṣetras*) they are immensely powerful and feared, more than any other deity that might also be worshipped there. Good harvests, the fertility of humans and animals, and the general well-being of the people as well as epidemics, droughts, floods and personal misfortunes are often attributed to the blessing or anger of these goddesses. As embodiments of *śakti*, a dynamic force associated with life, fertility, growth, sexuality and abundance, these goddesses have an ambivalent character which can either grant and sustain life or threaten and even destroy it. Several of these originally tribal deities have undergone various processes of Hinduization, leading, for example, to the gradual anthropomorphiza-tion of their non-iconical symbols. Minimal additions in this process of making a *mūrti*-like image out of their stones, trees etc. consist of the painting or plastering of eyes and a large protruding tongue upon the natural symbol. As far as their cults are concerned, the priests of these goddesses, though not themselves belonging to the Brahman caste, have adapted the Hindu form of worship called *pūjā* as their role model. However, the number of *pūjās* performed during a day and of the various offerings (*upacāras*) given to the deity are considerably smaller than in the case of a fully functioning

Hindu temple. Moreover, at certain times of the ritual calendar and in specific cases of emergency or gratitude, these goddesses are still offered blood sacrifices.[11]

Fifth Act. Time: Middle of the nineteenth century. Place: Bissamcuttack.

The priest of the Markama temple reported a legend to me according to which a king of Jeypore[12] once attacked the semi-autonomous *thātrāja* of Bissamcuttack because allegedly he had not paid tribute for several years. In the middle of the fight, when many soldiers of the *thātrāja* were losing their lives, Markama joined in. She disguised herself as a milkmaid and sold poisened curd to the soldiers of the king, whereupon they died and the fortune of the battle turned towards the *thātrāja*. One of the king's generals then inquired about the temple of this goddess, went there and shot her head off using a gun. But Markama took revenge by letting the general die soon afterwards. At this, the king of Jeypore considered it best to settle his disagreement with the *thātrāja* amicably, demanding no further payments of tribute. This story is not narrated in the family chronicles of the Jeypore kings.

Interludic remarks. In Orissa we encounter not only the theft of goddesses. Persons fighting for power and territorial sovereignty also attempted to obtain access to the temples of powerful local goddesses and to establish themselves as patrons of their cults. In this way they often managed to forge meaningful bonds with the earth and its inhabitants ruled or sought to be ruled over by them. Alternatively, they tried to destroy the tutelary deity of an enemy thus hoping to destroy a major source of his power. One of the major differences between the *mūrti*s of the goddess Durgā and tribal goddesses consists in their territoriality. The former are not indissolubly bound to a certain locality. Their force or *śakti* radiates from their statues and not, as is the case with most tribal deities, from the earth or locality they are standing on.

Sixth Act. Time: The mythical past, but also the time of the celebration of Durgā *pūjā*, a festival held annually in October at the end of the rainy season.

Once the demon king Mahisha succeeded in appropriating for himself Indra's place as supreme god and in ruling the world in his stead. As the other gods were worried about this state of affairs, particularly about their share in the sacrifices, they called on Durgā for help. In order to assist the goddess in restoring the cosmic order, they gave her several weapons, such as Shiva's trident, Vishnu's disc, Indra's thunderbolt and Varuna's snare, which can often be found depicted in paintings and sculptures of the goddess. Apart from this, the goddess holds in her twelve hands a bow and arrow, and, most significantly, the sword which she uses to cut off the demon's head when he tries to flee from his buffalo form.[13]

Interludic remarks. This killing of the buffalo demon, which is reported in classical writings such as the *Devī Māhātmya* and in innumerable folk stories, is ritually re-enacted during the eighth night of Durgā *pūjā.* As far as Jeypore is concerned, many of the buffaloes sacrificed each year were sponsored by the king, one or two of which he killed himself. Apart from being sacrifier and sacrificer, the king also established himself during the Durgā *pūjā* celebrations through a series of symbolic and ritual acts as Durgā's husband. In the myth and ritual of the destruction of demonic rule by Durgā and the king we encounter a social, political and also cosmic drama, during which an endangered world is saved and imbued with new order and power. Centrally to this process of restoration is the act of sacrifice.

Seventh Act. Time: October 1941. Place: Jeypore.

An Indian gentleman called Sahu describes the *dasarā* feast in Jeypore which is celebrated immediately after the nine nights of Durgā *pūjā* and closely linked to it in ritual and mythical terms in the following words: "The Dussara at Jeypore is a sight not only for me but for gods. (...) What a sight! People have thronged in their thousands. (...) They have come with their banners, their drums and flutes and various other musical instruments. Hundreds of ceremonies have gone on for the past seven days and ceremony after ceremony is going on. The Maharajah has been fasting in the midst of it; for religious ceremony requires it. And though he has been going through such purificatory penance, so to say, he bears it calmly without any show of it on his face. The procession begins. (...) The Maharajah Saheb will be coming. All are expecting him. (...) Well, thousands were raising their necks to have darsana [a view] of the Maharajah. I tried myself but utterly failed. Yet I was not disappointed. After all you see the Rajah in the Crowd and he is the symbol of the crowd."[14]

Interludic Remarks: The king was the central actor in this cultural performance of *dasarā*, not only on account of his being the head of the political system, but also because he functioned as Durgā's chief devotee and as patron of the ritual proceedings. In a Geertzian sense, he was the exemplary centre of the kingdom and the cosmos. In order to participate in the *dasarā* festivities, thousands of individuals were heading towards the politico-ritual centre of the kingdom, namely the royal palace, with its ceremonial hall and the temple of Durgā attached to it. Within the ceremonial hall the king was sitting on the throne together with Durgā whose *mūrti* was placed on a cushion next to him. He did not summon the arriving crowd, but attracted them by his charisma alone, like a magnet which attracts human beings. After an audience in the ceremonial hall for the most important functionaries and estate holders, who offered gifts and received in return the king's blessings and a *sari*, symbolizing their legitimacy as office holders, the procession started from the palace led by the king and Durgā, riding on an elephant, as if they were leading an army into war. They were followed by the holders of the various military fiefs and estates of the kingdom and by the foot-soldiers of these estates, who were holding flags (*jhaṇḍās*) symbolizing their territorial segments of the kingdom and its respective local tutelary deities like Markama.[15]

Eighth Act. Time 1568. Place: Cuttack and Puri in central Orissa.

In 1568, the army of the Afghan Kararani-Sultanate of Bengal defeated the army of the Gajapatis of Orissa in a decisive battle. Following his victory, the Afghan general immediately marched towards Cuttack, the royal capital of the Lord of the Elephants, and killed Gajapati Mukunda Deo. He then turned towards the pilgrimage centre of Puri, where he stormed the temple of Jagannath and stole the god's wooden effigy. This was taken north to the banks of the Ganges, where it was burnt. However, the temple chronicles of Puri, the so-called *Mādaḷā Pāñji*, report that an Oriya man succeeded in saving the inner essence of the god from the smouldering effigy. He buried this vital part of the god - the so-called *brahmapadārtha* substance which is stored in a cavity in the wooden god's belly - in a hole next to the village of Kujang in central Orissa. Thirty years later, when Orissa was still without a Gajapati and the temple of Jagannath, at least its main entrance, was still closed, Jagannath appeared to the King of Khurda in a dream, revealing the whereabouts of his *brahmapadārtha*. Thereupon this king, Ramachandra Deo, with the help of the priests of Puri found this live substance and had a new effigy of Jagannath built. This was installed first in Khurda and two years later in Puri. Ramachandra Deo thus managed to get himself acknowledged as the new Gajapati of Orissa, which was also aided by the Mughal emperor Akbar's (1558-1605) more tolerant ritual policy.

Interludic Remarks. Even after these events, during the period from the early seventeenth to the middle of the eighteenth century, Puri and the temple of Jagannath were repeatedly attacked and sometimes plundered by Muslim forces. However, the tragedy of 1568 did not occur again, because the priests of the temple and the various Gajapatis always succeeded in fleeing with the wooden effigy across the Chilka lake in time. On occasions, however, they only found time to take the vital substance with them. The deity's cult then continued in a clandestine way in some remote jungle kingdom until a safe return to Puri was possible.

Strategies of Ritual Enactments

In the preceding pages we have encountered eight different cases of the ritual enactment of power and authority. To start with, there was the Gajapati, who swept the floor in front of thousands of pilgrims and who then stole a bride, the beautiful Princess Padmabati. Then we met the jungle king of Jeypore, who captured the "golden" effigy of Durgā from his overlord, who himself had stolen it before from the rival king of Kanchipuram. Next a Brahman entrepreneur in danger of going bankrupt worshipped a local deity named Markama by personally conducting blood sacrifices in front of her image. This same goddess helped her patron, the rebellious *thātrāja* of Bissamcuttack, to win a battle against the king of Jeypore, after a general of this king tried to destroy her by shooting her with a gun. We also saw that the kings of Jeypore celebrated a grand Durgā *pūjā* festival around their *mūrti* each year, thus establishing themselves as politico-ritual centres of their kingdom and even of the cosmos. One must also include the demon king Mahishasura in this list, who in mythical times fancied this goddess and wanted to possess her sexually, but who was fought and slain by her. Finally, it was shown that in the history of Orissa several Mughal and Afghan leaders tried to subdue the kingdom of the Gajapatis by attempting to destroy the effigy of Jagannath.

Numerous other cases could be added. For example, the family chronicles of the jungle kings of Jeypore narrate that some time during the 18th century one bandit chief attempted (in vain) to steal the golden *mūrti* of Durgā from the kings. In another example, the *Indian Telegraph* of 20 February 1995 reports that the leader of the Orissan branch of the Janata Dal party opened the state elections of that year with a prayer within the Jagannath temple of Puri, followed by a speech in front the temple's main gate in which he claimed that Jagannath was his well-wisher for the coming election.[16] A third instance is recorded in the temple chronicle of Puri where the last Gajapati of the Ganaga dynasty, Bhanudev IV (1409-1434), is recorded as having been visited by Jagannath in a dream who advised him to nominate a beggar boy sitting in front of the temple as his successor on the throne (Kulke 1979). And, as a final and well-known example from outside Orissa, during the election campaign of 1991, L.K. Advani, a leader of the neo-Hinduist BJP, posed as the mythical god Rama, holding a bow and arrow while riding on a chariot.

All these acts have in common the fact that in them individuals or groups give spectacular expressions to their claims to power, authority and territorial sovereignty by getting close to a deity or stealing it, sometimes even attempting to destroy it. On the local and little kingdom levels the role of the contested deity was played by two different kinds or manifestations of the great Goddess (*Mahādevī*), one possessing a strong local rootedness, while the other has her *śakti* emanate from a mobile *mūrti*. In the two manifestations of the goddess as well as in their respective cults, we encounter different concepts of royal authority. These can be pinpointed with Stein, when he writes about the ritual politics of the mediaeval Chola: "On the one hand, there was a form of kingship which was universalistic, absolutistic, fiscally and extractively oriented; on the other hand, there was a form of lordship, very like kingship, but localistic, relativistic, or collegeal, and redistributivist" (Stein 1985: 408). If we here include Jagannath, that is the deity which was important on the level of the great kingdom or the region, it becomes obvious that ultimately we are not dealing with two strictly opposed concepts or, territorially speaking, with two different spheres of the expansion of royal and divine authority. The various territorial levels, starting from the estate of Bissamcuttack, through the little kingdom of Jeypore up to the regional empire of the Gajapatis (in conjunction with their various presiding deities, from Markama through Durgā to Jagannath), overlapped.[17]

At this point we have to ask about the character of the "stage" upon which these performances took place. It is perhaps best understood when seen as a field of energy which is open at its peripheries and which overlaps in places with other circles of the same kind or is encompassed by circles of higher orders. In the various centres of these circles we find deities who radiate energy and give force to their patrons and closest devotees. These deities were approached by bearers of royal authority, or by persons who strove for royal authority, in two essentially different ways: either they tried to establish themselves as a deity's patron and thus attempted to link their secular realm (*kṣatra*) with that deity's sacred realm (*kṣetra*); or else they tried to destroy the existing *kṣatra/kṣetra* symbiosis of an enemy by destroying or stealing the stone, *mūrti* or effigy of his tutelary deity. While the actors adopted these two main strategies in innumerable different concrete ways, the drama unfolded. Though the general outline of its plot was pre-determined by tradition and the power structure within which it took place, the details and the end of the story were far from being fixed or certain.

Moreover, the question of who was to play which character was open to some degree of competition, especially with regard to the the leading role of the aspiring chief devotee and patron of the deity. I have mentioned that with regard to certain passages and details of the play one can find both a policy of remembering and a policy of forgetting and concealment. Congruent with this, there is the fact that in some of the ritual enactments discussed here there were actors who, far from longing to play a role, refused to participate in the playacting or to assume the role ascribed to them by tradition or superior authority. One example is once again the *thātrāja* of Bissamcuttack, who practised some sort of ritual absenteeism when it came to participating in the King of Jeypore's *dasarā* celeberations, staging his own festival instead.[18] He thus forcefully expressed his claim to being a little king in his own right instead of being regarded as a feudal retainer of the Jeypore king. When these two protaganists failed to resolve their *dasarā* dispute among themselves, they finally resorted to fight it out in front of British colonial courts in a rather ruinous litigation which lasted from 1905 to 1926. It appears that, contrary to what the British felt their judicial system was there to achieve, the Indian actors used the courts as yet another stage and battle-field for the continuation of their former military, political and ritual battles. Their constant litigation thus represented a further manifestation of the ritual enactment of power and authority, only that it now had undergone a particular code-switching which adapted the form of the contest to the altered historical circumstances and the contingencies of colonial rule (Schnepel 1997: Chapter IV, 1998, 2000: Chapter IV).

Conclusions

In his model of the theatre state, which I introduced at the beginning of this paper, Geertz succeeds in showing that the symbolic aspects of power are more than "merely" symbolic, as is often thought by people who thus also believe that "really effective" politics is only to be found in economy, warfare and in some kind of Machiavellian *Realpolitik*. However, Geertz's model, with its image of a rather passive and immobile king viewed as "a sacred icon" (Geertz 1980: 108), was rightly criticized for the fact that it offers little room for the recognition of political conflicts and power struggles.[19] Geertz ignores non-ceremonial relations between kings on the one hand and the various office-holders and noble men on the other. Similarly, the relationship between the populace and the exemplary royal centre in this model appears to be no more than a rather artificial pageant in which actors and spectators hardly have any points of contact outside the drama. Ultimately, therefore, Geertz does not escape the rather problematic distinction between politics and religion as two functionally and substantially different domains. He reverses the relationship between power and pomp in a Copernican turning of more conventional interpretations of the role of ritual in politics, but this is ultimately neither questioned in essence nor taken apart altogether.

The ethno-historical data presented here strongly suggest that a more dynamic picture is needed if one wants to arrive at a sensible use of concepts like "theatre", "theatrality" or "performance" (and of models derived from these concepts) in social and cultural studies. It is necessary to put greater weight on the conflicts, contests, negotiations and strategies which accompany and inform these and similar cultural performances. And any interpretation needs to acknowledge the dynamic character and situational relativity of the groups or individuals specifically involved in each event. Power relations, positions of status and rank as well as political acts are not only theatralized, aestheticized, glorified and legitimized through cultural performances such as the ones discussed here; rather, power struggles are enacted and fought out through these performances, using them as their media and means to "make politics".

In this sense, many performances can only be interpreted sensibly when seen as polyphonic dramatic negotiations of diverse, changeable and contesting claims to power, authority and territorial sovereignty. Therefore, it is not enough to view them simply as stage plays in the narrow sense. We also have to pay attention to the power struggles, contests and negotiations which precede these performances, which help to form them, which find various forms of manifestation during them and which continue afterwards to be effective through their traditions and interpretations. Moreover, it is necessary to inquire whether there are also any counter-, subaltern or alternative dramatizations which reveal different and diverging interests or views.[20]

If ritual dramas are in a complex way the products and representations of social, political, cultural, economic, demographic, historical and other realities, this also means that they can provide us with valuable clues for the reconstruction and interpretation of these realities (and the plural form needs stressing). Such a view means abandoning the postmodern credo that there is no reality behind the "text" (and cultural performances are texts in this view) and that text and context basically fall into one another. But this does not mean going back to a naive pre-postmodern point of view, because when looking at ritual performances for a reconstruction of those realities which have brought them forth and of which they themselves are integral parts, it has to be emphasized that these performances are never neutral and never provide a direct path to, or a mirror-like reflection of, these realities. The ritual enactments of power and authority are as diffuse, polyphonic and contestatory as the realities themselves. Hence, they never are pure and simple representations; in fact, as manifestations of power struggles and conflicting views or interests they are often even deliberate misrepresentations of the realities.

We also have to bear in mind that these performances are not simply passive storers of clues leading us to these realities but that they construct, reconstruct, influence and change these realities themselves. They themselves possess agency or, to use Greenblatt's term, "social energy". Social energy, in Greenblatt's terminology, is "associated with repeatable forms of pleasure and interest, with the capacity to arouse disquiet, pain, fear, the beating of the heart, pity, laughter, tension, relief, wonder" (Greenblatt 1988: 6). If one adds the "belief in legitimacy" to Greenblatt's enumeration of sensations brought forth by social energy, then this concept can usefully be applied in the interpretation of the kinds of performance discussed here. However, it needs to be emphasized yet again that attention must be paid to the contests and negotiations which accompany attempts to acquire this social energy or, better, to acquire those storers of social energy, whether these are *mūrtis* of Durgā or stones representing local goddesses or rituals. Thus, it is also necessary to look for the strategies that are used to acquire social energy and for the resulting "circulation" of social energy.

The various ritual performances discussed here do not only *mean* something, they also attempt to *do* something. And they therefore not only allow a reconstruction of realities in the sense of a reconstruction of events as they actually are or, better, actually were, they also are documents of (a history of) ideas, ideologies and the ascription of meaning. It is especially with regard to this aspect that questions concerning the audience gain significance. Who is addressed by a specific cultural performance or ritual enactment and what are the specific intentions and dramaturgical means? How do the recipients receive what is being performed for them? Who attributes validity to these performances and who does not? Again, in most cases there will be no single, absolute sense of a performance in question. Meaning and validity, too, are given by negotiating the many varying, contesting and sometimes contradictory claims or views of both actors and spectators.

Moreover, for an understanding of the kind of ritual enactment discussed here, it is necessary to emphasize that we often only know about them through written or oral traditions. Again, these texts are not only passive reminders of the performances they remember and of the various realities integrally interconnected with these performances. These traditions, no matter whether they are orally transmitted or found on palm-leaf manuscripts or in temple inscriptions, are themselves agents within the various contestations for validity and meaning. Hence, like the stones of tribal goddesses, the *mūrtis* of Durgā or the celebration of the *dasarā* festival, these traditions, like the family chronicles of the Jeypore kings, are storers of social energy and as such agents of a politics of remembrance, but also of a politics of concealment and forgetting.

Why, one needs to ask further, did these enactments of power and authority revolve around deities, symbols, venerable women or religious values rather than focus directly on money, territory, cattle, grain and other material goods? As I have repeatedly argued,.this inclination toward the religious and symbolic does not mean that the enactments in question were "merely" religious and symbolic in character and had no effective political implications. Equally, my repeated emphasis on matters of power, authority and territorial sovereignty does not mean that these ritual enactments and negotiations were nothing but sham fights or a theatrical veil behind which we have to discern the "real" political and economic motives. Such a view would mean misunderstanding the complex relationship and interdependence between the domains of politics and religion in Hindu polities. More often than not, the actors themselves had truly religious motives and aims which cannot simply be reduced to representing a political strategy in disguise. For example, the jungle kings of south Orissa patronized tribal deities of their realms not only in order to find legitimacy in the eyes of the indigenous population but also – first of all – because they themselves believed strongly in the power of these deities and wanted to secure their divine blessing and aid.

Why then did these persons steal or even try to destroy the material representations of deities in their capacity of storers of *śakti* or energy? Why did they try to make symbolic conquests, to achieve prestige or to humiliate an enemy in the realm of ritual rather than to conquer his land, subdue him militarily and even kill him? Discussing historical events in early modern Europe Chartier arrives at some insights which help us understand the kind of performances discussed here: "The struggles within the realm of representations", he writes, "are no less important than the economic fights, if one wants to understand the mechanisms by which a group tries to prevail with its own view of the social world, its values and its rule" (Chartier 1992: 12; my translation). In this context Chartier also speaks of "battle zones" which are "the more decisive the less they can be grasped in a material way".

By stealing a *murti*, becoming the patron of a goddess or destroying the repository of an enemy's tutelary deity, it was possible in the Orissan context and beyond to conquer, subdue and dominate an enemy synecdochially and in a symbolic way. This statement should not be misunderstood in the sense that these conquests were "merely symbolic". They were actual conquests, but actual conquests by means of symbolic and ritual acts. In a sense, these ritual enactments of power and authority were more than "merely factual", because they occurred in a realm of values which possessed higher, timeless sanctions and validity. For this reason these ritual enactments were more effective and longer lasting than fights about material goods, which, to be sure, were also going on all the time.

Notes

1 See Kulke 1976, 1978f, 1980, 1984 a and 1984b. Shortly before I started my own research on the jungle kingdoms of south Orissa in the early nineties I read these articles, and it was only later that I fully realized how strongly they aided and guided me throughout my fieldwork and archival researches.

2 See, as one result, Kulke and Schnepel (eds.) 2000. Presently, we are mutually conducting, together with other colleagues, a research project on the former north Orissan kingdom of

Keonjhar. The present article presents a slightly rewritten English version of an article published in German in 1998.

3 On the history of the Jeypore kingdom, see Schnepel (1992, 1997: Chapter III, 2002: Chapter III), Senapati (1966) and Singh Deo (1939).

4 Here I use the terms "Hindu" and "tribal" in an ideal-typical sense to distinguish between the extreme poles of two forms of religion which in reality show many overlaps and borrowings from one another. The terms "Hinduization" and "tribalization" are used to denote movements between these poles. Here I am following Bailey (1961) and Eschmann (1978: 80-85).

5 For the distinction between these two kinds of legitimacy, see Kulke (1979: 26).

6 On the concept of "little kingdom", see Berkemer (1993), Cohn (2001a [1987]), Dirks (1987) and Schnepel (1997: Chapter 1, 2000: Chapter I).

7 In traditional Indian warfare knowledge that the "fame of a sword" was approaching could be decisive, and small skirmishes were often enough to decide the struggle for superiority between two warlords and their armies. Large-scale military encounters with hundreds killed were relatively rare. On this point, see Kolff (1990).

8 On the Kāñcī Kāverī legend, see *Kaṭakarājavaṁśāvali* (1987: 81-85).

9 On the "sweeping ritual", see Dash (1978: 214-219) and Kulke (1978c: 204-208; 1979: 71-75).

10 The *Kaṭakarājavaṁśāvali* (1987: 87) only reports that Purushottama "brought a statue of Lord Krishna ... as well as several other images".

11 On the cult of tribal goddesses, see Eschmann (1978), Kulke (1978f, 1980, 1984), Rath (1987: Chapters 9 and 11) and Schnepel (1993, 1997: Chapter V, 2002: Chapter V).

12 From historical sources available to me I assume that historically this king was Vikram Deo II (1825-60). See my discussion of Bissamcuttack's history in Schnepel (1997: Chapter IV).

13 On the battle between Durgā and Mahisha, see Berkson (1995), Coburn (1991) and Erndl (1993: 22-30).

14 Cited from Sahu (1942: 33-36). See also Francis (1907: 262-263).

15 A more detailed discussion of the *dasarā* festival in Jeypore can be found in Schnepel (1996 and 1997: Chapter VI, Section 3). For *dasarā* festivities in other parts of India, see Breckenridge (1977), Dirks (1987: 39-43, 90-91), Fuller (1992: 108-125), Jansen (1995: 139-177), Kane (1958: Chapter IX and X), Kinsley (1986: Chapter 7), Sontheimer (1981) and Toffin (1981).

16 One week later, the leader of the Congress Party also campaigned in Puri in a similar vein.

17 One might add yet another, higher level of political organization with the Mughal and, later, the British pan-Indian empires. The latter, as I found in some manuscripts, did not hesitate to place Queen Victoria in a role similar to, but more inclusive than, the one occupied by Durgā at the level of the little kingdom or the regional kingdom. Moreover, this role ascription was readily accepted and understood by those subordinate "princes" who felt compelled or, for various reasons, inclined to acknowledge British sovereignty. See Schnepel (1997: Chapter IV, 2000: Chapter IV).

18 His own *dasarā* centred not around a Durgā image but around the stone of Markama and reveals certain other characteristic differences when compared with the festival in Jeypore. On this point, see Schnepel (1997: Chapter VI, Section 4 and 1998).

19 For critics of this aspect of Geertz's work, see Dirks (1987: 401-402), Schulte Nordholt (1993), Tambiah (1985a) and Walters (1980).

20 Bailey (1996) discusses such a performance and counter-performance with regard to a conflict about entrance to a temple in a village in central Orissa.

On a tribal frontier – Aghriā-Gauntiā as Village Kings

Uwe Skoda

The little kingdom as framework

The "little kingdom" has been characterised in the relevant literature as a relational construct in which the position of the "little king" is determined by his relationship to the overlord(s) as well as to his subjects (Cohn 2001b [1962]: 488; Berkemer 1993: 319). Cohn (2001b [1962]: 485-486) distinguished several levels in the political system, with the "local level" – to use his term – as the lowest or basic administrative stratum, which according to him is constituted by local revenue collectors, indigenous chiefs and lineages. Furthermore, as Dirks (1979: 172) observed in reference to Hocart, the village community can be understood as a microcosm of the kingdom itself. The local level within the little kingdom seems, however, to have attracted much less attention than royal families and their relations to the overlord or secondary / imperial level. My paper will present an empirical example of revenue collectors from the Aghriā community and their position within the "little kingdom" of Bamra in Western Orissa. I will argue that these village headmen, known as Gauntiā, can be understood as "village kings", who – positioned between the "little king" and their own subjects – replicated royal functions in a ritual, political and economic sense as far as possible at village level. The data used here was collected during an 18-month anthropological field study among the Aghriā, but I will confine myself to an ethno-historical approach here, attempting a historical reconstruction of a situation prior to Indian independence and overlooking modern transformations and more recent phenomena of decline.

The Evolution and Spreading of the Gauntiā-System

The Aghriā probably migrated to a tribal area about 100 – 150 years ago from the north-western direction. According to their own mythology, having once been warriors they turned to agriculture following a verdict by Lord Jagannāth and acquired land rights by clearing the forest – the so-called *khuṇṭ katā gaunti*. *Khuṇṭ* stands here for stumps of trees that had to be cut (*katā* = to cut) in order to gain a headmanship or *gaunti* and become a *Gauntiā*. The rights were fixed in a formal document by the superior king – the so-called *gaunti paṭā*. As rather adventurous farmers, Gauntiā families began to spread throughout the area, taking up other headmanships for their sons. Most of the Gauntiā family histories show how the area, hitherto tribally dominated, was penetrated by new peasants, who were also influential in setting up state structures on the tribal frontier.[1] The king of Bamra certainly encouraged forest clearing, offering tax-reductions as a reward for turning "waste land" into fields. Earlier tribal headmen were superseded and their villages taken over by auction, if they were unable to pay the revenue demanded by the king.

External relations – The Gauntiā in Relation to His Overlord

Following Dirks' paradigm of the little kingdom as a system of redistribution processes of accumulation, both distribution and redistribution, which essentially constitute and express political, economic and ritual relations between the royal levels, great and small, must be analysed.[2]

Revenue Collection

The Gauntiā were formally recognised by the king of Bamra as their overlords in a document entitled *gaunti patā* or land deed given to them by the king. This document fixed both the obligations of a Gauntiā towards their superior king as well as their rights. Prior to receiving a *gaunti*, a potential Gauntiā had to deposit revenue for one year in advance. The most important obligation was certainly the collection of revenue fixed according to the *patā*. The revenue usually had to be brought to the capital or an office of a superior king. As a rule, it was paid in several instalments exactly laid down in the deed.[3] If the Gauntiā were unable to collect and pay the revenue, their *gaunti* was auctioned. Landlords who immigrated to the region and introduced profitable, modern methods or technologies certainly had an advantages over the more traditional tribal headmen, who often lost their office in favour of immigrants. In practice, however, there was a certain flexibility of payment in the sense that the king or his officers would have taken natural catastrophes such as damage caused by elephants etc. into consideration and allowed revenue reduction (*māph*), as elder villagers remember.

It seems to have been a privilege of the Gauntiā to distribute land in the village. Land not cultivated by anyone – particularly forest land – could be given to tenants selected by the landlord, who often had to first of all clear the forest.[4] Some people still gratefully remember certain headmen, who not only allowed them to stay in their villages but also provided them with land for cultivation. Gauntiā occasionally tried to attract members of their own community or certain service communities, such as leather workers, to settle in their village by offering them land. In many cases, Aghriā-Gauntiā invited other Aghriā families to stay with them and act as *jāti* – ritual witnesses. It might also have been necessary to some extent to draw tenants to the village to reduce the amount of revenue the headman had to pay – particularly if there was more land available than the headman could cultivate. A jamindār, king or British agent sometimes had to agree to land transfers, but purely as a formality. In cases where tenants were unable to pay revenue[5], the amount had to be put forward by the Gauntiā, who could then transfer the land to another tenant. Locals informed me that a Gauntiā had to inform the magistrate beforehand and wait for two years, up to which time a tenant had the opportunity of paying. In most cases, however, tenants unable to pay simply left the village and the Gauntiā offered the land to someone else. A paragraph of the *patā* that protected tenants seems to have had little significance, since there were cases where powerful Gauntiā simply forced tenants or *parjā* to sell him their land or their best cattle.

Services to the Superior King: Accommodating the King and His Officials

In addition, each Gauntiā had to accommodate the king, members of his family or any government servant on their journey throughout the kingdom. A special room known as *bai hak* close to the entrance of the Gauntiā house was usually reserved for such occasions. Meals were provided for the guests, the ingredients of which were listed precisely in a *patā* depending on the status of the guests. As well as this, the guests or government employees had to be provided with carriers / porters to the next village. Apart from royal guests and government servants in the respective village, food also had to be provided for large royal ceremonies such as weddings, when the Gauntiā were invited but had to bring milk, paddy etc. fixed prior to the function. The latter gifts are, however, not mentioned in a *patā*.

Socage / beṭhi and Gifts / bheṭi

Not mentioned in a *patā* either but still remembered by Gauntiā and villagers alike is socage or forced labour they had to carry out for the king and the Gauntiā. According to some people, *beṭhi* or *beṭh bigāḍi* was already abolished two or three years prior to independence, making it quite difficult to estimate its extent and characterise the system, since most people did not experience it personally. As both

Gauntiā and Kandh told me, *beṭhi* was primarily work for the king that was organised, managed and inspected by a Gauntiā. It included hunting elephants as well as constructing roads and ponds. Some of my informants remembered that the labourers were provided with neither money nor food. Others stated that the king paid minimal sums of money to the Gauntiā, which the latter then distributed among the villagers for their labour. An elder Gauntiā argued that the amount of *beṭhi* due to the king was calculated according to the village revenue, i.e., 10 Rs revenue was equivalant to one labourer or *beṭhiā* (= free, unpaid labourer, sometimes also called *butiyā*) working until a certain job, e.g., catching an elephant, was completed (the elephants were used or sold by the king later on). Hunting an elephant – considered by the villagers to be a form of punishment – required 10 to 15 days. In addition, certain roads were divided between neighbouring villages that were were responsible over the years for maintaining a fixed part of the road. Besides, in some cases the king and his administration ordered Gauntiā to provide certain materials such as firewood, e.g., for local jails, work that was also considered as *beṭhi*.

It seems that villagers were also forced to work for the landlord for a limited period without pay. Some pointed out that the Gauntiā used their labour or *beṭhi* to pay for dancers or meals at festivals such as *Śibrātrī*, to build ponds or wells, or for such pressing work as fire fighting or ploughing and sowing in the Gauntiā's own fields. In the latter case, villagers were occasionally provided with meals or a small sum of money. According to some Gauntiā, villagers were entitled in exchange for their labour to a gift at their wedding and a contribution in the case of illness. However, according to an elder Gauntiā, working for the headman during the sowing or harvest seasons was not regarded as *beṭhi* but as paid assistance to the Gauntiā.[6]

Bheṭi, gifts or tribute, should be distinguished from *beṭhi* or socage, which occasionally leads to confusion because it is to a certain extent closely related. In the case of a royal marriage or large function in the capital, Gauntiā were obliged to offer, particularly if invited, gifts of food such as milk, paddy, goats etc., which is fixed prior to the event. These gifts, a matter of prestige for the Gauntiā, were known as *bheṭi*. In some cases – as an elder Gauntiā related – villagers had to offer forest products like honey free of charge to the Gauntiā. This can also be regarded as *bheṭi*.

In his study of Gajapati court rituals, Hardenberg (2000: 126, 147-8) interpreted *bheṭi* – in his context, gifts of money offered during new year celebrations in particular – as a gift that produced an asymmetrical relation between giver and receiver, the latter standing in a higher position and bestowing titles or other honour on the Gajapati in return. The gifts represent both continuous relations between the king and his subjects as well as the land provided to loyal subjects protected by the king, the former offering gifts in exchange (ibid).[7] Here I want to argue that both forms – *beṭhi* and *bheṭi*, socage and gifts – constitute and express hierarchical relations from tenants to Gajapati. The village *parjā* working for the king of Bamra and the local Gauntiā, who also supervises work in the village, are responsible to the king; the Gauntiā, in turn, offers gifts to the king of Bamra and – as Hardenberg (2000: 143) notes – the king of Bamra provides *bheṭi* to the Gajapati, who in turn would offer it in a transcendental hierarchy to Jagannāth himself.

King's Land or Rent-free Land – bhogrā

A particular privilege enjoyed by the Gauntiā – directly linked to the *gaunti* – was the right to cultivate land formally belonging to the king. This land was rent-free in most cases and of very high quality (usually around ten acres). *Bhogrā* land could not be divided among sons but only transferred to the next Gauntiā, usually the eldest son, who received the *bhogrā* land as part of his *gaunti* in addition to his share of land inherited from his family. The counterpart of the *bhogrā* land that belonged to and symbolised the king of Bamra is the so-called *guti bunā* – land offered rent-free by the Gauntiā to loyal servants (Guti) for sowing (*bunā*), but belonging to the Gauntiā and registered in his name. Both can thus be termed "king's land".

Offering of Titles, Clothes and Other Symbols of Kingship

Apart from offering his land – the king's land – rent-free to the Gauntiā for cultivation, the overlord used to offer other symbols of his supremacy. Thus, the first matriculate in Bolangir State, an Aghriā who passed matriculation in 1895 in Calcutta, was honoured by the Bolangir king with the prestigious title of *S̱rī*, previously used by the kings of Sambalpur. The matriculate's family had previously used the title Patel, which was then abandoned in favour of *Sāe*. Furthermore, the king of Bamra occasionally offered clothes to his subjects, for instance a jacket presented by the king to a Gauntiā in Kuchinda, who is said to have been close to the king. The Gauntiā's name was stitched inside the jacket, which is still kept in the family. Similarly, the Gauntiā offered clothes – although much more basic, for instance a *lungi* (loin-cloth) – to loyal long-term or contract labourers (*Guti*) and house-servants.

Jagannāth-Cult – Sharing in the Authority of the Superior King

Sharing the authority of the superior king and deriving legitimacy for their own rule in the Jagannāth cult prevailed at all levels of kings and was perhaps even more significant than bestowing honours, such as titles. In the village context, the *Rath Jātrā* is an important festival traditionally sponsored by the Gauntiā, in which he explicitly replicates royal functions performed by both the king of Bamra and the Gajapati in Puri.

Sweeping in the village is performed with a new broom either by a Gauntiā, one of his brothers or a *Baḍ Parjā*.[8] *Bhog* – food for the lord – is prepared, for which the Gauntiā provides the ingredients.[9] By sponsoring the *Rath Jātrā*, the Gauntiā endeavours to share the ritual authority of superior kings to legitimise and consolidate his own rule, styling himself as the first servant of Jagannāth or "walking Viṣṇu" as the Gajapati does (Hardenberg 1999: 153). It is thus more than mere imitation of the overlord and could contain an element of rebellion or challenge, in an attempt by the Gauntiā to gain ritual sovereignty himself and effectively show that the performance of the *Rath Jātrā* is not bound to the superior level. In other words, an attempt to challenge the superiority of the king of Bamra or the Gajapati. The double-edgedness of royal symbols revealed during *Daśarā* had also been remarked on by Dirks (1979: 188), who observed that emblems can manifest royal authority but can also challenge that very authority by displaying them without permission. Similarly, while a Gauntiā may challenge a superior king, other villagers – *Baḍ Parjā* in particular – could contest the ritual authority of a Gauntiā, and there have been examples of the Gauntiā's role in ritual affairs being usurped by other villagers.

Internal Relations – the Gauntiā in Relation to His Subjects / Villagers
Signs of Prestige, Respect and Wealth

In the past, a headman was entitled to various signs of respect and obedience. Some of the latter were abolished, occasionally with the consent or support of headmen. Some simply disappeared and others again are quite common even nowadays. If a Gauntiā passed by, for instance, a *parjā* was obliged to stop his bicycle and show respect with the *namaskār* greeting. However, it was not necessary to do this if the Gauntiā was in a car. Villagers would stop and ask the Gauntiā about his family or his harvest if they saw him. Many of the older villagers still observe this tradition, albeit to a lesser extent. Furthermore, villagers had to shut their umbrella in the presence of the headman or were not even allowed to have one. A labourer (*Guti* or

Khamāri, see below) usually kept the umbrella for the Gauntiā. The Gauntiā and his family were the only villagers to wear shoes, trousers and shirts in the modern style, a custom that gradually changed later on as a result of colleges, where modern dress was obligatory. Some Gauntiā also say they encouraged other villagers to wear modern clothes. Nobody shouted in front of the Gauntiā, for fear as an elder Gauntiā explained. In the old days, when the Gauntiā or members of his family took a bath in their own pond, other villagers, who were generally allowed to use it too, had to wait till the Gauntiā was finished.

It was a matter of prestige for many Gauntiā that they were not obliged to seek work outside the house and that they had their own land to live on. Other potential sources of income were ignored as a result of the "landed gentry" image. Acknowledging failure to live off their own land would have been tantamount to a loss of prestige. Although this notion has changed considerably in recent years, it still prevails. Service jobs were not highly estimated – consistent with a *kṣatra-dharma*, which not only regards the *śudra* as universal servants within the *varṇa*-hierarchy, but from the kings' perspective places all other *varṇa* in a position of dependent servants (Trautmann 1995a [1981]: 284). A further privilege of the Gauntiā was the right to keep certain weapons. With the exception of the king and jamindār, Gauntiā were the only people allowed to keep a sword or *khandā*. Other weapons, however, such as a *gupti*, a bamboo stick roughly one and a half metres in length with a dagger half a metre long inside, were universally permitted. Up to the present day, many Gauntiā houses contain guns, which are ritually worshipped on *Rākhī Puni*.

Hunting constituted another essential element of the lifestyle of the Gauntiā as a local ruler. However, it was not an exclusive privilege of the Gauntiā, since hunting licenses were available to everyone from the magistrate (arms officer). While royal palaces often exhibit hunting trophies such as maneating-tigers, bison or other game in their rooms, Gauntiā houses display more modest trophies such as antlers – often used to build a table. In one particular case, the teeth of a tiger hunted by the father of a current Gauntiā were preserved and attached to a gold necklace worn on special occasions. Hunting symbols – a reminder of the royal conquest of the wilderness – certainly add to the prestige of the family, who imitate the habits of superior kings up to a point. Other status markers such as specific dishes, numbers of ploughs or polygyny could be added to the list.

Rākhī Puni / Rakṣā Bandhā as Durbar

The royal assembly or *durbar*, held for example in Bamra in the *durbar*-hall on *Daśarā*, forms an essential part of the constitution of kingship in India. Referring to the Mughal court, Cohn (1995 [1983]: 168) sees the act of incorporation as a central ritual of the *durbar*. Dignitaries seeking or forced to seek "incorporation" presented valuables carefully graded according to their rank and were subsequently honoured or incorporated with no less carefully ranked prestations – frequently clothes – as a sign of higher authority. Cohn (ibid.) notes:

> "Under the Mughals and other Indian rulers, these ritual prestations constituted a relationship between the giver and receiver, and were not understood as simply an exchange of goods and valuables. The khelat [prestation by Mughals – US] was a symbol 'of the idea of continuity or succession … and that continuity rests on a physical basis, depending on contact of the body of the recipient with the body of the donor through the medium of clothing'. The recipient was incorporated through the medium of the clothing into the body of the donor. This incorporation … rests on the idea that the king stands for a 'system of rule of which he is the incarnation … incorporating into his body … the persons of those who share his rule'. Those thus incorporated were not just servants of the king, but part of him …"

There is no direct equivalent to the described act of incorporation at the durbar at village level, in the sense that all the important subjects are physically assembled around a Gauntiā once a year, where they show their respect and obedience and are, in return, honoured for their loyalty. Similar processes exemplified, e.g., in gifts (*bheṭi*) and land transfer, have already been mentioned with regard to the relation between Gauntiā and overlord. Similar ideas are expressed at village level in a festival known as *Rākhī Puni*.[10] On this particular day, villagers present the Gauntiā with a *rākhī*, – a thread bound (*bandhā* = to bind) around his wrist. *Rākhī* are sometimes presented to other members of the Gauntiā's family, especially to his son as his future successor. *Rākhī* are offered to the Gauntiā in the form of an amulet to show respect and loyalty, but also dependence and as a plea for his protection. The villagers are also said to pray for the well-being of the Gauntiā on *Rākhī Puni*. In exchange for binding a *rākhi*, villagers who visit the Gauntiā house receive money and occasionally the raw ingredients for a meal (*kharchā*), coconuts, *murhi* or even a cloth (*dhoti*).[11]

The Gauntiā as Arbitrator and "Justice of Peace"

One of the prime royal functions deals with the protection to be offered by the king, which is essential in maintaining social order. The meaning at village level of *Rākhī Puni* as *durbar*, whereby villagers show their loyalty and respect and at the same time ask for the Gauntiā's protection, has just been referred to. The same idea is clearly expressed in the case of marriages in the village, when wedding parties coming to the village first call on the Gauntiā. As a rule, they give him a present of a cloth known as *gauntiā baraṇ*, which is meant as an invitation as well as a sign of respect and a request for security. In the same manner, others such as circus groups arriving in the village first pay their respects at the house of the Gauntiā, asking for permission to stay in the village and for his protection during their stay.

The function of a Gauntiā as the "Justice of Peace", however, even today still goes way beyond mere protection. He is actively involved in settling disputes – traditionally by punishing villagers who committed specific crimes such as adultery and theft. In cases of capital crime, in particular murder, the police are called. The Gauntiā deals with most minor crimes by using a stick to beat the defaulters, e.g., the stick used to drive bullocks, known as *pāchen bāri*. The beating frequently took place in public on the village road. Significantly, the most common stick used – the *pāchen bāri* – appears in their mythological story as having been offered to the Aghriā by the Gajapati after a divine verdict by Lord Jagannāth. Furthermore, the stick used by the Gauntiā is itself an expression of royal presence. Thus, a major part of the Mahabharat deals with the role of the king, who is supposed accept the use of his stick (*daṇḍa*) – as Arjuna tells Yudhiṣṭhira – in the world, since it corresponds to his *dharma* (Shulman in Hardenberg 2000: 21). In the same vein, to call for the police was – and still is – considered a *lāj* or shameful for the Gauntiā as well as the village. It means effectively that a Gauntiā is not in a position to maintain law and order in his respective area; it implies that a Gauntiā is incompetent and, ultimately, cannot fulfil his *dharma* – though some people also argued that villagers had no money to pay fines and it was too far to the next police station anyway.

Generally speaking, the verdicts of a Gauntiā were accepted and apparently there has never been a case where a villager tried to hit a Gauntiā, a possible indication of the villagers' fear of the Gauntiā and his power (*gaunti*).[12] His ability to enforce verdicts – the power of a Gauntiā – far exceeds that of a tribal headman, who could not achieve his objective in the same forceful way (Sahlins 1968). Most likely, it would have been possible in the past for a Gauntiā to put his tenant behind bars if he had wished to do so, but it seems that villagers also regarded it as a *pāp* (sin) to beat a Gauntiā. The method of settling disputes has changed considerably since the late 1960s – nowadays village meetings are arranged and often chaired by the Gauntiā.

The Gauntiā as Patron / Jājmān[13] *versus the Gauntiā as Master / Sāhu*

I will now turn to the complex network of relations between the Gauntiā and service castes, on the one hand, and between the Gauntiā and his labourers, on the other.

Since Wiser (1988 [1936]) these relationships – or rather this "system of interrelatedness" (ibid.: xxii) – have often been subsumed in the relevant literature under the term *jājmāni*-relations.[14] Wiser (ibid.: x, xix, 1, 56), describing a north-Indian setting, had stressed the element of reciprocity between the patron or *jājmān* and his servant or *kamin* – both sides having rights and responsibilities –, but also pointed to the asymmetrical nature of the power relationship. From the perspective of a Gauntiā, there are two significant types of relations:

The Gauntiā as Patron / Jājmān-Jājmāni-relations

Apart from acting as a sacrifier for the village, a Gauntiā maintained a wide range of ritual specialists and servants who contributed to certain rituals and were entitled to various payments. All these groups referred to the Gauntiā as jājmān. They include priest – Brāhmin / Tihāri (*purohit*), who performed life cycle rituals and received money (*bidāki, dakhiṇā*); ear guru / kān guru, who initiated the Aghriā by whispering a purifying mantra into their ear; also included in this category is the genealogist / dessondhi, who offered a special blessing at weddings (he receives *bhāg* = share). Furthermore, a washerman / dhobā, a barber / bandāri, a blacksmith / luhurā; a ferryman / ghaṇṭuāl; an oil-presser / teli and a potter / khumbā belong to the same category. They could all rightfully demand a payment known as *barttan*. Accordingly, the Gauntiā referred to them as *barttaniā*. While barbers and washermen were called upon particularly to remove ritual impurity during life-cycle rituals, oil-pressers and potters were essential, for example, in providing goods for a wedding such as oil for the torch lights of the groom's party and pots for the decoration of the wedding altar, respectively. The blacksmith had to supply the iron parts of the plough, which is also worshipped in certain rituals etc. In addition, they were entitled to receive gifts during the festivals (*jātrā dekhā*) and raw food for extra meals (*kharchā*) at certain times of the year (*Nuā Khāi, Rākhī Puni* etc). Only the priest – Brahmin or Tihāri – had the right to demand money. In all other cases – barber, washerman, dossondhi, ear guru, kālo, nariyā and labourer – there was only the right to demand paddy. The following picture emerges in summarising this first set of relations (the current relations I found are underlined):

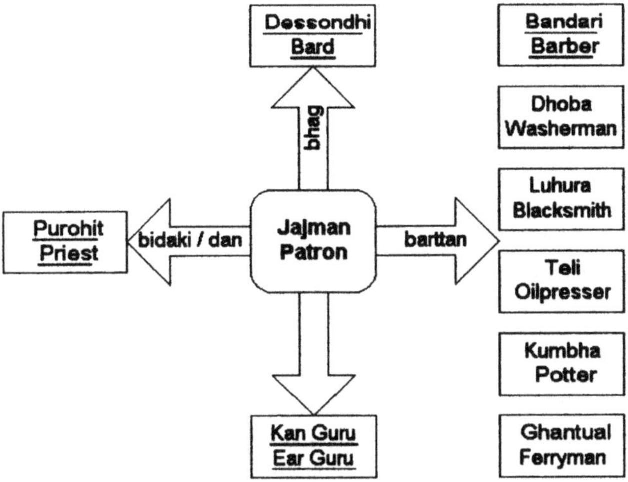

It was not necessary for all of these service relationships to be represented in the village itself. Even in the past, the only one of these nine relations that stayed in a certain village would have been the luhurā / blacksmith – the rest were external. This set of relationships actually falls into at least three sub-categories as far as gifts or payments are concerned, which cannot be discussed further at his point.[15]

The Gauntiā as Master / Sāhu[16]

A royal lifestyle also includes a wide network of servants, of which some will be mentioned here. Firstly, the storeroom keeper, revenue collector, treasurer – *khamāri*,[17] who also had to supervise the labourers, since the Gauntiā did not work in the fields himself. Loyal labourers were appointed, of course, but in some cases the job might have been inherited. Secondly, the confidential personal assistant, *bhitriā*, who was responsible for domestic affairs. The name literally denotes someone who is allowed to enter the inner rooms, a right other servants were denied. He used to be the right hand of the Gauntiā and some say he was even more powerful than a *khamāri*. Thirdly, a contract worker known as a *guti, haliā* (literally ploughman) or *kamihān* (literally worker derived from *kām* = work). A *guti* could be called in the middle of the night. His contract was renewed annually on *pous purnima*. The *guti* received the same payment as a daily labourer but was entitled to some advance payment (*nistar*). Furthermore, *guti* were invited to the landlord's family on *nuā khāi* and seen as part of the family. The *guti* was often addressed as *guti-puo*, as *guti*-son. A *guti* also receives cloth or money, particularly during festivals (*jātrā dekhā*) and used to receive some land for cultivation, known as *guti bunā* (*bunā* = to sow), from the landlord. Just as the Gauntiā received *bhogrā land* from the king, he himself offered *guti bunā* to his loyal servants. The *guti* was also provided with bullocks, ploughs and even seeds for cultivation. The *guti bunā* is also seen as a form of bonus. Fourthly, cattle herdsman or *narihā*, whose position is similar to a *guti*. Fifthly, maid servant / domestic servant or *ghar khiā*, who were not only entitled to food in the house, but also to other household necessities (soap etc). Sixthly, female domestic labourers or *kām karā* – usually women, forming to some extent an equivalent to the male contract labourers or *guti*. Seventhly, female water carrier or *pāenti* – women from the herdsmen caste (Gauḍen) engaged to bring water – particularly drinking water to the Aghriā-houses. Eighthly, night-guards or *suāti*: This kind of servant did not work manually but guarded the house at night. Frequently unmarried, guti acted as *suāti* too and used to stay in the sāhu's house during the night until they married. Ninthly, daily labourers or *butiyā* the term *butiyā* being derived from *buti* / wage - who were hired on a daily basis. The whole set of relations is summarised in a diagram below (servants currently found in a Gauntiā family are underlined). There is a certain flexibility in the system, which should be kept in mind, e.g., guti can act as suāti etc.

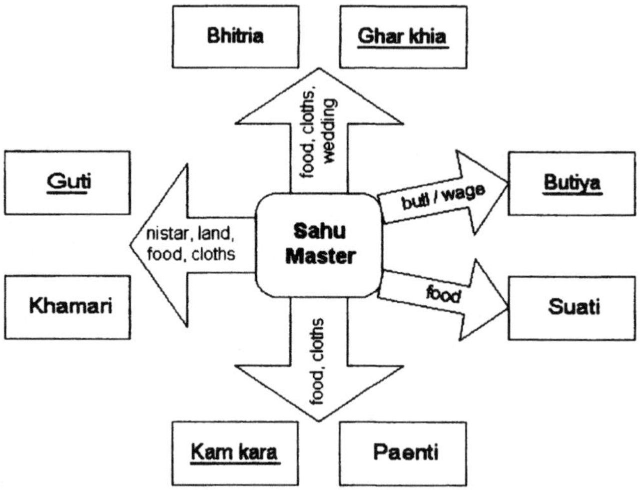

Relations between Gauntiā and Village Functionaries

Apart from these two networks, there are other village relations such as those between the Gauntiā and specific villagers that offer services to the entire village. These include a *Narihā* – a cattle herdsman; a *kālo* – a priest of the village goddess; a *beherā* – a village messenger; and a *pujāri* – a temple priest. All of them have often received land from the Gauntiā known e.g., as *narihā jāmi*, which could also be registered in the Gauntiā's name. As a rule, they were also entitled to receive gifts known as *jātrā dekhā* at festivals. However, their function is seen in relation to the whole village rather than merely to the Gauntiā.[18]

Analysis – Categories, Relations and Hierarchical Aspects

To begin with, both sets of relationships will be compared again. Firstly, the use of the terms *jājmān* and *sāhu* are common to both types of relations as a reference only. Secondly, while *jājmāni* relations are characterised by intervals, e.g., the barber comes once a week, relations with the *sāhu* exist on a day-to-day basis. Additionally, the *jājmāni* relations are conceived as permanent. Thirdly, all communities involved in *jājmāni* relations with the possible exception of the ferryman are involved in some way in rituals performed by the Gauntiā to remove impurity or attain purity. Alternatively, they offer products worshipped in the patron's house, e.g., the plough, pots used during weddings. Their higher status may be a result of this involvement. Relations to communities that refer to their patron as sāhu are of a more economic nature in the sense that no ritual impact could be detected.

Fourthly, another important distinction between the two sets of relations addresses the geographical area where communities with a *jājmāni* relation serve their patron exclusively. The right to this service can be – and usually is – inherited traditionally by the eldest son. These two aspects – the geographically fixed area, i.e., a certain number of villages or simply the *jājmāni*, and the right of the sons to inherit the service rights of their fathers to serve certain *jājmāns* – are absent from the relation between a *sāhu* and his labourers. Fifthly, there is a further distinction as far as status is concerned. Families, who refer to the patron as *jājmān*, are often ranked higher and get better treatment than communities serving on a daily basis. Thus, *jājmāni* relations are more valued and of higher status. Barbers, washermen etc. are considered more as guests than as servants in the strict sense, i.e., barbers etc. are treated more politely than labourers. The treatment of the former, however, is not as considerate as it is towards other patrons / *jājmān* in the village. Service is not generally valued highly from the point of view of the Gauntiā (although this is changing as far as bureaucracy is concerned). One could, therefore, derive the following hierarchy, which seems to correspond to concepts of wealth and prestige (whereby, of course, wealth and prestige are also seen here as relative):

Hierarchy

1. Gauntiā
2. Other Jājmān / Sāhu (Baḍ Parjā/upper castes)[19]
3. Barber, Washerman and other *barttaniā* (except Brahmin)[20]
4. Labourers: Guti/Butiyā

Leaving earlier discussions on the "exploitative" or rather "integrative" character of the *jājmāni* system aside (see Parry 1979: 76ff), I would like to underline that both sets of relationships are hierarchically ordered. In contrast to Wiser's primary focus on reciprocity, Dumont (1980 [1966]: 101f) emphasised the hierarchical order behind *jājmāni* relationships – the barber etc. serving only particular high-status communities. Here, not only are specific communities ordered by other communities that serve or refuse to serve them but two sets of relationships are ranked. *Jājmāni* relations conceptualised as permanent and hereditary and focused on the performance of rituals, for which a certain purity is essential, are more valued than short-term, contractual labour arrangements with far less ritual involvement. Thus, one might argue that the Gauntiā as *jājmān* encompasses the Gauntiā in his "*avatār*" as *sāhu*.[21] This, however, does not mean that there is a distinction between a somewhat religious level – *jājmāni* relations – and a second purely economic level.[22] Besides, these categories are not only hierarchised but also related through certain gifts – the receiving of *kharchā* (raw food for a meal) at *rākhī* and *pousa puni* as well as gifts during festivals such as *Śibrātrī* or *rath jātrā* and those known as *jātrā dekhā* (money, clothes), which is systematised below.

Thus, various sets of relations are interconnected by a Gauntiā or landlord, who as king had conquered the wilderness and gained "resources" including the services of conquered people (Falk 1973: 3). Furthermore, a Gauntiā as a prime donor fulfilling an essential royal function incorporates the servants.

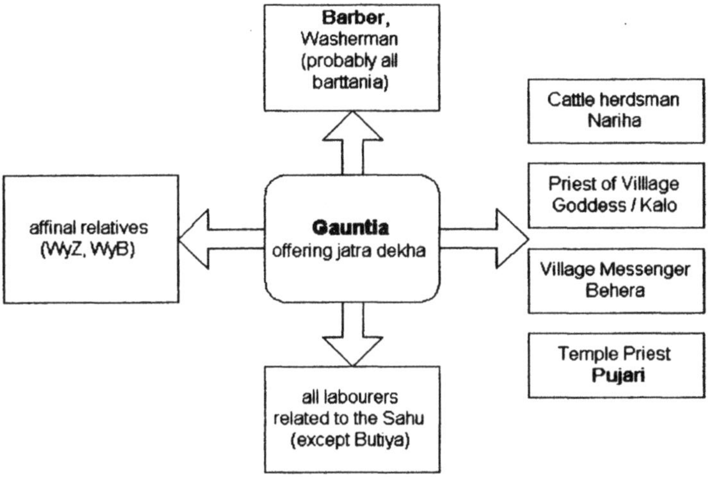

The Relation to the Village Goddess

The importance of a goddess – or more specifically an *iṣṭā devī* – in relation to kings has already been noted frequently in royal inscriptions (see e.g., *Lāngulesvara Itihāsa*) as well as the ethnographic and historical literature for India (Galey (ed.) 1990; Basu 2000) and Orissa in particular (Kulke 2001 [1978], Hardenberg 2000, Schnepel 2002). The relation between the Gauntiā and the village goddess mirrors the link between superior kings and their *iṣṭadevī*. In addition, their goddesses (and gods) could be put into a fairly consistent and analogous order, equivalent to the ranking of kings at various levels.

The Village Goddess and Her Priest – *Kālo*

The village goddess resides in a shrine known as *demul*[23] (*de* = god / goddess; *mul* = root / under a tree) in the sense of a sacred grove or abode of gods in the forest.[24] Her shrine is usually situated on the outskirts of the village, in a small forest near the village rather than deep in the jungle. The goddess is worshipped in the form of stones or termite hills. There are three major rituals for the village goddess, corresponding to the seasons: the *grām Śrī pūjā* after the harvest has been completed and before sowing, the *nisā-pūjā* (*nisā* = night) after cutting the paddy, and finally the *bihuḍā-pūjā* before transplanting and loosening the soil. All of these rituals contain blood sacrifices to the goddess – mainly billy-goats and cocks. The priest – not a professional in the sense of a Brāhmin but a peasant who additionally worships the village deities at intervals – usually has to belong to a high-status tribal community such as Kandh or Bhuyān and is chosen by the Gauntiā and the village community or *panchayat*. There is also an element of heredity attached to his post. Sometimes a Gauntiā or someone from his lineage acts as a priest of the village goddess, meaning that the kālo does not belong to a tribal community but to the Aghriā. In this case, the Gauntiā naturally increases his influence on the cult of the goddess – being simultaneously both patron and priest of the goddess.

The Role of the Gauntiā in the Cult of Grām Śri

The Gauntiā obviously has a very exalted position in the cult of the village goddess (or Mauli Mā etc.). He is the prime donor who offers the ritual items for worship, including valuable animal sacrifices. Additionally, there are stories circulating that the ritual cannot proceed properly without the Gauntiā's presence – a fact that privileges the Gauntiā further. Having privileged access to the goddess effectively means access to female power (*śakti*) embodied by the goddess. As Marglin (1989 [1985]: 300) noted in relation to the Gajapati, royal power is *śakti*-power, each Gajapati being "symbolically infused with the female procreative powers".[25] Therefore, not to worship the goddess ather shrine would mean to lose power and subsequently the kingdom.[26]

In some cases he even has the additional function of the priest and thus becomes the patron-servant (Tanabe 1996: 211) of the Grām Śri. The role of the Gauntiā in this regard resembles the situation of the Gajapati, who according to pontifical ideology is not only king but first servant of Lord Jagannāth and without whose presence and involvement as royal sweeper the *rath jātrā* cannot be conducted properly (Hardenberg 1999: 154).

Furthermore, the location of the goddess's shrine in the forest or sacred grove – in the wider sense in the wilderness – and the necessity for the Gauntiā to worship her at her shrine periodically hints at an age-old dilemma. This was already faced by kings in ancient scriptures and apparently by the Gauntiā as well. As Heesterman (1998: 22ff) argues, the conundrum of kingship lies in the fact that the "king has to be both part of the community and foreign to it" or to put it another way, his authority is based on the "alien, outside sphere of the jungle" (*araṇya*), while he is obliged to rule over the "settled, agricultural community" (*grāma*) (Heestermann 1998: 24). Therefore, according to Heesterman (ibid.: 30), the king alternates within the ritual cycle between these two spheres. In the same way – in an ancient royal fashion – the Gauntiā unites both elements, *bana* and *kṣetra* (Sontheimer 1994), by performing the rituals of the grām ŗri. Furthermore, the Gauntiā thus bridges the gap quite literally between caste society often associated with *kṣetra / grāma* and tribal society linked to *bana / araṇya* (Heesterman 1998: 24; Sontheimer 1994: 127ff). However, not only the alternating Gauntiā unites different spheres, but also the goddess herself, who resides within the village territory but in a part considered to be rather wild. "As such the shrine is a kind of preserve, a presence of the wilderness in more civilized areas." as Falk (1973: 4) observed. Thus both – the Gauntiā and the Goddess – incorporate aspects of liminality.

Conclusion: Relations between Gods, Kings and Subjects

I have tried to demonstrate the deep embeddedness of Aghriā-Gauntiā in concepts of kingship. Thus, the Gauntiā embodied kings following their *kṣatra-dharma* while conquering tribal land and cultivating the wilderness. Later on they institutionalised the alternating movement of the king between the settlement and the forest in the worship of the village goddess. In an arena of Hinduisation and Tribalisation, the Gauntiā acted as agents of change by building temples, inviting Brahmins and developing the land using new technologies. They thus played a decisive role in the process of "intensive propaganda" (Weber 1988 [1921]: 11) or "inner colonisation" and still do (Pfeffer 1978: 426; Kulke 2001 [1978]: 3).

Furthermore, Gauntiā manifested their *kṣatra-dharma* by becoming the supreme and universal donor on the village level – themselves integrated into the network of a superior king as a subject, but also integrating their own subjects on the lower level. Keeping in mind definitions of little kingdoms such as that proposed by Berkemer (1993: 13)[27] Gauntiā may well be understood as little kings within their own realm. Relations of a Gauntiā to the Raja of Bamra – of a little king to his overlord – are strikingly mirrored by relations between guti and Gauntiā, respectively. Both are bound to their superior king by sharing the king's land as well as by receiving gifts such as clothes. Gifting and sharing rights establishes the network of relations between the levels and more important, servants are incorporated into a royal body, becoming part of it (Cohn 1995 [1983]: 168). Therefore, the king may represent what Kantorowicz (1994 [1957]: 31ff) termed a *body politic*: the eternal, immortal, invisible, immaterial as well as collective, incorporating not only the actual king in his *body natural* or present appearance but also all subjects as imagined parts. Thus, the *body politic* – the idea of kingship – remains in existence even after the abolition of the kingdom or Gauntiā-system and survives the "absented throne" (Galey 1990b: 129), since it represents a whole from the king's perspective.[28]

There has been a long debate in the relevant literature on the question of superiority between king and Brahmin.[29] As Trautmann (1995a [1981]: 278ff), Galey (1990b: 169), Basu (2000: 163) and others have pointed out, there are different, contextual patterns of classification, depending on the perspective of the king or Brahmin, expressed in forms of exchange or rituals in the temple as opposed to rituals in the palace. While the Brahmin stands highest in a hierarchy of ritual purity, it is the king who, as supreme donor, ranks above all in a hierarchy of dependency.

On the village level the relation is manifested in certain ambivalences. On the one hand, the high status of Brahmin remains conspicuously absent during the *rākhī puni* rituals, arguing that he is not interested in the money offered by the Gauntiā in return for a *rākhī*. The motif of the Brahmin trying to avoid taking gifts in an attempt to maintain his independence seems obvious here, although they do take gifts on many other occasions. On the other hand, Aghriā-Gauntiā in neighbouring Chattisgarh (Sarangarh-area) relates that the Gauntiā – as their superior kings – do not show respect for the Brahmin by visiting their house in the form of *praṇām*, but only by providing a privileged seat next to the Gauntiā. However, Gauntiā in Kuchinda area and their family members carry out *praṇām*.[30] Furthermore, if tea is offered as usual on visiting the house of their *purohit*, it is the Gauntiā who washes up, although the *purohit* (Tihāri or Brāhmin) might protest. Not to wash one's own dishes on such an occasion would mean committing a *pāp* (sin) for the Gauntiā, who bears in mind the respective ritual purity. Thus, the ambivalent relation between king and Brahmin reflects that kingship and the royal network established and upheld by the Gauntiā is only one specific pattern ordering society. This can be dominant or subordinate depending on the context. In this article, however, I was concerned with the royal perspective only.

Finally, the relations of a Gauntiā to his superior kings and his subjects within a hierarchy of dependency (Trautmann 1995a [1981]: 278) as well as to the gods will be systematised here. Applying a model recently developed by Galey might help to place the Gauntiā in a wider sacred order. Beginning with kingship in Garhwal, Galey (1990b: 166ff) argued that royalty[31] could be defined as a combination of three ritual complexes: 1. the throne or *piṭha* as a seat of mastery into which a king married and was thus spatially rooted or rather attached to demarked soil; 2. the kingdom is ritually conceptualised as an active field or *kṣetra* animated by female potency (*śakti*) and embodied by a goddess to whom blood sacrifices are offered and 3. the king derives authority from his special relationship to a sovereign god, in whose cult he has a privileged position. The third element is regarded as particularly important for royal legitimation, since it places the palace within a space governed by the tutelary deity or *avatār* god in Galey's terms (*iṣṭadevtā, raṣṭradevatā*) – Viṣṇu in the form of Bhadrinath in the case of Garhwal. In relation to the *avatār* god expressed in the place of passage or *tīrtha*, the kingdom becomes a realm of order, a particular universe linked to the general universe or cosmos. Thus kingship is manifested by a complementarity of three elements: *piṭha* / mastery, *kṣetra* / potency and *tīrtha* / universality.

> "They associate the king in his palace with a throne, preside over the destiny of a kingdom which takes the form of a sacrificial area, before even inscribing it as a world of earthly limits and illimited potential" (Galey 1990b: 171)

Coming back to the Gauntiā, one could argue that a similar Vaishnava conception of kingship can be found at village level as well. First and foremost, the Gauntiā is linked to the Grām Śrī in relation to whom a *kṣetra*, an "arena of potency", is established. The Gauntiā derives *śakti* by offering blood sacrifices to the village goddess, who is related to fertility, auspiciousness etc. Being the prime donor in her rituals, the Gauntiā as symbolic head of the village is the direct counterpart of the goddess, who pours blood on her soil and "makes it possible for the procreative forces which lie in her womb to find an appropriate soil" (Galey 1990b: 168). The *śakti* of a Grām Śrī, however, locally or territorially fixed as it is, ranks lower in scale than that of Durgā – or her manifestation Kanak Durgā, who as *iṣṭadevī* of the Gajapati as well as Raja of Bamra constitutes a potency arena for and with them.

Furthermore, in some cases Gauntiā were able to link themselves directly to Lord Jagannāth (as a form of Viṣṇu), the *iṣṭadevatā* of their superior kings: the king of Bamra as well as the Gajapati. Ultimate legitimation derives from Lord Jagannāth as Lord of the Universe, whose title symbolises best the universality he embodies. Thus, on the one hand, a Gauntiā as village king does not derive his authority from Lord Jagannāth directly, but via his overlord(s) and fixed in a *patā* (skt. paṭṭa, land deed), making his authority secondary and indirect – in contrast to the primary *śakti* he derives from the village goddess. On the other hand, a Gauntiā can attempt to derive his authority directly from Lord Jagannāth by performing the *Rath Jātrā* himself. Thus by simultaneously imitating and rebelling against – or rather challenging – his overlords, a Gauntiā may try to style himself as a king or Gajapati and as a "walking Viṣṇu" (*calanti Viṣṇu*).

This leaves the question of Gauntiā's throne. Although there is no *gādī* (throne) as such, the relations – or mastery and dominance – a throne represents could well be found in a village. Galey (1990b: 171f) himself stresses this point:

> "The throne thus represents a mere relation than an object. Distinct in that from the tutelary temples, its reference is not one of concrete and permanent geography. Rather, its meaning lies more in the ceremonial display of items and actors than in the items and actors themselves."[32]

It has already been pointed out that the rituals of *rākhī puni* could be understood as royal *durbar*, where the Gauntiā once more acts as prime donor, thus binding loyal subjects to his "seat of mastery". Mastery seems to be expressed particularly by the role of the Gauntiā as *sāhu*, while the Gauntiā as *jājmān* tends to establish his links to or place in the cosmology. A Gauntiā embedded in a network of relations just described – to his subjects; to superior kings, for whom he is a subject; to Lord Jagannāth as well as a Grām Śrī – is shown in a diagram below, in which links, however, had to be simplified to some extent, since a Gauntiā might also try to establish relations to Durgā by performing rituals on *Daśarā*.[33]

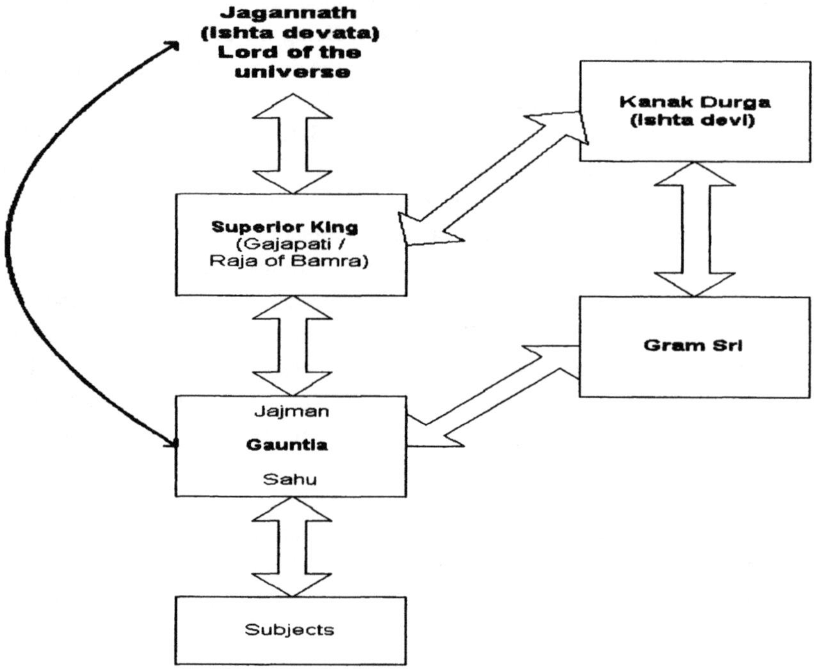

Notes

1 As Sahlins (1968: 5) pointed out, tribal society is characterised by a condition of permanent, latent war – or Warre in the sense of Hobbes –, while in peasant society, central institutions such as an appointed Gauntiā maintain law and order, guaranteeing the peace.

2 The distinction external versus internal relations is purely a matter of clear description but not made in the empirical context.

3 A long-term assessment of revenue collection was made by officers of the king, who used to revise the settlements every few years. Thus the revenue collection system seems to incorporate elements of both the Mughal and Maratha systems (Rothermund 1978: 36).

4 The timber logs were often taken over by the Forest Department to generate some extra revenue for the king.

5 Revenue as *rājasva* or *khajanā* (Oriya) or *māl bhujāri* (Sambalpuri).

6 Similar conditions were noted for neighbouring Chota Nagpur in late 19th / early 20th century by Schwerin (1977: 96, 117, 269ff), who argues that a scarcity of labour led to the introduction of socage. Forced labour varied from village to village, but higher castes – particularly Brahmins – were usually excluded from it. A traditional norm per year could consist of three days each of ploughing, digging, sowing / transplanting and harvesting, one or two days of threshing, a day for basket-making and seven to fifteen days transport work (Schwerin 1977: 271, see also 468). The landlords usually provided food and sometimes paid for the work, if it exceeded the traditional limit. In 1902, laws were introduced to turn socage into payment, although villagers were usually not able to pay any money. Although formally abolished. (ibid: 470ff), socage continued to exist around Ranchi until the 1940s. Thus, a service – possibly originally restricted to peasants settled by the landlord under this very condition – was changed into money rent (Rothermund 1978: 174f).

7 Schnepel (2002: 272) mentions that *bhet* – probably identical with *bheṭi* – was offered to the Queen in Jeypore by attending ladies during *Daśarā*.

8 There seems to be a tendency for Gauntiās to prefer to sprinkle water only and leave the sweeping to a brother or *Baḍ Parjā* – perhaps a rejection of an occupation conceived to be unclean.

9 The ingredients include rice (*aruā chāul*), molasses, milk, clarified butter (*ghī*), *mugdāl*, coconut, cardamom, gloves, raisins, cashew nuts and rice powder.

10 Also known as *Rakshā Bandhā* in Oriya and celebrated on full moon day in the month of Srābana.

11 Since the Gauntiā system is partly in decline, it is not surprising that nowadays fewer villagers visit the Gauntiā on this day than in the past. It should be noted that the festival is not exclusively centred around the Gauntiā, but rather shows various relations of dependency. Thus sisters fast during the day and bind a *rākhī* to their brothers, who with their wives bind *rākhī* to the ancestors and the different representations of Gods and Goddesses in the house. Thus, the Gauntiā not only incorporates villagers but the various levels of incorporation and superiority are quite literally bound or connected with a *rākhī*.

12 For a researcher staying at an influential headman's house, being associated with his family and often seen walking around with him or members of his family, it is obviously quite difficult to deal with critical remarks about the headman. There may, of course, be cases of opposition or envy towards him.

13 Pocock (1962: 81ff) noted that prior to Wiser's work, the term *jājmān* was less accepted and never universally known or used in India, instead of which the neutral term client was en vogue. However, I use it as an emic term.

14 Rothermund 1978, Pocock 1962.

15 Compared to other ethnographic cases, the service of carpenters, gardeners or astrologers are missing in the scheme presented. If such services are required, a price – *dām* – is paid, e.g., to

the *Jyotisiā* (astrologer), who writes horoscopes after the birth of a child and is consulted on constellations of stars prior to festivals or life-cycle rituals, all of which he does occasionally and in addition to his farm work. A Brahmin might also be asked about auspicious constellations of stars but not to write a horoscope. In two cases I encountered, Aghriā acted as *Jyotisiā*, which might be the reason why they were not in permanent jājmāni relations, including a gift exchange. As far as carpentry is concerned, every villager is free to pursue this profession and can sell his products, if they are of a certain quality.

16 In some cases the Gauntiā might have appointed other labourers / service-holders, e.g., people known as *Daḍhā* to collect revenue for him, if the village is very big. However, in most cases they collected it directly. In Sarangarh, a powerful Gauntiā had a representative in every hamlet (*sahi*) – not only to collect the revenue but also to convey his orders. The *Daḍha* resembles a Behera with wider functions but I did not come across any in present Orissa.

17 The name is derived from *khamār* or storeroom of a king.

18 They are not considered servants and relations between Gauntiā and Kālo are characterised by mutual respect. The Chamār serve the whole village but unlike the others receive neither land nor gifts.

19 In the village of Mundaloi, where I stayed, around 25 families who belonged to Aghriā, Māḷi, Gaṇḍ and Kandh maintained *jājmāni* relations.

20 On the relation between king and Brahmin, see conclusion.

21 The case of Kangra presented by Parry (1979: 59ff) hints at a similar situation. The *Purohit* – the barber being subsumed in this category too – is opposed to or rather tied to the *Jajman* in a "permanent alliance" (67). In contrast, the relation of the *Kamin* (craftsmen) – the term itself has "distinctly derogatory connotations and always applies to inferiors" (67) – to the *Zamindar* is more contractual, since unlike the *Purohit*, the *Kamin* has no right to serve ancestral property. Furthermore, while the *Purohit* receives gifts (*dān*), the Kamin receives payments. However, although Parry distinguishes between "priests" and "craftsmen" in the case I described, it is more a differentiation between "priests cum artisans" and "field-labourers cum domestic servants".

22 As Parry (1979: 79) argued, there is an on-going "extension of the 'economic frontier'", which means that even *jājmāni* relations constructed as permanent could be replaced by market-like relations, as seen in the case of potters, oil-pressers etc.

23 In one case, it was argued that the shrine of the village goddess can also be called *mer* and the sacrifice, *meriā* similar to the *mer khuṇṭ* at the centre of the threshing floor.

24 The village goddess does not usually remain alone, but is joined by other divine beings such as *Rākasbuḍhā* .

25 Marglin (1989 [1985]: 300) observed opposition between the royal power / *śakti* and the power of ascetic heat / *tapas*.

26 See Falk (1973: 4) for examples of this theme in ancient scriptures.

27 Berkemer (1993: 13) observed: "Ein politisches System, dessen Herrscher sich innenpolitisch als unabhängig betrachten kann, also zum Beispiel eine eigene Armee hält, Steuern einzieht, Tribute von kleineren Königen und chiefs empfängt und ihnen Titel verleiht, und der zudem eine unabhängige Ritualpolitik im Inneren seines Territoriums betreibt, aber zugleich einen politisch wie rituell über ihm stehenden, militärisch überlegenen Oberherrn anerkennen muß, dessen Autorität er teilt und zur Legitimation seiner eigenen Herrschaft nach innen hin benötigt, soll als little kingdom bezeichnet werden. " This definition fits the Gauntiā very well in a wider sense. Obviously Gauntiā do not command their own army, nor do they levy their own tax, but as shown, Gauntiā have rights to keep certain weapons and receive gifts or tributes etc.

28 See also Dirks (1979: 200), who argues that the alienation of land in particular symbolised "the personal authority of the king ... and ... represented a part of the whole which was symbolised by the king". Keeping in mind the holism of the caste system, Galey (1990b) proposed that the whole represented by the king stands in a hierarchically lower position to the

whole.

29 See Dumont (1980 [1966], Raheja (1988) et al. Intrinsically related to this question is the point of the sacrality of the king. While Hocart (1927: 1, 236f) argued that kingship is essentially divine, Dumont (1980 [1966]: 293) insisted on its secularisation, leaving the king the sole individual with magico-religious functions.

30 Some people also say that the Aghriā brides and grooms wearing a crown and symbolising Lakṣmī and Narāyaṇ should not do the *praṇām*. In practice, however, they usually do.

31 Galey (1990a, b) proposed a regional perspective on kingship in India. In my opinion, his theory is applicable to Orissa or more specifically to Western Orissa as well. However, for other regional concepts of kingship in India, i.e., Gujarat / Western India, see Basu (2000).

32 Furthermore, Galey (1990b: 172) pointed out that "Once united with the throne, the king is no longer the first among equals but "the whole and the parts" ritually acknowledged by all clans."

33 Lord Jagannāth as Lord of the Universe is not bound and therefore not put in a rectangle. Lord Jagannāth and Kanak Durgā are also related (Hardenberg 2000).

Validating "Tradition" . Revisiting Keonjhar and Bhuiyan Insurgency in Colonial Orissa[1]

Chandi Prasad Nanda

I

In tune with the stated objectives of the panel on "Little Kingdom" in South Asia, the following essay is a preliminary undertaking for a more elaborate study on the history of Keonjhar – an ex-feudatory Orissan state (*gadjat*; fort born). In fact, one of the most fundamental objectives is to explore the possibilities of tapping source materials pertaining to Orissan *gadjat* states of Orissa in archival collections, oral history and field surveys, backed by the characteristic professionalism of a student of history and social anthropology. In attempting a study of this nature, the thrust is not only to point to the empirical importance of these states in terms of possible collections of data, which have often been wished away or grossly underplayed. At the same time, it is equally important in the light of new sources to initiate an inter-disciplinary dialogue within the disciplines of history, anthropology and indology and thereby to revisit some of the existing historiographic approaches centring on the *gadjat* states. In this way, a study of this kind also has a restorative function.

Moreover, the actual rethinking of conventional methodological approaches to the study of these states can be of considerable help in updating the knowledge base on "little kingdoms" and contribute more profitably to existing scholarship on the nature of state in South Asia.

It is in this context that initial interest in locating and critically engaging with local chronicles or *Rājavaṁśāvali*s (Royal genealogies) essentially led us to focus on Keonjhar *gadjat* as an example of "little/jungle kingdoms" (Schnepel/Berkemer: n. d.) and to specifically consider its significance in terms of the hilly hinterland and its preponderant tribal population.[2]

The archival collections on these states in the 19th/20th century context make one sensitive to the barrage of information relating to the varied aspects of their royal administrative structures, popular resistance periodically organised against the "oppressive *rājā*s", colonial interventions vis-à-vis the states, ritual practices followed by the kings and subject populace (both caste and tribe) of the state in question and its linkage or otherwise with the "greater" religious traditions at the regional plane.[3]

It is of interest to note the nature and making of local chronicles on the *gadjat* states, mostly available in the shape of royal genealogies. These texts usually contain a substantially valorised piece of information on the ruling dynasties as well as bits of reference on the history, ecology, culture and people of these states.[4] "Biographies" of the "little/jungle kingdoms" characteristically betray a typical perception of the past and the associated time notion. The "multi-layered" past, as these texts reveal and Kulke has perceptively analysed, point to "three distinct" yet "interrelated" imagings of time in terms of an imagined pan-Indian past, constructed regional past and the remembered local past in swift succession (Kulke forthcoming b). Moreover, the more significant "contradictory" aspect of these texts is the "funnel-like" perceptions of "space and time". In other words, the very location of "sacred space" against the larger canvas of a mythologically imagined pan-Indian past is thinned down in subsequent stages and finally ends up with a vividly remembered local historical past.

However, the paper in its present form does not intend to dwell at length on any of the recently located chronicles or Keonjhar *Rājavaṁśāvali*s that have hitherto remained unexplored in terms of scholarly focus. On the other hand, it seeks to investigate some important issues in the context of Keonjhar state. First of all, it illustrates the process by which some tribal societies developed into "little kingdoms" or continued to retain their "symbolic sovereignty" over the king by installing or removing the latter, processes that were marked by elaborate rituals and phases of rebellion, respectively. This particular aspect is dealt with against the backdrop of the existing royal genealogical tradition of the state and what was referred to above as the vividly remembered local historical past. In a sense, a critical examination of the theme begs the other related issues that have been partly broached in the paper, such as the complex relationship between tribal groups and Hindu kings or how a little king's legitimatory ritual policy changes in the overall context of tribal ritual practices and beliefs.[5]

Although the present essay is not fully equipped at this stage to explain all the issues it confronts conceptually, it modestly ventures to map the nature of kingship or royal authority, the relationship between caste and tribe, domains of religion and politics, the nature and pattern of the transformation of "traditional" Indian society and its value system under the pressure of colonial rule. In dealing with aspects of tribal ritual practices and rebellion, the paper also attempts to examine the elemental structuring of popular consciousness.

In concrete terms, while weaving out a narrative on the *rājā* and rebels in the context of Keonjhar by primarily focusing on the "Bhuiyan rebellion" that sought to oppose and overthrow the Keonjhar *rājā* in the 1860s and 1890s, the paper proceeds to stress the fact that in tribal perception, the notions of "legitimacy" and "authority" remained symbolically dominant over the idea of "power and command" – the "actual political" sovereignty in which the kingship was embedded.[6]

II

We begin this narrative by taking a rather long extract from E. T. Dalton's account of the Bhuiyan community.

> "... They are then in Keonjhur, as in Bonai, a race whom you cannot help liking and taking an interest in from the primitive simplicity of their customs, their amenability, their anxiety to oblige; but unsophisticated as they are, they wield an extraordinary power in Keonjhur, and when they take it into their heads to use that power, the country may be said to be governed by an oligarchy composed of the sixty chiefs of the Pawri Desh, the Bhuiyan Highlands. A knotted string passed from village to village in the name of the sixty chiefs throws the entire country into commotion, and the order which is verbally communicated in connection with it, is as implicitly obeyed as if it emanated from the most potent despot. It is not because they are stronger, braver or better armed, that they exercise this supremacy; it arises from two causes, prestige and position. The Pawris dispute with the Juangs the claim to be the first settlers in Keonjhur, and boldly aver that the country belongs to them. They assert that the Raja is of their creation and that the prerogative of installing every new Raja on his accession is theirs and theirs alone. The Hindu population of Keonjhar is in excess of the Bhuiya, and it comprises Gonds and Kols, but the claim of the Pawris to the dominion they arrogate, is admitted by all; even Brahmans and Rajputs respectively acknowledge it, and the former, by the addition of Brahmanical rite to the wild ceremonies of the Bhuiyas, affirm and sanctify their installation..." (Dalton 1973: 144f)

The above characterisation of the Bhuiyans, a predominant tribe of Keonjhar state in terms of ritual tradition, integrally complex relationships with the Hindu caste system, kingship and above all of locating their consciousness, pointedly brings out the perceptions usually shared by colonial administrator-cum-historians and indologists.[7] However, such accounts are often found guilty of the typical limitations associated with colonial historiography and the blatant orientalist perspective such discourses display. The nationalist perspective, on the other hand, often tends to glorify individual kings and "valorise/celebrate" the cultural achievements of the princely states as pioneered by such kings. In contrast, Marxist historiography critically denigrates individual kings and seeks to explain or justify popular protest organised in opposition to the kings of such states, on the grounds of economic exploitation perpetrated by the latter on their subjects. Perspectives of this kind thus inevitably pound at the highly despotic nature of kingship in the erstwhile semi-feudal enclaves otherwise dubbed as *Andhari Mulak* (region of darkness).[8] They no doubt explain, but at the same time delimit the possibility of exploring the varied yet integrally complex relationships that exist between the domains of politics, religion and culture in the context of these states.

As observed earlier, the paper does not wish to trace the origin of the "little kingdom" by probing the authenticity of various genealogical traditions in regard to Keonjhar. Suffice it to mention here that Keonjhar's early history broadly coincides with that of Mayurbhanj district. We will briefly examine some of the traditions in the making of the Bhuiyan dynasty of Keonjhar. The discovery of the Asanpat inscriptions in this context is revealing in sofaras it dates the origin of the state back to the 5th-6th century A. D. (Senapati/Sahu (eds.) 1986: 42f). Further, it is well-known that the territory was called Vindhyatavi at the time and remained under the rule of a branch of the Naga dynasty. The donor "Maharaja Satrubhanja", son of "Maharaja Manabhanja", was of Naga lineage, born of Mahadevi Damayanti. Moreover, Manabhanja had defeated the Devaputras "Kushana Murundas" in hundreds of battles. Satrubhanja was perhaps succeeded by Disabhanja, whose name figures in the small inscription found in the Ravanchhaya cave shelter in Sitabinji near Keonjhar (Senapati/Sahu (eds.) 1986: 42f). It seems both these rulers remained patrons of Saivism – a fact testified by donations to Saiva *Matha*s and Saiva *Acharya*s by Satrubhanja and the subsequent emergence of Sitabinji as a major centre of Saivism. However, the history of Keonjhar remains obscure up to the advent of Adibhanja of Khijjinga Kota, who can be traced back to the 10th century A. D.

The Bhanjas of Khijjinga Kota ruled in all probability over an extensive territory comprising the modern districts of Mayurbhanj, Keonjhar and Singhbhu, known at the time as Khijjinga Mandala. In fact, Keonjhar belonged to the Southern part of the *Mandal*, known as Dakhina Khanda. It was also pointed out that Sultan Firuz Shah, who invaded Orissa through Khijjinga during the 14th century A. D., not only destabilised the empire but that this campaign forced the Bhanjas to shift their political headquarters from Khijjinga Kota (identified with Khiching) to Hariharpur. It was in this context perhaps that Keonjhar became a separate dominion under a chief named Jyoti Bhanja, who was apparently a scion of the Bhanja ruling family of Khijjing Mandala (Senapati/Sahu (eds.) 1986: 42f).

Another interesting tradition points to the Rajput origin of the state, which possibly gained currency in the late 19th century.[9] As per this tradition, one Jai Singh, son of Man Singh, a Kachua Rajput of the solar race and a Chief of Jeypore in Rajputana, visited Puri in the 11th century A. D. (1088 A. D.). He subsequently entered a matrimonial alliance with the Gajapati king of Puri and received Hariharpur as dowry. Later on, he was blessed with two sons named Adi Singh and

Jyoti Singh. The elder son Adi Singh, it has been told, displayed prowess in the war field by overpowering the troublesome chief Mayuradhwaja, an act that gained him the epithet "Bhanja" (*bhañjana* or to break) from the Gajapati ruler of Puri. Furthermore, Jai Singh had divided his territory into two parts before his death and put Adi Singh in charge of Mayurbhanj, who ruled from Adipur. Similarly, Jyoti Singh received the Keonjhar portion and ruled from Jyotipur, the headquarters named after the king himself. Although both headquarters initially remained on opposite sides of the river Baitarini, the two brothers subsequently shifted their capitals to more central areas. This tradition also suggests that the twenty-second Bhanja king, Gobind Bhanja, fell out with his father and left Keonjhar. He joined the service of the Puri ruler and was rewarded for the latter's victory in the battle of Kanchi Kaveriwith the *Zamindari* of Athagarh (now known as Anandpur) on his accession to the Keonjhar throne.

However, the fallacy of the tradition is clearly evident in the references to Kachua Rajput family, the town of Jeypore, and their linkage to the Gajapati king of Puri during the 11th century. Moreover, there is no reference to this tradition in the Sanskrit drama *Bhanja Mahodayam*, authored by the poet Narasingh Mishra in the early 19th century. The era of Gobind Bhanja cannot be as early as that of Gajapati Purushottama Deva (1467-1497 A. D.), the victor in the legendary battle of Kanchi Kaveri.

Yet another tradition locates the Bhanjas as the original inhabitants of Sonepur, Baud and Phulbani region, which comprised all of Khinjali-Mandala with its capital at Dhritipura, which corresponds to modern Baud. It is holds that when the Bhanja king Ranabhanja was defeated by the Somavamsi king Janmejaya I, a branch of the Bhanja family shifted to northern Orissa and established Khijjinga-Mandala comprising Mayurbhanj and part of Keonjhar district, with its capital at Khiching in Mayurbhanj. In fact, these Bhanjas of Bhanja Bhumi or Mayurbhanj were later split up into two territories under the respective rule of Adi Bhanja and Jyoti Bhanja, who ruled from Adipura and Jyotipur. The capital of Jyoti Bhanja was shifted, possibly for administrative convenience, to a place called Kendujhar (Sahu / Mishra / Sahu 1979: 171).

Similarly, mythological tradition has it that Virabhadra, also known as Adi Bhanja and supposedly born from the egg of a pea-fowl and nurtured by the sage Vasistha, became the founder of the state Khijjinga Mandala (Mishra n. d.).

III

We will now turn our attention to a local tradition that credits the Bhuiyan tribe with playing a decisive role in the formation of the state. According to this tradition, it was the Bhuiyans who effected the division of the Mayurbhanj state. Legend has it that the perils and hardships associated with the journey from the remote hills to the ruling chief of Mayurbhanj inspired the Bhuiyans with the idea of installing a chief of their own at Kendujhar. Hence, the Bhuiyans stole a small boy named Jyoti Bhanja from the Mayurbhanj ruling family, whom they nurtured from infancy and finally installed as the king of Kendujhar.

The indispensability of this tribe in the rituals concerning the installation of the Raja of Kendujhar and the continuance of the tradition is, in fact, suggestive of the dominant role it played in the making of the Bhanja dynasty of Kendujhar.[10] Considering the seemingly contestatory character of these traditions, it is worth noting the very nature of imaging the past history of the state.

The accounts reflect very distinct layers of mythological and legendary content in so far as myths relating to pan-Indian past are imagined and legends of the regional past constructed in the local-cultural matrix. Hence, rescuing the historicity of these traditions means examining the historical past of the locality, which is often inserted in the chronicles owing to local collective memory and a very lively oral tradition. It is precisely for this reason that we want to reflect on local tradition and examine its dominance, continuity and assertion as a form of discourse. Clearly, the Bhuiyan tribe stands at the centre of this discourse, in contrast to the pivotal positioning of the Hindu *Kṣatriyas* in various other accounts. Given the fact that the Hindu population of Keonjhar is in excess of the Bhuiyans and comprises other tribes such as Gonds and Kols, how did a discourse of this kind assume hegemonic popularity and wide circulation? Does it indicate a transformation process of tribal societies into "little kingdoms" and thus its popularity? This issue might well deserve a critical examination of the ritual practices and religious tradition of the Bhuiyan tribe. What also needs to be stressed is that explanations for Bhuiyan insurgency during the colonial period (1860s and 1890s) could partly be located in the *threatened subversion of a tradition* (emphasis added) that was so emotively defended by the tribe in the past. As the insurgent speaks loudest (Hardiman (ed.) 1993: 7) in terms of action and tradition, a detailed rethinking of the phases of Bhuiyan insurgency from the above standpoint might also provide substantial clues to an overall understanding of the proposed problem.

In dealing with this question, our effort in the following is to delineate the complexities of Bhuiyan ritual practice and, in particular, the overriding and dictatory association of the tribe in the royal coronation process. Further, by briefly analysing the context and the nature of the Bhuiyan rebellion during the 19th century, we seek to explore religious consciousness and the "elementary aspects" of insurgent consciousness.

In this connection, the following observations make quite valuable reading,

> "... Keonjhar, however, has always been the stronghold of the Bhuiyans, and in this state they are undoubtedly the dominant race. They claim to be the children of the soil (*bhui*, earth), and to possess full proprietary rights over the soil in the same manner as other aborginal tribes always term themselves Zamindars. Though the Hindu population in Keonjhar far outnumbers that of the Bhuiyas yet the claim of the hill (Pahāriā or Pauri) Bhuiyans to be the dominant race is admitted without question even by the Brahmans and Rajputs. In Keonjhar they claim the indefeasible right to install the chief on his *gadi* and in Bonai this right is similarly claimed by the Saonts, a thoroughly Hinduised portion of the clan. There are two broad distinctions between the members of the clan viz. the Bhuiyas of the hills and the Bhuiyas of the plains : the latter form the feudal militia of the state and hold their lands on service tenure and are supposed to be prepared to take up arms for their chief whenever required, though they are equally prepared to turn their arms against an unpopular chief. The true hill (Pahāriā or Pauri) Bhuiyas are not however bound to fight for their chief, though they are perfectly prepared to take up arms against him. The duty of the hill Bhuiyas, is to attend the chief on his journey and act as transport. In Keonjhar, the hill Bhuiyas wield an extraordinary power and are capable at any moment of setting the county in a blaze of insurrection and revolt ... such outbreaks have not been uncommon..." (Cobden Ramsay 1982: 43)

The right of the Bhuiyans to rule over the land through a process of exercising choice in the selection of their chief and installing him on the throne, sanctified by elaborate rituals, remained a time-honoured tradition. This same tradition not only sought legitimation by appropriating Brahmanical rites at the Bhuiyan ceremony of royal installation, but likewise ensured "respectful acknowledgement" by the tract's "Brahman and Rajput" populace. Conspicuous in this context are the social divisions and attendant customs of the Bhuiyans in Keonjhar, which were reinforced by the degree of connectivity with their Hindu neighbours and the latter's influence on them. The four principal clans that constitute the Bhuiyan populace are *Mul*, *Desh*, *Paharia* and *Pawri*, whereby the latter, inhabitants of the mountain tracts, claim to be the superior clan. They are the Bhuiyans of the country or the *Desh-lok*. The *Rajkuli* Bhuiyans, on the other hand, are supposedly descendants of the Raj family from a Bhuiyan concubine and can thus boast of a royal connection. Even the creation of this category of Bhuiyans points to the overarching influence of Hinduism and the process of Hinduisation in the 19th century. Moreover, the linkage between this category of Bhuiyans and the Rajput origin of Keonjhar state is worth pondering. The tradition further holds that the Bhuiyans "stole" the child from the Mayurbhanja Raja family, nurtured him and finally made him Raja. The young Raja was "freely admitted to intercourse with Bhuiyan girls, and the children of this intimacy are the progenitors of the Rajakuli" (Dalton 1973: 145; Mishra n. d.). These divisions are followed by *Rautali* and *Pabna-ansha*, who are smaller in number compared to the first two but characterised by a greater degree of intimacy with Hinduism.

The local chronicle, the Keonjhar *Rājavaṁśāvali*, presents a valorised account of the "determination and deeds" of Bhuiyans who, braving all odds, stole the child from the Mayurbhanj royal family, grooming the infant with tremendous care so they could install their Raja at a later date, endowed with royal qualities.[11] The account also brings out how Jyoti Bhanja, the first king of Keonjhar, was installed on the throne accompanied by a meticulous celebration of the rites and rituals fundamental to a royal coronation. In this connection, the detailed description of the ceremony, an eye-witness account by the colonial administrator Dalton, merits attention. Referring to the coronation ceremony of Dhanurjaya Narayan Bhanja, the 36th king of the Keonjhar royal line, he notes:

> "... A large shed attached to the Raja's palace and ordinarily used as lumber room, was cleared out, swept and garnished, spread with carpets, and otherwise prepared for the occasion. A number of Brahmans were in attendance in sacerdotal costume, seated amidst the sacred vessels and implements, and articles for offerings used in the consecration of Rajas, according to the ceremonies prescribed in the Veds.
>
> Beyond the circle of the brahmanical preparations a group of the principal Bhuiyas were seated, cleanly robed for the occasion and garlanded.
>
> When the company were all seated and these arrangements complete, the young Raja Dhananjai Bhanj entered and distributed pan, confections, spices, and garlands, and retired. Then after a pause there was heard a great crash of the discordant but wild and deep-toned wind instruments and drums of the Bhuiyas and other tribes, and the Raja entered mounted on the back of a strongly-built Bhuiya chief, who plunged and pawed and snorted under him like a fiery steed. Moving to the opposite side of the brahmanical sacred circle, followed by a host of the tribe, one of them placed himself on a low platform covered with red cloth, and with his body and limbs formed the back and arms of the throne on which the Raja, dismounting from his biped steed, was placed. Then the attendant Bhuiyas each received from the Raja's usual servants extemporized imitations of the insignia of royalty, banners, standards, pankhas, chaurs, chhatras, canopies, and thirty-six of the tribe as hereditary office-bearers, each with his symbol, ranged themselves round their chief.
>
> There was a temporary hitch in consequence of the unexpected absence of the hereditary sword-bearer, but after a slight delay a deputy was found and the ceremony proceeded, not however, until the Bhuiyans had protested against such an irregularity being admitted as a precedent. Then one of the principal Bhuiyan chiefs, taking a light flexible jungle creeper of considerable length, binds it round the Raja's turban as the "siropa', or honorary head dress,

> conferred by them. The bands strike up whilst this is done. Bards chant hymns of praise, and Brahmans recite from the Shama Veda, and a leading chief of the clan, Bamdeo Ranha, dipping his finger into the saucer of sandalwood essence, makes on the forehead of the Raja the mark called "tika'. The Brahman priest, the Prime Minister or Bewurtha, and others then repeat the ceremony of giving the "tika', so that a considerable amount of such sealing is required to constitute a Raja of Keonjhar. The Brahmanical ceremony of consecration had been duly solemnized on a previous occasion by the Brahmans, but a portion of this ceremony, omitting the anointing with clarified butter, etc., was now again performed by the priests, ratifying and rendering sacred the act of Bhuiyas.
>
> Then the sword, a very rusty old weapon, is placed in the Raja's hands, and one of the Bhuiyans, named Anand Kopat, comes before him and kneeling sideways, the Raja touches him on the neck with the weapon as if about to strike off his head, and it is said that in former days there was no fiction in this part of the ceremony. The family of the Kopat hold their lands on the condition that the victim when required shall be produced. Anand, however, hurriedly arose after the accolade and disappeared. He must not be seen for three days; then he presents himself again to the Raja as miraculously restored to life.
>
> The Bhuiya chiefs next make offering to the Raja, rice, pulse, pots of ghee, milk, honey, and other things, each article being touched by all the Sirdars before it is presented. The chief sirdars now solemnly address him, and telling him they have, under the authority exercised by them and their ancestors from time immemorial, made over to him the realm and the people therein, enjoin him to rule with justice and mercy. It was a long speech, of which I could catch but little. The ceremony was then concluded with a salute of guns. The Raja arose and again mounted on his curvetting and frisky biped steed, left the assembly surrounded and followed by all the Bhuiyan office-bearers with their insignia, and was thus escorted to his own apartment in the palace.
>
> Soon after – it may be on a subsequent date – the Bhuiyas do homage to the Raja elect. They come in a body bringing in as gifts, produce, gourds, fruits, Indian corn, and laying them at the Raja's feet, they ask after his health, his establishment, his horses and his elephants and in return the Raja inquires after their crops, cows, fowls, and children. This over, each sirdar prostrates himself, and taking the Raja's foot in his hand places the royal toe first on his right and then on his left ear, and then on his forehead ..." (Dalton 1973: 146f).

Similarly, Cobden Ramsay draws our attention to some stimulating observations on Bhuiyan rites with regard to royal installation. He also notes how "Goalas" (milkmen) and other required Hindu castes were imported to the hills to help nurture the royal child until he became installed as king. This is again suggestive of the tribe's actual process of Hinduisation, which may have been further reinforced when the Bhuiyans provided the young chief with their own concubines, from which unions the *Rajkuli* Bhuiyan originated. To understand the rites observed at the time of the king's coronation and emphasise the continuance of this tradition during the rule of Dhanurjaya, we quote Ramsay's account here at length. Furthermore, it provides us with interesting clues in exploring their consciousness, particularly in the context of their insurgency in the 19th century.

> "... The site then chosen by the Bhuiyans as the *garh* for their chief has remained unchanged ever since and it is here that the Bhuiyans install each successive chief, claiming that until the chief has been actually invested by them, the installation is not complete. The Bhuiyas desire in their chief a leader to whom they can appeal and obtain advice and have no desire for independence : they claim, however, a prescriptive right to approve of or resent the administrative acts of the chief whom they have themselves created; the periodical rebellions which have taken place have been due to dislike of the individual ruler by the Bhuiya clans. This attitude was manifest in the rebellion of 1890-1893 when the chief fled to Cuttack leaving his family in the *garh* which could easily have been taken by the Bhuiyas. The Bhuiyas, however, made no attack on the *garh* as they had no animosity against the family of the chief, but only against the chief himself, who had fled. The Bhuiya *pirs* (tracts) have always been the property of the Rani of the state, and the Bhuiyas hold her in high veneration, styling her "the mother". In one of their rebellions the Bhuiyas entered the *garh* seeking for the *Bawarta* (prime minister), they found him in the Rani's apartments, where he had fled for sanctuary: horrified at the sacrilege that he should have seen the face of their revered mother they put him to death" (Cobden Ramsay 1982: 45f).

In his note on religion, Dalton further mentions that for the Bhuiyans, the tutelary goddess *Thakurani Mai* in a way anticipated the origin of Kali, worshipped by the Hindus. This again suggests the tribal linkage of Hindu religious tradition. The custom of human sacrifice before the *Thakurani* was not only prevalent in Keonjhar but in Bamra, Bonai and Gangpur – the tracts largely populated by Bhuiyans. Possibly crucial in this context is that the act of murdering the Raja's assistant and presenting the leader of the insurrection with his head in the course of the Bhuiyan rebellion in the 1860s could be seen as a form of sacrificial offering to the *Thakurani*.

How should the implications of the rites performed by the Bhuiyans be read? The authoritative accounts by Dalton and Cobden Ramsay thoroughly explore Bhuiyan perceptions of kingship, their idea of independence, the primordial right over the land, the prescriptive right to approve or resent the activities of the king emanating from their inevitable right to choose the leader as the founder-creator of the institution called kingship.

However, these apparently assertive and pronounced tribal rights as observed in the dialogue of Bhuiyan chiefs with the king or during the *tika* ceremony (emblem investiture), where the Bhuiyan chief not only solemnly presents the king with *siropa* or the honorary head dress on behalf of the community but also symbolically imposes thereby the first stamp of investiture. The rituals invest the king's authority with legitimacy, which is symbolically enacted by the king sitting on the Bhuiyan leader's lap. This form of community consciousness is stitched and coloured with yet another form of consciousness, clearly evident in the shape of the tribe's reverential empathy for the king. The overall celebratory spirit of the community expressed by the playing of drums, by shouting or by the fiercely symbolic act of Bhuiyans carrying the king on their back or prostrating themselves before the king, while raising his foot, placing it on their shoulder and touching it with their forehead remain an annually repeated affair, demonstrating signs of reverence and obedience with great clarity. Similarly, the carrying of a pumpkin by the Bhuiyan leader is a symbolic token indicative of submission and allegiance to authority and reinforces the idea of royal "dominance and sovereignty" .

In the light of Dalton's observations, it should be underlined that the repetition of the *tika* ceremony by the Brahman priest, the Raja's assistant or *bewarta*, and others following the Bhuiyan pomp and glory, or the Brahminical attempt "to render sacred the act" of the Bhuiyans by "anointing with clarified butter" powerfully bring out the delicately woven balance between the upper castes and the tribe in the context of this kingdom.

Similarly, the reference to "symbolic human sacrifice" by the king as he places the sword at the neck of the kneeling Bhuiyan leader in both accounts may hint at genuine human sacrifice in the days of yore. At the same time, the victim's "symbolic disappearance followed by reappearance as miraculously cured" could be an indication of other impressions. One, for instance, that in the final analysis all human sacrifice is intended as an offering to the "blood-thirsty goddess" of the Bhuiyan to sustain the regenerative process on earth. The element of reappearance in the rite is a possible interpretation of this. Alternatively, it could mean that any form of royal oppression including killing is to be resisted by Bhuiyan subjects, perhaps in response to the blessing by the mother goddess. The reappearance of the victim before the king could also be interpreted as a strategy of resistance, having been "miraculously healed' by it. It could well be asked in this context if there was a link between the killing of Ratna Naik, the leader of the Bhuiyan insurgency in the 1860s, and the reappearance of Dharnidhar Naik in the 1890s. As has been stressed earlier, the Bhuiyan reverence for "the mother" by the Bhuiyans led them to treat their land as the property of the *Rani* of the state. Their veneration for "the mother" was so intense that the Bhuiyans would hardly have tolerated the king's *bewarta* (prime minister) entering the *Rani*'s apartment to seek refuge when the Bhuiyans under Ratna Naik targeted their enemies during the rule of Dhanurjaya Bhanja. More important to note in this context is that Rani Bishnupriya, who remained opposed to Dhanurjaya Bhanja's accession to the throne of Keonjhar, continued to evoke respect and mass support from the tribal community, since she was seen as "the mother" of the Bhuiyan *pirs* (tracts).

IV

The context and nature of the "Bhuiyan rebellion" of Keonjhar during the 19th century will be touched on very briefly here.[12] The death in 1861 of Gadadhar Bhanja, the thirty-fifth king of Keonjhar, spelt a crisis for the kingdom, as he died without leaving a "legal heir" to the throne. Gadadhar Bhanja had, in fact, two queens. The chief queen Bishnupriya was barren, while the younger queen (a concubine) had a son named Dhanurjaya Bhanja. Rani Bishnupriya, however, was not reconciled to Dhanurjaya's claim to the throne of Keonjhar, declaring the latter as an "illegitimate" heir. Instead, the Rani solemnly tried to install Brundaban Bhanja, the grandson of the "Maharaja" of Mayurbhanj on Keonjhar *gadi*, claiming Brundaban as the adopted son of her deceased husband and thus the legitimate successor. This plea was, however, turned down by the colonial authorities, who on the other hand strongly backed Dhanurjaya's claim to the Keonjhar throne. The Mayurbhanj Raja had in the meanwhile appealed to the High Court in Calcutta and the Privy Council to have Brundaban Bhanja's claim to the throne recognised, but to no avail. It was in this context that Rani Bishnupriya appealed to the Bhuiyan *sardars* to recognise Brundaban as the Raja of Keonjhar and sent a deputation of Bhuiyan *sardars* to meet the Lieutenant Governor of Bengal. However, since the court of law favoured Dhanurjaya, he refused to recognise Brundaban.

The announcement of Dhanurjaya's succession was the signal for organised opposition on the part of Rani Bishnupriya with the active support of the Bhuiyan and Juang tribes, who remained devotedly attached to her. In response to the Rani's appeal, the Bhuiyans vowed to resist Dhanurjaya's installation to the hilt. They targeted the pro-Dhanurjaya forces and sought to obstruct the entry of the colonial troops to Keonjhar, who had declared their support for Dhanurjaya. It was during this phase that Ratna Naik emerged as the leader of the Bhuiyans.

In the meantime, the colonial authorities sought to bring the other tribes of the Keonjhar state, such as the Juangs and Saonts, into submission, resorting to either cajoling or coercion. However, the Bhuiyans under the leadership of Ratna Naik stoutly held out against the combine of Raja and colonial authorities. The colonial masters attempted to organise Dhanurjaya's installation ceremony in December 1867, which was, of course, completely boycotted by the Bhuiyans. The installation ritual, which took place without the approval of the Rani, was marked by "abuse of the Rani and her women".

These developments set the context for a serious backlash in the months that followed, unleashed by the colonial forces. The Rani was demoralised to the extent of being pressured "to release the Bhuiyans from their oath", and "consented to invest Dhanurjaya with the usual insignia of her acquiescence in his succession, and to withdraw from all further interference". This finally paved the way for the "second and real" installation of Dhanurjaya on the Keonjhar throne, the coronation rituals of which were accompanied by the Bhuiyans. The ceremony itself, this time in February 1868, was organised under the watchful eye of the colonial authorities and carried out in the presence of Colonel Dalton, Commissioner of Chota Nagpur, and Ravenshaw, Superintendent of Tributary States. It must be emphasised here that it was now the turn of the colonial masters and no longer that of the Brahmans and Rajputs, who had traditionally put the seal of approval/legitimacy on the process of royal installation in the "little kingdom". The Rani Bishnupriya, now entirely cowed, conferred a *Shiropa* on the new Raja as a "token of acknowledgement of his succession". On the other hand, she was granted a pension and opted to leave Keonjhar for Puri on a pilgrimage.

This was, however, merely a temporary lull on the part of the Bhuiyans. Around April 1868, the insurgency of the Bhuiyans once again gathered momentum and militancy. Ratna Naik, who had hitherto remained underground, now strove to mobilise the Bhuiyan *sardars*, making them withdraw their allegiance to the new Raja. The Bhuiyan chiefs reassembled in armed bands, guarding the passes leading to Keonjhar and resorted to "plundering and burning" the houses of Pro-Dhanurjaya elements in the villages. On 1st May, the Bhuiyans under Ratna Naik's leadership marched forward to take the Raja's palace in Keonjhar. In this bid, they not only overpowered the Raja's police guards but also carried off his *bewarta* and officials to the hills. The *bewarta* was finally murdered by the Bhuiyans, perhaps a sacrifice to propitiate the *Thakurani Mai* of the tribe. For the Bhuiyans, the *bewarta* had turned out to be the "most hated creature", as he remained at the forefront of frustrating attempts to make Brindaban the Raja. For some time, the Bhuiyans succeeded in setting up a "provisional government" in Keonjhar.

In fact, this phase of Bhuiyan triggered off an even more ferocious colonial backlash, so that by August 1868, the rebellion had petered out fully. The colonial forces ably backed by the support of the neighbouring Rajas of Bonai, Pal-lahara, Dhenkanal, Mayurbhanj and Udaipur had quelled the rebellion. Ratna Naik along with six of his principal associates was captured and sentenced to death. About one hundred others suffered various terms of imprisonment.

However, Bhuiyan resistance to the king assumed a different dimension in the 1890s. The context of opposition had changed by then and the Bhuiyans were ensconced in resisting the feudal oppression of the king, perpetuated by the system of *bethi* (forced labour). Indeed, when the king had planned to extract *bethi* from the Bhuiyans in order to build a canal for the state, it was enough to provoke them into open rebellion. This time it was Dharanidhar who took the lead in mobilising the Bhuiyans, a man who had been educated at Cuttack and appointed as the state surveyor. Gopal Naik, the younger brother of Nand Naik and one of the prime associates of Ratna Naik, also exerted tremendous influence on Dharanidhar during this phase of insurgency. He had continued to carry the banner of revolt against the Raja in the Bhuiyan community despite the violent liquidation of the first phase of Bhuiyan insurgency. During the 1880s, the Bhuiyans under Dharanidhar and Gopal Naik once again succeeded in almost waging war against the king by looting granaries, procuring guns and cannons and, above all, by planning to organise a provisional government. The colonial authorities swung into action again in the face of these developments, and unlike in the 1860s, this phase of counter-insurgency was curiously marked by the support of the "native middle-class intelligentsia", who essentially represented the forces of modernity. Fakir Mohan Senapati, for instance, who had all along remained an ideologue of Keonjhar Raja, and Madhusudan Das, who had defended the Raja's case in the legal battle in Cuttack against the Bhuiyan leader, Dharnidhar, were among the representatives of this force.

Certain aspects regarding the nature of Bhuiyan insurgency merit critical consideration, against the backdrop of the usual historiographical explanations such as the sheer economic exploitation of the people by the Raja in these kingdoms or the often valorised emphasis on a specific tribe's notion of independence.

That the Bhuiyans would never tolerate the breach of a "highly sanctified time immemorial tradition" (emphasis added) in terms of their primordial and prescriptive rights vis-à-vis the kingship and the kingdom (land/*pirs*) seems obvious from the above account. Moreover, the time-honoured religious tradition of venerating and propitiating the tutelary mother goddess almost spiritually endowed the community with the right to wage war against the new king. The Rani was the goddess incarnate in the community's perception. The departure of Rani Bishnupriya from the royal palace of Keonjhar to Puri and the subsequent killing of the *bewarta* by Ratna Naik could perhaps be seen symbolically as a "sacred performance to propitiate the terribly anguished mother". In the same vein, the killing of Ratna Naik and the subsequent appearance of Dharanidhar on the scene could also be considered to have emanated from the conviction embedded in the Bhuiyan tradition that if a subject was killed as a result of royal despotism and injustice, he was likely to reappear (through a process of miraculous healing) before the king. In fact, in the symbolic act of sacrifice associated with the process of royal installation, the victim reappears after three days and, remarkably, Dharanidhar reappeared three decades after Ratna's disappearance.

We have attempted to show the elements of reverence and assertion that broadly characterised Bhuiyan consciousness. What can also be discerned as the "underlying structure" of this consciousness were the aspects of "negation, ambiguity, modality, solidarity, territoriality and transmission".[13] In fact, it has been aptly remarked that "by reading their actions (peasants/ tribal), one could start to understand their minds" (Hardiman (ed.): 1993).

The colonial authorities not only fully recognised the hold of tradition as far as legitimacy for kingship in the kingdom was concerned. Along with the colonial policy of terror and violence, the authorities desperately sought the stamp of approval from the Bhuiyan community in order to "really" install Dhanurjaya on the throne. Hence, the *tika* ceremony for Dhanurjaya had to be organised a second time by the community to ensure their involvement in the royal rituals under the watchful guidance of the colonial officials, who had by then emerged as the "new avatars" of legitimacy alongside the Brahmans and Rajputs. And as we noted above, the native middle-class intelligentsia also joined the above sections shortly afterwards and seem to have positioned themselves ambiguously vis-à-vis tribal community tradition. As the so-called forces of "modernity", their ambiguity partly sprang from the unresolved contradiction between the upholding and subversion of tradition.

This paper has, at a preliminary level, attempted to grasp a particular tribal ritual policy in the actual context of a politico-economic domain instead of treating both aspects as isolated. Secondly, it also sought to locate the sources and notions of honour, legitimacy and authority as upheld by the community in the context of a "jungle kingdom" in contrast to the traditionally assumed notion of relations of power, i.e., command and obedience.

Notes

1 Acknowledgement: I am grateful to Georg Berkemer and Hermann Kulke for inviting me to present this paper at the 17th ECMSAS Conference in Heidelberg. I am equally indebted to Berkemer for his critical comments on the first draft.

2 "Being the third largest of the Orissa ex-feudatory states, Keonjhar was bounded on the north by Singhbhum district; on the east by Mayurbhanj state and Balasore district; on the south by Cuttack district and Dhenkanal state; and on the west by Dhenkanal, Pal-lahara and Bonai states. Divided into two widely dissimilar tracts, Keonjhar consists of two parts; Lower Keonjhar (region of valleys and low lands) and Upper Keonjhar (mountainous high lands) ... the chief among the tribes are Bhuiyas, Juangs ..." (Cobden Ramsay 1982: 212f).

3 The District Records category in the archival collections at Orissa State Archives,

Bhubaneswar, are undoubtedly a valuable source for any study on "little kingdoms".

4 Apart from existing sources on the royal genealogy of Keonjhar, genealogical accounts on Keonjhar can be found in the following texts: Mishra (n. d.), Mishra (1933), *Brief History of Keonjhar (1901)*.

5 Dirks' views on rituals as cited in Schnepel/Berkemer (n. d.).

6 Cohen and Stein's model on state formation as cited in Schnepel/Berkemer (n. d.).

7 Reference can be made to the following texts: Risely (1891), Cobden Ramsay (1982), Russel/Lal (1916).

8 The major representative of nationalist historiographic accounts on *gadjat* states is available in Mahtab / De (eds., 1957-1959); however, for an alternative understanding based on broad left historiographic tradition, see Pati (1993) and Nanda (1998).

9 Cobden Ramsay (1982). The thesis on Rajput origin is discernible in this account.

10 This fact is attested to in the existing writings on Keonjhar state, such as Mishra (n. d.), Dalton (1973), Cobden Ramsay (1982), Senapati / Sahu (1986).

11 A detailed account on this is available in Mishra (n. d.).

12 Detailed accounts on Bhuiyan Rebellion of Keonjhar from a nationalist historiographic perspective can be found from Mahtab / De (1957-1959) to Mishra (1983).

13 We wish to elaborate on these aspects of insurgent consciousness in more detail in future. For a critical analysis of the nature of peasant insurgency and consciousness in colonial India, see Guha (1983) and Hardiman (ed., 1993: 7).

The Gajapati's Game

Maria Schetelich

Texts on Dharmaśāstra and Nītiśāstra are indispensable manuals of proper rule in pre-modern Indian society. They provide an indigenous "theory" of royalty and the state and supply a shared code of conduct for great kings, little kings and would-be-kings alike. In this essay, it will be shown that certain parts of medieval Rājanīti-śāstras can be used as "textbooks" for heirs and pretenders. At the same time, these pieces prove that in this struggle for power even losers can win their rājadom if they succumb to the right victor. This is expressed inter alia in the myth and ritual of the struggle between Hari and Hara, which is described as a courtly game in am Orissan Nītiśāstra text.

Medieval India not only abounds in kingdoms, both large and small, but also in works on *rājanīti* (*rājanītiśāstra*), more often than not written by ministers, *rāja-gurus* or kings. The authors of such treatises usually drew on the two famous works of the "great tradition", the Kamandakīya Nītisāra (KN) and the Kauṭalīya Ar-thaśāstra (KA), for their basic concepts. From about the 9th century onwards, when new forms of kingship developed giving the king the "monopoly of political au-thority as a sovereign ruler, deputy of the state deity, whose absolute power he claims to enforce, authority over all those who are devotees of the god, making use of the integrative power of the central cult" (Kulke 1978b: 139), this also had its impact on the science of politics. In the age of constant armed conflicts and inter-necine wars that followed the defeat of Pṛthivīrāj Chauhan and his allies by the Muslims in 1192, the design of relations between the king and his political partners and adversaries was of first-rate importance. According to the new trend in political science, a king no longer derived his fame and image primarily from his *dharma-rāja* qualities,[1] but from his *prabhāvotsahamantraśakti*, his power and efficiency effected by majesty, energy and constant deliberation on political matters.[2]

In spite of changed notions of kingship, no genuinely new political theory was worked out in medieval times. Medieval political *śāstras* are didactic manuals of applied (classical) political theory, responding to the exigencies of the day, and medieval teachers of political science drew quite freely and highly selectively on the classical treatises, choosing only concepts or topics that fitted into the concrete political context of their respective times, thereby dwelling in great detail on one subject and abridging others.[3] The most important concept, as of old, is that of the political "energetic field" (*rājamaṇḍala, sāmantacakra*). The instruments of politics and diplomacy are, as before, the four *upāyas*, *sāma* (conciliation), *dāna* (gift), *bheda* (sowing dissension) and *daṇḍa* (military action). War remains the last political resort to be applied should the other three fall short. Historical reality, however, has a way of shining through. *ṣāḍguṇyam*, the sixfold policy in times of conflict, is very often treated more elaborately than the *upāyas*. Of the seven elements of political rule (*saptāṅgarājya*), the king (*svāmi*) and the military force (*bala, daṇḍa*) rank highest in importance, followed by the minister (*amātya*). *Prabhāva* (majesty), *utsaha* (energy) and *mantra* (deliberation) are the paramount forces (*śakti*) or qualities (*guṇa*) a king should possess.

Conforming to the spirit of their time, almost every Rājaśāstra dedicates far more space than classical texts not to the army as such, but to elephants and horses (*gajavidyā, aśvavidyā*), the most expensive element of an army, not to mention the most auspicious and prestigious. *Dhanurvidyā* (science of arms) and *ratnaparīkṣā* (inspection of precious stones) were introduced as separate (and sometimes quite prominent) topics, for more often than not, the political destiny of a medieval king depended on his success at war. Topics of courtly life (*vihāra, vinoda, sevyasevakopadeśa, puruṣa- und strīlakṣaṇa,* omina) have their place in these texts, for the king's person now deserved more attention. This was not only because he was seen as the receptacle of *prabhāva-* and *utsahaśākti* and the representation of Viṣṇu on earth (*calanti Viṣṇu*), but also because of his more intense relation to the *rāṣṭradevatā,* be it Jagannātha, Śrīnāthji, Bhavānī, Kāmākṣī, Virūpākṣa or others, and finally because the political destiny of those present at his court depended on his favour or disfavour. To what extent the respective traditional subjects are treated and what a Rājanīti author adds or stresses, i.e., the kind of knowledge he considers necessary to teach, varies from from one work to another. It is almost possible to glean political attitudes or personal, dynastic preferences or politics from these texts, if the political and cultural background is known.

From the 11th century onwards, almost every region in India contributed to the production of Rājaśāstras or Rājanītiśāstras in one form or another, but the significance of this genre as a source of regional history has up to now attracted no more than the scant attention of the historian. One work that exemplifies how the knowledge of political science was transported at that time is the Orissan Sanskrit text Hariharacaturaṅga (HHC) by Godāvara Miśra.[4] According to the text, the author was a poet and scholar of great fame, minister (*mantrin*) and *rājaguru* to Pratāparudradeva (the last of the three great Sūryavaṁśī kings of Orissa, 1504-1537), who is supposed to have bestowed him with the right to bear his own white umbrella adorned with four gold lions and the sign of the golden jar, known as Meghāḍambara.[5]

Godāvara Miśra is most probably identical with the *rājaguru* of Pratāparudradeva's father Puruṣottamadeva, Godāvarīśa, mentioned in the context of the "Kāñci-Kāverī legend" in Kaṭakarājavaṁśāvalī (KRV) chapter 64 A,[6] an interpolated and apparently somewhat corrupted section, missing in one of the two existing manuscripts of the text. It tells how this Brahmin made the river swell by magic and thus saved Puruṣottama and his army from being chased by the Kāñci king after Puruṣottama had abducted his daughter. This fits in well with the fact that Godāvara Miśra is credited with the authorship of the Śāradārcanapaddhati, a Tantric text (Panda 1987: 121).[7]

The title of the work suggests a focus on military science and the art of war and, indeed, seven of eight chapters deal with the four parts of the Indian army (*caturaṅga*), with knowledge of arms and the tactics of fighting (*yuddha*). The last chapter describes "the game" (*krīḍā*) – a battle between the two gods Hari (Viṣṇu) and Hara (Śiva) played with 64 pieces and eight heralds on a board of 14x14 = 196 fields. The text abounds in *itihāsa* citations from Mahābhārata and epic Kṛṣṇa mythology. There is an obvious weighing of subjects. The chapter on *nīti* is much shorter (503 *ślokas*) than the chapters on elephants (*gajapariccheda*, 813 *ślokas*) and horses (*aśvapariccheda*, 837 *ślokas*) and only slightly longer than that on arms (*dhanurveda*, 399 *ślokas*), but twice as long as the *yuddha* (196 *ślokas*) und *krīḍā* (165 *ślokas*) chapters.

In the preface to his edition, S.K. Ramanatha Sastri classifies the HHC as a work on *rājanīti*.[8] Yet, from the structure of the text and the introductory verses in particular, it is quite evident that the author did not simply want to expose politics or military science. The topics he chose and the way he treats them point to his intention to furnish the reader with the basic *rājanīti* knowledge required to appreciate and play the *caturaṅga* game taught in the last chapter, from which the work got its name. Strictly speaking, chapters 1-7 could almost be regarded as accessory to chapter 8, and to a certain extent, the "table of contents" (verses 1-23) confirms this impression:

Pratyūhapratināgendravāraṇaṃ vāraṇānanam | vande candanasindūrabindubhiścitritānanam || 1 ||
Vande Hariharau vīrau caturaṅgabalānvitau | Bāṇāsurapure pūrvaṃ yudhyamānau raṇapriyau || 2 ||
Śrīdurgācaraṇāmbhojadvandvacandanabindunā | kṛtir Godāvareṇeyaṃ tatprasadād viracyate || 3 ||
Dhīragodāvarasye[yaṃ]daṃ kṛtir āstāṃ mude satām | pareṣāṃ guṇakāsāre nīradhā-viva garjatām || 4 ||

dhanurvidyādikaṃ tadvad vinā yuddhaṃ bhaven na hi | yuddhasya sādhanatvena tad apy atrābhidhāsyate || 8 ||
anītikasya rājño hi prārambho viphalo bhavet | granthe 'tra nītiśāstrārthaṃ saṃgṛhyātaḥ pravakṣyate || 9 ||
saṃpūrṇacaturaṅgasya dhanvino nītivedinaḥ | nṛpater vakṣyate yuddhaṃ saprakāraṃ yathāśrutam || 10 ||
vakṣyate yuddhaśikṣārthaṃ yoddhṛharṣavivarddhanam | kṛtāv asyāṃ manohāri krīḍāyuddham api sphuṭam || 11 ||

kuśale nṛpatau sarve narāḥ kuśalino yataḥ | nṛpeṇāpekṣitaṃ tasmād atra granthe 'bhidhāsyate || 5 ||
paripālayatā rājño prajāḥ poṣyāḥ kuṭumbavat | caturaṅgaṃ yatas tasmād āvarṇyate tad yathākramam || 6 ||
dviṣadbhyastrātukāmena prajās tadvijigīṣuṇā | caturaṅgeṇa yoddhavyam iti yuddhaṃ pravakṣyate || 7 ||

caturaṅgādikaṃ yadyapy anyeṣām api sambhavi | anuktvā svāminaṃ cāpi tadvaktuṃ śakyate 'pi ca || 12 ||
tathāpi śrīhariharasvāmikaṃ vakṣyate yataḥ | prasaṅgāt kīrttanaṃ dhyānaṃ darśanaṃ puṇyadaṃ tayoḥ || 13 ||

I praise the remedy against obstacles, the best of elephants, the elephant-faced (god) whose face is adorned with spots of sandal paste and vermilion.
I praise Hari (i.e. Viṣṇu/Kṛṣṇa) and Hara (Śiva), the two heroes, possessing armies (and) eager for battle who in the past fought against each other in Bāṇāsura's city.
This work has been composed by Godāvara who reveres the pair of lotus-feet, adorned with spots of sandal paste, of Śrīdurgā, by her favour.
This work of Godāvara shall contribute to the pleasure (happiness) of the righteous roaring at the enemies who are sitting, as it were, in a (mere) pool of good qualities (while they themselves sit) in an ocean (of such qualities).
(Then) the battle will be explained, for the would-be-emperor king has to fight with the help of an army in order to save his people from enemies.

And because no fight can be undertaken without (the knowledge of) the science of the bow (and other weapons), this (science) will also be treated here, for the sake of success in fighting.
Indeed, any undertaking of a king without *nīti* (politics, also: morals, clever acting) cannot bear fruit. That is why a concise exposition of the main points (*artha*) of the Nītiśāstra will also be given here.
After that will be explained the battle of a king possessing a complete army, bowmen (or: shrewdness) and knowledge of *nīti* with all its ways and conforming to tradition.
Then in this work, to teach the rules of war and to increase the excitement.
All the subjects prosper if the ruler prospers. That is why (everything) required by a ruler will be taught in this book.
Because the king is protecting (his) subjects, nourished (by him) like a family, the army etc. will be treated here in due order.

There is nothing exceptional in Godāvara Miśra's describing a game (and a *caturaṅga* game in particular) in the context of political science. Other Rājanīti authors include "games of intelligence" (*buddhikrīḍā)* among the subjects taught. Nīlakaṇṭha Bhaṭṭa, in Nītimayūkha (NM) or Somadeva in Mānasollāsa (M) teach the game(s) of *caturaṅga* as part of the knowledge requirements for royal courtly life, whose different aspects they discuss *in extenso*. Yet, the HHC is the only work that confines itself to topics related to the game in some manner. It is usually the other way round, even in Nītimayūkha (NM), where the exposure of Rājanīti also ends with "the game", i.e., two-handed chess.

The description of games in the context of the Rājanītiśāstras is a medieval phenomenon that occurred for the first time in the Mānasollāsa (1925-37). Up until then, games (*dyūta*) were spoken of in the śāstras with a negative connotation. On the one hand, they were mentioned as a vice of the king that could be indulged and tolerated only to a certain measure and, on the other hand, in the *dyūtasamāhvayam* precept, as one of the "criminal passages" from a total of 18 precepts on duties in the Dharmaśāstras. This precept deals with fraud, betting, stakes (Nārada, Yājñavalkya, Kātyāyaṇa, Bṛhaspati usw.) and the ensuing profit drawn on by the king. It primarily concerns all games involving dice and combat. The player is called *dyūtaka* or *kīṭaka*.

Gaming becomes a teaching subject in its own right only when the Rājanītiśāstras shifted their focus to sketching courtly life and the instruction of the exemplary life of a Hindu king. In doing so, they amend the traditional topics of *daṇḍanīti* with courtly matters – *strīpuruṣalakṣaṇa*, witty conversation at the *rājā*'s court, dress code etc. Four-handed and two-handed chess were taught in this context (or later) in separate treatises for entertainment and ritual use as part of Lakṣmī- and Bali-Pūjā in the months of Āśvina and Kārttika.

The *caturaṅga* taught in the HHC is definitely constructed along the model of Indian two-handed chess. It is played on a square board divided into two halves that symbolise the two kingdoms, and the board has 14x14 fields instead of the usual 8x8. The number of game pieces is larger (32 pieces on each side) and unlike the stereotyped set of chess pieces reflects a real army. The set of one party consists of a king (*svāmi*), crown prince (*yuvarāja*), counsellor (minister, *mantrin*), general (*vahinīpati*), four elephants (*gaja, hasti*), four chariots (*syandana*), four horses (*vāji, aśva, haya*), and (in the role of pawns), four sword-men (*khadgin*), four bowmen (*dhanvin*), four lancers (*śaktika*) and four soldiers for mechanical contrivances (*yantrika*) (8. 5-8). There are four more pieces not found in any other variant of Indian chess, i.e., the "heralds" (*vādyakāriṇaḥ*), again four on each side (8. 9) for the four wings of the army (8. 22-23: *baladeśe ca catvāraścatvāro vādyakāriṇaḥ* I *gajam ekaḥ samārūḍho hayam ekas tathā parau* II *pattis syātāṁ yatheccham ca vādya eṣāṃ prakalpayet* I *yodhā eva rathe śaṅkhavādyakarāḥ prakīrtitāḥ* II). They are not directly involved in the game but evidently have to announce the changes in putting up the different *vyūha*s of the army during the game (see below).

– The pieces are not coloured (Indian chess pieces are usually red and green) but the parties, i.e., the armies, have to have the same attributes as their respective lord (*svāminor ubhayayos sainyaṃ sarvaṃ svasvāmirūpakam*, 8. 24 ab).
– The shape of the different pieces is not only de-, but prescribed and the king pieces (Viṣṇu and Śiva), must have the iconographically correct form (8. 12-21).[9]

Both gods have four arms and ride their vehicles, the Garuḍa and the bull, and each of them has his usual attributes: Hari has the *śrīvatsa* mark on his breast and in his hands *śaṅkha, cakra* and bow. He is clad in two yellow garments.

> Śiva, with a blue throat, the half-moon, the third eye on his forehead and braided hair held by a "turban" (*śirodāman*), wears his tiger skin and holds the javelin, the *ḍamaru* drum and bow and arrows in his hands.
>
> While Garuḍa is adorned with the *kaustubha* juwel, Nandin bears the name (of Śiva). Both gods bear the parasol (*chattra),* the obligatory sign of royal dignity.

– Although the parties are not distinguished by colour, there is a visual difference between them. The crown prince (in this context known as *sūtrī*), for explanation see below), minister and general of one party are seated on aerial chariots (*vyomayāna*), while the "officials" of their enemy have to use elephant, chariot and horse, their normal vehicles (8. 20).
– Moves and range of the pieces differ from those of the "standard" *caturaṅga.*[10] The king can move ad libitum towards all sides and thus becomes the most efficient, in short the most important piece. The moves of the "officials" cover six fields. The move of the horse is a combination of six instead of two fields straight and two sideways.
– The course of the game is mainly determined by the skilled deployment of the ten different battle arrays of the army (*vyūha*) explained *in extenso* (8. 34-99) for which a good knowledge of the rules of attack (*dāna*), defence (*rakṣaṇa)* and blocking (*bandhana*) is indispensable.[11]

Considering the emphasis on the deployment of *vyūha*s on the battle field, the deviations from familiar types of Indian chess and the intention of Godāvara Miśra to combine the teaching of war tactics with the visualisation of a war between the two gods with their armies, the *Hariharacaturaṅga* game could indeed support Renate Syed's hypothesis that Indian chess was originally invented as a "sand-table exercise" for the sake of training strategic military skills with a didactic game Syed 2001: 10-12)[12] – if it were not for specific details contained in the text. In the introductory verses of chapter 1 (1. 13, not included into his German translation by Bock-Raming), the game is said to serve, among other things, the veneration of Hari and Hara through praise, memorising, sight of the gods and *pūjā.* This suggests at least a partly religious connotation of the game, and when the introduction to chapter 8, verse 4 cd, mentions that the battle of the gods "is written down here in concise form as a game *kautukād api"*, then the game could well be understood as a kind of visual *itihāsa,* a visualised example from the mythological past that was and still is generally taken in India to have been real history. *Kautukāt,* then, might not only mean "out of vehement desire, curiosity, interest in anything" (A.

Bock-Raming 2001), but "for the purpose of a show, festivity, festival, spectacle, solemn ceremony" or, as is also possible, "for relaxation or amusement". Performing the deeds of the gods in song, dance and stage shows with live actors or puppets before the deities is still quite common and an element of many festivals as well as the daily routine of service to the gods.[13] Entertaining the gods or celebrating their deeds on special days in the yearly cycle of festivals or of their biography and as part of certain rituals is held to be a particularly auspicious form of veneration, beneficial to both performers and spectators. The king or queen playing board games with their *kuladevatā* on certain occasions or fixed times of the day is a frequent theme in art and mentioned in medieval literature. Lack of evidence forbids us to claim that the *Hariharacaturaṅga* game was intended for such occasions, but it was certainly not simply a didactic game.

Another striking detail appears in chapter 1. 2 cd, where Bāṇāsurapura is mentioned as the place where Hari and Hara originally fought their battle. This brings us to a myth prevalent in Śaiva and Vaiṣṇava tradition (and here related particularly to Hari, Viṣṇu in his Kṛṣṇāvatāra). The myth of Bāṇāsura is familiar in two versions, a "northern", centring on Viṣṇu-Kṛṣṇa and a "southern", centring on Śiva and the Devī in her form as Kanyā, the virgin girl. Both versions existed side by side in South and Central India from the 8th to the 9th century at least.

According to the southern version, the *asura*-king Bāṇa, the eldest son of Bali Vairocana, armed with thousands of weapons and always eager to wage war, oppressed the world at the end of a former Yuga. The gods could not overcome him because through the power acquired by revering Śiva and by the austerities he practised, Brahma had granted him the boon that neither god nor man but only a small girl could conquer him. Viṣṇu then chose the Devī, who as a young girl had practised penance at the seashore with the desire to marry Śiva. To prevent her from achieving this aim (which would have robbed her of her virgin power and thus made her unable to vanquish Bānāsura), the sage Nārada had fixed midnight as the auspicious hour for the marriage ceremony. In order to deter Śiva, who was already approaching the Devī's place with marriage presents and utensils, Nārada let a cock crow to announce the coming of daybreak. Śiva, assuming that the auspicious moment had passed, returned to his place, leaving the Devī-Kanyā disappointed and with the resolution to spend her life as a virgin at the seashore. When Bānāsura heard this, he came to win her in marriage but, trying to do this by force, aroused her wrath. A battle took place between them in which Bāṇāsura was slain. The place where it occurred was, according to tradition, Kanyākumārī (Cape Comorin), the southernmost tip of India where three oceans meet. At Vijayadaśamī, the tenth day of Navarātri (known as Durgāpūjā in the North), the story of the battle is enacted in connection with a procession of the goddess at several places in South India up to this day.

The "northern" version, related in the Harivaṁśa and the Viṣṇupurāṇa is much more complex, as can be seen from a 10th century South Indian *yamaka* poem, the Śaurīkathodaya of Vāsudeva, one of the numerous Sanskrit *kāvyas* that recount episodes from the Mahābhārata. The Bāṇāsura legend is told in Canto 6. 56-107:[14]

56. Then at one time a certain 'asura' was born on earth who provided the gods with equal battle (?). He, Bāṇa by name, who was of incomparable strength, made the heaven free from gods.
He (Bāṇa) who possessed the thousands of hands which made (his) enemies bow down, acquired a progeny from Śiva by means of most laborious ('sutata-ayena') excellent austerities.
The city of whom (Bāna), which was abounding in cloves, cardamom and fields of corn, (was situated) in the proximity of the Kailāsa mountain. And him, who wore an armlet of good conduct around his arm (?), they called the son of Bali possessing great strength.
A most desired excellent girl, Uṣā by name, with limbs of radiant lustre was born to him (Bāṇa) who was in charge of the lordship of the 'daityas'. There was no (other) such exquisite woman.
One day Umā with the most shining moon-face, who had resorted to a forest region, was observed by Uṣā while sporting together with her joyful lord (Śiva).
Beholding these two (Umā and Śiva) with respect, she whose face resembles the moon (Uṣā) thought langourously in her passion: "If such a one would become my husband then my eyes would be blessed with good fortune."
The goddess (Umā) who was born as the consort of the god (Śiva) and who is worthy to be known by the (whole) ascetic community, accomplished everything that was in the mind of Uṣā who is praised by the gods.
(Umā said): "The beloved young man, who will arrive at (your) beautiful palace at night and who will enjoy you when you are being absorbed in sleep after your garment has been removed, he will become yours."
Thus having heard the utterance of Gaurī, Uṣā with much passion, overcome by joy and filled with enthusiasm because of these words, betook herself again from there to her own dwelling.
Then at night, during her sleep, the girl experienced the reality of that most excellent utterance of Ambā (Umā). Awakening, however, and not seeing the young man present, Uṣā, having an emaciated body, started to weep.
(Then) a certain friend, Citralekhā by name, who was incomparable in drawing pictures said to her beloved (Uṣā), whose lotus-face was overflowing with tears.
(Citralekhā) always possessing good conduct, was the foremost daughter of Bāṇa's minister Kumbhāṇḍa who, being a vessel of the nectar of pure insight, had resorted to the earth.
Weeping (Citralekhā said): "O Uṣā, you spoil our happiness. Which is the arrow (piercing) your heart? Enough of concealment here. I who have beautiful eyes will remove your sorrow."
Thus having heard (these) most cherished words she (Uṣā) said with her mind filled with distress: "O friend, this attainment of an urgent matter cannot be accomplished even it can be reflected upon in the mind. O you who has beautiful teeth (Citralekhā)! This handsome thief with bristling hair on (his) chest came during night and (having) arrived he disappeared

(after) giving me much joy.
O Citralekhā! Being abandoned by this dear person who had entered (my) heart, I am not capable of supporting (my) body which has fallen into unequalled afflictions."
Having heard the sweet Uṣā's words – (Uṣā who was like) a jewel-box of good qualities – she (Citralekhā) drew on a spotless cloth the different people in all the worlds who were full of splendour.
Seeing Aniruddha, who was shining with various kinds of garlands, in the picture which had a brilliant splendour and which was pure and wonderful, she (Uṣā), who possessed much beauty, showed him to (her) friend (Citralekhā).
She (Citralekhā) having gone immediately with great speed to Dvāravatī due to her excellent yoga, took him (Aniruddha), who was asleep and brought him to Uṣā's place – (Uṣā) who excelled the gods in beauty.
He, the wise one, who possessed much human beauty, sported together with Uṣā. There (in Uṣā's place) he was recognized by a group of spies who had orders from the 'asura' (Bāṇā) and were not known by other people.
Bāṇa, having heard that, became terrified in his heart – (he) who strived for the happiness of his family – and having drawn (his) sword from ist sheath, ordered the masses of (his) troops, who were eager to fight against him (Aniruddha).
The darling of Pradyumna, full of strength and rapture, destroyed that army which arrived. At that moment Bāṇa reached him – (Bāṇa) who possessed bow and arrow and had an angry mind.
He (Aniruddha) attacked him (Bāṇa) who uttered a drawn-out growl and made him distraught. But he (Aniruddha) was seized by (his) foe (Bāṇa) with a power that had equalled (that of) all his enemies.
Bāṇa whose behaviour was evil, exposed Aniruddha to (much) distress on account of the obstruction of (his) spies and there he (also) fettered the love-stricken Uṣā who had the same guilt.
Due to irresistibility he (Bāṇa) felt much itching pain for battle and in a firm state of confidence ('a-mṛdu-āsthatayā') he said to Śaṅkara (Śiva) who stood (near) in the guise of a guard at the door:
"O Lord Śiva! In order that I may not still more have an overwhelmingly strong itching for battle, quickly grant me a great fight with the enemy ('para-mahā-samaram') which will afford me (the) utmost laughter ('datta-parama-hāsa')".
Thus addressed by Bāṇa, who through his words had given a number of offerings, the Supreme Spirit (Śiva),who removes the ignorance of his devotees and is free from confusion, said full of laughter:
"When the banner which is marked with the peacock and destroys the lives of (your) enemies, definitely falls, a very harsh battle will take place which will lend splendour to your face which is (now) pale."
Thus addressed with compassion by the enemy of Pura (Śiva), Bāṇa, who is the protector of the 'daityas', longed for the breaking of that banner.
Then the lord (Kṛṣṇa), even though he possessed the supreme most exalted consciousness and had resorted to human 'māyā' went in the night into a state of despondency, his mind depressed on account of the separation from Aniruddha.
The abode (of Aniruddha) for whose sake the Yadu people became subdued with hundreds of cries of affliction, Nārada himself spoke about to the protector of the Yadus (Kṛṣṇa) – (Nārada) who is constantly resourceful.
The lord thought of the foremost of birds (Garuḍa) who arrived quickly and together with that famous one Hṛṣikeśa (Kṛṣṇa) went to the town of the enemy with much haste.
The mighty gods headed by Hara (Śiva), bearing bows and destruction for (their) enemies, guarded the four gates (of Bāṇa's town), whose entrances were beautiful with (their) arches of jewels.

In the morning, he (Kṛṣṇa) arrived rapidly to the eastern 'gopura' which was surrounded by a multitude of enemies ('ari-saṃyad-vari') and whose door (was guarded) by Maheśvara (Śiva) who afforded (it) protection and is always intent upon the satisfaction of the 'dānavas'.
There the feast-like battle took place between the two armies for the sake of Bali (Bāṇa) – the armies which purified the hearts of the worshippers ('iṣṭa-āśaya-śodhanayoḥ') and (offered) no small amount of honour and wealth ('akṛśa-yaśas-dhanayoḥ') and the minds of whom (those in the armies) were free from fault and great fear ('gatamatidoṣorubhayaḥ').
Then the battle (at the same time) wonderful and dreadful between Viṣṇu and Maheśvara, the two esteemed deities of the world, proceeded and the host of gods became rapidly much terrified.
There Kapālin (Śiva) let loose a shower of arrows against the agitated Kṛṣṇa. They became moths in his (Kṛṣṇa's) shining splendour, something which was not possible at another place.
Kṛṣṇa's arrows which desired to go to Iśvara (Śiva) who was in the battle, reached the end of the horizon ('dig-antam'). They (the arrows), the frightening ones of Kṛṣṇa, also suffered annihilation in his (Śiva's) splendour.
Thus, this proper (event) took place between Kṛṣṇa and Sthāṇu (Śiva), these two were equal in battle – the two Ancient Beings who on account of their identity are praised in the Vedas.
Thereafter a severe fever from Hara (Śiva) called Raudra, which was intent upon injury, fell rapidly on Hari (Kṛṣṇa) and a great fever from Viṣṇu reached quickly that of Śiva, which was falling swiftly.
Then it blazed around these two (Kṛṣṇa and Śiva) who had burning ashes on their hands and who had vanquished (their) enemies – these two who have identical bodies, possess great fevers and engage in battle-activities.
Due to the wind (from the battle) the earth shook and the moon and the fire did not produce light and the sun entered visibly into darkness. Śiva's fever fled away here (in the battle).
Then the Lord Viṣṇu, who as one should know, according to his nature ('anu-rūpāya'), is greatly resourceful in his activities, stupefied Śiva ('īśāna') with his weapon, injuring ('lambhayan') Ganeśa ('gaṇīśānam').
The Supreme Being, who with hundreds of arrows had stupefied Kālī, Vahni and Guha, who brings death to (his) enemies and who has a voice like the rumbling of a cloud approached Bāṇa who had defeated the gods and engaged in battle with him.
Piercing Bāṇa with his arrows – (Bāṇa) who possessed a horrible desire for creating trouble – Hari cut off his (Bāṇa's) hands with the discus – (Bāṇa) who possessed a mass of shining splendour ('sphurita-mahā -styānasya').
Out of great anger Kṛṣṇa raised (his) discus to finally kill Bāṇa. Śitikaṇṭha (Śiva) (then) smiling, with compassion indicating good fortune (for Bāṇa), said:
"Not so! Do not kill this Bāṇa! He has come to me for refuge." (Then) Hari said to Hara who was speaking – (Hara) who engages in battles out of favour to his devotees:
"He (Bāṇa) is (already) granted you, the Lord, because of whom worship spreads day by day. Those who worship your name and my own or you worship also me."
Thus saying, he (Kṛṣṇa) released Aniruddha and (his) wife who had been kept in prison and went joyfully to Dvāravatī together with him (Aniruddha) who was in company with Uṣā.
He (Bāṇa) entered his (own town) from the battle. Then on account of his dancing before Śambhu (Śiva), Bāṇa, who was no longer lord of the 'dānavas', gained the lordship of the attendant of Śiva ('prāptaṃ ... gāṇapatyam').
The shining lord, the purifier of the earth which had been full of 'asuras' and which

was (now) free from the stain of the Kali age, lived at his own pleasure in the town of the Vṛṣṇis which (already) before was sacred to Viṣṇu.
Viṣṇu, a (genuine) forest fire for the forest of (his) enemies on account of (his) noble activities ('su-apadānatayā'), sported (thereafter) in Dvāravatī – (Viṣṇu) to whose feet the Yādavas bowed down.
Thus Ends Canto Six and This Book as Well.[15]

The Bāṇāsura myth in both its versions is part of the group of myths circling around the *asura*-king Bali Vairocana, from whom Viṣṇu in his incarnation as the dwarf Vāmana won back the sovereignty over the three worlds, but granted him rule over the netherworld as a favour. Bali's family comprises five generations of kings: Hiraṇyakaśipu, Prahlāda, Virocana, Bali and Bāṇa, and each of them is connected to one of Viṣṇu's *avatāras* as Lord of the Universe (Matchett 2001: 150-158). In the Bāṇa myth where the story of the 5th generation is told and that of the 6th generation heralded, the old controversy between *asura* and the *deva* is replaced by the integration of the *asura* world into the Hari fold. Thus, after Bāṇa is rescued by Śiva, first from his excessive bellicosity and then from death at the hands of his adversary, Kṛṣṇa, he is made to serve by his own consent both Hara and (first and foremost) his former enemy Hari until death. Aniruddha, Kṛṣṇa's grandson, marries Uṣā, the *asura* king's daughter, and takes her to his place, Dvāraka. Could there be a greater promise for future harmony and stability of the universal order? The legend thus marks a real turning point in Viṣṇu mythology:

The Harihara concept with its original domination of Śiva over Viṣṇu has been changed in favour of a Viṣṇu/Kṛṣṇa, now the Lord who reigns over all three worlds. At the same time, the method of subduing the *asuras* has changed from deceit, previously applied by Viṣṇu, to heroism in battle, i.e. from overwhelming the enemy by the power of *buddhi* to fighting for victory. This matches the religious situation in most parts of Central and part of South India at the time of Godāvara Miśra, where Viṣṇu and Śiva temples are found side by side and both gods are worshipped equally (Stietencron 1978b). The most remarkable site in our context is, of course, Mahabalipuram with its Shore temple, where Viṣṇu and Śiva have their temples side by side and where several reliefs of other temples contain Bali scenes. On the rock depicting Arjuna's penance there is a scene, according to Jagadisa Ayyar (1920: 171ff) showing "king Bali holding *darbar* attended by warriors, Rajas and several wild animals in Patālaloka, his underground kingdom ... A historical dynasty claiming to be Bāṇa's descendants went by the name Vanas, and these had their own connection with Mahabalipuram or the Seven Pagodas. Their flag displayed a black buck and their crest was the bull. Many of their inscriptions are found at Tiruvallam, North Arcot District, known also as Vānapuram (Banapuram) situated in Perum-Banappadi, the great Bāṇa country where they settled later on." Thus, in this sphere too, there is an intermingling of both Bali and Bāṇa tradition.

Two more examples can be added. Remarkably enough, there is a "family identity" at work in the Bali/Bāṇa legends, which to a certain extent blurs the distinction between Bali and Bāṇa. This is also true for the distinction between Hari and Vāmana. To quote only a few instances: in verse 90 of the Śaurīkathā cited above, the battle between Kṛṣṇa and Bāṇa is fought "for the sake of Bali". A legend gives the reason (among others) for the ritual burning of twigs (*chokkappañci*) as part of the *Karttikai vratam* on Kārttika full moon day. It is told that it was first done by Mahabali as a remedy for getting rid of a burning sensation in his body (Jagadisa Ayyar 1920: 155) – but in literary tradition it is Bāṇa who is driven into an aggressive mood by the itching all over his body (Śaurīkathā verses 90ff).

According to HHC 8. 12-13, the piece representing Viṣṇu is to be made with oblong eyes and elongated earlobes ending in lotos buds (see above). This form of ear is typical for Vāmana sculptures (Gail 1997: 763f).

Given all this, the HHC *devayuddha* game itself could well have been invented to serve as a variant of the (*caturaṅga*) game that has to be played on Balipratipad (the first day of Kārttika *śuklapakṣa*, also called Dyūtapratipad), which in the annual festival cycle marks the end of the three days of Bali's rule over the earth and the forthcoming awakening of Viṣṇu (*viṣṇuprabodhinī*) from his cosmic sleep Raghavan (1979: 237) mentions a *caturaṅga* text giving details of the game on this day, which unfortunately has not yet been accessible).

Thus, to the many spheres where Bāṇa-Bali are represented in medieval Central and South India, the HHC perhaps adds one more. Further research is needed, however, to turn this hypothesis into data based fact.

Conclusion

Bāṇa is the pre-ordained loser in this legend. He, a demon and a king on earth, attempts to play in the same league as Śiva and Viṣṇu and must eventually pay the price for his hybris. His scheme to outmanoeuvre the two great gods does not materialise, but in fact he loses nothing. In the end, he is exactly what he used to be, the guardian of Śiva's abode.

If we shift from the narrative mode of religious legend to that of political legitimation, we can also interpret Bāṇa's attempt as the struggle of a little king for sovereignty. By pitching two great kings against each other, he endeavours to be the third party that comes out best in the matter. Although he fails and is himself threatened with death by Kṛṣṇa, his former loyalty to Śiva saves him. He thus received the treatment described in Samudragupta's Allahabad inscription: defeated, released and re-instated (*-grahaṇa-mokṣa-anugraha-*, Fleet 1888; Chhabra/Gai 1981: lines 19-20).

Notes

1 The principal duty of a *dharmarāja* and source of his legitimation according to Kauṭilya (Arthaśāstra [KA] 1.3, part. 1.3. 16-17) and Manu (Mānavadharmaśāstra, ch. 7.) was to create social harmony by establishing the order of the four *varṇas* (*varṇadharmasthiti)* and prevent *varṇasaṁkara* (distortion of *varṇas* by intermingling of their members) in his kingdom.

2 See e.g., the portrait of Acyutarāya in Tirumalāmbaradevī (1970).

3 Medieval political didactic texts can roughly be classified: a) nibandha work, in which *nīti* is taught as theory only or in connection with or parallel to other traditional sciences of governance (*vyavahāra* etc.); b) separate Rājanītiśāstras teaching predominantly Kaliyugadharma; c) works with selected topics suited to practical needs or reflecting the image of the king such as, for example, Lokaprakāśa, Nītivākyāmṛtam of Somadeva Sūrī (10th cent.), Mānasollāsa of Bhūlokamalla Somadeva (12th cent.), Nītikalpataru of Vyāsadāsa Kṣemendra (11th cent.), Nītimayūkha of Bhaṭṭa Nīlakaṇṭha (17th cent.), Rājanītiratnākara of Caṇḍīśvara (14th cent.), Śukranīti (11th cent?) or Rājadharmakaustubha of Anantadeva (14th cent.).

4 Ed. from a single Grantha ms. in the Govt. Oriental Library Madras by S.K. Ramanatha Sastri in 1950. According to A. Bock-Raming (2001), who translated Chapter 8 of the HHC, there are two more ms. of the text in Śāntiniketan and the Orissa State Museum respectively.

5 (... *srīmānmahārājādhirājagajapatiPratāparudradevasvahastadhāritakanakakesaricatuṣṭayāveṣṭitaśātakumbhamayakumbhasaṃbhṛtameghāḍaṃbarābhidhānasitātapatraśobhamānakavipuṃgavapaṇḍitarājaguruvājapeyayājimantrivara* ...). The editor comments: *ayaṃ rājo Gajapatipratāparudradevasya mantrī, guruśca bhūtvā tena nitarāṃ bahumānitaśca asādhāraṇāi rājabahumānaiḥ* I *asadhāraṇaścāyamupacāraḥ – yat poṣako mahārāja eva Meghaḍāmbaranāmakaṃ kanakakesaricatuṣṭayāveṣṭitahemakalaśāṅkaṃ sitātapatraṃ svayaṃ svapoṣyāya dhārayati*I *kiṃca kavipuṁgava iti paṇḍitarājā iti ca virudadvayaṃ vaiduṣyāvedakaṃ, vājapeyayājī ityetadapi svajanmādhikārakarmakāritvamavagamayati* I *Pratāparudrasya mantrī tatkāle vartamana eva syāt* I

6 KRV 64*: *tata āgatam* I *Godāvarītīre sthitvā Kañcīrājā sainyaṃ gṛhītvā yathārtham-āgatam* I *tacchrutvā sainyair-uktam – asmin balaṃ nāsti* I *brāhmaṇena daivabalaṃ kṛtam* I *tacchrutvā Godāvarī-rājaguruḥ Godāvarīm – āvāhayitvā (= āvāhya) Godāvarīṃ pūritavān* I *taddṛṣṭvā rājā svadeśaṃ gataḥ* I
„While retreating, the king camped [on the northern] bank of the Godāvarī [where his soldiers relaxed]. In the meantime, the king of Kanchi [chasing Puruṣottamadeva] appeared in person [on the southern bank of the river]. When the soldiers came to know of this, they refused to fight saying that they had no more strength in their limbs. The Brahmin [Priest of the king], thereupon, put his supernatural powers to use. Having learnt of the plight of the soldiers, the royal preceptor, Godāvarī[śa Mahāpatra] invoked the river -goddess Godāvarī and caused the basin of the river filled up [with waters]. Having seen this [and realizing that the Godāvarī has now become unfordable for his soldiers] the king [of Kanchi] went back to his country" (Translation by G.Ch. Tripaty).

7 See P.K. Panda, Contribution of Orissa to Sanskrit Literature, p. 121

8 „If Kauṭilya's celebrated treatise contains rules for Government in times of peace and war, this work furnished the rules for warfare and military matters including array of troops con-

sisting of four divisions ... His work covers a wide field of ripe experience in warfare and political administration. Such books help us to penetrate into the past glory of our land and get a glimpse of the duties of an able and successful king" (Ramanatha Sastri 1950: Vf).

9 *caturbhujaṃ Hare rūpaṃ kuryāt śrīvatsa vakṣasam* | *śaṅkhacakraṃ śārṅgadharaṃ dadhānaṃ karapallavaiḥ* || 12 ||
vasānaṃ vāsasī pīte Garuḍoparisaṁsthitam | *nalinīdalavistīrṇakarṇāntavyāpidṛgyugam* || 13 ||
śastrair nānāvidhair yuktavāhanaṃ kaustubhānvitam | *kirītānvitamūrdhānaṃ ratnacchatravirājitam* || 14 ||
dhātudantendhanādyais tu prakṛtīr daivabhedataḥ | *kuryād devau Hariharau varṇenecchanurūpataḥ* | *caturbhujaṃ Haraṃ kuryād āsīnaṃ vṛṣabhāsane* ||15 ||
dadhānaṃ sulabhra[ḍa]maru pinākeśu karāmbojaiḥ | *kapardinaṃ nīlakaṇṭham adhacandravibhūṣitam* || 16 ||
śirodāmnā śobhamānaṃ netratrayādi [netratrayavi]bhūṣitam | *śastrair nānavidhairyuktavāhanaṃ nāmabhūṣanam* || 17 ||
vyāghracarmāmbaradharaṃ ratnachattravirājitam | *yuvarājastathā mantrī vāhinīnāyakastathā* || 18 ||
rāgā[jā]rohāḥ syandinaḥ sādinaḥ svāminor dvayaḥ[yoḥ] | *dhanurbāṇāṅgulitrāṇakarāḥ kāryāḥ kirītinaḥ* || 19 ||
sūtrimantricamūnāthāḥ vyomayānaṃ samāśritāḥ | *śiṣṭā viśeṣanipuṇāḥ gajasyandanavājiṣu* || 20 ||
nitriṁ[striṁ]śaśaktinārācakuntakhadgāṅkitāsanāḥ | *yuvarājādayas sarve bhaveyur yuddhasajjitāḥ* || 21 ||

10 HHC 8. 100-116. For diagrams, see the German translation by Bock-Raming (2001).

11 *jñatvā ca vyūhasaṃsthānaṃ padaṃ pādaṃ ca rakṣakam* | *ruddhatvaṃ ga[cā]ruddhatvaṃ dānarakṣakayos tathā* | *balābalaṃ tayos tadvad uccanīcapadaṃ tathā* || *jayāyādvaitadānaṃ ca krīḍāṃ kuryān na cānyathā* |

12 Syed 2001, p. 10 ff.

13 Raghavan 1979; Welbon/Yocum 1982; Entwistle 1987, 1997.

14 Carl Suneson, Śaurikathodaya, a Yamaka Poem by Vāsudeva. Edited with Translation, Notes and Introduction. Second Revised Edition Stockholm 1986, pp.178-186. In the section from canto 6 cited above, the notes have been left out.

15 Vāsudeva (1986: 178-186). In the part of canto six cited above the notes have been left out. Translation and marking of Sanskrit words by Carl Suneson.

Little Kings or Little Kingdoms? Some Unresolved Questions

Georg Berkemer

A friend of mine recently described how one of her colleagues had reacted to her Lit D thesis on the issue of political formations in the Vedas. The said colleague, long since retired, had looked through the manuscript and exclaimed: "But how can you do this, it's history!" This took place in the former GDR. However, if the Indianists of the two Germanys ever did have something in common, it was their suspicion of anything that smelt of theory. In a review of my own PhD thesis, a colleague of my generation wrote that the little king model had about the same heuristic value as the existence of little green men. Germany may not be the only positivist refuge, but the faction dead set against synthetic thinking of any kind is still going strong, even in the age of post-modernity. Admittedly, the term "little kingdom" may sound somewhat odd to some people. As a non-native English speaker, I will refrain from comment. The term is just there, it is used and has its history as a technical term. It is striking how widely it is used in the Internet – from the "very little king Herod" of the Bible to several historic medieval rulers, and "little king Loc" of children's stories, from historic kingdoms like Judah and Israel to sectarian congregations and esoteric circles. For historians of South Asia, it is a familiar term and has a specific, albeit not particularly well-defined, meaning.

As far as I know, it has been used in the field since 1959 (Cohn 1959) and became popular in the 1960s (Cohn 2001b [1962]). Being of the opinion that the "byzantine", imperial Islamic and Western state models did not really fit, Bernard Cohn and Burton Stein developed their own versions to accommodate data from their own respective regions of research, the Benares region and Tamil Nadu. I will not dwell on the details here as they have been discussed above (The Role of Hermann Kulke and History of the Model). Suffice it to say here that both models have four common features: 1) they try to avoid using European pre-modern state models, 2) they are based on regional, not all-Indian data, 3) they emphasise segmentation and the existence of multiple political units, 4) they use hierarchy and stress the fact that system levels are mutually interdependent.

For a long time thereafter, when talking of the political structures that B. Cohn called "little kingdoms", that is "rajadoms, jagirs and talukas" (Cohn 2001b [1962]: 489), scholars such as B.D. Chattopadhyaya, André Wink, Susan Bayly and

Nicholas Dirks always referred to the lowest level of a political hierarchy. It could be said that the typology of the little kingdom extended to the end of the 1980s. Typologies were developed from regional data, including from Tamil Nadu, Rajasthan, Oudh and Maharashtra. The weakness of many of the outstanding regional history publications was apparent when the authors attempted to provide a theoretical framework that was not only applicable to their region, but to all of India. The result was usually a failure.

Typologies tend to emerge in the first stage of a new model or theory, when people are still trying to come to grips with the source material they intend to systematise. They consist basically of lists and as such are one-dimensional. Cohn's four levels for the eighteenth-century political system is one example and, as Nicholas Dirks has shown, the whole British local administration set-up in South India was based on colonial typologies of this kind, hierarchical models into which the little kingdoms of the time had to fit in order to survive. If he is right, the present caste system is based on a colonial typology of this kind that turned virulent.

Thus, typology helps only to a certain extent. It is a tool to understand the basics, but only on a regional level. Since students of South Asian history usually end up concentrating on a certain region, there is much to be learned from this approach. However, the shortcomings are obvious when an attempt is made to apply the findings of one author's research region and time frame to another regional and temporal context. What, for instance, could be of use in B. Cohn's late Mugal context in describing the contemporary situation of Assam or Kerala? What is the common denominator of the 11th century Cola state and 17th century Maratha kingdoms? Can the political situation of early 20th century Gilgit, Chitral or Bolor be compared with the desert states of colonial Rajasthan?

The paradigmatic little kingdom, N. Dirks' Putukottai of the 19th century (Dirks 1987), is an isolated political unit within the Madras Presidency. What do we learn from this about the dozens of little kingdoms in the power pyramids of such diverse regional empires as Orissa, Karnataka or the Sultanate of Gujarat, to mention only a few?

Those who study these phenomena know that all the instances I mentioned have something in common, namely that they are more closely linked to each other than they are to contemporary political structures in the Near East, China or Europe. I believe the difficulty in pinpointing common features lies in the polythetic nature of their sets. Polythetic classifications, which are also typologies, are open-ended. Rodney Needham (1979, following Sokal 1974) and Gabriella Eichinger Ferro-Luzzi (1989) used them to describe various cultural phenomena both in and outside of South Asia. Polythetic sets have in common that there is no finite class of statements adequate to describe the elements of each set. Elements are not part of a set because they are the same kind of phenomenon or because they can be reduced to a certain essential. On the contrary, they belong to a given set because there are rules that describe their relations to each other.

Applying this polythetic approach, we can say that a little kingdom is not "little" because it is small, i.e., under a given number of square kilometres or bags of rice per annum or head of soldiers, but because it has a specific relationship to a greater kingdom. The historical roots and regional characteristics of this relationship make it easy to recognise as a little kingdom situation, but often difficult to say exactly why this is so without being an expert on the particular regional history.

As I see it, little kingdoms can be recognised as such by looking at groups of states within cultural regions and imperial and/or regional power pyramids. If two or more political units with ties of a politico-religious, kin-based, military and economic nature that share a common legitimatory meta-narrative and endo-historical time are reviewed, a little kingdom relationship is certain to emerge. Although the little king may be lower in the hierarchy, absolutes are not implied. Hierarchic relations can run in circles or fade out in sub-networks, depending on the histories of the particular claims of supremacy or such banal things as language boundaries and mountain ranges that impede communication.

Many scholars, anthropologists and historians have carried out research on topics related to little kingdoms, some using the term, others not. I could mention among many others Susan Bayly, Pamela Price, Henri Stern, Dirk Kolff, Surajit Sinha, Cynthia Talbot, Jean Claude Galey, David Shulman, Amalendu Guha, Richard Emerson, Richard Fox.

Since the conference was convened in Heidelberg, let me concentrate on the German contribution to little kingdom studies, foremost on Hermann Kulke and his school of thought. I should also mention Akio Tanabe, who is well known for his studies on the Orissan kingdom of Khurda/Puri and will present us with his ideas today, and C. P. Nanda from Sambalpur who gives the subaltern a voice and occasionally reveals the ugly side of the little kings.

But back to the 1980s: the next step in the history of our paradigm is linked to the name of Hermann Kulke. We, his students in the 1980s in Heidelberg, learned from him that a region's political system could be far more diverse, more dynamic, and of greater depth in time than previously appreciated. In Orissa he faced a cultural region that was multi-centred in itself, had a temporal depth of two millennia and consisted of culturally heterogeneous populations. In other words, it was an area that contained all the problems of the early little kingdom model in a nutshell.

In his writings, Kulke concentrated on formation and transformation processes that ranged from tribal chief, military leader and robber baron to Hindu raja, on the spread of the notion of a Hindu kingdom in previously untouched areas, and on the foundation of ruling families, temples, villages etc. in the process. He saw that this pattern of formation and settlement, of Hinduisation and integration into existing power pyramids had been repeated hundreds of times and for hundreds of years. The resulting political systems were often short-lived, although some lasted for several centuries. They shared a common political structure and were centred towards the great regional temples and cities. This process of change and re-formation never ceased. Even the structure itself was subject to change, albeit on a much larger time scale. Here we encounter the dimension of long duree, which must also be taken into account when talking of little kingdoms. This process of formation, fission, integration and destruction so crucial to the history of Orissa and the formation of its regional identity, changed continuously in size and speed and was simultaneously influenced by contingent factors such as the politics at imperial level, new religious movements, the increase or decrease in population and available surplus goods.

To sum up, it can be said that Kulke introduced important analytical tools with his processural model of the little kingdom, such as the shift from the single kingdom to the group, to the process rather than the historical moment, to the variant scales of temporal depth, and – most important of all – to the nuclear areas that share a similar cultural background but have their own sub-regional identities and are politically separate, inasmuch as they are not integrated into a generally short-lived empire. These are the stages at which the history of the little kingdom unfolds and from where the idea of the Hindu kingdom gradually spread into new areas.

As a result of Kulke's studies and those of Indologist Günther Sontheimer and sociologist Jakob Rösel of Freiburg, the younger generation here in Heidelberg learned to apply the various models of traditional political systems to our own region of study. The more historically inclined among us, such as Swapna Bhattacharya, began comparisons with Europe or in the case of Stanley Tambiah, with Buddhist Asia, while others again, like Tilman Frasch, were more interested in an anthropological point of view. However, the book on *Political Systems of Highland Orissa* has yet to be written. Some of those who took up studies of other Indian regions are represented in this volume.

I must now confess to having smuggled one of my own ideas into the above historiographical account of the little kingdom model – the radical relationalism that highlights the links between phenomena as opposed to their substance or essence. Although fully aware that it does not elicit a very positive response from many colleagues, I would argue that the entire model stands or falls with this approach, built on the assumption that Indian kingship is fundamentally different to its Europan counterpart. Based on a hierarchy of kings, as distinct from nobles under one king, it lacks the rigidity of the European medieval feudal systems. As Bernhard Cohn once remarked, "system-wide values set the common goals and provide a framework and a set of ground rules through which the competing segments, both vertically and horizontally, are integrated into the political system" (p. 484). In Europe, vertical competition is much less evident than in India, where all rulers are kings, or kings of kings. Since the elements of the system are basically the same, it is their relationships that render them differ from each other.

I would suggest, for instance, that no power pyramid contains a single lowest little king. There is always a legitimatory narrative for a ruler, which is sufficient to prove the existence of somebody lower in the neighbourhood.

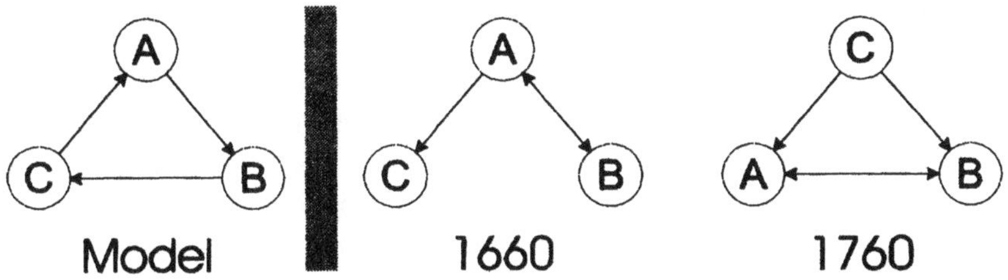

Fig. 1: Circular claims of higher status. To the left the model, next two historical situations from south Orissa, where three "little Gajapatis" Jeypur (A), Parlakimedi (B) and Vizianagaram (C) expressed their claims for hierarchical supremacy according to their respective political fortunes (Berkemer 1997, forthcoming a, b).

Little king status is relational rather than given or inherited by substance, such as kinship, jati or rank in a closed social environment such as a village. This implies that little kings do not come from a given social stratum. As we know from the Puranas, there are Brahminic complaints that with the commencement of the Kali yuga almost anyone, whether Sudra, Brahman, Nishadas or Mlecchas, can become kings. No distinction is made here between great and little kings. On the contrary, the Brahman writers of the Vaṁśa-anucarita of the Purana texts complain about is that they see the office of king as being ostensibly wide open.

There is a clear distinction between the status of a Kṣatriya, the almost extinct ancient nobility of Aryan pre-state tribal societies and the new elites, both local and immigrant, in the various regions of the subcontinent.

A newcomer acknowledges the status of a subordinate king by accepting symbols, such as titles, material gifts or offices from a more powerful ruler. The relationship established in this manner, however, is not necessarily permanent. There are numerous examples of insubordination and rebellion. Absenteeism from royal festivals and the resultant non-performance of the required rites of obeisance, issue of an era and a currency, marriage relations with other great kings, palace revolts in the overlord's capital and open war against a weak overlord all crop up in medieval sources.

Many kings who are economically just not strong enough to establish an empire of their own tell stories about their "conquests" of sovereignty symbols, such as the famous Kanaka Durgā of the Gajapatis of Orissa (Schnepel 2002).

Little kings of this kind have almost all the prerequisites for an empire. They have status and the respect of both their subjects and their own little kings, and have at their disposal well-established foreign relations, a network of temples and other sacred sites, a routine-based system of surplus-collection, and a semi-divine status among the tribal population of their realm. They simply cannot afford an army strong enough to overthrow the established overlord, even in phases when the empire is in a critical state. Such kings can destroy a state but they will never be able to establish one of their own, with the possible exception of taking over a stable empire from within. Evidence of the latter can be found in Vijayanagar and the Gajapati empire, where powerful military leaders established themselves as kings and founded a new dynasty. The great Kapilendra of Orissa and the even greater Krishnadevaraya of Vijayanagar, who is the son of a successful usurper, are examples of this

The relational model implies of necessity a large amount of scale invariance, i.e., regardless of the hierarchy level in the power pyramid, the structural features are basically the same. Since we are looking at kings and kings of kings, we are also looking at kingdoms and kingdoms within kingdoms. The mental map of any of these states within a cultural region is basically identical. 18th century Orissa constantly reveals palace and temple, Brahman agrahāra and forest stronghold, Rājput origin myth and copper plate inscriptions, as well as cadastral procedures and historigraphical techniques of collective memory. Muthadār and deśmukh, forest chief and merchant prince have one thing in common with the descendants of the imperial rulers of Gaṅga, Gajapati, Bhañja, Cauhan and Cālukya origin: if they can lay their hands on enough money and muscle, they can rise in status, give the right donations to Brahmans, patronise the right temples and festivals, and acquire the necessary reputation as protectors of their subjects, managers of state affairs and army leaders. They will find someone to invent a heroic history of their own, while marriage relations will settle them firmly in the upper ranks of the power pyramid, provided someone equally shrewd and ambitious does not appear on the horizon a few years later. A glance at the local chronicles reveal that this process and its variants are repeated over and over again and we have no reason to doubt that it was exactly the same centuries earlier. The inscriptions of medieval kings and the chronicles of their early modern successors give us at least some indication of this process (Berkemer 1997, 1999).

Thus, our model is based on the principles of relationality and scale invariance. But what is it good for? Where are its limits?

I admit to not being able to answer these questions fully. Nobody has ever used the model in order to prove it wrong, since it has not been taken very seriously outside the Kulke group. There are a few indicators, however, that may help.

1) The epistemological limits: what I am talking about is a model, not a theory. It cannot predict much, as a good theory should, and lacks a set of precise statements about its abilities and inabilities. A good theory will always include the rules for its own falsification. The little kingdom model does not, at least not explicitly. So it is best described as a tool, a label we sometimes require to indicate what we are talking about. Little kingdoms do not exist, they are mental constructs. Their place is on the historian's desk and not in the plains and jungles of India.

2) So far, there has been no adequate analysis of the structural constants that implicitly underlie the model. As I mentioned earlier, it could be understood as a set of polythetic classifications. We would, however, need several classifications and in hierarchical order: one to describe the phenomena that allow us to recognise a little kingdom situation from our observations, sources and secondary texts, a second one for the changes in time, a third for the power pyramid, a fourth for the imperial level, a fifth for the long duree, and so on. This, of course, would only provide us with a regional set, not one for the whole of India.

3) Since we can communicate about little kingdoms, the model helps us to understand something. But what? So far, we have compared regions and historical situations. They seem – at least to my knowledge – to have the following in common: they are geographically located in South Asia, they exist in a Hindu context with its dharmśāstra and nītiśāstra texts, they are pre-modern, they are regional, they all include nuclear areas of surplus production, and communication is more intensive within the power pyramid than without and includes channels such as diplomacy, festivals, ritual submission, kinship, warfare, gift-giving, tribute, plunder and trade.

4) There seems to be an upper and lower time limit in which the model is useful: in his Putukottai, Dirks deals with a kind of relic that has outlived itself. It exists without a living context in a colonial environment and I wonder how far we can go in deriving general or regional conclusions from this type of little kingdom. It seems to me that the end of the old regime is also the end of the little kingdom. For some

little kingdoms, this end came in the 19th century, for others only around 1950 (Berkemer: forthcoming b).

On the other end of the time scale, things are more difficult. Let us therefore return to the regional level. For Orissa we can assume that a little kingdom situation first came into existence between the time of the Gupta empire and the 7th century. The same seems to be true of Andhra and Karnataka. It was at a time when the idea of Hindu kingship spread widely in the area and was used on various integrated levels of political domination. I doubt that the Maurya or Śātavāhana states had already developed the necessary level of grass-root kingship that became the trademark of the little kingdom situation in early medieval India. Two more factors should be taken into account: the urbanisation crisis in the Ganges plain in the second half of the first millennium AD that forced Brahmans to seek employment beyond the realm of Aryavarta (Nandi 1986, 2000; Witzel 1985), thus spreading the idea of dharmic kingship, and secondly, the availability of a Puranic model of historical narrative that could be used by experts to create an all-Indian idea of a proper local past. Both factors coincided in time.

5) But what about non-Hindu polities? Can there be little kingdoms in an Islamic or Buddhist context? Rajasthan, Gujarat, Vijayanagar and the Benares region suggest that it might work. Here, however, Islamic states were planted on old Hindu soil. What about Indus Kohistan, Bolor, Baltistan, Citral? Are they simply small states at the borders of empires or are they little?

What about the Persian empire? The omnipresent royal formula mahārāja-adhirāja was derived from the Persian shah-anu-shahi, king of kings. So in what sense were the states of Judah and Israel,[1] the Greek states of Asia Minor or the polities on the western borders of the Subcontinent little kingdoms in relation to the empire of Cyrus, the Babylonians or the Seleucids?

At present I cannot answer these questions, but it seems to me that a model that gives rise to so many questions cannot be bad. Maybe some of them can be answered in the future.

Notes

1 These, as well as the successor kingdoms of the Roman Empire in Britain, might well be an ultimate source of the term "little kingdom".

The Great Afterword

Heiko Frese

Looking at all these essays, it is futile to ask whether it really makes sense to speak of *little kings* and their *kingdoms*. After all, had the category not existed, this volume would have created it, a category that will now be waiting even more eagerly for further definition and discussion. Nevertheless, when asked to contribute a paper, I hesitated: firstly, because the topic did not exactly touch the centre of my studies, and secondly, because I see severe problems.

This does not, of course, imply that the phenomenon of relatively little rulers at the regional or local level were non-existent in India – their importance for India's history is commonplace in science since Nicholas Dirks' pioneering work on Putukkottai (Dirks 1987).[1] To me, the term little king, understood as a category, sounds both wrong and misleading. It may be clear to everyone else and not worth even a footnote, but why then is it still in use, and why is made the focus of conference panels and books, why a (beginning of) discourse? To illustrate what I mean, let me introduce a metaphor.

One of the essays in Jorge Luis Borges' famous "Fictions",[2] written in the 1940s, contains a story about a certain Pierre Menard and his legacy of unpublished works that include, as the narrator detects, referring to it as the "invisible work", the 9th and 38th chapter of Don Quijote by Miguel de Cervantes. This information is accompanied by the extremely puzzling fact that the chapters are not copies. Indeed, the narrator continues, Menard had planned to write the Quijote. Not another Quijote but *the* Don Quijote. He had not planned a mechanical transcription, had not wanted to copy the original. His incredible ambition was to produce a few pages that coincided word for word with those written by Cervantes. His intention was to write an existent novel in a language that was foreign to him.

In the following years, Menard learned Spanish, returned to Catholicism, fought against the Turks and forgot the history of Europe between 1602 and 1918 (in which year he began his enterprise). And although the task was difficult, he prevailed in the end. He succeeded in composing a second Quijote, which in many aspects, as the narrator claims, surpassed even the original. Menard's fragmentary Quijote (fragmentary because most of it was lost) turned out to be more subtle than that of Cervantes. The latter, for example, contrasts the fictions of knighthood with the poor reality in the province of his country – which, one could argue, lacked a certain subtlety. Menard, on the other hand, selects the country of Carmen in the 16th century as his background, carefully avoiding stereotypes such as conquistadors, mystics or Philip II, and thus creating a new feeling for the historical novel. In the end, a sense of triumph prevails as the author demonstrates why two Quijotes are better than one.

Little kings also rewrite a text. They "learn" Sanskrit like Menard learned Spanish, they often adopt Hinduism as he "returned" to Catholicism, and they fight against the enemies of their overlords like Menard fought against the Turks. And they "forget" parts of their histories by incorporating Hindu myths into their historiography, again like Borges' protagonist, who deleted part of his cultural memory.

They do not copy great kings but make every effort to become the centre of power in the largest possible kingdom. There are numerous little kings and each has in theory the potential to become a great king. To continue the metaphor, many Quijotes have been written by many authors, each of whom could in principle be Cervantes at times. The others are known as *little* Cervantes, as long as their texts are less complete than that of the great Cervantes; if this pattern were to change, their identities would change with it.

Yet, what is their identity? Or, in other words, do little kings have an identity at all? According to the only existing definition of the term little king

> "a political system whose ruler can consider himself in domestic politics to be independent and who also pursues a ritual policy within his own territory, but who at the same time must recognise an overlord who is both politically and ritually above him and militarily superior, whose authority he shares and who needs him for the acknowledgement of the authority of his own rule within his own kingdom and in his dealings with other little kings, should be considered a little kingdom.
>
> ...Once his [the little king's] relationship to the overlord has been established in a single routine interaction (for example through participation in a marriage or in a military parade) and through a clear assignment of the rank of those involved, the positions must constantly be redefined through rituals, gifts, marriages or even through warfare, as there is *no categorical difference between overlord and little king* [my italics]." (Berkemer 1993: 320-322)[3]

I see none. Neither does Berkemer. A little king is a great king is a little king is a great king. If the term is understood as a category, it leads nowhere, since little kings or little kingdoms do not work as theories. It resembles the notion of filling a container with something that, if it fits or is made to fit and the author rests content, eventually emerges as a little king – per definition, as it were. *Little* can only be an expression of demarcation, not of classification. It *could be defined* in the sense of performance or *interpreted* as an emphasis on the dynamics of history in association with events portrayed in narratives. If it is to be used as a term, then as a relational one, similar to how colour works in football shirts for the spectators, i.e., as an indicator of the opposition that enters the game once the performance begins and leaves when it is over. In this case, it exists as a fleeting tool of recognition, not as a marker that distorts reality. One cannot "speak of" little kings. However, if they are a matter for discussion, some indeed may be little in relation to others. Little kings do not exist, they co-exist.

Needless to say, the term itself is a Western construct that has nothing to do with India. Let me focus on *little* for a moment and repeat that little kings cannot exist without (great) kings, and (great) kings need little kings to become what they are. Could a (great) king exist if there were no little kings? While there is no doubt that (great) kings did exist (everyone recognises titles such as *mahārāja* and *mahārājādhirāja*), I am certain that no king in the history of India ever defined himself a little king or spoke of his little kingdom.

And they were not *kings* either. The connotations attached to this term in English are certainly quite different to what is transported by *zamindār, sāmanta rāja, ināmdār, tribal chief* or – of course – *rājā*. Admittedly, *rājā* has commonly been translated as *king*, but would it not be far more adequate to speak of *rulers* and thus avoid the entire conglomeration of possible links to the Western/European world?[4] Thus, only the genuine orientalist will detect little kings in the history of the Indian subcontinent.

One cannot speak of a clearly demarcated identity in referring to the category of little king/little kingdom. As shown above, the definition is not without its pitfalls. Even if it were to be *de-defined* as or into a relational term, the result would hardly be satisfactory. It could only lead to the ultimate trivial statement that some kingdoms are smaller than others and some rulers less powerful.

The most straightforward method of creating a term is presumably to produce a definition and then start looking for things that "fit" – be it from history or from other fields of study. However, even if the term *had* a working definition or *did not* sound misleading, I still have a point to make: I would very much prefer to enter a discourse "from the back", to "sneak into" it rather than stand at its centre or worse still, trigger it off.[5] By this I mean to enter the world of the protagonists as far as possible, using their language. Little kings are events that come from outside and create their own realm.

Events – understood as "the usurpation of power, the appropriation of a vocabulary turned against those who had once used it, a feeble domination that poisons itself as it grows lax, the entry of a masked 'other'", and not as a treaty, a battle or a reign (Foucault 1997: 124f)[6] – should in fact be at the centre of the historian's work. Yet, it should not be his task to create them.

I came here with faltering steps. I still doubt whether my contribution to this volume carries "enough substance" to deserve the attention of the reader, who expects to learn something about an Indian phenomenon, about Indian history. Behind the term around which all these articles revolve there are very real events and I am sure that *they* are the focus of the authors' interest, not the fictional concept. Thus, having added profoundly to a discourse I already found too powerful, I will now be quiet. Nevertheless, I hope I have done my little best to put a stop to it.

Notes

1 Dirks 1987.
2 Borges (2001: 35-45); the reference is to the German edition.
3 Berkemer 1993, pp. 320-322.
4 For the etymological discussion of the term rājan, see Mayrhofer (1996: 444-446).
5 The principle of this way of looking at things is very eloquently formulated by M. Foucault in his work *L'ordre du discours* (Foucault 1972).
6 Foucault 1997, p. 124-125.

Bibliography

Administrative Report, 1914-18: Administrative Report of the Bashahr State for the Sambat Years 1970-73 (Mar 1914-15 to Mar 1917-18). Simla: Army Press.

Ahluwalia, Manjeet Singh, 1978: Muslim Expansion in Rajasthan. The Relations of Delhi Sultanate with Rajasthan, 1206-1526. Delhi: Yugantar Prakashan.

– 1993: History of Himachal Pradesh. New Delhi: Intellectual Publishing House.

Ali, Daud, 2000: Royal Eulogy as World History. Rethinking Copper Plate Inscriptions in Cola India. In: Inden, R. / Walters, J. / Ali, D. (eds.), Querying the Medieval. Texts and the History of Practices in South Asia. Oxford: Oxford University Press, pp. 165-230.

Arthaśāstra 1969 / 1972: The Kauṭilīya Arthaśāstra. Kangle, R. P. (ed.), Part I: A Critical Edition with a Glossary. Part II: An English Translation with Critical and Explanatory Notes. Bombay: University of Bombay.

Arunima, G., 1992: Colonialism and the Transformation of Matriliny in Malabar 1850-1940. Cambridge: University of Cambridge, PhD thesis.

– 1998: A Vindication of the Rights of Women: Families and Legal Change in Nineteenth-Century Malabar. In: Anderson, M. R. / Guha, S. (eds.), 1998: Changing Concepts of Rights and Justice in South Asia. Delhi: Oxford University Press, pp. 114-139.

Aung-Thwin, Michael, 1981: Jambudipa: Classical Burma's Camelot. In: Contributions to Asian Studies, Leiden 16 (1981), pp. 38-61.

– 1983: Divinity, Human and Spirit: Conceptions of Classical Burmese Kingship: In: Gesick, L. (ed.), Centers, Symbols and Hierarchies. New Haven: Yale University Press, p. 45-85.

– 1998: Myth and History in the Historiography of Burma. Singapore: Inst. of Southeast Asian Studies.

Avalon, Arthur [Woodroffe, John George], 1982 [1933]: Śārada-Tilaka Tantra. Text with Introduction. Delhi: Motilal Banarsidass.

Axel, Brian Keith, 2001: The Nation's Tortured Body: Violence, Representation, and the Formation of a Sikh "Diaspora". Durham / London: Duke University Press.

Bailey, Frederick George, 1961: 'Tribe' and 'Caste' in India. In: Contributions to Indian Sociology, Paris 5 (1961), pp. 6-19.

– 1996: Cultural Performance, Authenticity, and Second Nature. In: Parkin, D. / Caplan, L. / Fisher, H. (eds.), 1996: The Politics of Cultural Performance. Providence / Oxford: Berghahn Books, pp. 1-17.

Bakker, Hans T. (ed.), 1992: The Sacred Centre as the Focus of Political Interest, Groningen: Egbert Forsten.

Ballhatchet, Kenneth / Taylor, David (eds.), 1984: Changing South Asia: Religion and Society. London: University of London.

Banerji, Rakhal Das, 1928: Rajput Origins in Orissa. In: Modern Review, Calcutta 43 (1928) March, pp. 285-291.

Basu, Helene, 2000: Die Göttin und die Charan – Das Gedächtnis des Königtums, Verwandtschaft und Askese in Kacch (westl. Indien). Berlin: unpublished habilitation thesis, Dept. of Anthropology, Free University, Berlin.

Bataille, George, 1976: Theorie de la religion. In: Oeuvres Completes VII. Paris: Gallimard, pp. 281-345.

Bayly, Chris A., 1992 [1983]: Rulers, Townsmen and Bazaars: North Indian Society in the Age of British Expansion, 1770-1870. Delhi: Oxford University Press.

– 1996: Empire and Information: Intelligence Gathering and Social Communication in India, 1780-1870. Cambridge / New York: Cambridge University Press.

– 1998: Origins of Nationality in South Asia. Patriotism and Ethical Government in the Making of Modern India. Delhi: Oxford University Press.

Bayly, Susan, 1989: Saints, Goddesses and Kings. Muslims and Christians in South Indian Sociey 1700-1900. Cambridge: (Cambridge University Press).

– 1994: Cults and Warrior Kingdoms in South India. In: Thomas, N. / Humphrey, C. (eds.), Shamanism, History and the State. Ann Arbor: University of Michigan Press, pp. 117-132.

Becher, Matthias, 1999: Karl der Große. München: C. H. Beck.

Behera, Sarat Chandra, 1982: Rise and Fall of the Śailodbhavas. History and Culture of Ancient Orissa from 550 A.D. to 736 A.D. Calcutta: Punthi Pustak.

Berkemer, Georg 1992: The 'Centre out There' as State Archive. The Temple of Siṃhāchalam. In: Bakker, H. (ed.), 1992: 119-130.

– 1993: Little Kingdoms in Kalinga. Ideologie, Legitimation und Politik regionaler Eliten. Stuttgart: Steiner.

– 1997: The Chronicle of a Little Kingdom: Some Reflections on the Tekkalī Tālūka Jamīṃdārla Vaṁśāvali. In: Kölver, B. (ed.), 1997: 65-95.

– 1998: Literatur und Geschichte im vormodernen hinduistischen Südasien. In: Rüsen, J. / Gottlob, M. / Mittag, A. (eds.), Die Vielfalt der Kulturen. Frankfurt am Main: Suhrkamp, pp. 145-190.

– 1999: No Heroes in Kaliṅga? On Death in Kaliṅga Inscriptions. In: Schömbucher, E. / Zoller, C. P. (eds.), Ways of Dying. Death and Its Meanings in South Asia. New Delhi: Manohar, pp. 179-189.

– 2001a: Banausia and Endo-history: European Conceptions of Indian Historical Consciousness. ASAFAS Special Paper, Graduate School of Asian and African Area Studies, Kyoto University.

– 2001b: Political Systems and Political Structure of Medieval South India. In: Berkemer, G. / Frasch, T. / Kulke, H. et al. (eds.), Explorations in the History of South Asia. Essays in Honour of Dietmar Rothermund. New Delhi: Manohar, pp. 121-137.

– forthcoming a: Jaipur – Parlakimedi – Vizianaragaram: The Southern Gajapatis. In: Beltz, J. / Frese, H. / Malinar, A. (eds.), forthcoming: Text and Context. New Delhi, Manohar.

– forthcoming b: The King's Two Kingdoms – Or: How the Maharaja of Parlakimedi finally became the Ruler of Orissa. In: Pfeffer, G. (ed.), forthcoming: Periphery and Centre. New Delhi, Manohar.

Berkson, Carmel, 1995: The Divine and Demoniac: Mahisa's Heroic Struggle with Durga. Delhi: Oxford University Press.

Berreman, Gerald, 1963: Hindus of the Himalayas. Berkeley / Los Angeles: University of California Press.

Bhatt, L. B., 1980: India and Indian Regions: A Critical Overview. In: Sopher, D. E. (ed.): An Exploration of India. Geographical Perspectives on Society and Culture. Ithaca: Cornell University Press, pp. 35-61.

Bhattacharya, Swapna, 1989: Landschenkungen und staatliche Entwicklung im frühmittelalterlichen Bengalen. Stuttgart: Steiner.

Biller, Stefan, 1986: Zur Entstehung von Herrschaft und Staat. Das Beispiel des indischen Regionalreiches Orissa. Freiburg: Hochschulverlag.

Bock-Raming, Andreas, 2001: Das 8. Kapitel des Hariharacaturaṅga: ein spätmittelalterlicher Sanskrittext über eine Form des „Großen Schachs". Annotierte Übersetzung und Interpretation. In: Board Games Studies - International Journal for the Study of Board Games, Leiden 4 (2001), p. 85-127.

Boholm, Åsa (ed.), 1996: Political Rituals. Gothenburg: Institute for Advanced Studies in Social Anthropology.

Borges, Jorge L., 2001: Fiktionen. Erzählungen 1939-1944. Frankfurt am Main: Suhrkamp.

Breckenridge, Carol A., 1977: From Protector to Litigant: Changing Relations between Hindu Temples and the Raja of Ramnad. In: Stein, B. (ed.), 1977: 76-106.

Brief History of Keonjhar, 1901: Brief History of Keonjhar, with Genealogy, Statistical Accounts and Geographical description, 1901, Acc. No. 1150Kr, Bhubaneswar: Orissa State Archives.

Briggs, John, 1981 [1829]: History of the Rise of Mahomedan Power in India. New Delhi: Ajanta Publishers.

Burghart, Richard, 1978: Hierarchical Models of the Hindu Social System. In: Man, London 13 (1978), 519-536.

Chartier, Roger, 1992a: Kulturgeschichte zwischen Repräsentationen und Praktiken. In: Chartier 1992b: 7-23.

– 1992b: Die unvollendete Vergangenheit: Geschichte und die Macht der Auslegung. Frankfurt am Main: Fischer.

Chattopadhyaya, Brajadulal, 1976: Origin of the Rajputs: The Political, Economic and Social Processes in Early Medieval Rajasthan. In: Indian Historical Review, Delhi 3 (1976), pp. 59-82.

– 1983: Presidential Address. Political Processes and Structure of Polity in Early Medieval India: Problems and Perspective. In: Proceedings of the Indian History Congress, Burdwan 44th Session (1983), pp. 1-34.

– also in: Chattopadhyaya, Brajadulal, 1994a: The Making of Early Medieval India. Delhi: Oxford University Press, pp. 183-222

– and Kulke (ed.), 1995: 195-232.

– 1994b: The Emergence of the Rajputs as Historical Process in Early Medieval Rajasthan. In: Schomer, K. / Erdman, J. / Lodrick, D. O. et al. (eds.), 1994: 161-191.

– 1997: "Autonomous Spaces" and the Authority of the State: The Contradiction and Its Resolution in Theory and Practice in Early India. In: Kölver, B. (ed.), 1997: 1-14.

Chhabra, Bahadurchand / Gai, Govind Swamirao (eds.), 1981: Allahābād Stone Pillar Inscription of Samudragupta. In: Corpus Inscriptionum Indicarum, Vol. 3 (rev. ed.). New Delhi, Archaeological Survey of India, Inscr. No. 1, pp. 203-220.

Chutintaranond, Sunait, 1990: "Mandala", "Segmentary State" and Politics of Centralization in Medieval Ayudhya. In: Journal of the Siam Society, Bankok 78 (1990) 1, pp. 89-100.

Claus, Peter, 1978: Oral Traditions, Royal Cults and Materials for a Reconsideration of the Caste System in South India. In: Journal of Indian Folkloristics, Mysore 1 (1978) 1, pp. 1-25.

Cobden Ramsay, L. E. B., 1982 [1910]: Feudatory of Orissa. Calcutta, Firma KLM.

Coburn, Thomas B., 1991: Encountering the Goddess: A Translation of the Devī-Māhātmya and a Study of Its Interpretation. Albany: State University of New York Press.

Cohn, Bernard S., 1959: Some Notes on Law and Change in North India. In: Economic Development and Cultural Change, Chicago 8 (1959) 1, pp. 79-93.

– 1995 [1983]: Representing Authority in Victorian India. In: Hobsbawm, E. / Ranger, T. (eds.), 1995: The Invention of Tradition. Cambridge: Canto, pp. 165-209; also in Cohn 2001a: 632-682.

– 2001a [1987/1990/1993]: An Anthropologist among the Historians and Other Essays. New Delhi: Oxford University Press.

– 2001b [1962]: Political Systems in Eighteenth-Century India: The Benares Region. In: Cohn 2001a: 483-499.

– 2001c [1960]: The Initial British Impact on India: A Case Study of the Benares Region. In: Cohn 2001a: 320-342.

– 2001d [1977]: African Models and Indian Histories. In: Cohn 2001a: 200-223.

– 2001e [1962]: An Anthropologist among the Historians: A Field Study. In: Cohn 2001a: 1-17.

– 2001f [1980]: History and Anthropology: The State of Play. In: Cohn 2001a: 18-49.

– 2001g [1981]: Anthropology and History in the 1980s: Towards a Rapprochement. In: Cohn 2001a: 50-77.

Comaroff, John L. / Comaroff, Jean, 1987: The Madman and the Migrant: Work and Labour in the Historical Consciousness of a South African People. In: American Ethnologist, Washington, D. C., 14 (1987) 2, pp. 191-209.

– 1992: Ethnography and the Historical Imagination. Boulder: Westview Press.

Coombe, Rosemary J. / Stoller, Paul, 1994: X Marks the Spot: The Ambiguities of African Trading in the Commerce of the Black Public Sphere. In: Public Culture, Durham 7 (1994), pp. 249-274.

Dalton, Edward T. 1973: Tribal History of Eastern India. Delhi: Cosmo.

Dash, Gagan N., 1978: The Evolution of Priestly Power. The Sūryavaṁśa Period. In: Eschmann / Kulke / Tripathi (eds.), 1978: 209-221.

Deleuze, Gilles / Guattari, Félix, 1987: A Thousand Plateaus: Capitalism and Schizophrenia. Minneapolis: University of Minnesota Press.

Deyell, John S. / Frykenberg, Robert E., 1982: Sovereignty and the ‚SIKKA' under Company Raj: Minting Prerogative and Imperial Legitimacy in India. In: Indian Economic and Social History Review, New Delhi 19 (1982), pp. 1-25.

Dīgha Nikāya, 1890-11: Dīgha Nikāya. Vol. 1-3. Rhys Davis, T. W. / Carpenter, J. E. (eds.). London: Oxford University Press.

Dirks, Nicholas B., 1976: Political Authority and Structural Change in Early South Indian History. In: Indian Economic and Social History Review, New Delhi 13 (1976) 2, pp. 125-157.

– 1979: The Structure and Meaning of Political Relations in a South Indian Little Kingdom. In: Contributions to Indian Sociology (N. S.), New Delhi 13 (1979) 2, pp.169-204.

– 1982: The Pasts of a Pāḷaiyakkārar: The Ethnohistory of a South Indian Little King. In: Journal of Asian Studies, Ann Arbor 41 (1982), pp. 655-683.

– 1985: Terminology and Taxonomy; Discourse and Domination: From Old Regime to Colonial Regime in South India. In: Frykenberg, R. F. / Kolenda, P. (eds.): Studies of South India. An Anthology of Recent Research and Scholarship. Madras / Delhi: New Era / American Institute of Indian Studies, pp. 127-149.

– 1986: From Little Kingdom to Landlord: Property, Law, and the Gift under the Madras Permanent Settlement. In: Comparative Studies in Society and History, Cambridge 28 (1986), pp. 307-333.

– 1987 (second edition 1993): The Hollow Crown. Ethnohistory of an Indian Kingdom. Cambridge: Cambridge University Press.

– 1989a: The Invention of Caste: Civil Society in Colonial India. In: Social Analysis, Adelaide / New York 25 (1989), pp. 42-52.

– 1989b: The Original Caste: Power, History and Hierarchy in South Asia. In: Contributions to Indian Sociology (N. S.), New Delhi 23 (1989), pp. 59-77.

– 1992a: Castes of Mind. In: Representations, Berkeley 37 (1992) Winter 1992, pp. 56-78.

– 1992b: From Little King to Landlord: Colonial Discourse and Colonial Rule. In: Dirks, N. B. (ed.): Colonialism and Culture. Ann Arbor: University of Michigan Press, pp. 175-208.

– 1993: Colonial Histories and Native Informants: Biography of an Archive. In: Breckenridge, C. A.; van der Veer, P. (eds.): Orientalism and the Postcolonial Predicament: Perspectives on South Asia. Philadelphia: University of Pennsylvania Press, pp. 279-313.

– 1994: Guiltless Spoliations: Picturesque Beauty, Colonial Knowledge, and Colin Mackenzie's Survey of India. In: Asher, C. B. / Metcalf, T. R. (eds.): Perceptions of South Asia's Visual Past. New Delhi: Oxford & IBH Publishing Co., pp. 211-232.

– forthcoming: Colonial Rule and the Ethnographic State in India. In: Kimura / Tanabe (eds.): forthcoming.

Diskalkar, Dattareya Balkrishna, 1977: Selections from Sanskrit Inscriptions, 2nd to 8th Century A. D. New Delhi: Classical Publishers.

Dowson, John, ^{10}1961: A Classical Dictionary of Hindu Mythology and Religion. Geography, History and Literature. London: Routledge & Kegan Paul.

Drekmeier, Charles, 1962: Kingship and Community in Early India. Stanford: Stanford University Press.

Dumont, Louis, 1962: The Conception of Kingship in Ancient India. In: Contributions to Indian Sociology. Paris 6 (1962), pp. 48-77. Reprinted in and cited from Dumont 1980: 287-313.

– 1970 [1966]: Homo Hierarchicus. The Caste System and Its Implications. London: Paladin / Chicago: University of Chicago Press.

– 1980 [1966]: Homo Hierarchicus.The Caste System and Its Implications. Chicago: University of Chicago Press (rev. ed.).

Duroiselle, Charles, 1921: List of Inscriptions Found in Burma, Rangoon: Superintendent of Government Printing.

Eichinger Ferro-Luzzi, Gabriella, 1989: The Polythetic-prototype Approach to Hinduism. In: Sontheimer, G. D. / Kulke, H. (eds.), Hinduism Reconsidered. New Delhi: Manohar, pp. 187-195.

Encyclopedia of Indian Temple Architecture, 1983: Encyclopedia of Indian Temple Architecture: South India, Lower Draviḍadeśa 200 B.C.-A.D. 1234. Philadelphia: American Institute of Indian Studies, University of Pennsylvania Press.

Entwistle, Alan W., 1987: Braj, a Centre of Krishna Pilgrimage. Groningen: Egbert Forsten.

Erndl, Kathleen M., 1993: Victory to the Mother: The Hindu Goddess of Northwest India in Myth, Ritual and Symbol. Oxford: Oxford University Press.

Eschmann, Anncharlott, 1978: Hinduization of Tribal Deities in Orissa: The Śākta and Śaiva Typology. In: Eschmann / Kulke / Tripathi (eds.), 1978: 79-97.

Eschmann, Anncharlott / Kulke, Hermann / Tripathi, Gaya C. (eds.), 1978: The Cult of Jagannath and the Regional Tradition of Orissa. New Delhi: Manohar.

Falk, Nancy E., 1973: Wilderness and Kingship in Ancient South Asia. In: History of Religions, Chicago 13 (1973) 1, pp. 1-15.

Fleckstein, Josef, 1991: Karl der Große. In: Bautier, R.-H. / Auty, R. / Angermann, N. (eds.), Lexikon des Mittelalters, Vol. 5. München / Zürich: Artemis, cols. 955-959.

Fleet, John F., 1888: Allahabad Posthumous Stone Pillar Inscription of Samudragupta. In: Fleet, J. F. (ed.), 1888: 1-17.

– (ed.), 1888: Corpus Inscriptionum Indicarum, Vol. 3. Inscriptions of the Early Gupta Kings and their Successors. Calcutta: Government Press.

Fortes, Meyer, 1953: The Structure of Unilineal Descent Groups. In: American Anthropologist, Washington, D. C., 55 (1953), pp. 17-41.

Foucault, Michel, 1972: L'ordre du discours. Paris: Gallimard.

– 1979: The History of Sexuality, Vol. 1. London: Allen Lane.

– 1983: The Subject and Power. In: Dreyfus, Hubert L. / Rabinow, Paul: Michel Foucault: Beyond Structuralism and Hermeneutics. Chicago: University of Chicago Press.

– 1997: Nietzsche, Genealogy, History. In: Jenkins, K. (ed.), The Postmodern History Reader. London: Routledge, pp. 124-125.

Fox, Richard G., 1971: Kin, Clan, Raja, and Rule. State Hinterland Relations in Preindustrial India. Berkeley: University of California Press.

– (ed.), 1977: Realm and Region in Traditional India. Durham: Duke University Press; also New Delhi / Bombay / Bangalore: Vikas

Francis, W., 1907: Madras District Gazetteers: Vizagapatam. Madras: Government Press.

Frasch, Tilman, 1996: Pagan. Stadt und Staat. Stuttgart: Steiner.

– 1998: King Nadaungmya's Great Gift. In: Robinne, François / Pichard, Pierre (eds.), ńtudes birmanes: en hommage R Denise Bernot. Paris: ńcole Française d'ExtrĻme-Orient, pp. 27-35.

– 2000: A Note on the Mahabodhi Temples at Pagan. In: Lobo, Wibke / Reimann, Stephanie (eds.), Southeast Asian Archaeology. Proceedings of the 7th Conference of the European Association of Southeast Asian Archaeologists, Berlin, 31 August - 4 September 1998. Hull: Centre for South-East Asian Studies, pp. 41-50.

– 2002a: Anuradhapura - Angkor - Pagan. Versuch eines strukturgeschichtlichen Vergleichs. In: Feldbauer, P. (eds.), Die vormoderne Stadt. Asien und Europa im Vergleich. München / Wien: Verlag für Geschichte und Politik, pp. 32-59.

– 2002b: Coastal Peripheries during the Pagan Period. In: Gommans, Jos / Leider, Jacques (eds.), 2002: The Maritime Frontier of Burma. Amsterdam: Koninklijke Nederlandse Akad. van Wetenschapen, pp. 59-78.

Fraser, James Baille, 1982 [1820]: The Himala Mountains. Delhi: Neeraj Publishing House.

Freed, Ruth S. / Freed, Stanley A., 1964: Calendars, Ceremonies, and Festivals in a North Indian Village: Necessary Calendric Information for Fieldworkers. In: Southwestern Journal of Anthropology, Albuquerque 18 (1964), pp. 246-277.

Frenz, Margret, 2000: Vom Herrscher zum Untertan. Spannungsverhältnis zwischen lokaler Herrschaftsstruktur und der Kolonialverwaltung in Malabar zu Beginn der britischen Herrschaft (1790 - 1805). Stuttgart: Steiner.

– 2003: From Contact to Conquest. Transition to British Rule in Malabar. New Delhi: Oxford University Press.

Fukazawa, Hiroshi, 1982: Agrarian Relations and Land Revenue: The Medieval Deccan and Maharashtra. In: Raychaudhuri, T. / Habib, I. (eds.): The Cambridge Economic History of India, Vol. 1: c. 1200-c. 1750. New Delhi: Orient Longman / Cambridge University Press, pp. 249-260.

Fuller, Christopher J., 1991: Servants of the Goddess. The Priests of a South Indian Temple. Delhi: Oxford University Press.

– 1992: The Camphor Flame: Popular Hinduism and Society in India. Princeton: Princeton University Press.

Gail, Adalbert, 1997: Image and Meaning: The Buddha in Hindu Art and the „Buddhist Vāmanāvatāra". In: Allchin, R. / Allchin, B. (eds.): South Asian Archaeology 1995. Proceedings of the 13th Conference of the European Association of South Asian Archaeologists 1995, Vol. 2. Cambridge / New Delhi: Oxford & IBH / Science Publishers, pp. 795-768.

Galey, Jean-Claude, 1980: Le Créancier, le Roi, la Mort. Essai sur les Relations de Dépendance au Tehri-Gahrwal. in: Puruṣārtha, Paris 4 (1980), pp. 93-163.

– 1986: Totalité et Hiérarchie dans les Sanctuares Royaux du Tehri-Gahrwal. In: Puruṣārtha, Paris 10 (1986), pp. 5-56.

– 1990a: Introduction: Kingship in the Leeway of Scholarship. In: Galey (ed.), 1990: 1-29.

– 1990b: Reconsidering Kingship in India: An Ethnological Perspective. In: Galey (ed.), 1990: 123-188.

Galey, Jean-Claude (ed.), 1990: Kingship and the Kings. History and Anthroplogy, Vol. 4. Chur: Harwood Academic Publishers.

Ganshof, François, 1961: Feudalism. New York: Harper & Row

Geertz, Clifford, 1966: Person, Time, and Conduct in Bali. An Essay in Cultural Analysis. New Haven: Yale University.

– 1980: Negara: The Theater State in Nineteenth-Century Bali. Princeton: Princeton University Press.

Glass Palace Chronicle, 1923: The Glass Palace Chronicle of the Kings of Burma. Luce, G. H. / U Pe Maung Tin (transl.). London: Oxford University Press.

Godāvara Miśra, 1950: Hariharacaturaṅgam. Critically edited with introduction by S. K. Ramanatha Sastri. Madras Government Oriental Series, No. 17. Madras: Government Oriental Manuscripts Library.

Gopal, Lallanji, 1963: Sāmanta – Its Varying Significance in Early India. In: Journal of the Royal Asiatic Society, Cambridge (1963), pp. 21-37.

Greenblatt, Stephen, 1988: Shakespearean Negotiations. The Circulation of Social Energy in Renaissance England. Berkeley: University of California Press.

Guha, Ranjit, 1983: Elementary Aspects of Peasant Insurgency in Colonial India. Delhi / London: Oxford University Press.

Gutschow, Niels, 1996: Bisketjātrā of Bhaktapur – Continuity and Change of an Urban Ritual. In: Lienhard, S. (ed.), 1996: Change and Continuity. Studies in the Nepalese Culture of the Kathmandu Valley. Torino: Edizioni dell'orso, pp. 285-302.

– forthcoming: Ranpur Resolved. Spatial Analysis of A Town in Orissa, Based on A Chronicle. In: Beltz, J. / Frese, H. / Malinar, A. (eds.), forthcoming: Text and Context. New Delhi, Manohar.

Gutschow, N. / Vasavada, R., 2001: Temples of Jagannāth in Puri and Ranpur, Orissa, India. A Preliminary Typological Comparison. In: Beiträge zur Allgemeinen und Vergleichenden Archäologie, Mainz 21 (2001): 59-74.

Habib, Mohammad 1981: The Campaigns of Ala-ud-din Khilji. In: Habib, M. / Nizami, K. A. (ed.), 1981: Collected Works of Professor Mohammad Habib. Vol. 2: Politics and Society During the Early Medieval Period. Delhi: People's Publishing House, pp. 181-201.

Hall, Kenneth R., 1980: Trade and Statecraft in the Age of the Cholas. New Delhi: Abhinav Publications.

Hamilton, Francis B., 1971 [1819]: Account of the Kingdoms of Nepal and the Territories of the Dominion by the House of Gurkha. New Delhi: Manjusri Publishing Co.

Hamilton, Walter, 1820: A Geographical, Statistical, and Historical Description of Hindostan and the Adjacent Countries, 2 Vols. London: John Murray.

Hardenberg, Roland, 1999: Die Wiedergeburt der Götter. Ritual und Gesellschaft in Orissa. Hamburg: Kovac.

– 2000: Die Ideologie eines Hindu-Königtums. Struktur und Bedeutung der Rituale des Königs von Puri, Orissa / Indien. Berlin: Das Arabische Buch.

Hardiman, David (ed.), 1993: Peasant Resistance in India (1858-1914). Delhi: Oxford University Press.

Harvey, David, 1989: The Condition of Postmodernity: An Inquiry into the Origins of Cultural Change. Oxford / Cambridge, Mass.: Blackwell.

Heesterman, Jan C., 1985: The Inner Conflict of Tradition: Essays on Indian Ritual, Kingship, and Society. Chicago: Chicago University Press.

– 1998 [1978]: The Conundrum of the King's Authority. In: Richards (ed.), 1998: 13-40.

Henige, David P. 1974: The Chronology of Oral Tradition: Quest for a Chimera. Oxford: Clarendon Press.

– 1975: Some Phantom Dynasties of Early and Medieval India: Epigraphic Evidence and the Abhorrence of a Vacuum. Bulletin of the School of Oriental and African Studies, London 38 (1975), pp. 525-549

Hocart, Arthur. M., 1927: Kingship. Oxford: Oxford University Press.

– 1950 [1938]: Caste: a Comparative Study. London: Methuen.

– 1970 [1936]: Kings and Councillors. An Essay in the Comparative Anatomy of Human Society. Chicago: Chicago University Press.

Hopkins, Edward Washburn, 1915: Epic Mythology. Strassburg: Trübner.

Hubert, Henri / Mauss, Marcel, 1964 [1898]: Sacrifice: Its Nature and Function. Chicago: University of Chicago Press.

Inden, Ronald B., 1990: Imagining India. Oxford: Basil Blackwell.

– 1998 [1978]: Ritual, Authority, and Cyclic Time in Hindu Kingship. In: Richards (ed.), 1998: 41-91.

– (ed.), 2000: Querying the Medieval: Texts and the History of Practices in South Asia. Oxford: Oxford University Press.

Jagadisa Ayyar, P. V., 1920: South Indian Shrines. Madras: Madras Times Printing and Publishing Co.

– 1921: South Indian Festivities. Madras: Higginbothams.

Jansen, Roland, 1995: Die Bhavani von Tuljapur: Religionsgeschichtliche Studie des Kultes einer Göttin der indischen Volksreligion. Stuttgart: Steiner.

Juergensmeyer, Mark, 1993: The New Cold War? Religious Nationalism Confronts the Secular State. Berkeley: University of California Press.

Kamandaka 1961: The Nītisāra or the Elements of Polity by Kamandaki. Mitra, R. L. (ed.). Bibliotheca Indica Vols. 19 /179. Calcutta: Baptist Mission Press.

Kane, Pandurang Varman, 1958: History of Dharmaśāstra. (Ancient and Medieval Religious and Civil Law in India), Vol. 5, 2 Pts. Poona: Bhandarkar Oriental Research Institute.

Kantorowicz, Ernst H., 1957: *The King's Two Bodies: A Study in Medieval Political Theology*. Princeton: Princeton University Press.

– 1994 [1957]: Die zwei Körper des Königs. Eine Studie zur politischen Theologie des Mittelalters. München: dtv.

Karan, R., no date: History of the Rathors. Calcutta: no publisher

Karashima, Noboru (ed.), 1999: Kingship in Indian History. New Delhi: Manohar.

Kaṭakarājavaṁśāvali, 1987: Kaṭakarājavaṁśāvali: A Traditional History of Orissa with Special Reference to Jagannātha Temple, Vol. 1. Tripathi, G. C. / Kulke, H. (eds.). Allahabad: Vohra Publishers.

Kielhorn, Friedrich, 1905: Junagadh Rock-Inscription of Rudradaman; The year 72. In: Epigraphia Indica, Calcutta 8 (1905), pp. 36-49

Kimura, Masaaki / Tanabe, Akio (eds.), forthcoming: The State in India. Past and Present (Proceedings of a conference in Kyoto, December 1999).

Kinsley, David, 1986: Hindu Goddesses. Visions of the Divine Feminine in the Hindu Religious Tradition. Berkeley: University of California Press [reprint Delhi: Motilal Banarsidass 1987].

Kolff, Dirk H. A., 1990: Naukar, Rajput and Sepoy: The Ethnohistory of the Military Labour Market in Hindustan, 1450-1850. Cambridge: Cambridge University Press.

Kölver Bernhard (ed.), 1997: Law, the State and Administration in Classical India. München: Oldenbourg.

Kosambi, Damodar Dharmanand, 1956: An Introduction to Indian History. Bombay: Popular Book Depot.

Kotani, Hiroyuki, 2002: Western India in Historical Transition: Seventeenth to Early Twentieth Centuries. New Delhi: Manohar.

Krishnamachariar, Madabhushi, 1937 [1906]: History of Classical Sanskrit Literature. Madras: Tirumalai-Tirupati Devasthanam Press.

Kulke, Hermann, 1974: Kings without a Kingdom: The Rajas of Khurda and the Jagannatha Cult. In: South Asia, Armidale 4 (1974), pp. 60-74.

– 1976: Kshatriyaization and Social Change: A Study in Orissa Setting. In: Devadas Pillai, S. (ed.), 1976: Aspects of Changing India. Studies in Honour of Prof. G. S. Ghurye. Bombay: Popular Prakashan, pp. 398-409.

– 1977: Tempelstädte und Ritualpolitik – Indische Regionalreiche. In: Gutschow, N. / Sieverts, T. (eds.): Urban Space and Ritual. Darmstadt: Technische Hochschule, pp. 68-73.

– 1978a: Royal Temple Policy and the Structure of Medieval Hindu Kingdoms. In: Eschmann / Kulke / Tripathi (eds.), 1978: 125-137.

– 1978b: Early Royal Patronage of the Jagannātha Cult. In: Eschmann / Kulke / Tripathi (eds.): 139-155.

– 1978c: Jagannātha as the State Deity under the Gajapatis of Orissa. In: Eschmann, Kulke, Tripathi (eds.): 199-208.

– 1978d: The Struggle between the Rājās of Khurda and the Muslim Subahdārs of Cuttack for Dominance of the Jagannātha Cult. In: Eschmann / Kulke / Tripathi (eds.): 321-342.

– 1978e: "Juggernaut" under British Supremacy and the Resurgence of the Khurda-Rājās as "Rājās of Puri". In: Eschmann / Kulke / Tripathi (eds.): 345-357.

– 1978: Early State Formation and Royal Legitimation in Tribal Areas of Eastern India. In: Moser / Gautam (eds.), 1979: 29-37.

– 1979: Jagannātha-Kult und Gajapati-Königtum: Ein Beitrag zur Geschichte religiöser Legitimation hinduistischer Herrscher. Wiesbaden: Steiner.

– 1980: Legitimation and Town-Planning in the Feudatory States of Central Orissa. In: Pieper, J. (ed.), 1980: 30-40.

– Reprint in: 1982a: Legitimation and Town-Planning in the Feudatory States of Central Orissa. In: Kulke / Rieger / Lutze (eds.), 1982: 17-38.

– 1982b. Fragmentation and Segmentation Versus Integration? Reflections on the Concepts of Indian Feudalism and the Segmentary State in Indian History. In: Studies in History, New Delhi 4 (1982), pp. 237-264.

– 1982c: Gibt es ein indisches Mittelalter? Versuch einer eurasiatischen Geschichtsbetrachtung. In: Saeculum, Freiburg / München 33 (1982) 3/4, pp. 221-239.

– 1984a: Local Networks and Regional Integration in Orissa: Ritual Privileges of the Feudatory Rājās of Eastern India in the Jagannātha Cult of Puri. In: Ballhatchet / Taylor (eds.), 1984: 141-148.

– 1984b: Tribal Deities at Princely Courts: The Feudatory Rājās of Central Orissa and their Tutelary Deities (iṣṭadevatās). In: Mahapatra, S. (ed.), 1984: 13-24. (Reprinted in Kulke 1993: 114-136.)

– 1985: Die frühmittelalterlichen Regionalreiche: Ihre Struktur und Rolle im Prozess staatlicher Entwicklung Indiens. In: Kulke / Rothermund (eds.), 1985: 77-114.

– 1987: The Chronicles and the Temple Records of the Madala Panji of Puri. A Reassessment of the Edivence. In: Indian Archives, New Delhi 36(1987) 1, pp. 1-24.

– 1992a: Kṣatra and Kṣetra: The Cult of Jagannātha of Puri and the "Royal Letters" (chāmu ciṭaus) of the Rājās of Khurda. In: Bakker, H. (ed.): 131-142. (Reprinted in Kulke 1993, pp. 51-65.)

– 1992b: Periodization of Pre-Modern Historical Processes in India and Europe: Some Reflections. In: Indian Historical Review, Delhi 19 (1992) 1/2, pp. 21-36.

– 1993a: Kings and Cults: State Formation and Legitimation in India and Southeast Asia. Delhi: Manohar.

– 1993b: Kṣetra and Kṣatra: The Cult of Jagannath of Puri and the Royal Letters of the Rajas of Khurda. In: Kulke, H. (ed.), 1993a: 51-65.

– 1993c: Reflections on the Sources of the Temple Chronicles of the Mādaḷā Pañji of Puri. In: Kulke 1993a: 137-158.

– 1995a: Introduction: The Study of the State in Pre-modern India. In: Kulke, H. (ed.), 1995: 1-47.

– 1995b: The Early and the Imperial Kingdom: A Processural Model of Integrative State Formation in Early Medieval India. In: Kulke, H. (ed.), 1995: 233-262.

– 1997: Some Observations of the Political Functions of Copper-Plate Grants in Early Medieval India. In: Kölver, B. (ed.), 1997: 237-244.

– 1998: Geschichtsschreibung als Heilung eines Traditionsbruches? Überlegungen zu spätmittelalterlichen Chroniken Südasiens. In: Rüsen, J. / Gottlob, M. / Mittag, A. (eds.): Die Vielfalt der Kulturen. Frankfurt am Main: Suhrkamp. pp. 422-440.

– 2001a [1993]: Kings and Cults. State Formation and Legitimation in India and Southeast Asia. Delhi: Manohar.

– 2001b [1978]: Royal Temple Policy and the Structure of Medieval Hindu Kingdoms. In: Kulke, H., 2001a: pp. 1-16.

– 2001c: Historiography and Regional Identity. The Case of the Temple Chronicles of Puri. In: Kulke / Schnepel (eds.), 2001: 211-225.

– forthcoming a: The Integrative Model of State Formation in Early Medieval India. Some Historiographic Remarks. In: Kimura, M. / Tanabe, A. (eds.): forthcoming.

– forthcoming b: The Making of a Local Chronicle: The Raṇapur Rājavaṁśa Itihāsa. In: Beltz, J. / Frese, H. / Malinar, A. (eds.), forthcoming: Text and Context. New Delhi: Manohar.

Kulke, Hermann / Rothermund, Dietmar, 1982: Geschichte Indiens. Stuttgart: Kohlhammer.

Kulke, Hermann / Rothermund, Dietmar, 1986: A History of India. Beckenham / London / Sidney: Croom Helm.

Kulke, Hermann (ed.), 1995: The State in India, 1000-1700. Delhi: Oxford University Press.

Kulke, Hermann / Rieger, Hans Christoph / Lutze, Lothar (eds.), 1982: Städte in Südasien. Geschichte, Gesellschaft, Gestalt. Wiesbaden: Steiner.

Kulke, Hermann / Rothermund, Dietmar (eds.), 1985: Regionale Tradition in Südasien. Stuttgart: Steiner.

Kulke, Hermann / Schnepel, Burkhard (eds.), 2001: Jagannath Revisited. Society, History and Culture in Orissa. Delhi: Manohar.

Langulesvara Itihasa, n. d.: Langulesvara Itihasa, etc. Copied from Local Records, Vol. 37 (pages 409-498), Govt. Oriental Manuscripts Library, Madras. (Translated into English from Telugu). n. d. n. p.; Typoscript, Heidelberg: Orissa Archive, Library of the South Asia Institute.

Lansing, Stephen, 1991: Priests and Programmers: Technologies of Power in the Engineered Landscape of Bali. Princeton: Princeton University Press.

Leider, Jacques, 1994: Le passe de Am (Arakan): Contribution R̠ l'étude d'une route terrestre entre la Birmanie et le Golfe du Bengale. In: Journal Asiatique, Paris 282 (1994) 2, pp. 335-370.

Lingat, Robert, 1973: The Classical Law of India. Berkeley: University of California Press.

– 1989: Royautés Bouddhiques. Aśoka et la Fonction royale R̠ Ceylan. Deux études éditées par Gérard Fussman et Eric Meyer; préface de Louis Dumont. Paris: Editions de l'Ecole des hautes études en sciences sociales.

Logan, William, 1989 [1887]: Malabar, 2 Vols. New Delhi / Madras: Asian Educational Services.

Luce, Gordon H. / Tin, U Be Maung (eds.), 1933: Inscriptions of Burma, Vol. 1. Rangoon: University of Rangoon.

Mādaḷā Pāñjī, 1940: Mādaḷā Pāñjī, Rājbhog Itihās. Mahanti, Arttaballabha (ed.). Kaṭaka: Prāci Samitīi.

Mahalingam, Teralundur Venkatarama, 1972: Mackenzie Manuscripts. Summaries of the Historical Manuscripts in the Mackenzie Collection, Vol. 1: Tamil and Malayalam). Madras: University of Madras.

– 1988: Inscriptions of the Pallavas. New Delhi: Indian Council of Historical Research.

Mahapatra, Lakshman K., 1977: Gods, Kings and the Caste System in India. In: David, K. (ed.): The New Wind: Changing Identities in South Asia. The Hague: Mouton, pp. 159-178.

Mahapatra, Sitakant (ed.), 1984: Folk Ways in Religion: Gods, Spirits and Men. Cuttack: Institute of Oriental and Orissan Studies.

Mahtab, Harekrushna / De, Sushil Chandra (eds., for the State Committee for the Compilation of the History of Freedom Movement, Orissa, India), 1957-59: History of Freedom Movement in Orissa, 5 Vols. Bhubaneswar: State Govt. of Orissa.

Majumdar, Dhirendra Nath, 1960: Himalayan Polyandry: Structure, Functioning and Cultural Change: A Field Study of Jaunsar-Bawar. New York: Asia Publishing House.

Mānasollāsa, 1925-1937: Mānasollāsa, Vol. 1-3. Ed. by Someśvara Bhūlokamalla. Gaekwad Oriental Series 28. Baroda: Oriental Institute.

Mānavadharmaśāstra, 1991: The Laws of Manu. Doniger, W. / Smith, B. K. (trnsl.). Harmondsworth: Penguin.

Marglin, Frédérique A., 1989 [1985]: Wives of the God-King. The Rituals of the Devadasis of Puri. Delhi: Oxford University Press.

Marty, Martin E. / Appleby, R. Scott (eds.), 1991: Fundamentalisms Observed. Chicago: University of Chicago Press.

– 1993a: Fundamentalisms and Society: Reclaiming the Sciences, the Family, and Education. Chicago: University of Chicago Press.

– 1993b: Fundamentalisms and the State: Remaking Polities, Economies, and Militance. Chicago: University of Chicago Press.

– 1994: Accounting for Fundamentalisms: The Dynamic Character of Movements. Chicago: University of Chicago Press.

– 1995: Fundamentalisms Comprehended. Chicago: University of Chicago Press.

Massey, Doreen, 1992: Power-geometry and a Progressive Sense of Place. In: Bird, J. / Curtis, B. (eds.): Mapping the Futures: Local Cultures, Global Change. London: Routledge, pp. 59-69.

Matchett, Freda, 2001: Kṛṣṇa: Lord or Avatāra? The Relationship Between Kṛṣṇa and Viṣṇu. London: Curzon Press.

Mayer, Peter B., 1993: Inventing Village Tradition: The Late 19th Century Origins of the North Indian "Jajmani System". In: Modern Asian Studies, Cambridge 27 (1993) 2, pp. 357-395.

Mayrhofer, Manfred, 1996: Etymologisches Wörterbuch des Altindoarischen, 2. Band. Heidelberg: Winter.

Meister, Michael W., 1994: Art Regions and Modern Rajasthan. In: Schomer, K. / Erdman, J. / Lodrick, D. O. et al. (eds.), 1994, Vol. 1: 143-176.

Mishra, Kshetramohan, 1933: Keonjhar Rajavamshabali. Keonjhar: The Author.

Mishra, Madan Mohan, n. d.: Keonjhar Rajavamshabali. Unpublished Manuscript.

Mishra, Prasanna Kumar, 1983: Political Unrest in Orissa in 19th Century (Anti-British, Anti-Feudal and Agrarian Risings). Calcutta: Punthi Pustak.

Mita, Masahiko, 1999: Polity and Kingship of Early Medieval Rajasthan: An Analysis of the Nadol Cāhamāna Inscriptions. In: Karashima, N. (ed.), 1999: 89-117.

Monier-Williams, Sir Monier 1993 [1899]: A Sanskṛit-English Dictionary. Etymologically and Philologically Arranged. Delhi, Varanasi, Patna: Motilal Banarsidass.

Moorcroft, William / Trebeck, George, 1841: Travels in the Himalayan Provinces of Hindustan and the Punjab. London: John Murray.

Moser, Rupert R. / Gautam, Mohan K. (eds.), 1979: Aspects of Tribal Life in South Asia I. Strategy and Survival. Studia Ethnologica Bernensia 1. Bern: University of Bern.

Mukherji, Ramaranjan / Maity, Sachindra Kumar (eds.), 1967: Corpus of Bengal Inscriptions Bearing on History and Civilization of Bengal, Calcutta: Mukhopadhyay.

Munn, Nancy, 1992: The Cultural Anthropology of Time: A Critical Essay. In: Annual Review of Anthropology, Palo Alto 21 (1992), pp. 93-123.

– 1996: Excluded Spaces: The Figure in the Australian Aboriginal Landscape. In: Critical Inquiry, Chicago 22 (1995/96), pp. 446-465.

Nagar, Vandana, 1985: Kingship in the Śukranīti. Delhi: Pushpa Prakashan.

Nanda, Chandi Prasad, 1998: Towards Swaraj: Nationalist Politics and Popular Movements in Orissa. Ludhiana: Kalyani Publishers.

Nandi, Ramendra Nath, 1986: Social Roots of Religion in Ancient India. Calcutta, New Delhi: K.P. Bagchi & Co.

– 2000: State Formation, Agrarian Growth and Social Change in Feudal South India. C. AD 600-1200. New Delhi: Manohar.

Narayana Rao, Velcheru / Shulman, David / Subrahmanyam, Sanjay, 1992: Symbols of Substance. Court and State in Nāyaka Period Tamilnadu. Delhi: Oxford University Press.

– 2001: Textures of Time. Writing History in South India 1600-1800. Delhi: Permanent Black.

Narayanan, Muttayil Govinda M. S., 1996: Perumals of Kerala. Political and Social Conditions of Kerala under the Cēra Perumals of Makotai (c. 800 AD-1124 AD). Calicut: The Author.

Nath, Ram, 1999: Chittorgadh Kīrtti-Stambha of Maharana Kumbha. New Delhi: Abhinav Publ.

Needham, Rodney 1979: Symbolic Classification. Santa Monica: Goodyear Publications.

Nīlakaṇṭha Bhaṭṭa, 1925: Nītimayūkha. Sanskrit Text. A Treatise on Rules of Polity. Girgaon / Bombay: J. R. Gharpure.

Nilakanta Sastri, K. A., [4]1975: A History of South India from Prehistoric Times to the Fall of Vijayanagar. Madras, Delhi, Bombay: Oxford University Press.

– 1984 [[2]1955]: The Cōḷas. Madras: University of Madras.

Njammasch, Marlene, 1997: Staatliche Strukturen im Reich der Maitrakas von Valabhi. In: Kölver (ed.), 1997: 111-124.

Padmanabha Menon, K. P., 1989 [1924]: History of Kerala. Written in the Form of Notes on Visscher's Letters From Malabar, 4 vols. Reprint, New Delhi / Madras: Asian Educational Services.

Paḻaśśi Rēkhakaḷ, 1994: Paḻaśśi Rēkhakaḷ, Zacharia, Scaria (ed.). Kottayam: D. C. Books. (Partly translated into English in: Frenz, M. 2000.)

Panda, Pradipta Kumar, 1987: Contribution of Orissa to Sanskrit (Creative Literature). Delhi: Pratibha Prakashan.

Panda, Sisir Kumar, 1986: Herrschaft und Verwaltung unter den späten Gangas (ca. 1038-1434). Stuttgart: Steiner.

Parkin, David / Caplan, Lionel / Fisher, Humphrey (eds.), 1996: The Politics of Cultural Performance. Oxford: Berghahn Books.

Parry, Jonathan, 1979: Caste and Kinship in Kangra. New Delhi: Vikas.

Pathy, Dinanath, 2001: Art: Regional Traditions. The Temple of Jagannatha. Architecture, Sculpture, Painting. Ritual, New Delhi: Sundeep Prakashan.

Pati, Biswamoy, 1993: Resisting Domination: Peasants, Tribals and the National Movement in Orissa 1920-1950. New Delhi: Manohar.

Peabody, Norbert, 1991a: Koṭā Mahājagat, or the Great Universe of Kota: Sovereignty and Territory in 18th Century Rajasthan. Contributions to Indian Sociology (N. S.), New Delhi 25 (1991) 1, pp. 29-56.

– 1991b: In Whose Turban does the Lord Reside? The Objectification of Charisma and the Fetishism of Objects in the Hindu Kingdom of Kota. In: Comparative Studies in Society and History, Cambridge 33 (1991) 4, pp. 726-754.

– 2003: Hindu Kingship and Polity in Precolonial India. Cambridge: Cambridge University Press.

Perlin, Frank, 1993: Invisible City: Monetary, Administrative and Popular Infrastructures in Asia and Europe, 1500-1900. Aldershot: Variorum.

– 1994: Unbroken Landscape: Commodity, Category, Sign and Identity: Their Production as Myth and Knowledge from 1500. Aldershot: Variorum.

Peterson, Peter, c. 1890: A Collection of Prakrit and Sanskrit Inscriptions. Bhavnagar: State Print.

Pfeffer, Georg, 1978: Puri's Vedic Brahmins. Continuity and Change in their traditional Institutions. In: Eschmann / Kulke / Tripathi (eds.), 1978: pp. 421-437.

– 2003: Hunters, Tribes, Peasants: Cultural Crisis and Comparison. Dr. Ambedkar Memorial Lectures. Bhubaneswar: NISWASS.

Pieper, Jan (ed.), 1980: Ritual Space in India: Studies in Architectural Anthropology. London: aarp (Art and Anthropological Research Papers) 17.

Pocock, David F., 1962: Notes on *Jajmani* Relationships. In: Contributions to Indian Sociology, Paris 5 (1992), pp. 78-95.

Pugh, Judy F., 1981: Person and Experience: The Astrological System in North India. Unpublished Doctoral Dissertation. Chicago: Department of Anthropology, University of Chicago.

– 1983. Into the Almanac: Time, Meaning and Action in North Indian Society. In: Contributions to Indian Sociology, New Delhi 17 (1983) 1, pp. 27-49.

Punjab Government Records, 1911: The Delhi Residency and Agency Records: 1807-57, Vol. 1. Lahore: Punjab Government Press.

Quigley, Declan, 1993: The Interpretation of Caste. Oxford: Clarendon Press.

Raghavan, Venkatarama, 1979: Festivals, Sports and Pastimes of India. Ahmedabad: B. J. Institute of Learning and Research.

Raheja, Gloria G., 1988: The Poison in the Gift. Chicago: University of Chicago Press.

Ramanatha Sastri, S. K., 1950: Introduction. In: Godāvara Miśra (1950).

Rath, Ashoka K., 1987: Studies on Some Aspects of the History and Culture of Orissa. Calcutta: Punthi Pustak.

Ray, Hem Chandra, 1936: The Dynastic History of Rajasthan, Vol. 2. Calcutta: Calcutta University Press.

Reu, Bisheshwar Nath, 1938/40: Mārvā kā Itihās. 2 Vol. Jodhpur: Jodhpur Archaeological Department.

Rice, Benjamin Lewis, 1983 [1879]: Mysore Inscriptions. Delhi: Navrang.

Richards, John F. (ed.), 1998 [1978]: Kingship and Authority in South Asia. Delhi: Oxford University Press.

Risley, Herbert H., 1891: Tribes and Castes of Bengal, Vol. 1. Ethnographic Glossary. Calcutta: Bengal Secretariat Press.

Rothermund, Dietmar, 1978: Government, Landlord, and Peasant in India. Agrarian Relations under British Rule 1865-1935. Wiesbaden: Steiner.

– 1994: Nation and Region in Indian Historiography. In: The East and the Meaning of History. International Conference (23rd-27th Nov. 1992). Rome: Bardi, pp. 253-262.

– 1995; Geschichte als Prozeß und Aussage. Eine Einführung in Theorien des historischen Wandels und der Geschichtsschreibung. München: Oldenbourg.

Rottler, Johann Peter, 1790: Herrn Rottlers Reise nach Ceylon und der Malabarküste vom 2ten Januar bis 4ten August 1788. In: Neuere Geschichte der evangelischen Missions-Anstalten zur Bekehrung der Heiden in Ost-Indien, 8 Vols. 1770-1848, Vol. 4, 37th piece (1790). Halle: Verlag des Waisenhauses, pp. 27-94.

Russel, Robert V. / Lal, Hira, 1916: The Tribes and Castes of the Central Provinces of India, 4 Vols. London: Macmillan.

Sahlins, Marshall D., 1968: Tribesmen. Englewood Cliffs: Prentice Hall.

– 1983: Other Times, Other Customs: The Anthropology of History. In: American Anthropologist, Washington, D. C., 85 (1983) 3, pp. 517-544.

– 1985: Islands of History. Chicago: University of Chicago Press.

Sahu, Lakshmi N., 1942: The Hill Tribes of Jeypore. Cuttack: Orissa Mission Press.

Sahu, Nabin Kumar / Mishra, Prabodh Kumar / Sahu, Yajñakumara , 1979: History of Orissa. Cuttack: Nalanda.

Sarma, Ramanatha N., 1938: Jayapura Raja Vamsyavali: A History of the Solar Dynasty of Jeypore-Orissa. Madras: Vavilla Press.

Śaurīkathā: cf. Suneson (1986).

Sax, William, 2002: Dancing the Self: Personhood and Performance in the Pandav Lila of Garhwal. Oxford: Oxford University Press.

Scharfe, Hartmut, 1989: The State in Indian Tradition. Leiden: Brill.

Schmidt, Bettina E. / Münzel, Mark (eds.), 1998: Ethnologie und Inszenierung. Ansätze zur Theaterethnologie. Marburg: Curupira.

Schmidt, P. W. 1906: Buch der Ragawan, der Königsgeschichte. In: Sitzungsberichte der philosophisch-historischen Classe der Kaiserlichen Akademie der Wissenschaften zu Wien, Wien 151(1906) 3.

Schnepel, Burkhard, 1988: In Quest of Life: Hocart's Scheme of Evolution from Ritual Organization to Government. In: Archives Européennes de Sociologie, Cambridge 29 (1988), pp. 165-187.

– 1992: The Nandapur Suryavamshis: Origin and Consolidation of a South Orissan Kingdom. In: Orissa Historical Research Journal, Bhubaneswar 38 (1992), pp. 170-199.

– 1993: Die Schutzgöttinnen: Tribale Gottheiten in Südorissa (Indien) und ihre Patronage durch hinduistische Kleinkönige. In: Anthropos, St. Augustin 88 (1993), pp. 337-350.

– 1995a: Durga and the King: Ethnohistorical Aspects of the Politico-Ritual Life in a South Orissan Jungle Kingdom. In: Journal of the Royal Anthropological Institute (Man), Oxford 1 (1995) 1, pp. 145-166.

– 1995b: Twinned Beings: Kings and Effigies in Southern Sudan, East India and Renaissance France. Göteborg: The Institute for Advanced Studies in Social Anthropology at Göteborg University (Sweden).

– 1996: The Hindu King's Authority Reconsidered: Durga-pūjā and Dasarā in a South Orissan Jungle Kingdom. In: Boholm (ed.), 1996: 126-157.

– 1997: Die Dschungelkönige. Ethnohistorische Aspekte von Politik und Ritual in Orissa. Stuttgart: Steiner.

– 1998: Der Raub der Göttin. Rituelle Inszenierungen von Macht und Autorität in Orissa, Indien. In: Schmidt / Münzel (eds.), 1998: 459-488.

– 2001: Kings and Rebel Kings. Rituals of Incorporation and Dissent in South Orissa. In: Kulke / Schnepel (eds.), 2001: 271-295.

– 2002: The Jungle Kings. Ethnohistorical Aspects of Politics and Ritual in Orissa. Delhi: Manohar.

Schnepel, Burkhard / Berkemer, Georg.n. d.: Little Kingdom Symposium: An outline for the 2002 Panel at the EASA Conference (unpubl. manuscript).

Schomer, Karine / Erdman, Joan / Lodrick, Deryck O. et al. (eds.), 1994: The Idea of Rajasthan. Explorations in Regional Identity, 2 Vols. New Delhi, Manohar.

Schulte-Nordholt, Henk, 1993: Leadership and the Limits of Political Control: A Balinese 'Response' to Clifford Geertz. In: Social Anthropology, Cambridge 1 (1992/93), pp. 291-307.

Schwerin, Dagmar Gräfin, 1977: Von Armut zu Elend. Kolonialherrschaft und Agrarverfassung in Chota Nagpur, 1858-1908. Wiesbaden: Steiner.

Senapati, Nilamani / Sahu, Nabin Kumar (eds.), 1986: Orissa District Gazetteers 6: Kendujhar. Cuttack: Gazetteers Unit, Dept. of Revenue, Govt. of Orissa Press.

Sharma, Ram Sharan, 1980 [1965]: Indian Feudalism. Madras: MacMillan.

– 1993: The Segmentary State and the Indian Experience. In: Indian Historical Review, Delhi 16 (1993), pp. 81-110.

She-haung Myanma Kyauksa-mya [Old Burmese Inscriptions, abbrev. OBI], 1972-83: She-haung Myanma Kyauksa-mya, Vol. 1-3. Rangoon: Archaeology Department.

Shulman, David D., 1980: On South Indian Bandits and Kings. In: Indian Economic and Social History Review, New Delhi 17 (1980), pp. 283-306.

– 1985: The King and the Clown in South Indian Myth and Poetry. Princeton: Princeton University Press.

Singh, Mian Goverdhan, 1982: History of Himachal Pradesh. Delhi: Yugbodh Publishing House.

Singh Deo, Bidyadhar Kumar, 1939: Nandapur: A Forsaken Kingdom. Cuttack: Utkal Sahitya Press.

Sinha, Surajit C. 1962: State Formation and Rajput Myth in Tribal Central India. In: Man in India, Ranchi 42 (1962), pp. 35-80.

– 1987: Introduction. In: Sinha, S. (ed.), 1987: Tribal Polities and State Systems in Pre-Colonial Eastern and North Eastern India. Calcutta: Bagchi & Company, pp. ix-xxvi.

Sircar, Dines Chandra, 1965: Indian Epigraphy. Delhi: Motilal Banarsidass.

– 1969: The Guhilas of Kiskindha. Calcutta: Sanscrit College.

– 1982: The Emperor and the Subordinate Rulers. Santiniketan: Visva-Bharati.

Sokal, Robert 1974: Classification: Purposes, Principles, Progress, Prospects. In: Science, Princeton 185 (1974), p. 1117.

Somani, Ram Vallabh 1976: History of Mewar. Jaipur: Ranka.

– 1993: History of Rajasthan. Jaipur: Jain Pustak Mandir.

Sontheimer, Günther D., 1981: Dasarā at Devaraguḍḍa. Ritual and Play in the Cult of Mailār / Khaṇḍobā. In: South Asian Digest of Regional Writing, Heidelberg 10 (1981), pp. 1-28.

– 1994: The Vana and the Kṣetra: The Tribal Background of Some Famous Cults. In: Tripathi, G. C. / Kulke, H. (eds.), 1994: Religion and Society in Eastern India. New Delhi: Manohar, pp. 117-164.

Southall, Aidan B., 1956: Alur Society. A Study in Process and Types of Domination. Cambridge: Heffer & Sons.

– 1987: The Segmentary State in Africa and Asia. In: Comparative Studies in Society and History, Cambridge 30 (1987), pp. 52-82.

Spencer, George W., 1969: Religious Networks and Royal Influence in 11th Century South India. In: Journal of the Economic and Social History of the Orient, Leiden 12 (1969), pp. 42-56

– 1976: The Politics of Plunder: The Cholas in Eleventh-Century Ceylon. In: Journal of Asian Studies, Ann Arbor 35 (1976), pp. 405-449.

– 1984: Heirs Apparent: Fiction and Function in Chola Mythical Genealogies. In: Indian Economic and Social History Review, New Delhi 21 (1984) 4, pp. 415-432.

Srinivas, Mysore Narasimhachar, 1989 [1952]: Religion and Society among the Coorgs of South India. Bombay: Media Promoters & Publishers PVT. LTD.

Stein, Burton, 1977: The Segmentary State in South Indian History. In: Fox (ed.), 1977: 3-51.

– 1980: Peasant State and Society in Medieval South India. Delhi: Oxford University Press.

– 1985: State Formation and Economy Reconsidered. In: Modern Asian Studies, Cambridge 19 (1985), pp. 387-413.

– 1989: Eighteenth Century India: Another View. In: Studies in History, New Delhi 5 (1989) 1, pp. 1-26.

– 1998: All the King's Mana: Perspectives on Kingship in Medieval South India. In: Richards (ed.), 1998: 133-188.

Stein, Burton (ed.), 1977: South Indian Temples. In: Indian Economic and Social History Review, New Delhi 14 (1977), theme volume.

Sterling, Andrew, 1904 [1822]: An Account (Geographical, Statistical, and Historical) of Orissa proper or Cuttack with Appendices. Calcutta: Bengal Secretariat Press.

Stietencron, Heinrich von,1978a: The Jagannātha Temples of Contemporary Orissa. In: Eschmann / Kulke / Tripathi (eds.), 1978: 469-475.

– 1978b: The Advent of Viṣṇuism in Orissa. In: Eschmann / Kulke / Tripathi (eds.), 1978: 1-31.

– 1996: Die Zusammenkunft der Götter. Ein Bericht über das Doḷasaṃmelaṇa Fest in Orissa. In: Kapp, D. B. (ed.), 1996: Nānavidhaikatā, Festschrift für Hermann Berger. Wiesbaden: Harrassowitz, pp. 214-247.

– 2001: A Congregation of Gods: The Doḷameḷaṇa Festival in Orissa. In: Kulke, H. / Schnepel, B. (eds.), 2001: 363-401.

Subbarayalu, Y., 1973: Political Geography of the Chola Country. Madras: State Department of Archaeology, Government of Tamilnadu.

Subramanian, Vadakaymadam Krishnier, 1990 [1980]: Maxims of Chanakya (The Crystallized Wisdom of the Indian Macchiavelli). Delhi: Motilal Banarsidass.

Subrahmanyam, Sanjay, 1986: Aspects of State Formation in South India and Southeast Asia, 1550-1650. Indian Economic and Social History Review, New Delhi 23 (1986), pp. 357-377.

– 1998: Hearing Voices: Vignettes of Early Modernity in South Asia, 1400-1750. In: Daedalus, Cambridge, Mass. 127 (1998) 3, pp. 75-104.

– 2001: Penumbral Visions. New Delhi: Oxford University Press.

– forthcoming: Market and State Formation in Late Pre-Colonial India. In: Kimura M. / Tanabe, A. (eds.): forthcoming.

Subrahmanyam, Sanjay / Shulman, David D., 1990: The Men Who Would Be King? The Politics of Expansion in Early Seventeenth-Century Northern Tamilnadu. In: Modern Asian Studies, Cambridge 24 (1990) 2, pp. 225-248.

Śukranīti, 1968: Śukranīti, ed. with the Vidyotini Hindi Commentary by Śrī Brahmaśaṅkara Miśra. Kashi Sanskrit Series Vol. 185. Varanasi: Chowkhamba Sanskrit Series Office.

Sutherland, Peter, 1998: Traveling Gods and Government by Deity: an Ethnohistory of Power, Representation, and Agency in West Himalayan Polity. Unpublished Doctoral Dissertation. Oxford: Institute of Social and Cultural Anthropology, Oxford University.

– (forthcoming): Traveling Gods and Political Location: Himalayan Counterhistories on the Margins of the State.

Syed, Renate, 2001: Kanauj, die Maukharis und das Caturanga. Der Ursprung des Schachspiels und sein Weg von Indien nach Persien. Kelkheim: Förderkreis Schach-Geschichtsforschung.

Talbot, Cynthia, 1991: Temple Donors and Gifts: Patterns of Patronage in 13th century South India. In: Journal of Asian Studies, Ann Arbor 50 (1991), pp. 308-340.

– 2001: Precolonial India in Practice: Society, Region, and Identity in Medieval Andhra. New Delhi: Oxford University Press.

Tambiah, Stanley J., 1976: World Conqueror and World Renouncer: A Study of Buddhism and Polity in Thailand against a Historical Background. Cambridge: Cambridge University Press.

– 1985a: Culture, Thought, and Social Action: An Anthropological Perspective. Cambridge: Harvard University Press.

– 1985b: The Galactic Polity in South East Asia. In: Tambiah 1985a: 252-286.

– 1985c: A Reformulation of Geertz's Conception of the Theater State. In: Tambiah 1985a: 316-338.

Tanabe, Akio, 1996: Indigenous Power, Hierarchy and Dominance: State Formation in Orissa, India. In: Claessen, H. J. M. / Oosten, J. G. (eds.): Ideology and the Formation of Early States. Leiden: Brill, pp. 205-219.

– 1998: Ethnohistory of Land and Identity in Khurda, Orissa: From Pre-colonial Past to Post-colonial Present. In: Journal of Asian and African Studies, Tokyo 56 (1998), pp. 75-112.

– 1999a: Kingship, Community and Commerce in Late Pre-colonial Khurda. In: Karashima, N. (ed.), 1999: 195-236.

– 1999b: The Transformation of *Śakti*: Gender and Sexuality in the Festival of Goddess Ramachandi. In: Tanaka, M. / Tachikawa M. (eds.), 1999: Living with *Śakti*: Gender, Sexuality and Religion in South Asia. Osaka: National Museum of Ethnology, Osaka, pp. 75-112.

– 2000: Early Modernity and Colonial Transformation: Rethinking the Role of the Little King in Eighteenth and Nineteenth Century Orissa. ASAFAS Special Paper, Graduate School of Asian and African Area Studies, Kyoto University.

– 2003: Early Modernity and Colonial Transformation: Rethinking the Role of the Little King in the 18th-19th Century Orissa. In: Hayami, Y. / Tanabe, A. / Tokita-Tanabe, Y. (eds.): Gender and Modernity: Perspectives from Asia and the Pacific. Kyoto: Kyoto University Press / Melbourne: Trans Pacific Press.

– forthcoming: The Structure of Local Community in Pre-colonial Khurda: the Case of 'The System of Entitlements' in Garh Manitri. In: Nayak, P. K. / Parkin, R. (eds.): Rethinking Orissa: Society, Culture and History (provisional title). New Delhi: Manohar.

Tanaka, Masakazu, 1991: Patrons, Devotees, and Goddesses: Ritual and Power among the Tamil Fishermen of Sri Lanka. Kyoto: Institute for Research in Humanities, Kyoto University.

Tessitori, Luigi P., 1918: A Descriptive Catalogue of the Bardic and Historical Survey of Rajputana, Manuscripts. Calcutta: Asiatic Society.

Teuscher, Ulrike, 2000: Staat und Königtum in Mewar, Rajasthan. Kiel: Kiel University, Dept. of History, unpublished doctoral dissertation.

Thapar, Romila, 1979: Ancient Indian Social History. Delhi: Orient Longman.

– 1984: From Lineage to State. Delhi: Oxford University Press.

Tirumalāmbā, 1970: Varadāmbikā Pariṇaya Campū of Tirumalāmbā, ed. by Suryakanta Shastri. Chowkhamba Sanskrit Studies Vol. 79. Varanasi: Chowkhamba Publ. Office.

Toffin, Gerard, 1981: Culte des Désses et Fete du Dasai chez les Newar (Nepal). In: Puruṣārtha, Paris 5 (1981), pp. 55-81.

Trautmann, Thomas R., 1995a [1981]: Dravidian Kinship. New Delhi: Vistaar.

– 1995b: Indian Time, European Time. In: Hughes, D. O. / Trautmann, T. R. (eds.), 1995: Time: Histories and Ethnologies. Ann Arbor: University of Michigan Press, 1995.

U Kala [Kulāḥ, Ūḥ], 1960: U Kula mahayazawinkyi [Mahārājavaṅ krīḥ]. Rankun: Haṃsāvatī piṭakat puṃ nhip tuik.

Underhill, Muriel M., 1921: The Hindu Religious Year. Calcutta: Association Press / London: H. Milford / Oxford: Oxford University Press.

van der Veer, Peter, 1988: Gods on Earth: The Management of Religious Experience and Identity in a North Indian Pilgrimage Centre. London / Atlantic Highlands: Athlone Press.

– 1994: Religious Nationalism: Hindus and Muslims in India. Berkeley / Los Angeles: University of California Press.

Vāsudeva, 1986: Śaurikathodaya, a Yamaka Poem by Vāsudeva. Ed. with Translation, Notes and Introduction by Carl Suneson. 2nd rev. ed. Stockholm: Department of Indology, University of Stockholm.

Veluthat, Kesavan, 1993: Political Structure of Early Medieval South India, Hyderabad: Orient Longman.

Vidal, Dennis, 1982: Le Culte des Divinités Locales dans une Région de l'Himachal Pradesh. Paris: Unpublished Dissertation. Laboratoire d'Ethnologie et de Sociologie Comparative. Université de Paris X.

Vishnupurāṇa, 1980 [1840]: Vishnupurāṇa: A System of Hindu Mythology and Tradition, Vols.I & II. Translated by H. H. Wilson. Delhi: Nag Publishers.

Walters, Robert G., 1980: Signs of the Times: Clifford Geertz and Historians. In: Social Research, New York 47 (1980), pp. 537-556.

Weber, Max, 1988 [1921]: Gesammelte Aufsätze zur Religionssoziologie, Vol. 2. Tübingen: UTB

Welbon, Guy R. / Yocum, Glenn E., 1982: Religious Festivals in South India and Srī Lankā. New Delhi: Manohar.

Welch, Stuart Carey (ed.), 1997: Gods, Kings and Tigers. The Art of Kotah. Munich / New York: Prestel.

Wink, André, 1984: Sovereignty and Universal Dominion in South Asia. In: Indian Economic and Social History Review, New Delhi 21 (1984) 2, pp. 265-292.

– 1986: Land and Sovereignty in India: Agrarian Society and Politics under the Eighteenth-Century Maratha Svarājya. Cambridge: Cambridge University Press.

– 1990. Al-Hind: the Making of the Indo-Islamic World, Vol. 1. Delhi: Oxford University Press.

Wiser, William H., 1988 [1936]: The Hindu Jajmani System. A Socio-economic System Interrelating Members of A Hindu Village Community in Services. New Delhi: Munshiram Manoharlal.

Wittfogel, Karl, 1957: Oriental Despotism: A Comparative Study of Total Power. New Haven: Yale University Press.

Witzel, Michael, 1985: Regionale und überregionale Faktoren in der Entwicklung vedischer Brahmanengruppen im Mittelalter. In: Kulke / Rothermund (eds.) 1985: 57-76.

Index

108 (symbolic figure) 138, 139, 143-150
108 gods 139, 149, 150

accounts, paurāṇic 68
agency, ritual 39
ʿAlaʾ al-Dīn Khaljī 63, 72
Āṇahilla 70
Adi Singh 208
Ādibhañja 208
Ādityas 77
Advani, L.K. 174
ādya sevāyat 119
Agañña-Sutta 93
Aghriā community 181
Aghriā-Gauntiā 181, 183, 197, 198
agrahāras 93
Ahar 66
Ahila 70
Alaungsithu 99
Alhaṇa 69, 70
Alur 22
Amber 76
Anandapura 74
Anawrahta 98, 103
Andhra 18, 26, 82, 244
Angkor 108
anthropologists/anthropology 7, 8, 11, 19, 22, 31, 32, 40, 61, 115, 205, 239
Anuradhapura 109
areas, nuclear 14, 23-26, 96, 222, 240, 243
areas, peripheral 65
Arakan 99, 100
Aravalli mountains 65
architecture 8, 23, 31
archives 18, 31, 50, 84
Arthaśāstra 28, 42, 93, 221, 233
Ashoka 94
Aṣṭamātṛkā 137
Aśvapāla 70
Athagarh 209
authority, ritual 13, 123, 186
authority, royal 13, 17-19, 118, 122-124, 126, 165, 175, 186, 206
authors, Brahman 68

Babylon 148
Babylonians 244
baḍadaṇḍa 139, 141, 155
bakhan 35, 36, 54-57
Bali Vairocana 227, 231
ballads, local 18
Baluṅkeśvara 140-143, 146
Bamra 181, 182, 185-187, 197, 199, 214
Banas plain 69
Bāṇa-Bali 232
Bāṇāsura 224, 227, 228, 231
Bāṇāsurapura 227
Bappa 71, 74, 76
barber 121-126, 190, 193, 194
Bardic literature 72-77
Bashahr 33-41, 46, 50-52, 55-59, 62
Bāṣpa 76
Bayly, Christopher A. 117, 125
Bayly, Susan 237, 239
bāyoling 45
Benares 8, 12, 237, 244
Bengal 26, 96, 99, 109, 110, 173, 216
Berkemer, Georg 8-11, 18, 21, 23, 27, 28, 41, 86, 181, 197, 205, 219, 237, 241-248
beṭhi 183, 184, 185
bewarta 215-218
Bhagavatam, Oriya 119, 140
Bhagavatamaṇḍapas 140
Bhairava 148
bhakti 119, 127, 130
Bhanja Mahodayam 209
Bhañjas 208, 209
Bhānudeva IV 174
bhaṭṭāraka 86
Bhīmākālī 51, 52, 56
bhoga 121-124
bhogrā 185, 192
bhoktṛ 66
Bhubaneswar 137
Bhuiyan insurgency 210, 215, 218
Bhuiyan sardars 216, 217
Bhuiyans 207, 210-218
bhūmi devī 47
bhūt-pret 43
Bhuvaneśvarī 140, 156
Bibi of Kannur 87
Bissamcuttack 169, 171, 174, 175
BJP 174
Bodhgaya 99
Bonai 207, 211, 214, 217, 219
boning 41

Bon-Po 57
Borges, Jorge L. 245, 246, 248
Borobudur 150
boundary 37, 49, 104, 108
brādarī 46
Brāhmaṇīdevī 140, 156
Brahmans 17, 43, 49, 57, 64, 68, 71, 77, 93, 95, 124, 125, 137, 141, 150, 197, 201, 207, 211-213, 217, 219, 242, 244
brahmapadārtha 173
British colonial courts 176
British East India Company 37, 81, 89, 90, 137
British India 97
British rule 16, 17, 23, 32, 34, 37, 38, 53
brotherhoods of gods 47, 56
brothers, younger 67, 73
Brundaban Bhanja 216
Buddhism 82, 93, 94, 100, 150
Burma 8, 98-110
Byzantine empire 22

Cāhamāṇas 65, 69, 70, 74
Cāhamāṇas of Marwar 70
Cāhamāṇas of Śakambharī 69, 70
Caitanya movement 119
cakravartin 14, 64, 94
calanti Viṣṇu 199, 222
calendar 34-36, 48, 56-58, 86, 139, 142, 148, 151, 171
calendar, festival 40, 62
Calukyas 25
Cāmuṇḍā 75
candravaṁśa 76
Candeśvara 140
car festival (ratha yātra) 139, 168, 186, 199
caste system 13, 16, 17, 42, 207, 238
caturaṅga 223-226, 232
Caulukyas 65, 67, 69-72
Cēramān Perumāḷ 82, 83, 85-90
Cervantes, Miguel de 245, 246
Chamba 39
Chamu citaus 27
Chartier, Roger 179
Chattopadhyaya, B.D. 15, 65, 66, 77, 237
Chaupal 54
cherā pāhamrā 168
chess 224, 225, 226
Chidambaram 22
chiefs, „tribal" 25
chiefdom 117, 118
China 36, 100, 103, 106, 238
chronicles, family 18, 171, 174, 178
chronopolitics 35
Ciṟakkal 87
circumambulation 41, 44, 49, 51
classifications, polythetic 243
Clastres, Pierre 50
clothes 185-188, 194, 197
Cobden Ramsay, L.E.B. 211-214, 219
Cohn, Bernard S. 7-9, 12, 13, 16, 22, 24, 27, 32, 33, 36, 42, 48, 52, 84, 181, 188, 197, 237, 238, 241
Colas 25, 96
community, sacrificial 117, 120, 126, 130-132
contestation 18
criticism, textual 18
cults, local 8
Cuṇḍa 75
cycles, rhythmical 36
cycles, temporal 34, 35

Dalton, Edward T. 207, 212-217
Daṇḍabaluṅkeśvara 140, 143
daṇḍanāyaka 68
Dasara 51, 52, 57,120, 125, 126
Daurā 41
Dehra Dun District 37
deity, dominant-caste 41
deity, family (kuladevatā) 26, 42, 75
deity, favourite (iṣṭadevatā) 117, 149, 151, 169, 195, 199
deity, government by 31, 33, 34, 36, 38, 42-44, 48, 53-57, 62
deity, Hinduised tribal 26, 137, 150
deity, jungle 139
deity, local 121, 124, 126-128, 131, 171, 178
deity, rural 34, 39, 62
deity, tutelary 117, 118, 125, 126, 138, 149-151, 160, 169, 171, 175, 179, 198, 214
deity, village 169, 193-199
Delhi 37, 55, 56, 63, 69, 72
Delhi Sultan 63, 69
deoālī 45
dēśavāḻis 89
devatā kā rāj 31, 33, 38
dhammarāja 94, 101
Dhammayazika stupa 99
Dhanurjaya Narayan Bhanja 212-219
dharmaśāstra 84
dharmbhai 46
Dharnidhar Naik 215
Dhauladhar range 46

Dhenkanal 217, 219
Dhuhar 75
Dirks, Nicholas B. 9, 16, 17, 24, 27, 39, 62, 81, 97, 98, 130, 169, 181, 182, 186, 238, 243, 245, 248
doḷameḷaṇa 143, 149, 150, 151, 157
dolapūrṇimā 144, 157, 161
dostī 46
Drekmeier, Charles 18
Dumont, Louis 13, 16-18, 21, 48, 57, 194, 203
Durgā 48, 49, 52, 62, 120, 148, 156, 163, 168-175, 178, 199, 200
Durgā, Kanaka 242
Durgā Pūjā 120, 153, 227
Dyora 54

East India Company, British 37, 81, 89, 90, 137
Ekaliṅga 74
Ekliṅgji 74
Emerson, Richard 239
empire, Persian 244
empire, regional 25, 175, 238
endo-history 8
energy, social 26, 177, 178
entitlements 118, 125-132
ethnicity 15
exchange, dyadic 45, 46

families, royal 25, 27, 65, 67, 71, 181
Ferishta, Mahomed Kasim 75
feudalism 14, 23, 94, 96
Firuz Shah 208
Foucault, Michel 18, 128, 129, 247, 248
Fox, Richard G. 239
France 23
Frasch, Tilman 8, 93, 240
Frenz, Margret 8, 9, 11, 19, 21, 28, 81, 89
Frese, Heiko 9, 28, 245

Gadadhar Bhanja 216
gaḍajāta 115, 137
Gahāḍavāla 75
gajapati 16, 115, 165, 208, 209
Galey, Jean-Claude 17, 19, 20, 62, 195, 197, 198, 199, 239
games of intelligence 224
Gaṇeśa 140, 148
Gangas 26
Gangpur 214
Garh Manitri 116, 120, 122
Garhwal 20, 31, 38, 39, 198
gāṃ muha 121
Gauntiā 181-191, 193-199, 201
Geertz, Clifford 9, 27, 62, 166, 176
genealogical lists 64
genealogical part of the inscription 70
genealogies, Brahmanic 77
genealogists 68, 70, 76
geometry of assembly 49, 51
ghori 41, 42, 45
gifts 19, 172, 183, 184, 188, 190-198, 213, 241, 246
Gobind Bhanja 209
Godāvara Miśra 222-224, 226, 231
Gonds 207, 210
Grām Śri 196
group identities 15
Guṇḍīcā 139, 155
Guha, Amalendu 239
Guhilas 65, 67, 69, 70-74, 76
Gujarat 65, 67, 72, 75, 110, 238, 244
Gupta empire 25, 54, 244
Gurjara-Pratihāras 65
Gutschow, Niels 9, 137, 161, 163, 164

Habudasinghī 140
Haladia rāja 118
Hanol 52, 53, 54, 55
Hara 221-231
Hari 121, 221-232
Hariharacaturaṅga 222, 226
Harihareśvara 140, 143, 154
Harita 71, 74
Harivaṁśa 228
heroes, mythical 70, 71
Heesterman, Jan C. 18, 196
Hegel, Georg Friedrich Wilhelm 21, 48
hegemony, ritual 13, 16
Heidelberg 11, 28, 219, 239, 240
Himachal Pradesh 28, 37, 39
Hinduisation 170, 197, 211, 213, 240
hierarchies, patrilinear 84
history, colonial 21
history, European conceptions of 7
history, periodisation of 22, 110
history, post-colonial 21
history, Rajput 8
historiography 7, 8, 23, 68, 105, 207, 246
historiography, post-modern 7
Hseittaung 103

Ikṣvākus 76, 77

incorporation, rituals of 17
Inden, Ronald B. 18, 33-36, 39, 42, 51, 55, 56, 59, 62
India, mediaeval 16
India, Western 63-65, 71-73, 76, 77
Indian society, Orientalist view of 17
indology 11, 21, 205, 207
influence, spheres of 14
inscriptions 25, 63-77, 84, 86, 93-106, 108, 110, 166, 178, 195, 208, 231, 242
insignia, royal 82, 83
iṣṭadevatā 117, 149, 151, 169, 195, 199
institutions, monarchical 69

Jagannātha 16, 25, 116, 118, 119, 125-132, 137-149, 153-157, 160, 161, 165, 168, 173-175, 222
jagir 42
jājmān 43, 190, 193, 194, 199, 201
janapada 42, 53
jātra 41
Jaunsar-Bawar 31, 39
Jayavarman VII 108
Jeypore 166, 168, 169, 171, 172, 174, 175, 178, 201, 208, 209
Jeyyasingha 99, 101, 102, 108
Jodha 75
Jodhpur 75
Juangs 207, 216, 219
Jumna 36
Jyoti Bhanja 208, 209, 210, 212
Jyoti Singh 209

Kacchvāhas 76
Kaivarta uprising 96
Kakātiyas 87
Kalinganagara 26
Kamandakīya Nītisāra 221
kamin 190
kaṅ-sū-krī 103
Kanait 39, 42, 47, 52-54, 62
Kanauj 75
Kāñci-Kāverī legend 209, 223
Kanchipuram 168, 174
Kangra 37
Kapilendra 242
Kararani-Sultanate 173
Kashmir 35-38, 52, 53, 59
Kathmandu Valley 148
Kaṭakarājavaṁśāvali 27, 29, 223
Kaṭattanāṭu 85
Kaṭudeva 69
Kaurava cousins 54
kāyasthas 93
Keonjhar (Kendujhar) 205-219
Kerala 28, 82, 84, 86, 87, 89, 90, 238
Khaṇḍāyats 125
Khash-Rājpūts 42, 43
Khijjinga Kota 208
Khiḷāmuṇḍa 138
Khond priest 121, 124, 125
khunds 38, 39, 41, 42, 44-52, 55-58
Khurda 24, 27, 115-118, 126, 130-132, 137, 152, 173, 239
khvaṅ 103
kingdoms, divine 39
kingdoms, imperial 24
kingdoms, jungle 20, 165, 179, 205, 206
kingdoms, regional 133, 180
kingdoms, subregional 26
kingdoms, transregional 14
kings, feudatory 116
kings, great 8, 13, 18, 26, 37, 52, 65, 81-90, 166, 167, 175, 221, 232, 242, 246
kings, hierarchy of 64, 241
kings, jungle 25
kings, virtual great 81, 88, 90
kingship 7, 9, 16, 18, 19, 28, 36, 38, 39, 43, 48, 51-53, 56, 59, 64, 66, 90, 93, 94, 96, 97, 100, 101, 104, 106, 110, 115-118, 120, 121, 128, 130-132, 137-140, 145, 147, 165, 175, 187, 196-199, 206, 207, 214, 218, 219, 221, 241, 244
Kinnaur 41, 46
knowledge, Brahmanical 64
kṣatra-dharma 187, 197
Kṣatriya 74, 76, 241
Koḷḷaṃ era 85
kṣetra 147, 170, 175, 196, 198, 199
Kṣetrasiṃha 76
Kolff, Dirk H. 15, 239
Kols 207, 210
Konnilakkonadiri 82, 83, 85
Kēraḷa Varmma Paḷaśśi Rājā 87, 88
Kopat, Anand 213
Koraput District 166
Kosambi, D.D. 14, 94, 110
Koḻikkōṭu 82, 85, 89
Krishnadevaraya 242
Kṛṣṇa 139, 140, 142, 143, 146, 147, 160, 223, 224, 227, 229-232
Kṛṣṇa mythology 223
Kublai Khan 100
Kurumpranāṭu 85, 87, 88

Kuśa 77
Kujang 173
kula 42, 43
kuladevī 75
Kulke, Hermann 8, 9, 11, 14, 16, 21-29, 62, 81, 95, 110, 119, 137-139, 149, 150, 165, 174, 179, 195, 197, 206, 219, 221, 237, 239, 240, 243
Kullu kings 37
Kumaon 37
Kumbha 74-76
Kumbhalameru 75
Kurumpranāṭu 85, 87, 88
kūṭṭaṃ 88
Kyanzittha 99, 103
Kyazwa 100, 102, 106

Lāngulesvara Itihāsa 195
Laws of Manu 42
leader, military 240, 242
legitimacy 12, 13, 68, 69, 70, 74, 88, 126, 128, 131, 172, 177, 179, 186, 206, 215, 217, 219
legitimacy, emblems of 13
lineage past 68
lineage, younger 67, 70, 73
lineages, royal 67, 71, 93
Lingat, Robert 18, 101, 110
linguistics 18, 22
lipirekhas 93
little king, lowest 241
little kingdoms, anthropology of 19
little kingdom 7-9, 11-13, 15-19, 24, 27, 32, 33, 36-39, 42, 50, 62, 72, 81, 84, 87-90, 96, 107, 115-117, 165, 168, 174, 181, 182, 197, 205-208, 210, 217, 237-240, 243-247
little kingdoms, ethnohistory of 19
long duree 24, 28, 240, 243

Mackenzie, Colin 27, 81-83, 86, 90
Mackenzie Collection 27, 82, 86
Madhusudan Das 218
Mahabali 232
Mahābhārata 38, 223, 228
Mahabodhi temple 99
mahādān 101, 102, 106
Mahādevī 174
mahāmaṇḍaleśvara 67
māhāpraśād 118
mahārāja 26, 66, 83, 84, 86, 90, 233, 244, 247
mahārājādhirāja 69, 76
mahārājakula 67
mahārāvala 67
mahāsamantādhipati 67
mahāsammata 94
Mahāsu 34
māhātmya 74
Mahendra 70
Mahiṣa 171, 174
Maisūr 89, 90
Malabar 19, 81-90
Malayāḷam manuscripts 81
mālī 38
Mali community 143
Malinowski, Bronislaw 68
Malwa 65, 72
Mānasollāsa 224, 225, 233
Mānavadharmaśāstra 233
maṇḍala 14, 72, 149, 150, 160
māṇḍalika 66, 67, 69, 71
Maṇḍavyapura 75
Maṇḍovarapura 74, 75
Maṅgalā 140, 156
Maṇināga 137-139, 144, 147-150, 153-160, 163, 164
Mañjuśrī 148
Manu 233
Marathas 15, 115, 137, 138, 167, 169-175, 201, 238
marriage 47, 57, 65, 74, 122, 129, 168, 184, 227, 242, 246
Marwar 65, 67-70, 74, 76
Marx, Karl 21, 48, 94, 110
Massey, Doreen 31, 40, 49
Maturai 87
Mayurbhanj 208-210, 212, 216, 217, 219
Mecca 82, 83, 85, 86
memory 32, 34, 35, 36, 37, 51, 55, 59, 62, 86, 89, 105, 142, 169, 210, 242, 246
methodology 9, 21
Mewar 65, 67, 69, 70, 72-77
Mewar genealogies 70
micro-kingdoms 38-40, 44, 49, 52, 56, 58, 62
milin 47
military 15, 240, 242
Mīnākṣi temple 87
model, anthropological 9
model, Hindu state 27
model, historical 22
model, little kingdom 7-9, 11, 24, 27, 81, 237, 239, 240, 243
model, relational 242

modernity 21, 22, 40, 110, 116, 117, 119, 120, 125, 128, 130, 218, 219, 237
modernity, paradox of early 120
monarchy, European absolute 131
Mongolia 149, 150
Mongols 100, 103, 150
Mount Abu 71
Mount Meru 55
Mughal empire 32, 63, 110
Mughals 12, 73, 77, 115, 167, 188
Muktāpīda Lalitāditya 59
Mukunda Deo 173
Mussoorie 36
myth, ancestral 70
myth, Rajput 8

Naḍol 69
Nagda 66
Nanda 9, 28, 205, 239
Nārada 225, 227, 229
Narapatisithu 99, 102, 105, 106, 108
Narasihapati 100-102, 106
Narasingh Mishra 209
Narayana Rao, V. 18, 87
Nārāyaṇī 140
nāṭuvāḻis 89
nāṭus 96
Navarātri 227
Nawab of Oudh 12
Nāyaka dynasty 87
Nāyars 83, 85
Negara 166
negotiation 18, 47
negotiations , dramatic 177
neighbouring rulers 88, 95, 96, 109
Nepal 57, 148
Newars 148
Nilakanta Sastri, A.K. 22
Nīlakaṇṭha Bhaṭṭa 224
Nītimayūkha 224, 233
Nītiśāstra 221, 224

oracle 33, 38, 43, 47, 54
Orientalism 17
origin, Brahmanic 71
origin, Kṣatriya 76
Orissa 9, 18, 19, 23-29, 81, 115-120, 127-132, 137-143, 148, 149, 165-174, 179, 181, 195, 205, 208, 209, 219, 222, 233, 238-242, 244
Orissa projects 9
Oriya Bhagavatam 119
overlord 13, 64, 67, 68, 77, 94, 95, 174, 181, 185, 186, 188, 197, 199, 242, 246

Pagan 98-109
Pahārī religion
pāikas 122
Palas 25
Pal-lahara 217, 219
Pāndavas 54
pan-Indian mythic genealogies 71
pañcadoḷayātrā 144, 145, 158-160, 162
paradigm, shifts of 21
Paramāras 71, 72
pargana 41, 42
parjā 183, 185, 186
Pati, Biswamoy 28
patron 43, 69, 70, 125, 172, 174, 175, 179, 190, 193, 196
Paḻaśśi Rājā 87, 88, 89
Paḻaśśi Rēkhakaḷ 81
paurāṇic accounts 68
Payyermola 85
Peabody, Norbert 19, 169
Pegu 100
performance 32, 49-52, 54, 62, 83, 124, 127, 131, 139, 167, 168, 172, 176, 178, 186, 194, 218, 242, 246
performances, ritual 177, 178
Perlin, Frank 117
phīr 49
pilgrimage 55, 104, 150, 173, 217
polity, galactic 14, 97, 107
Polonnaruwa 99, 109
polycentric realms 14
power pyramid 26, 27, 238, 239, 240-243
prabhāvotsahamantraśakti 221
practice, historical 33, 35, 59
praśasti 26, 70, 74-77
pratihāra 86
prestige 12, 50, 53, 105, 106, 125, 179, 184, 187, 194, 207
Price, Pamela 239
priest, „tribal" 25, 121, 141
privileges, ritual 13
processional itineraries 39, 59
processional practices 32, 34, 36
processual model 16, 27, 28, 96, 98
production of time in space 36
Prome 101, 104
Pudukkottai 16, 24, 39, 97, 238, 243
pūjā 118, 121, 123, 124, 126, 169, 170, 171, 172, 174, 195, 226

puñji 121
Puri 22, 27, 118, 137, 140, 142, 146, 150, 168, 169, 173, 174, 186, 208, 209, 217, 218, 239
purohita 43, 49, 190, 198
Puruṣottamadeva 168, 223, 233

Quigley, Declan 7, 9

Rājā of Kocci 89
rājādhirāja 64, 247
rājamaṇḍala 72
rājanīti 221, 223
rājāṅka khaṇḍā 121
rājaputra 66, 67
rājās, feudatory 116
Rajasthan 15, 28, 65, 72, 73, 238, 244
Rājataraṅgiṇī 35, 111
Rājavaṁśāvali 206, 212
Rajkuli Bhuiyan 211, 213
Rajputs 8, 15, 16, 28, 44, 49, 52, 57, 62, 63, 71, 72, 75-77, 207-209, 211, 217, 219
rākash 39, 43
rākhī puni 198, 199
Rāma 76, 154, 174
Rāmacandra 77
Ramachandi festival 116, 120, 130, 131
Ramachandra Deo 173
Ramapala 96
rāṇā, rāṇaka 67
Ranpur 137-154, 158, 159, 160, 162, 164
rāṣṭradevatā 26, 118, 168, 222
rāṣṭrakūṭa 86
Rāṣṭrakūṭas 25
ratha yātrā (car festival) 139, 168, 186, 199
Rāṭhoḍs 74, 75, 76
Ratna Naik 215-218
rāutta 67
Ravenshaw, T.E. 217
Rawain 38, 54
rebellion 15, 107, 186, 206, 211, 214, 216-218, 242
rebels 15, 18, 206
relationality, principles of 243
revenue collection 201
rituals 14, 17-19, 25, 32, 35, 107, 118, 131, 138-140, 148, 151, 166, 178, 184, 190, 193-196, 198, 199, 206, 210-212, 214, 217, 219, 227, 246
robber baron 240
Rottler, Johann Peter 82
royal redistributive system 119

sacrifice 39, 43, 49-52, 55, 57, 117, 118, 121-126, 131, 169, 172, 214-218
sacrifice, animal 122, 196,
sacrifice, peace 49
sacrificer 117, 120, 123, 126, 127, 128, 130-132, 169, 172
sacrificer state 117, 126, 130, 132
ṣāḍguṇyam 222
Saiva Mathas 208
Śakambharī 65
śakti 34, 40, 49, 53, 54, 58, 121, 122, 170, 171, 174, 179, 196, 198, 199, 222
sāmantacakra 14, 222
samantaization 95
sāmantamaṇḍala 67
sāmantas 95
samsāra 36, 62
Samudragupta 24, 233
sangera 48
śant 49-51, 55, 57
śānt yajña 49
Saonts 211, 216
Saora medium 121, 124
saptāṅgarājya 222
Sarahān 51
Śāsana villages 141
Satrubhanja 208
sauri khaṇḍāyat 118
Śaurīkathodaya 228
Saw Lu 98
sāza 55-57
scale invariance 242, 243
Schetelich, Maria 221
Schnepel, Burkhard 11, 18-20, 27, 41, 63, 165, 169, 176, 179, 195, 201, 205, 242
Seleucids 244
self-criticism, methodological 21
Senapati, Fakir Mohan 208, 218
seniority 66, 68, 69
service, military 15
Sharma, Ram S. 94, 96, 110
Shulman, David D. 18, 87, 189, 239
Sīha Rāṭhaḍ 75
Śīlāditya 76, 77
Simla Hills 31, 32, 34, 39, 40, 52
Singhbhum 219
Sinha, Surajit 239
Sitabinji 208
Skoda, Uwe 28, 181
socage 183-185, 201
social system, commercialisation of the 119
society, matrilineal 83

society, „tribal" 16, 20, 206, 210, 241
Somadeva 224, 233
Somavamsa dynasty 26
sources, written 23
Southall, Aidan 22
Southeast Asia 14, 93, 97, 110, 165
sovereignty 13, 17, 31, 33, 39, 50-52, 54, 59, 115, 116, 121, 130, 167, 171, 174, 177, 178, 206, 207, 215, 231, 232, 242
sovereignty, ritual 13, 186
sovereignty, shared 33, 49
space, bounded 14, 45
space, centre-oriented 14
Sri Lanka 99, 109
state, medieval south Indian 13
state deity 26, 132, 137, 138, 168, 221
state formation 14, 15, 24, 27, 65, 81, 97, 119
state, galactic 14, 97, 107
state, Hindu 25, 27, 31, 34, 35, 37, 50, 51, 59, 62
state, segmentary 13, 16, 24, 96
state, theatre 27, 166, 176
states, feudatory 137, 152, 219
states, jungle 137
states, princely 23, 24, 26, 81, 145, 166, 207
state model, centralised 12
Stein, Burton 13, 16, 22, 24, 62, 96, 97, 104, 175, 237
Stern, Henri 239
Stietencron, Heinrich von 142, 146, 150, 231
sū-krways 105
subaltern groups 18
Subrahmanyam, Sanjay 18, 87, 110, 133
succession, matrilineal 84
śūprī 47
Sutherland, Peter 31, 39
Sutlej 36, 37
Svapneśvara 140, 143, 144, 146, 157
sword 82, 86, 121-126, 131, 148, 163, 171, 187, 212, 213, 215, 225, 229
Syed, Renate 226
system, local political 7, 13

Tala 100
talavāra 86
Talbot, Cynthia 96, 239
taluka 42, 84
Tambiah, Stanley 14, 45, 62, 97, 240
Tamil Nadu 26, 82, 87, 90, 237, 238
tāmūtiri 83, 90
Tanabe, Akio 19, 28, 115, 116, 118, 119, 120, 129, 196, 239
Tanjavur 96
Tariṇī 140
Tayokpye Min 100
temples 18, 25, 26, 41, 55, 87, 93, 96, 99, 103, 132, 139, 140, 143, 144, 145, 150, 154, 156, 171, 197, 199, 231, 240, 242
temporalization 31, 36, 59
tenants 182, 185
Tessitori, Luigi P. 72, 75, 76
Teuscher, Ulrike 16, 28, 63
texts, classical 18, 222
thākur rājā 119
ṭhakura 67
Thakurani 214, 217
thāt 47
thātrāja 171, 174, 175
thaur 47
theft of the mūrti 169
theories, grand 21
Theravada Buddhism 99
timescapes 34, 59
Ṭippu Sulttān 89
titles 13, 15, 19, 67, 86, 95, 105, 106, 184, 186, 241, 247
tradition, Indological 21
tradition, Nepali shamanic 57
tradition, oral 18, 178
tradition, purāṇic 84
traditional Hindu polities 39
translocality 39
Tribalisation 197
tuiṅ 103
Tukpā 41, 46
typologies 22, 238

Udaipur 217
Udayasiṃha 69, 71
upāyas 222

Vagor 73
Vāmana 231, 232
varṇa-hierarchy 187
Vasiṣṭha 71
Vāsudeva 228
vihāras 93
Vijaya Chandra 168
village council 104
village headman 104, 105, 181
village kings 181
Vīra Varmma of Kurumpranāṭu 87

Viṣṇu 55, 142, 143, 146, 147, 160, 186, 198, 199, 222-227, 230-232
Viṣṇupurāṇa 228
Visscher, C.J. 82

wazīr 43
Weber, Max 21, 128, 197
Wink, André 15, 59, 110, 237
Wittfogel, Karl 35

yātra 41
year, conquest of the 35
yuga 62, 241
yuvarāja 69, 225

zamīndārs 15
zamorin 83
zātra 41

List of Contributors

Georg Berkemer teaches pre-modern South Asian History at the South Asia Institute, Heidelberg.

Tilman Frasch is Research Fellow at the Department of History and Economic History at Manchester Metropolitan University.

Margret Frenz is Research Associate at the Centre for Modern Oriental Studies, Berlin.

Heiko Frese is presently working in a research project on historiography in 17th to 20th century Orissa sponsored by the German Research Council.

Niels Gutschow works as an architect and architectural historian.

Chandi Prasad Nanda is lecturer in History, Sambalpur University, Orissa.

Maria Schetelich was associate professor at the Institute of Indian and Central Asian Studies, Leipzig University.

Burkhard Schnepel is Professor of Anthropolgy at the Martin-Luther-University, Halle.

Uwe Skoda is research scholar with the Orissa Research Project of the German Research Council.

Peter Sutherland is Director of International Studies, Louisiana State University, Baton Rouge.

Akio Tanabe is Associate Professor at the Department of South and West Asian Area Studies, Graduate School of Asian and African Area Studies (ASAFAS) at Kyoto University.

Ulrike Teuscher is presently working in tourism management and doing research on temples and literature in Rajasthan.

Reihen des Zentrums Moderner Orient (Auswahl)

ARBEITSHEFTE

Nr. 2 HEIKE LIEBAU: Die Quellen der Dänisch-Halleschen Mission in Tranquebar in deutschen Archiven. Ihre Bedeutung für die Indienforschung (1993)

Nr. 4 GERHARD HÖPP: Arabische und islamische Periodika in Berlin und Brandenburg, 1915 - 1945. Geschichtlicher Abriß und Bibliographie (1994)

Nr. 5 DIETRICH REETZ: Hijrat: The Flight of the Faithful. A British file on the Exodus of Muslim Peasants from North India to Afghanistan in 1920 (1995)

Nr. 6 HENNER FÜRTIG: Demokratie in Saudi-Arabien? Die Āl Saʿūd und die Folgen des zweiten Golfkrieges (1995)

Nr. 7 THOMAS SCHEFFLER: Die SPD und der Algerienkrieg (1954-1962) (1995)

Nr. 8 ANNEMARIE HAFNER (Hg.): Essays on South Asian Society, Culture and Politics (1995)

Nr. 9 BERNT GLATZER (Hg.): Essays on South Asian Society, Culture and Politics II (1998)

Nr. 10 UTE LUIG/ACHIM VON OPPEN (Hg.): Naturaneignung in Afrika als sozialer und symbolischer Prozess (1995)

Nr. 11 GERHARD HÖPP/GERDIEN JONKER (Hg.): In fremder Erde. Zur Geschichte und Gegenwart der islamischen Bestattung in Deutschland (1996)

Nr. 12 HENNER FÜRTIG: Liberalisierung als Herausforderung. Wie stabil ist die Islamische Republik Iran? (1996)

Nr. 14 DIETRICH REETZ/HEIKE LIEBAU (Hg.): Globale Prozesse und "Akteure des Wandels": Quellen und Methoden ihrer Untersuchung (1997)

Nr. 15 JAN-GEORG DEUTSCH/INGEBORG HALENE (Hg.): Afrikabezogene Nachlässe in den Bibliotheken und Archiven der Bundesländer Berlin, Brandenburg und Mecklenburg-Vorpommern (1997)

Nr. 16 HENNER FÜRTIG/GERHARD HÖPP (Hg.): Wessen Geschichte? Muslimische Erfahrungen historischer Zäsuren im 20. Jahrhundert (1998)

Nr. 17 AXEL HARNEIT-SIEVERS (Hg.): Afrikanische Geschichte und Weltgeschichte: Regionale und universale Themen in Forschung und Lehre (2000)

Nr. 18 GERHARD HÖPP: Texte aus der Fremde. Arabische politische Publizistik in Deutschland, 1896-1945. Eine Bibliographie (2000)

Nr. 19 HENNER FÜRTIG (Hg.): Abgrenzung und Aneignung in der Globalisierung: Asien, Afrika und Europa seit dem 18. Jahrhundert (2001)

Nr. 20 JAN-GEORG DEUTSCH/BRIGITTE REINWALD (Hg.): Space on the move : transformations of the Indian Ocean space in the nineteenth and twentieth century (2002)

Nr. 21 THOMAS ROTTLAND: Von Stämmen und Ländern und der Macht der Karte. Eine Dekonstruktion der ethnographischen Kartierung Deutsch-Ostafrikas (2003)

STUDIEN

Bd. 1 JOACHIM HEIDRICH (Hg.): Changing Identities. The Transformation of Asian and African Societies under Colonialism (1994)

Bd. 2 ACHIM VON OPPEN/RICHARD ROTTENBURG (Hg.): Organisationswandel in Afrika: Kollektive Praxis und kulturelle Aneignung (1995)

Bd. 3 JAN-GEORG DEUTSCH: Educating the Middlemen: A Political and Economic History of Statutory Cocoa Marketing in Nigeria, 1936-1947 (1995)

Bd. 4 GERHARD HÖPP (Hg.): Fremde Erfahrungen: Asiaten und Afrikaner in Deutschland, Österreich und in der Schweiz bis 1945 (1996)

Bd. 5 HELMUT BLEY: Afrika: Geschichte und Politik. Ausgewählte Beiträge 1967-1992 (1996)

Bd. 6 GERHARD HÖPP: Muslime in der Mark. Als Kriegsgefangene und Internierte in Wünsdorf und Zossen, 1914 – 1924 (1997)

Bd. 7 JAN-GEORG DEUTSCH/ALBERT WIRZ (Hg.): Geschichte in Afrika. Einführung in Probleme und Debatten (1997)

Bd. 8 HENNER FÜRTIG: Islamische Weltauffassung und außenpolitische Konzeptionen der iranischen Staatsführung seit dem Tod Ajatollah Khomeinis (1998)

Bd. 9 BRIGITTE BÜHLER: Mündliche Überlieferungen: Geschichte und Geschichten der Wiya im Grasland von Kamerun (1998)

Bd. 10 KATJA FÜLLBERG-STOLBERG/PETRA HEIDRICH/ELLINOR SCHÖNE (Hg.): Dissociation and Appropriation: Responses to Globalization in Asia and Africa (1999)

Bd. 11 GERDIEN JONKER (Hg.): Kern und Rand. Religiöse Minderheiten aus der Türkei in Deutschland (1999)

Bd. 12 REINHART KÖßLER/DIETER NEUBERT/ACHIM V. OPPEN (Hg.): Gemeinschaften in einer entgrenzten Welt (1999)

Bd. 13 GERHARD HÖPP/BRIGITTE REINWALD (Hg.): Fremdeinsätze. Afrikaner und Asiaten in europäischen Kriegen, 1914 - 1945 (2000)

Bd. 14 PETRA HEIDRICH/HEIKE LIEBAU (Hg.): Akteure des Wandels. Lebensläufe und Gruppenbilder an Schnittstellen von Kulturen (2001)

Bd. 15 DIETRICH REETZ (Hg): Sendungsbewußtsein oder Eigennutz: Zu Motivation und Selbstverständnis islamischer Mobilisierung (2001)

BD. 16 GERHARD HÖPP (Hg.): Mufti-Papiere. Briefe, Memoranden, Reden und Aufrufe Amīn al-Ḥusainīs aus dem Exil, 1940-1945 (2001)

BD. 17 KATJA FÜLLBERG-STOLLBERG: Amerika in Afrika. Die Rolle der Afroamerikaner in den Beziehungen zwischen den USA und Afrika (2003)

BD. 20 GEORG BERKEMER/MARGRET FRENZ: Sharing Sovereignty. The Little Kingdom in South Asia (2003)

In Vorbereitung:

BRIGITTE REINWALD: Lebensstrategien westafrikanischer Weltkriegsveteranen der französischen Kolonialarmee

GERHARD HÖPP/PETER WIEN/RENÉ WILDANGEL: Arabische Begegnungen mit dem Nationalsozialismus

SCHRIFTEN DES ARBEITSKREISES MODERNE UND ISLAM

Bd. 3 GERHARD HÖPP/NORBERT MATTES (Hg.): Berlin für Orientalisten. Ein Stadtführem (2001)

Bei Fragen zur Produktsicherheit wenden Sie sich bitte an:
If you have any questions regarding product safety,
please contact:

Walter de Gruyter GmbH
Genthiner Straße 13
10785 Berlin
productsafety@degruyterbrill.com